Identity, Reconciliation and Transitional Justice

D1739203

Building upon an interdisciplinary synthesis of recent literature from the fields of transitional justice and conflict transformation, this book introduces a groundbreaking theoretical framework that highlights the critical importance of identity in the relationship between transitional justice and reconciliation in deeply divided societies. Using this framework, Aiken argues that transitional justice interventions will be successful in promoting reconciliation and sustainable peace to the extent that they can help to catalyze those crucial processes of 'social learning' needed to transform the antagonistic relationships and identifications that divide post-conflict societies, even after the signing of formal peace agreements. Combining original field research and an extensive series of expert interviews, Aiken applies this social learning model in a comprehensive examination of both the South African Truth and Reconciliation Commission and the uniquely 'decentralized' approach to transitional justice that has emerged in Northern Ireland. By offering new insight into the experiences of these countries, Aiken provides compelling firsthand evidence to suggest that transitional justice interventions can best contribute to post-conflict reconciliation if they not only provide truth and justice for past human rights abuses, but also help to promote contact, dialogue and the amelioration of structural and material inequalities between former antagonists.

Identity, Reconciliation and Transitional Justice makes a timely contribution to debates about how to best understand and address past human rights violations in post-conflict societies, and offers a valuable resource to students, scholars, practitioners and policymakers dealing with these difficult issues.

Nevin T. Aiken is Assistant Professor in the Department of Political Science and Global and Area Studies at the University of Wyoming. He researches and teaches in the areas of transitional justice, genocide studies, peace and conflict studies and international relations.

Transitional Justice
Series Editor: Kieran McEvoy
Queen's University Belfast

The study of justice in transition has emerged as one of the most diverse and intellectually exciting developments in the social sciences. From its origins in human rights activism and comparative political science, the field is increasingly characterised by its geographic and disciplinary breadth. This series aims to publish the most innovative scholarship from a range of disciplines working on transitional justice related topics, including law, sociology, criminology, psychology, anthropology, political science, development studies and international relations.

Titles in this series:

Transitional Justice, Judicial Accountability and the Rule of Law
Hakeem O. Yusuf (2010)

The Era of Transitional Justice: The Aftermath of the Truth and Reconciliation Commission in South Africa and Beyond
Paul Gready (2010)

The Dynamics of Transitional Justice
Lia Kent (2012)

Forthcoming titles in the series:

Corporate Accountability in the Context of Transitional Justice
Sabine Michalowski

The Judiciary and the Politics of Transition: Saviours, Scoundrels, Scapegoats
Marny Requa

Truth, Denial and Transition: The Contested Past in Northern Ireland
Cheryl Lawther

Families of the Missing
Simon Robins

Gender Politics in Transitional Justice
Catherine O'Rourke

The Concept of the Civilian
Claire Garbett

Transitional Justice and the Arab Spring
Edited by Kirsten Fisher and Robert Stewart

Transitional Justice Theories
*Edited by Susanne Buckley Zistel, Teresa Koloma Beck, Christian Braun
and Friederike Mieth*

Identity, Reconciliation and Transitional Justice

Overcoming intractability in divided societies

Nevin T. Aiken

Routledge
Taylor & Francis Group
a GlassHouse Book

First published 2013
by Routledge
2 Park Square, Milton Park, Abingdon, Oxon OX14 4RN
A GlassHouse Book

Simultaneously published in the USA and Canada
by Routledge
711 Third Avenue, New York, NY 10017

Routledge is an imprint of the Taylor & Francis Group, an informa business

British Library Cataloguing in Publication Data
A catalogue record for this book is available from the British Library

Library of Congress Cataloging in Publication Data
A catalog record for this book has been requested

ISBN (hbk) 978-0-415-62833-4
ISBN (pbk) 978-0-415-81237-5
ISBN (ebk) 978-0-203-06935-6

Typeset in Garamond
by RefineCatch Limited, Bungay, Suffolk

Because of Jules

Contents

Foreword by Professor Brandon Hamber   x
Acknowledgments   xii
Abbreviations   xiv

1   Introduction   1

2   Identity, reconciliation and transitional justice   13

3   A social learning model of transitional justice   31

4   Transitional justice in Northern Ireland and South Africa   54

5   Instrumental learning   74

6   Socioemotional learning   111

7   Distributive learning   162

8   Conclusion: social learning and reconciliation in
    divided societies   195

    Appendix: interviewees   222
    Bibliography   226
    Index   252

Foreword

Violent conflict destroys infrastructure and livelihoods, but also seriously damages intercommunity relationships and social connections. To address this, it is widely argued that strategies aimed at politically, physically and economically reconstructing society are needed, as well as mechanisms aimed at restoring the social fabric and rebuilding intergroup relations. Justice for human rights violations is also critical, and it is often postulated that this is essential to dealing with pervasive violence, preventing repetition of that violence and addressing fractured relationships. It is through attempts to settle past grievances and deliver justice, primarily to victims of mass atrocity in societies emerging from conflict, that the field of transitional justice has emerged.

Considerable strides have taken place in the field of transitional justice with the emergence of different mechanisms aimed at delivering justice ranging from trials and truth commissions through to interfacing these with traditional forms of justice. The intersection between transitional justice and other processes such as security sector reform, development and memorialization are now also being explored. The notion of reconciliation has also long been associated with transitional justice, but as noted in this book, exactly how reconciliation and addressing relationships between former adversaries are related to transitional justice remains underdeveloped.

Indeed, as Nevin Aiken observes here, the relationship between transitional justice, reconciliation and sustainable peace, as well as the actual processes underlying this relationship, have been left "surprisingly unspecified and undertheorized" in the literature to date. In particular, he illustrates that there has been insufficient consideration "given to studying empirically the linkages between institutional mechanisms and the social and psychological changes that are ultimately necessary to facilitate processes of reconciliation in post-conflict societies."

Aiken explores these issues in an eloquent and empirical way. His book, built on extensive fieldwork and desktop research, outlines the critical need for instrumental, socioemotional and distributive learning as key components of reconciliation. In this way, Aiken demonstrates that a range of factors including, but not limited to, dealing with justice and truth is needed to build reconciliation in divided societies. This includes promoting contact and dialogue between former adversaries as well as structural change that ameliorates inequality between divided communities. Aiken formulates this thinking into a model that is persuasive and soundly argued, and that will no doubt be useful to practitioners, policymakers and academics.

The model is then tested through an examination of the two case studies of Northern Ireland and South Africa. In each case study, convincing evidence is found to emphasize the crucial importance of each of these distinct aspects of social learning. Essentially, Aiken argues that a broad range of processes and mechanisms will ultimately be necessary to ensure reconciliation in divided societies. These processes and mechanisms may be needed differently at different times (sequential and simultaneous, he writes). As a result, Aiken argues that reconciliation and transitional justice should not be viewed in a narrow sense (that is, only about justice, or focused on a specific modality of transitional justice) if intergroup reconciliation is to be fostered and sustained.

To this end, Aiken neatly makes a case for a need to focus on what transitional justice processes *do* rather than what they *are*. In doing so, his book provides one of the first concerted studies of the relationship between transitional justice processes and intergroup relations, and provides the reader with a framework for understanding how transitional justice might deliver reconciliation in a real and practical sense.

Professor Brandon Hamber
Director, International Conflict Research Institute (INCORE)
University of Ulster, Northern Ireland
15 September 2012

Acknowledgments

The author wishes to extend his sincere thanks to all those who made this book possible.

First, I would like to express my appreciation for all those individuals in Northern Ireland and South Africa who agreed to be interviewed for this study. The 'insider's perspective' that these interviewees provided proved to be an invaluable resource and this study greatly benefitted from their time and generosity.

Second, particular gratitude is due to my PhD dissertation committee, including Professors Richard Price, Diane Mauzy and Brian Job from the University of British Columbia and Brandon Hamber, Director of INCORE at the University of Ulster, who served as an external examiner. This project is much richer for their thoughtful comments, critiques and suggestions.

Third, I would like to thank Dr. Joanna Quinn from the University of Western Ontario, who first introduced me to the field of transitional justice and who has been a constant source of support ever since.

Fourth, I also wish to extend my gratitude to the Transitional Justice series editor, Kieran McEvoy, and the excellent editors at Routledge, including Commissioning Editor Colin Perrin and Editorial Assistant Melanie Fortmann-Brown, for all of their help and guidance along the way.

Finally, my deepest thanks to Julia C. Obert of the University of Wyoming, whose encouragement, advice and countless hours of editorial assistance helped shape this project from concept to completion.

Substantial funding for this project came from a variety of sources. Support included a CGS Doctoral Scholarship from the Social Sciences and Humanities Research Council of Canada (SSHRC), a Security and Defence Forum Doctoral Scholarship from the Canadian Department of National Defence, a Human Security Fellowship from the Canadian Consortium on Human Security (CCHS), and a Kugelman Citizen Peacebuilding Fellowship from the Center for Citizen Peacebuilding at the University of California, Irvine. Special thanks are also due to Dr. Cecelia Lynch and the Center for Global Peace and Conflict Studies at the University of California, Irvine, who, in addition to extending financial support, also provided a stimulating environment for research and writing by generously hosting the author as a Visiting Research Fellow from 2006 to 2010. Last but not least, many thanks to the Department of Political Science and the Global and Area Studies Program at the University of Wyoming, which together provided a wealth of support and collegiality as this project was seen through to completion.

Portions of this work were first published as an article entitled "Learning to Live Together: Transitional Justice and Intergroup Reconciliation in Northern Ireland" in the *International Journal of Transitional Justice* 4, no. 2 (2010) and appear here with the generous permission of the editors and Oxford University Press.

Abbreviations

AC	Amnesty Committee (South African TRC)
ACP	Ardoyne Commemoration Project
ACT	All Children Together
ANC	African National Congress
APLA	Azanian People's Liberation Army
BEE	Black Economic Empowerment
BFA	Belfast (Good Friday) Agreement
BIP	Belfast Interface Project
BSI	Bloody Sunday (Saville) Inquiry
CAIN	Conflict Archive on the Internet
CCR	Centre for Conflict Resolution
CAJ	Committee on the Administration of Justice
CFNI	Community Foundation for Northern Ireland
CGPNI	Consultative Group on the Past Northern Ireland
CRC	Community Relations Council
CRJI	Community Restorative Justice Ireland
CRO	Community Relations Officer
CRU	Community Relations Unit
CSVNI	Commission for Victims and Survivors (Northern Ireland)
CSVR	Centre for the Study of Violence and Reconciliation
DCCRP	District Council Community Relations Programme
DUP	Democratic Unionist Party
FAIR	Families Acting for Innocent Relatives
GEAR	Growth, Employment and Redistribution Initiative
GNI	Government of Northern Ireland
GSA	Government of South Africa
HET	Historical Enquiries Team
HRVC	Human Rights Violations Committee (South African TRC)
HSRC	Human Sciences Research Council
HTR	Healing Through Remembering
ICTJ	International Center for Transitional Justice
ICPNI	Independent Commission on Policing for Northern Ireland

IDASA	Institute for Democracy in South Africa
IFB	Intermediary Funding Body
IFP	Inkatha Freedom Party
IHOM	Institute for the Healing of Memories
IJR	Institute for Justice and Reconciliation
INCORE	International Conflict Research Institute
INLA	Irish National Liberation Army
IRA	Irish Republican Army
IRG	Interim Reparation Grants
MK	Umkhonto we Sizwe
NIA	Northern Ireland Alternatives
NIACRA	Northern Ireland Civil Rights Association
NIACRO	Northern Ireland Association for the Care and Resettlement of Offenders
NICIE	Northern Ireland Council for Integrated Education
NIHE	Northern Ireland Housing Executive
NILT	Northern Ireland Life and Times Survey
NIMF	Northern Ireland Memorial Fund
NIO	Northern Ireland Office
NIPB	Northern Ireland Policing Board
NISRA	Northern Ireland Statistics and Research Agency
NP	National Party
NPA	National Prosecuting Authority of South Africa
OFMDFM	Office of the First Minister and Deputy First Minister
OPONI	Office of the Police Ombudsman for Northern Ireland
PAC	Pan Africanist Congress
PEACE	EU Programme for Peace and Reconciliation
PFC	Pat Finucane Centre
PIRA	Provisional Irish Republican Army
PRG	Peace and Reconciliation Group
PSNI	Police Service of Northern Ireland
PUP	Progressive Unionist Party
RDP	Reconstruction and Development Programme
RFJ	Relatives for Justice
RIRA	Real IRA
RRC	Reparations and Rehabilitation Committee (South African TRC)
RUC	Royal Ulster Constabulary
SACP	South African Communist Party
SACTJ	The South African Coalition for Transitional Justice
SAHA	South African History Archive
SARB	South African Reconciliation Barometer
SDLP	Social Democratic and Labour Party
SF	Sinn Fein

TRC	South African Truth and Reconciliation Commission
UDA	Ulster Defence Association
UDR	Ulster Defence Regiment
UIR	Urgent Interim Reparations
UUP	Ulster Unionist Party
UVF	Ulster Volunteer Force
UVP	Unionist Voice Party
VLU	Victims' Liaison Unit

Chapter 1

Introduction

The field of transitional justice has emerged in recent years as a distinct area of scholarship concerned with the study of the processes and mechanisms used by local communities, states or international actors to provide justice and accountability in the wake of gross violations of human rights. While the modern roots of transitional justice can be traced back to the Nuremberg Trials following the Second World War, the growth in scholarly interest in these mechanisms only began in earnest following an exponential increase in their use in the early 1990s (Hayner 1994; 2002). No longer subject to the exigencies of Cold War politics, a number of states began 'transitioning' away from histories of government repression and internal conflict towards commitments—at least in theory—to democracy and sustainable peace. A key component of these transitions for many states has involved finding new and innovative ways to deal with issues of accountability for the legacies of violence, human rights abuses and acts of mass atrocity carried out in the past. In many cases, these legacies involved the commission of crimes such as mass murder, forced 'disappearances,' mass rape, war crimes, ethnic cleansing, acts of genocide and other crimes against humanity (Newman 2002).

In part, the drive to deal with these crimes was a function of an emerging norm of accountability within the international community following the Second World War, a norm linked to the formation of the United Nations and the creation of an international human rights regime based on the concept of universal human rights (Donnelly 2003). In essence, this new norm of accountability placed both a moral and a legal duty on states to end impunity and bring to justice individuals who committed gross human rights abuses within their borders, and these obligations were codified over time in an emerging body of international human rights law. Where states were unable or otherwise unwilling to provide justice, the international community itself increasingly assumed this responsibility, as evidenced both by the United Nations' founding of the International Criminal Tribunals for the Former Yugoslavia and Rwanda during the 1990s and the more recent establishment of the International Criminal Court in 2002.

However, the increased use of transitional justice strategies has also been tied to a growing consensus among both scholars and practitioners in the field that such strategies have crucial parts to play in supporting processes of reconciliation in transitional societies. In particular, the literature has recognized that these justice mechanisms are key to achieving sustainable peace in post-conflict societies, as they can help to prevent past abuses from serving as the basis for future returns to violence. Additionally, transitional processes can facilitate societal reconciliation by helping those divided by past violence to put aside their antagonisms and to begin to build new, more conciliatory relationships with one another. Nonetheless, while there is virtual consensus that a relationship exists between transitional justice, reconciliation and sustainable peace, to date the actual processes underlying this relationship have been left surprisingly unspecified and undertheorized in the literature. Indeed, reflecting on the current state of the field of transitional justice, Audrey Chapman (2009: 143) notes that "there is little agreement on how to promote reconciliation or on how to conduct research to assess the status of the reconciliation process in deeply divided societies undergoing transitional justice processes." In particular, insufficient consideration has been given to studying empirically the linkages between institutional mechanisms and the social and psychological changes that are ultimately necessary to facilitate processes of reconciliation in post-conflict societies. As a direct result, there is still no clear understanding of what best practices might be drawn from existing strategies and adapted to guide policy in future societies seeking to use transitional justice mechanisms to facilitate reconciliation. This book begins to address these critical gaps.

I contend that these gaps can be attributed to two interrelated factors. First, I argue that much of the existing transitional justice literature tends to overlook the collectivized nature of the mass violence, repression and gross human rights violations to which transitional mechanisms respond. As legal scholar Mark Drumbl (2007) has noted, the extraordinary crimes for which transitional justice mechanisms provide accountability are extraordinary not just for the scope of their violence, but for the fact that they are inherently tied to group membership and committed on the basis of collective religious, ethnic, national or political identity. Such violations are almost exclusively carried out in the service of the persecutor's own group, and they target victims not because of their individual characteristics, but because of their perceived membership in a denigrated group. However, when most of the studies in the field consider the appropriate design of justice strategies for addressing these crimes and the ways in which these strategies might contribute to reconciliation in deeply divided societies, attention to the communality of mass violence seems to wane. While the literature suggests that large-scale violence demands different approaches to justice than those normally employed for the rule-breaking behavior of 'ordinary' domestic crime, rarely does it reflect on the role that these justice mechanisms must play in directly challenging the collective animosities linked to identity in order to move divided societies toward reconciliation and sustainable peace.[1] Accordingly, I contend that in order to uncover the relationship between transitional justice and reconciliation, the literature must undertake a reconsideration of institutional design that begins by engaging the fundamental issues of collective identity at the root of gross human rights violations. Additionally, scholars and practitioners must consider how the strategies employed by transitional institutions might contribute to overcoming antagonisms linked to group identifications that might otherwise threaten to incite future returns to violence.

Second, I suggest that the inherently comparative and institutional focus of much of the existing transitional justice literature may have inadvertently prevented fruitful engagements with other disciplines that have closely investigated issues of identity and reconciliation. In particular, there exists to date very limited dialogue between transitional justice scholars (the majority of whom come from traditions of legal scholarship and human rights advocacy, as well as from practitioner backgrounds) and the growing body of 'conflict transformation' scholarship developed by academics working in the related disciplines of political science, peace and conflict studies and social psychology. Recent conflict transformation work engages directly with the complex dynamics of how post-conflict societies are able to move towards more reconciled relations. In particular, it highlights the central role that group or collective identity plays in the commission and perpetuation of ethnonational violence within the state, and indicates the need to transform these identities and their antagonistic relationships in pursuit of intergroup reconciliation and sustainable peace (Lederach 1997; Kelman 1999; 2001; Bar-Tal 2000; Bar-Siman-Tov 2004). However, no attempt has yet been made to synthesize the structural and institutional insights of transitional justice and the social and psychological theories of identity and intergroup reconciliation developed in the conflict transformation literature. This study brings these two bodies of literature into dialogue with one another, contending that such theoretical cross-fertilization and interdisciplinary analysis is required in order to trace the causal path between transitional justice and reconciliation in divided societies.

A social learning model of transitional justice

This book aims to contribute to the burgeoning field of transitional justice by developing a new and innovative theoretical framework that seeks to open the 'black box' surrounding the relationship between transitional justice and reconciliation in societies that have been deeply divided by histories of violence between collective identity groups. In so doing, it also helps to provide a much-needed standard by which the relative utility of different justice strategies might be assessed. Following on the work of conflict transformation scholars, this theoretical model contends that the crucial connections between transitional justice and reconciliation can be uncovered by analyzing how transitional mechanisms interact with the 'politics of identity' in post-conflict societies. In particular, it investigates how the tactics employed by transitional justice strategies can work to impede or impel the transformation of the antagonistic identifications and relationships between former enemies ultimately required for intergroup reconciliation and sustainable peace (Eriksen 2001; Eder et al. 2002).

I argue that the causal path connecting transitional justice and reconciliation depends on the ability of these tactics to serve as catalysts for 'social learning' in transitional societies (Aiken 2010). Social learning is defined here as the set of social and psychological processes by which former enemies come to reassess the hostile perceptions and negative beliefs they once held about one another and to create a more positive system of relationships governing their interactions. These processes are crucial steps on the road to intergroup reconciliation in divided societies, offering the means for former antagonists to be brought together to condemn past abuses and to challenge—and potentially transform—the entrenched mistrust, hostility and prejudice that might otherwise threaten to incite future returns to violence. By building on a synthesis of insights derived from the conflict transformation and transitional justice literatures, this study introduces a new theoretical model outlining a set of key mechanisms of social learning that are widely identified as being necessary, if perhaps not sufficient, conditions for fostering intergroup reconciliation in post-conflict environments. Accordingly, the model proposes these mechanisms of social learning as the central causal processes mediating the link between transitional justice and reconciliation in divided societies.

While this social learning model is taken up in much greater detail in Chapter 3, the key causal mechanisms it examines essentially fall into three broader categories or processes of social learning.[2] The first, 'instrumental learning,' refers to interventions that focus on rebuilding relationships and perceptions between previously divided groups. The foremost of these instrumental learning mechanisms is the promotion of new forms of positive contact between former antagonists. This argument draws on insights from the long-standing 'contact hypothesis' in social psychology that suggests how renewed interaction can facilitate reconciliation by helping to rebuild trust, reduce prejudice, and challenge misperceptions about former enemies. Providing opportunities for sustained positive contact is therefore the first step in moving divided groups in post-conflict societies away from polarized 'Us versus Them' identities towards an increasingly inclusive sense of 'We' that allows more cooperative relationships to become the norm. The second of these instrumental learning mechanisms is often directly tied to contact, and it involves efforts to renew meaningful dialogue and communication across group boundaries. Nearly all conflict transformation scholars agree that dialogue is vital for breaking down negative beliefs between former enemies and for developing a more inclusive sense of shared identification.

The next broad category of social learning processes falls under what I call 'socioemotional learning'—efforts centered on reducing grievances, anger and negative beliefs between groups tied to past violence, with the aim of providing both 'justice' and 'truth.' These interventions must try to reduce the sense of injustice caused by past abuses by acknowledging the worth of victims and the wrongness of the harms done to them, and by in some way also taking action to prevent impunity by holding perpetrators accountable for their actions. In addition to justice, there is a growing consensus that social learning also requires the establishment of a mutually acceptable—or at least mutually tolerable—'truth' about what actually transpired during past violence in order to counter any myths or biased memories that may have developed between former antagonists. This is a key step in breaking down polarized identifications and beliefs about the past and about the 'Other' that might otherwise sustain societal divisions and provide a ready basis for future violence.

Finally, the third broad category is 'distributive learning,' which involves interventions designed to ameliorate structural and material inequalities that may continue to exist between divided groups in post-conflict societies. Distributive learning is tied to the recognition that the social and psychological aspects of social learning must also be matched by concrete changes in the daily lives of former antagonists. These kinds of interventions might include provisions for reparations or compensation for those who experienced severe disadvantage in the past, or broader recommendations and reforms designed to work towards reducing inequality. Left unaddressed, continued social, economic or political inequalities in divided societies have been shown to preclude opportunities for meaningful contact and communication, serve as sources of continued feelings of victimization and injustice, and otherwise hinder the development of social learning and intergroup reconciliation.

In summary, the theoretical framework developed in this study indicates that transitional justice strategies can be most successful in promoting intergroup reconciliation and sustainable peace in post-conflict societies if they actively catalyze instrumental, socioemotional and distributive processes of social learning by encouraging contact, dialogue, 'truth,' and 'justice,' and by ameliorating material inequalities. Importantly, this model also proposes that these three types of social learning are deeply interrelated and are mutually dependent upon and mutually constitutive of one another. This study therefore suggests that all three of these elements will likely need to be addressed concurrently either within or alongside transitional justice strategies to successfully advance processes of intergroup reconciliation in divided societies.

Research design and methodology

While this contribution to theoretical development is important, the principal aim of this study is to empirically test the ability of the proposed social learning framework to shed new light on the causal linkages between transitional justice and intergroup reconciliation in deeply divided societies. Accordingly, the majority of this book is given over to evaluating the social learning model through a qualitative assessment of the case studies of Northern Ireland and South Africa—an assessment that combines elements of both within-case and cross-case analysis (George and Bennett 2004: 18; Backer 2009). This form of theory-oriented small-n analysis is appropriate to this investigation for a number of reasons. First, conventional quantitative or statistical methods can prove unwieldy in attempting to trace the complicated causal structures at work in intricate processes such as societal reconciliation where direct claims about correlation are easily confounded by interaction effects and path dependence (Ragin 1987; Pierson 2004; Hall 2007). Second, as there currently exists little agreement as to the actual causal connections between transitional justice and reconciliation, limiting the scope of analysis to a smaller number of cases allows for a more intense and focused examination of these connections, and may offer greater opportunity for drawing causal inferences (Chapman 2009). Third, this type of small-n analysis allows both for the kind of in-depth exploration required for assessing complex causal relations, and for comparisons enabling contingent and preliminary generalizations (George and Bennett 2004: 19–32).

This study also employs a research methodology of process-tracing in order to explore the causal path linking transitional justice and intergroup reconciliation in divided societies. Instead of seeking to establish a simple correlation between two variables, process-tracing "attempts to identify the intervening causal process—the causal chain and causal mechanisms—between an independent variable (or variables) and the outcome of the dependent variable" (George and Bennett 2004: 206). More specifically, this study uses a form of process-tracing known as theoretically-oriented systematic process analysis, which is recognized as being particularly well suited to testing complex causal theories through small-n case study designs (Hall 2007). In essence, as Peter Hall notes, this type of process-tracing begins by "formulating a set of theories that identify the principal causal variables said to conduce to a specific type of outcome to be explained as well as an accompanying account . . . about how those and other variables interact in the causal chain that leads to the outcome" (2004: 6). This initial stage of theory development is taken up in Chapters 2 and 3, in which the social learning model is introduced in detail.

In Chapters 5 through 7, the predictions made regarding the role of instrumental, socioemotional and distributive learning are tested against empirical observations drawn from a comparative assessment of the key case studies of Northern Ireland and South Africa. Process-tracing, which relies on drawing inferences not from the correlative terms of the conventional comparative method but from a detailed examination of the causal chain at work within a particular context, is not dependent to the same extent upon the need to select representative cases for study (Hall 2007: 6). Nevertheless, if contingent generalizations are to be drawn from such studies, it is doubly important that the chosen cases conform to a specific type or subtype of the broader phenomena being explored. Accordingly, this study limits its case selection to deeply divided, post-conflict societies that have implemented transitional justice strategies to deal with their legacies of past violence. This choice therefore necessarily brackets similarly divided countries in which overt intergroup violence has not yet ceased and which may be involved in earlier stages of conflict management or resolution.

While the scale and scope of past violence differs greatly between Northern Ireland and South Africa, both cases nonetheless have histories of protracted conflict and gross human rights violations enacted along the lines of relatively clearly defined group identities that are explored in Chapter 4. In Northern Ireland, the violence of the 'Troubles' was primarily committed between two communities divided by a set of overlapping religious and national identifications—namely, Catholics/nationalists and Protestants/unionists.[3] In South Africa, under the system of apartheid and the ensuing liberation struggle, societal divisions fell along legally defined categories of racial identity, with lines being most starkly drawn between communities of 'white' and 'black' South Africans.[4] Further, both of these cases involve post-conflict societies in which the commission of overt violence between identity groups has now largely ceased and has been replaced by at least a 'negative peace' following negotiated peace processes carried out during the 1990s. Finally, following their respective peace agreements, both Northern Ireland and South Africa employed transitional justice strategies to deal with the legacy of past violence and to foster sustainable peace and reconciliation among formerly divided communities. Northern Ireland has pursued a largely decentralized transitional justice approach that has combined a series of discrete government programs with a widespread base of 'bottom-up' efforts by civil society and local community actors. In contrast, in the case of South Africa, the transitional justice process has largely focused on the South African Truth and Reconciliation Commission (TRC), a highly centralized truth-recovery initiative undertaken by the government to investigate the history of human rights abuses committed during the apartheid era.

Moreover, as this study undertakes the initial development and inaugural testing of the proposed social learning framework, further pragmatic considerations informed its case selection. First, these cases were chosen because they appear to share a particular outcome on the dependent variable. Both Northern Ireland and South Africa are widely considered to have achieved at least some level of societal reconciliation following their respective transitional justice interventions. In other words, these countries were selected as 'most likely' cases in which the proposed causal relation between transitional justice and reconciliation might hold. While this does raise concerns of selection bias, it has increasingly been recognized that selecting on the dependent variable may in fact be entirely appropriate with process-tracing methodologies if the study's purpose is theory development. This is because this kind of selection better allows for "identifying the potential causal paths and variables leading to the dependent variable of interest" or testing which variables are not necessary or sufficient conditions in the causal chain leading to the selected outcome (Dion 1998; George and Bennett 2004: 121–122). In addition, Northern Ireland and South Africa were chosen, at least in part, because there exists a wealth of primary and secondary information on each of these cases, thereby providing the opportunity for ready access to the depth and breadth of data ultimately required for an effective use of the process-tracing methodology.

Finally, it should be noted that the case study of Northern Ireland was selected, in particular, because it offers the additional opportunity to gain insight about how a decentralized transitional justice program might impact processes of social learning in divided post-conflict societies. Northern Ireland has received relatively little attention to date in the transitional justice literature as a result of the field's tendency to focus on more centralized or institutionalized justice mechanisms like trials, tribunals or truth commissions (Aiken 2010). By including Northern Ireland as one of its two initial case studies, this study therefore also provides new knowledge about how such decentralized approaches might serve to impede or impel reconciliation.

The observations drawn from the case studies of Northern Ireland and South Africa are intended to achieve two interrelated goals. First, these observations provide a qualitative test of the social learning framework presented in Chapter 3 by examining whether the causal processes and interactions the model predicts are present in each of these cases. In essence, the observations derived from within-case analyses can help to "establish whether the causal chain that [the] theory anticipates is present in the cases [under study]" (Hall 2007: 8). A secondary aim of these observations is the genesis of contingent generalizations about the causal relationship between transitional justice and intergroup reconciliation by way of cross-case comparison. This analysis can inform 'best practices' for future justice interventions in deeply divided societies. This study's findings can therefore provide a stable platform for the cumulative development of knowledge through potential future studies of transitional justice and reconciliation in other deeply divided societies.

The observations themselves are drawn from two main sources. The first is desk research—a review of the wide range of primary and secondary materials available in both Northern Ireland and South Africa, many of which engage with topics directly related to this study's interests in identity, reconciliation and transitional justice. This existing research was an invaluable resource for this study, particularly as much of it addresses—albeit in a discrete and often disconnected fashion—the presence and impact of what this study identifies as the key causal variables of instrumental, socioemotional and distributive social learning. In fact, a number of prominent academic and governmental studies have used empirical survey work to measure the relative impact of aspects of transitional justice strategies on reconciliation in both Northern Ireland and South Africa (Bell 2002; Hamber 1998; Gibson 2004; Chapman and van der Merwe 2008a). Additionally, numerous publications have addressed the status of intergroup reconciliation in each of these countries, and this material greatly assisted in providing a solid qualitative measure of the dependent variable. A key resource in this regard was the ready availability of longitudinal survey data in both cases on key indicators of intergroup reconciliation. When coupled with more qualitative findings, access to this survey data allowed for an important degree of methodological triangulation that served to further strengthen the validity of this study's assessments of reconciliation (Putnam 1993; Olson 2004).

This study's observations are also based on periods of field research carried out in both Northern Ireland and South Africa in 2008. In Northern Ireland, this fieldwork was conducted during a two-month period between February and April 2008 and was based primarily in the cities of Derry and Belfast.[5] Additional interviews were also conducted during this period in the Irish Republic in the cities of Limerick and Dublin. A similar two-month period of research was carried out in South Africa in June and July 2008, centered largely on the cities of Cape Town, Johannesburg and Pretoria. In both cases, in addition to engaging in a limited amount of archival research, the primary purpose of this fieldwork was to carry out a series of expert interviews with those select academics, government officials, civil society representatives, former combatants and non-governmental community leaders best positioned to provide a solid qualitative measure of the contribution that their country's transitional justice program has made to social learning and ongoing processes of intergroup reconciliation.

Expert interviewees were selected via a 'key informant' sampling method which "targets individuals who are particularly knowledgeable about the issues under investigation" and who are therefore uniquely positioned to provide substantial insight into the causal processes under study (Schutt 2009: 173). This included interviews with those directly involved in the transitional justice interventions in both South Africa and Northern Ireland, including, for example, several prominent former TRC Commissioners. The selection of interview subjects also involved an element of 'snowball sampling' in which interviewees themselves helped to identify other potential contacts (idem: 174). In total, 83 in-depth expert interviews were carried out as part of this study, 44 in Northern Ireland and 39 in South Africa. In each country, in the interest of securing a degree of representativeness and limiting bias, these samples included international observers as well as individuals drawn from nationalist and unionist backgrounds (Northern Ireland) or who self-identified as white or black (South Africa). While conducting additional interviews is always desirable, the numbers collected in each case were deemed sufficient to approximate the levels of 'completeness' and 'saturation' desired in qualitative interviewing (Rubin and Rubin 1995: 66–73). A full list of interviewees is provided in an index at the end of the volume.

The interviews themselves were conducted for approximately 1.5 hours each and, with few exceptions, were audio recorded. The interviews involved a semi-structured series of questions designed to gauge individual qualitative evaluations of the relative importance of each of the mechanisms of social learning identified in the theoretical model (namely contact, dialogue, truth, justice and the amelioration of distributive equality) to processes of inter-group reconciliation. Questions also targeted interviewees' assessments of whether instrumental, socioemotional and distributive forms of social learning were impeded or impelled by the transitional justice strategy employed in their country. Where appropriate, interviewees were asked to discuss what 'interaction effects,' if any, they saw occurring between these types of social learning. In addition, using the key definitional 'markers' of reconciliation identified in Chapter 2, interviewees were posed a series of questions designed to assess their perceptions of levels of intergroup reconciliation both before and after the implementation of their country's transitional justice strategy.

Finally, interviewees were asked to provide a broader evaluation of the relative impact, or lack thereof, of these transitional justice initiatives on advancing intergroup reconciliation. This included several open-ended questions designed to address the most positive and negative aspects of these initiatives with regard to intergroup reconciliation, as well as what future challenges remain to be addressed. These questions allowed for the possible identification of new crucial intervening variables or hypotheses that had not previously been identified in the proposed theoretical model—an important component of testing and refining new causal theories through the case study approach (George and Bennett 2004: 20).

The information derived from these interviews was then transcribed and analyzed. This initially involved coding the data gathered under key 'thematic' categories centered on each of the distinct areas of questioning listed above (Rubin and Rubin 1995: 203). Data within each of these categories was then further examined in order to identify strong points of consensus that emerged in interviewees' assessments. Selected direct quotations were chosen for inclusion in each case study chapter to serve as illustrative or representative examples of these points of consensus. Overall, the information gained through these expert interviews offered invaluable new data about the causal processes at work between transitional justice and intergroup reconciliation in the cases under study, providing insiders' insights about these relationships that would likely have been inaccessible through desk research alone.

The final stage of systematic process analysis involves drawing conclusions based on a comparison between the data obtained through observations and the predictions made by the theoretical framework being tested in the study. These findings are presented in Chapters 5, 6 and 7. In Chapter 8, individual within-case conclusions based on the application of the social learning model to the transitional justice processes in Northern Ireland and South Africa are considered, including a summary of the ability of each country's transitional justice strategy to advance aspects of instrumental, socioemotional and distributive learning and the consequent implications for intergroup reconciliation. Second, building on a cross-case comparison of the findings drawn from both Northern Ireland and South Africa, Chapter 8 also considers the potential importance of the social learning model presented in this study and its implications for 'best practices' in the design of future transitional justice interventions in divided societies.

However, while this study offers an important first step towards opening the 'black box' that currently surrounds the causal relationship between transitional justice and reconciliation, it is also important to underscore the inherent limitations of the conclusions reached in the following pages. It is readily recognized that much more work—both qualitative and quantitative—remains to be done before it will be possible to speak conclusively about the validity of the social learning model presented here. That said, it is hoped that this initial study will be only the first building block of a larger research project within the field of transitional justice, and that future studies will be able to test this causal model against cases in which there is greater variation both on the dependent variable and on the type of transitional justice approach used. The following chapter begins to lay the groundwork for this larger project by introducing the crucial dynamics of collective identity and social learning that underpin the relationship between transitional justice and reconciliation in divided societies.'

Notes

1   That said, there are several notable exceptions. Transitional justice scholars who have begun to focus on the relation between identity and reconciliation in divided societies include Fletcher and Weinstein (2002); Gibson (2004); Weinstein and Stover (2004); Drumbl (2007); Aiken (2008; 2009; 2010); Chapman (2009); and Arthur (2010).

2   The labels for these three types of social learning are adapted from Arie Nadler and Nurit Shnabel (2008).

3   Throughout this volume, the terms 'unionist' and 'nationalist' will be used to describe these communities, with the recognition that these political labels closely—but do not exactly—overlap with the respective religious identifications of Protestant and Catholic. Following Brendan O'Leary and John McGarry, this recognizes that the fundamental antagonism in Northern Ireland has been "between two (internally divided) national communities rather than between two religious communities" (1993: 3).

4   While individual designation in each of these categories was ostensibly based on racial background, evidence shows designation of racial identity under apartheid was often as much a product of social construction and perception as it was linked to the possession of objective physical traits. Further, it should be noted that major internal divisions existed (and continue to exist) within each of these broader racial categorizations in terms of major ethnic, linguistic and political cleavages. Nonetheless, the starkest economic, political and social divisions during apartheid existed between those identified as belonging to the white majority or the black majority. Further, the majority of gross human rights violations committed during apartheid-era violence occurred among individuals from these two racial groups. Accordingly, while it is important not to discount the involvement of other racial groups or the presence of internal divisions within racial categories, this volume follows others who have examined processes of post-apartheid reconciliation in South Africa by focusing primarily on the changing nature of relations between 'black' and 'white' South Africans (Gibson 2004; Chapman and van der Merwe 2008a).

5   Notably, the deep divisions in Northern Ireland are reflected in ongoing debates about the name of the city of Londonderry/Derry, with most unionists preferring the use of Londonderry and most nationalists preferring Derry. Legally the city and county are called Londonderry while the local government district/city council is called Derry, though in practice the two are often used interchangeably both in the media and in everyday parlance. Following those experts interviewed and my experience of common usage within the city itself (among both unionists and nationalists), 'Derry' will be used in all future references to the city in this volume.

Chapter 2

Identity, reconciliation and transitional justice

In this chapter, the relationship between transitional justice, identity and intergroup reconciliation in deeply divided societies is explored. This exploration begins with a discussion of recent theories from social psychology and related disciplines that point to the central role played by perceptions of group or collective identity in both the instigation and evolution of intrastate conflict. The chapter shows how antagonistic identities, polarized over the course of intergroup conflict, can contribute directly to the commission of mass violence and gross human rights abuses. Second, the concept of reconciliation, understood as both a process and an outcome, is examined in detail, including its relationship to intergroup identity in deeply divided societies. Drawing on recent insights from the field of conflict transformation, the chapter asserts that the potential for the transformation of these identities and the creation of more peaceful and reconciled relationships between former antagonists always remains open. It stresses the crucial part that institutions can play in the processes of 'social learning' identified by conflict transformation scholars as critical to the development of reconciliation and sustainable peace. Building on this groundwork, I argue that transitional justice mechanisms can contribute to the processes of social learning ultimately required to facilitate intergroup reconciliation in divided societies by bringing together former enemies to challenge and potentially transform the nature of their relations.

The politics of identity in deeply divided societies

The concept of 'social,' 'group,' or 'collective' identity has received increased attention in recent years within political science, and is now widely considered one of "the most normatively significant and behaviorally consequential aspects of politics" (Abdelal et al. 2006: 695) and a key variable in explaining the complex dynamics of violence and peace both internationally and within the state (Horowitz 2002; Bruland and Horowitz 2003). While studies have drawn upon various understandings of collective identity to account for political behavior, most recent scholarship has adapted the prominent Social

Identity Theory (SIT) approach from social psychology, promoting this approach as the most effective means of explaining patterns of peace and conflict (Monroe et al. 2000; Gross-Stein 2002). The SIT approach focuses on studying 'the group in the individual,' looking at the ways in which individuals come to define significant portions of their identities in terms of their social group memberships (Tajfel 1982; Tajfel and Turner 1979; Hogg and Abrams 1998). Under SIT, 'social identity' is understood as "the individual's knowledge that he belongs to certain social groups together with some emotional and value significance to him of the group membership," and 'identity groups' are defined as "two or more individuals who share a common social identification of themselves, or . . . [who] perceive themselves to be members of the same social category" (Hogg and Abrams 1998: 15). As Michael Hogg and Dominic Abrams note, the SIT approach views group belonging largely as a psychological state that forms part of personal cognition, but one that extends beyond the individual to the society around her to confer a "shared or collective representation of who one is and how one should behave" (idem: 3). Indeed, group identities do not only provide a sense of belonging, but also imply conformity to a set of normative standards which both describe the criteria tied to one's inclusion and prescribe rules of 'acceptable' or 'appropriate' behavior—guidelines that are binding to the extent that an individual considers herself to be part of that collective identity (idem: 159, 170).

This kind of group categorization has been shown to be a universal cognitive tool used by individuals to help make sense of the world around them, effectively providing parsimonious shorthands via schemas and stereotypes and holding members of one's 'ingroup,' the 'Self,' in contrast to all those belonging to an 'outgroup' or externalized 'Other' (Brewer and Campbell 1976; Brewer 2001). Further, SIT centrally contends that, due to our innate psychological need for self-affirmation, individuals tend to extend positive perceptions of themselves to all members of the social group(s) of which they are a part. This, in effect, creates a "benign cycle of positive affect" in which mutual regard, trust, empathy and cooperative relations come to be shared among all those belonging to the ingroup (Brewer 2001: 22–23). However, while these findings of ingroup positivity are frequently taken to assume relations of hostility and negative regard for the outgroup—a kind of virulent 'universal ethnocentrism'—more recent studies have established that this is not the case.[1] Rather, ingroup perceptions of the Other and subsequent relations have been shown to be heavily dependent on structural, environmental and situational conditions, and also, most importantly, on the nature of past and current intergroup social interactions (Brewer and Campbell 1976; Kriesberg 1982; Hogg and Abrams 1998; Brewer 2001; Gross-Stein 2002; Gibson 2004). Therefore, as these studies illustrate, intergroup hostility is only one of many options that exist on the "continuum of possible relations between groups," with potentials ranging from trust, friendship and altruism to extreme suspicion, enmity and violence (Brewer 2001: 19).[2]

The central insights of SIT are particularly important to analyzing the dynamics of conflict and reconciliation in societies that are deeply divided along existing fault lines of collective identity centered on ethnicity, nationalism, race or religion. Significantly, other scholars working in the social sciences have similarly suggested that collective identities and the relationships between them cannot be viewed as essential or primordial facts. Rather, these identities are typically viewed as fluid and malleable, shaped by the intentional actions of elites, by ongoing contestation among group members themselves, by group members' relations with members of the 'Other,' and even by the structural and normative influences of broader society (Horowitz 1975; 1994; 2000; Hobsbawm and Ranger 1991; Connor 1994; Lake and Rothchild 1996; Anderson 1997; Hastings 1997; Levine 1997; Fearon and Laitin 2000; Kaufman 2001). Klaus Eder and others have labeled these processes the 'politics of identity,' defined as "the construction of the symbolic boundaries and collective identities which provide the cognitive basis for normative order and social integration" (2002: 4).[3] However, this is not to say that such identities are always entirely fictive or that they are easily invented and changed. Indeed, collective national, ethnic and religious identities have an inordinately strong pull on the hearts and minds of individuals, as they are often based on a shared sense of kinship and are frequently tied to territorial belonging (Smith 1986). Accordingly, while they may be almost entirely socially constructed, over time these identities can come to be perceived by group members as relatively stable 'truths' or 'social facts' (Durkheim 1984; Wendt 1994; 2000).

Similarly, the nature of the relations between different ethnic, national or religious identity groups are also recognized as being the products of social construction, with patterns of intergroup animosity in deeply divided societies frequently triggered by certain conducive conditions (Coleman 2002). These conditions can include the active efforts of ethnonational elites or 'entrepreneurs' to foster intergroup tensions either by banding a group together to compete for resources and other instrumental gains, or by actively vilifying the Other through propaganda, negative labeling or discriminatory narrative (Rabushka and Shepsle 1972; Brass 1994; Ronnquist 1999; Fearon and Laitin 2000). Further, structural and material threats to the basic human needs of group members are major contributors to the potential for intergroup enmity in multicommunal societies, as is the breakdown of centralized authority structures in weak or failed states (Azar 1990; Staub 1989; Staub and Bar-Tal 2003). Finally, the experience of hostility or threat in prior interactions or a past history of marked intergroup domination, injustice or violence has been shown to contribute to antagonistic relations between identity groups (Kriesberg 2005). Over time, these relations can take on a seemingly self-fulfilling quality as the experience of negative interaction leads to the creation of schemas, stereotypes and prejudices about the Other that color all future exchanges with expectations of prejudice and antagonism

(Gross-Stein 2002: 294). In such cases, multicommunal societies can become deeply divided, characterized by the perception of incompatible goals, values and ideologies between groups, as well as by intergroup relationships marked by deep distrust, threat, animosity and underlying devaluations of the Other that can serve to legitimize intergroup violence (Ryan 1995; 2007; Lederach 1997; Oberschall 2007).

The onset of overt physical violence in divided societies can itself increase polarization and deepen antagonisms between identity groups, resulting in protracted and seemingly intractable communal identity conflicts (Northrup 1989; Kriesberg 1998; Bar-Tal 2000). At this stage, entrenched ethnonational identities typically take on a monolithic quality and come to permeate all facets of social, economic and political life (Coleman 2002). First, violence breaks down the levels of 'social capital' that exist between identity groups, causing the decline of meaningful contact and communication across group boundaries and destroying essential networks of trust and reciprocity that enable more cooperative intergroup interactions (Colletta and Cullen 2000: 4).[4] A rise in segregation among identity groups often accompanies the onset of violence, as individuals seek to distance themselves from the threat posed by the Other and to band together for safety with members of their own community (Shirlow 2001; Shirlow and Murtagh 2006; Oberschall 2007). This distance, in turn, limits any potential for groups to challenge their negative perceptions of one another, as it "foster[s] mutual ignorance and suspicion, maintain[s] prejudice and negative stereotypes, and reinforc[es] group boundaries" (Gallagher 1995 as cited in Tausch et al. 2007: 66).

Second, the dynamics of violence render it increasingly difficult for members of the ingroup to empathize or identify meaningfully with the Other, as groups often develop 'ideologies of antagonism' that hold all members of the Other responsible for the suffering of the Self and therefore turn those individuals into justifiable targets for violence (Staub 2000; Bar-Tal 2000; Bar-Tal 2003; Staub and Bar-Tal 2003). In the worst instances, this heightens the potential for members of the Other to become dehumanized and excluded from the 'moral universe' governing acceptable behaviors and obligations among the ingroup, with the result that "principles of morality no longer apply to them and moral restraints against killing are more readily overcome" (Kelman 1973: 48). This dehumanization or delegitimization and the associated disruption of the 'moral order' between groups have been widely recognized within the literature as necessary permissive conditions for the escalation of intergroup violence, repression and other gross human rights violations committed on a mass scale (Duster 1971; Staub 1978; 1989; Northrup 1989; Mack 1990; Montville 1990; Ball 1999; Fein 1999; Petonito 2000; McCauley 2002; Minow 2002; Cobb 2003; Staub and Bar-Tal 2003).

Third, over the course of protracted violence, groups can develop antagonistic myths, collective memories or communal narratives that reinforce biased conceptions of the Self as a victim of injustice while portraying the Other as an intractably evil enemy, effectively glossing over any complicity that the ingroup may have had in past violence (Mack 1990; Bar-Tal 2000; Minow 2002; Cairns and Roe 2003; Devine-Wright 2003). These myths about the nature of the Self and the Other can therefore further polarize perceptions of identity and ossify hostile relationships, blocking the potential for the future development of empathy and reinforcing existing fears, prejudices and stereotypes. Further, such beliefs are actively socialized among younger generations and even in the absence of overt conflict, they may legitimize future violence and cycles of revenge (Bar-Tal 2003).

Finally, protracted intergroup violence has been shown to almost inevitably retrench material disparities between identity groups. This occurs as group identity gains increasing salience in discriminatory distributions of social, economic and political power—factors which may themselves have been central to the initial development of intergroup hostility. Additionally, the devastation wrought by mass violence can not only amplify antagonism by increasing the difficult life experiences of identity groups, but can also shrink the total 'resource pie' available to a society and thereby increase the likelihood of future conflict and competition over diminished supply (Homer-Dixon 1994; 1999).

Ultimately, the initiation of physical violence typically presses identity conflicts into ever-worsening cycles of violence, moving along a 'continuum of destruction' in which each act of violence makes future aggression more likely (Staub 1989: 208). Over time, the evolution of identity-based conflict in deeply divided societies can culminate in acts of intergroup mass violence, including large-scale repression, killing, genocide, ethnic cleansing or other gross human rights violations carried out by "individuals who injure, kill and murder" on the basis of group membership (Staub and Bar-Tal 2003: 710). Such acts of mass violence represent "intergroup behavior at its most horrific extreme," with people being targeted not because of any individual characteristic, but because of their inclusion in an identifiable and maligned social category (Hogg and Abrams 1998: 1). Accordingly, the mass atrocities and gross human rights violations committed in deeply divided societies are remarkable not just for the scope and duration of their violence, but for the fact that they are inherently tied to group membership and committed on the basis of collective identity. Indeed, as Mark Drumbl has noted, in deeply divided societies, such 'extraordinary crimes' are almost exclusively carried out against "large numbers of individuals based on their actual or perceived membership in a particular group that has become selected as a target on discriminatory grounds," with individual victims being targeted for persecution solely because of their identified group membership (Drumbl 2007: 4).

Reconciliation: transforming deeply divided societies

While all these factors contribute to making identity-based mass violence in deeply divided societies notoriously difficult to resolve, this does not mean that these animosities are inevitable or that they cannot be replaced by more peaceable relations. Indeed, as Tarja Väyrynen and other scholars have argued, since identities are constructions that are constantly created and re-created by social practices, the "space for innovation" for their transformation is never fully closed (Väyrynen 1999: 139).[5] What this analysis does suggest, however, is that any effort at reconciliation and building a sustainable peace among enemies previously engaged in gross human rights violations will need to directly address, and significantly alter, the antagonistic perceptions of group identity and the hostile system of relationships dividing Self from Other that make such mass violence possible.

Reconciliation, understood both as a theoretical concept and an empirical goal, has attracted increased attention throughout the body of literature engaged in the study of peace and conflict, and has gained particular prominence among scholars concerned with the ways in which groups might be brought to live peacefully together following the conclusion of protracted conflict. However, as a concept, reconciliation has tended to remain murky and resistant to clear definition, with every author having slightly different understandings of what exactly needs to take place during processes of reconciliation, what the 'successful' outcome of reconciliation processes would look like, and whether reconciliation occurs at the interpersonal, intergroup or intersocietal level (Oduro 2007; Chapman 2009). Despite this variability, it is generally accepted that the process of reconciliation might be defined as the act of creating or rebuilding "friendship and harmony between rival sides after resolution of a conflict, or transforming the relations between rival sides from hostility and resentment to friendly and harmonious relations," a long-term endeavor that will require former enemies to "form new relations of peaceful coexistence based on mutual trust and acceptance, cooperation, and consideration of each other's needs" (Bar-Siman-Tov 2004: 72).

In this way, reconciliation is understood to entail a movement beyond the mere absence of conflict and situations of 'thin' or 'negative' coexistence, requiring deeper changes to the underlying ways in which former enemies perceive one another and their relationships (Kriesberg 1998; 2001; 2004; Lederach 1997; Weiner 1998; Bar-Tal and Bennink 2004; Kelman 1999; 2004; 2008). Indeed, the 'thick' social and psychological changes associated with reconciliation are commonly acknowledged as the elements ultimately needed for the foundation of sustainable peace, as they create the opportunity for relations of insecurity and animosity to be replaced by those of cooperation, mutual respect and a commitment between former enemies to settling future conflicts without recourse to violence (Reychler and Paffenholz 2001;

Wilmer 2002; Bar-Siman-Tov 2004). These observations indicate that neither the initial termination of hostilities nor the signing of formal peace agreements will themselves be enough to "overcome the bitterness and grievances inherent in a protracted conflict, nor the perceptions and mutual fears" these conflicts engender among former enemies—factors that will otherwise continue to prevent more cooperative relations and could bring about a renewal of violence (Bar-Siman-Tov 2004: 61). In other words, former enemies' entrenched animosities will not fade easily with the passage of time, but rather will require extended reconciliation processes to be challenged and overcome (Staub 2001: 17). Accordingly, nowhere are such reconciliation efforts more important than in the context of deeply divided societies seeking to overcome legacies of mass intergroup violence between heavily polarized identity groups—especially if the goal is to have these former enemies peacefully reintegrated and living together in a single state, as is often the case.

Reconciliation in divided societies is thus understood as a fundamentally transformative process, one that requires "changing the motivations, goals, beliefs, attitudes, and emotions of the great majority of society members regarding the conflict, the nature of the relationship between the parties, and the parties themselves" (Bar-Tal and Bennink 2004: 12). This conception underlies a growing body of 'conflict transformation' literature that has emerged within and among the related fields of political science, conflict resolution and peace studies (Lederach 1997; Miall et al. 2000; Miall 2004; Ryan 2007). Often drawing heavily on studies in sociology and social psychology, this work argues that successful reconciliation in divided societies necessarily involves an element of 'social learning' between former enemies, namely "an active process of redefinition or reinterpretation of reality—what people consider real, possible, and desirable—on the basis of new causal and normative knowledge" (Adler and Barnett 1998: 43). Social learning processes engage former enemies in redefining the antagonistic identities and belief systems motivating past violence and in (re)creating a more positive system of relations governing their interactions (Bar-Siman-Tov 2004: 71). Indeed, as the distinguished social psychologist Herbert Kelman argues, given that collective identity is recognized as a prime contributor to intergroup conflicts in divided societies, so too will it have a central role to play in the processes of social learning required for their reconciliation. As he contends, "identities have to change, at least tacitly, if protracted identity conflicts are to be settled and, certainly, if they are to be resolved in a way that transforms the relationship and opens the way to reconciliation" (2001: 194).

There is a growing consensus among conflict transformation theorists as to what successful reconciliation, understood as the outcome of such 'identity negotiation,' might entail in deeply divided societies. While this is by no means an exhaustive list, five widely accepted indicators of successful social learning and intergroup reconciliation in formerly divided societies are identified below.[6] However, it should be noted that, within the literature, all of these elements are considered to be highly interrelated and mutually constitutive. Further, it has been recognized that social learning processes cannot be limited to decision-makers or elites alone if they are to successfully effect the kind of broader transformation required to achieve reconciliation and sustainable peace in divided societies. That said, such high-level 'strategic learning' has been noted as an important first step in the right direction (Bar-Siman-Tov 2004: 70). However, as Yaacov Bar-Siman-Tov and others have noted, to achieve the goal of sustainable peace it is ultimately necessary that these changes "penetrate deep into the societal fabric" and effect a broader reconciliation "involving the whole society or at least a majority in the reconciliation process" (idem: 73).

First, reconciliation is marked by social learning that develops mutual trust among former enemies (Lederach 1997; Bar-Tal and Bennink 2004; Amstutz 2005; Jeong 2005; Nadler and Liviatan 2006; Oduro 2007). The creation of such trust centers on replacing past feelings of fear, threat and suspicion of the Other with the belief that future relations will be governed by amicable reciprocity and reasonable expectations of cooperative interaction. While largely marked by cognitive and affective change, this trust is a direct product of social interaction, built up over time through sustained experiences of positive and reciprocated contact and communication with the Other (Kelman 2008). Notably, the creation of mutual trust is also necessarily tied to reduced levels of discriminatory bias and prejudice, as well as to the amelioration of negative stereotypes that reproduce simplistic, and often hostile, misperceptions about the Other's actions, intentions and inherent trustworthiness (Gross-Stein 2002).

Second, reconciliation in divided societies involves processes of social learning that develop a broader sense of collective identification in which the cognitive boundaries of the Self are expanded to include the Other, replacing previous divisions with a sense of shared identity, friendship, trust and common interest (Kelman 1999; 2004; 2008; Schirch 2001; Bar-Siman-Tov 2004; Bar-Tal and Bennink 2004; Stover and Weinstein 2004; Kruger 2006; Oberschall 2007). To be clear, this does not entail the elimination of existing group identities as such, but is rather a process of 'identity widening' that moves towards a more inclusive perception of 'superordinate' or 'transcendent' identity marked by more peaceful and cooperative relations and within which common normative structures apply (Ellis 2006).[7] This point is succinctly made by Terrell Northrup, who notes that reconciliation entails replacing the rigid divisions of Self and Other that defined past conflict with a more inclusive common identity in which a "sense of 'we' replaces the 'us/them' split" (Northrup 1989: 81). However, as she notes, "this does not imply that the parties become like each other but that they accept their differences [and] possibly even value them" (ibid.).[8] The kind of collective identification associated with reconciliation therefore involves the creation of a more inclusive sense of moral and political community among former enemies, one that doesn't require the "elimination of existing cultural and ethnic loyalties and identities," but rather facilitates the "creation of regions of social cognitive and normative bonds that can encourage peoples to identify, and to expect their security and welfare to be intimately intertwined, with those that exist on the same side of spatial and cognitive borders" (Adler and Barnett 1998: 59).

Third, the kind of reconciliatory social learning required in divided societies must also include a corresponding change to the antagonistic societal beliefs that enemies hold about one another and that reinforce their relations of enmity. Political psychologists Ervin Staub and Daniel Bar-Tal have emphasized the need to transform the corrupted ideologies, normative structures and value systems developed over the course of conflict between identity groups, arguing that if these beliefs are left unaddressed, they will continue to reinforce the devaluation or delegitimization of the Other and to maintain perceptions that the outgroup is a justifiable target for violence (Staub and Bar-Tal 2003: 731). Reconciliation therefore requires an extension of the boundaries of moral community among former antagonists such that members of the Other are effectively 'rehumanized' (Kelman 1973; 1999; 2004; Mack 1990; Schirch 2001; Bar-Siman-Tov 2004; Bar-Tal and Bennink 2004; Kruger 2006; Aiken 2008). In essence, this entails the development of a more equitable moral order that values difference but also recognizes a common humanity among former enemies—the notion that Self and Other should be accorded equal moral worth and are therefore entitled to the same ethical considerations. Most notably, this process involves replacing the previous 'culture of violence' with a new 'culture of human rights' under which both Self and Other are perceived to be equally entitled to fundamental human rights protections (Aiken 2009). This process of rehumanization centrally involves a broadening of empathy beyond the boundaries of the ingroup to incorporate members of the Other and to reverse the patterns of moral exclusion tied to past conflict (Halpern and Weinstein 2004; Stover and Weinstein 2004; Nadler and Liviatan 2006).

Fourth, successful reconciliation is distinguished by social learning that leads to perceptions of the illegitimacy or 'unthinkability' of the use of violent force to resolve future disputes among former enemies (Boulding 1978; Northrup 1989; Adler and Barnett 1998; Kriesberg 1982; 1998; Elshtain 2001; Bar-Siman-Tov 2004). As noted peace scholar John Paul Lederach suggests, the key to reconciliation lies in altering the system of social and psychological relationships that exist between identity groups, and so approaches to post-conflict peacebuilding must seek to "transform a *war-system* characterized by deeply divided, hostile and violent relationships into a *peace-system* characterized by just and interdependent relationships with the capacity to find non-violent mechanisms for expressing and handling conflict" (Lederach 1997: 84). To be sure, this is not to assert that no conflict and competition will exist in this new relationship or that reconciliation entails the goal of perfect harmony. Rather, based on a foundation of mutual trust, shared moral order, and a more inclusive and amicable sense of common identification, the kind of reconciliation envisioned here entails a mutual expectation that all future conflicts will be settled peacefully and by means other than violence—in effect, reflecting the fact that former enemies "ha[ve] become integrated to the point that there is a real assurance that the members of that community do not fight each other physically, but will settle their disputes in some other way" (Adler and Barnett 1998: 6).

Fifth, and finally, changes in structural and material conditions are also considered necessary components of social learning and successful reconciliation in divided societies. Indeed, it is now widely recognized that reconciled relations between former enemies cannot be effectively sustained if gross disparities in economic well-being or inequitable access to social and political rights persist. Among conflict transformation scholars, addressing structural and material divisions is therefore considered essential to social learning and reconciliation, both for creating the sense of equality needed for collective identification and for ensuring that these disparities do not serve as points of contention that could provide the basis for future conflict (Azar 1990; Kriesberg 1998; 2004; Staub 1989; 2000; 2006; Staub and Bar-Tal 2003; Bar-Tal and Bennink 2004; Jeong 2005). While reconciliation is unlikely to make for exact symmetry between groups, more equitable relations improve chances for reconciliation and the creation of a sense of shared identity, while gross and systematic disparities between groups are more likely to prevent opportunities for more reconciled relations between former antagonists (Bar-Siman-Tov 2004: 65).

However, to make the argument that identities are socially constructed and always in process, and therefore that conflictual relations can be transformed, is not to suggest that this is an easy task or that it might even be a viable possibility during all stages of intergroup conflict. Due to the ways in which the commission of violence retrenches group boundaries, mutual vilification and perceptions of the Other as enemy, it remains unlikely that reconciliatory social learning and the development of peaceable collective identities can be effected during periods of overt conflict. Hostile relations tend to be path-dependent, and during protracted conflicts, in particular, the identification of the Other as an externalized enemy may come to be viewed as a solidified 'social fact' or virtual objective truth governing intergroup relations. The argument made here therefore self-consciously brackets cases of ongoing violence to focus on practices of reconciliation in post-conflict societies, forwarding the more limited claim that if divided societies exist in a minimal state of 'negative peace' in the aftermath of intergroup violence, the potential exists for the reconstruction of identity through social learning and the subsequent development of a more 'positive' and sustainable peace (Galtung 1985). That said, to begin theorizing the causal connections between institutions of transitional justice and reconciliation in divided societies, a new line of dialogue must be opened between conflict transformation scholars' insights about social learning and the burgeoning field of transitional justice.

Transitional justice

The term 'transitional justice' refers to "the full range of processes and mechanisms associated with a society's attempts to come to terms with a legacy of large-scale past abuses, in order to ensure accountability, serve justice, and achieve reconciliation" (Annan 2004: 4).[9] In recent years, the field of transitional justice studies has emerged as a distinct area of scholarship concerned with the study of the various judicial and non-judicial strategies that have been used by community, state and international actors to provide accountability for gross human rights violations in societies transitioning away from legacies of internal conflict and/or state repression. To date, these strategies have included a wide range of institutional responses, including domestic trials, international tribunals, truth commissions, amnesties, reparations programs and more 'traditional' justice methodologies (Kerr and Mobekk 2007). For the most part, the body of transitional justice scholarship that has emerged since the mid-1990s has centered largely on a series of comparative institutional analyses of the various approaches that have been used to account for past abuses within different countries as a way of helping these countries successfully transition towards democracy and sustainable peace (Kritz 1995; Hamber 1998; Minow 1998; Rotberg and Thompson 2000; Teitel 2000; Biggar 2001; DeBrito et al. 2001; Hayner 2002; Schabas and Darcy 2004; Sriram 2004; Weinstein and Stover 2004; Sarat et al. 2005; Borer 2006; Elster 2006; Philpott 2006; Roht-Arriaza and Mariezcurrena 2006; Quinn 2010). While a consensus exists within this work that the unique context of each society's transition means that no 'one-size-fits-all' strategy can be usefully employed across all cases, the field has nonetheless been largely defined by a series of debates as to which institutional strategies might best achieve the goals of justice and reconciliation in transitional societies (Roht-Arriaza 2006; Kerr and Mobekk 2007).

The first of these debates is that of 'trials' versus 'truth'—a recurring disagreement between those scholars who advocate criminal prosecutions or other legal sanctions against the perpetrators of violence and gross human rights violations as an essential means of re-establishing law and order in transitional societies, and those proponents of 'truth-recovery' or 'truth-telling' frameworks who hold that the full acknowledgment and explication of past conflict are more essential elements of justice and reconciliation (Hayner 1994; 2002; Minow 1998; Van Zyl 1999; Rotberg and Thompson 2000; Freeman and Hayner 2003; Schabas and Darcy 2004; Gibson 2004; Braham 2007). A second, and closely related, debate over 'retributive' and 'restorative' approaches has further divided the transitional justice literature. This argument concerns the underlying philosophy of justice that should inform accountability for past violence, and is usually drawn in rather stark contrast. Very broadly, proponents of retributive justice argue for punishment as a response to mass violence, emphasizing the need for deterrence, individual criminal liability, and the reestablishment of the rule of law, processes that may require legal sanctions and criminal prosecutions to be carried out in national and international courts (Orenlichter 1991; Osiel 2000; Auckerman 2002; Snyder and Vinjamuri 2003; Drumbl 2007; Mallinder 2007). Advocates of restorative justice, on the other hand, argue that legal punishments sought against perpetrators must be limited in favor of rebuilding social connections and relationships that may have been damaged over the course of the conflict and involving victims and perpetrators of past violence as cooperative partners in reparative processes (Zehr 1990; Van Ness and Strong 1997; Minow 1998; Llewellyn and Howse 1999; Kiss 2000; Van Ness 2002; Llewellyn 2006; 2007; Johnstone and Van Ness 2007; Aiken 2008).

Finally, there exist long-standing debates in the literature surrounding the most effective locations, mandates and compositions of transitional justice institutions. These arguments take up the relative efficacy of pursuing justice and accountability primarily through community-based mechanisms, national institutions or international organizations, and ask whether the ultimate authority and responsibility for these transitional justice approaches should rest with local, national or international officials (Sarkin 2001; Bell 2003; Des Forges and Longman 2004; Peskin 2005; Kerr and Mobekk 2007; Lundy and McGovern 2008; McEvoy and McGregor 2008; Waddell and Clark 2008; Aiken 2010). Sparked by recent experiences in countries such as Uganda, Rwanda and East Timor, there is also a growing body of work examining the utility of incorporating more traditional, indigenous or informal practices in transitional justice strategies (Burgess 2006; Baines 2007; Quinn 2007; Clark 2008, 2010; Huyse and Salter 2008). Recently, however, these debates have evolved, as a growing number of transitional justice scholars have sought to move beyond this kind of diametrical thinking and to explore the potential benefits of more 'holistic' institutions—mechanisms that combine elements from each of these traditional debate axes. Institutionally, this has been reflected in the design of 'hybrid' strategies involving combinations of both national and international structures and officials, 'mixed' mechanisms, which incorporate both restorative and retributive aspects of truth and trial processes, and even 'mixed/hybrid institutions,' which combine components of all of these strategies in some complementary or sequential arrangement (Dickinson 2003; Evenson 2004; Reiger 2006; Roht-Arriaza 2006; Schabas 2006; Kerr and Mobekk 2007).

However, despite the existence of these debates regarding institutional design, scholars and practitioners working within the field remain united in their agreement that transitional justice is an integral component of post-conflict reconciliation processes in societies struggling to overcome legacies of past violence (Kerr and Mobekk 2007; Leebaw 2008; Lambourne 2009; Aiken 2008; 2010). A recent survey of transitional justice literature undertaken by the Canadian International Development Research Centre concludes that reconciliation, in tandem with justice, remains a fundamental aim of almost all transitional justice processes, and that preventing the recurrence of violence and stabilizing a post-conflict peace are the "ultimate goals" of transitional justice (Oduro 2007: 3). Further, recent studies have suggested that the use of some form of transitional justice strategy to account for past atrocities may be a necessary component of the development of sustainable peace in post-conflict societies, particularly in societies that have been deeply divided along lines of entrenched identity cleavages (Lederach 1997; Miall et al. 2000; Huyse 2003; Long and Brecke 2003; Bar-Siman-Tov 2004; Kriesberg 2004; Oberschall 2007). However, despite the strong connection drawn in the literature between transitional justice, reconciliation and lasting peace, the causal processes underlying these connections are left largely unspecified and undertheorized. For instance, while proponents of truth commissions and other restorative mechanisms argue that bringing former enemies together and revealing truths about past events can help to heal broken relationships, and advocates of trials and retributive justice strategies forward the necessity of criminal punishment for societal reconstruction, to date insufficient consideration has been given to theorizing and studying empirically how these institutional components actually contribute to the psychosocial processes of intergroup reconciliation (Fletcher and Weinstein 2002; Weinstein and Stover 2004; Braham 2007; Chapman 2009).

I argue that what may be required by way of uncovering the relationship between transitional justice and reconciliation is a reconsideration of institutional design that begins by engaging the fundamental issues of collective identity at the root of mass violence, and that examines how the specific strategies employed by various institutions might contribute to transforming underlying identity-based antagonisms that might otherwise threaten to incite future returns to violence. This reconceptualization offers an opportunity to move beyond traditional comparative examinations of transitional justice mechanisms based on assessments of structure and arguments as to the efficacy of various institutional designs in providing justice and reconciliation in divided societies. Indeed, the literature's recognition of the highly contextualized nature of conflict, and its consensus that no one model of transitional justice will be universally effective, already inherently limit the utility of such approaches. The argument advanced here, on the other hand, seeks to change the terms of transitional justice debates. Ultimately, asking whether any one kind of institution—be it indigenous, retributive or hybrid—is intrinsically 'better' than another seems less important than asking whether the processes and mechanisms employed by such strategies serve to impede or impel the transformation of communal identities and relationships through the kinds of social learning ultimately required for reconciliation. To be clear, this is not to make the claim that transitional justice is all relative or that institutional design is unimportant. In fact, quite the opposite—it may be that institutional design is of the greatest importance in determining whether a transitional justice strategy is able to contribute positively to reconciliation in post-conflict societies. Rather, I suggest that by reorienting our attentions from structure to process and concentrating on what transitional institutions *do* rather than what they *are*, we can gain greater insight into how transitional justice interacts with the politics of identity in divided societies, and how it directly impacts thereby the potential for reconciliation and sustainable peace.

Identity, reconciliation and transitional justice

The argument that transitional justice can have a causal effect on promoting social learning and intergroup reconciliation is fundamentally predicated on the logic underpinning the identity-based arguments advanced by conflict transformation theorists. As discussed, these theories assert that neither the content of collective identities nor the nature of relations between them exist as reified structures, but are rather social creations, constructed and reconstructed through ongoing processes of social interaction. Following from this premise, the transformative potential for developing more peaceful relations among even the most intractable of former enemies can exist if antagonistic conceptions of Self and Other are challenged by new patterns of social interaction and identification.[10] Indeed, several scholars working in this conflict transformation tradition have noted that the systemic changes, societal upheaval and altered relationship dynamics associated with the post-conflict environment mark an 'innovative space' in which the existing politics of identity can be challenged and changed in divided societies (Coleman 2002; Eder et al. 2002; Wilmer 2002). In other words, the initial cessation of overt conflict can bring with it a unique transformative moment: a narrow window for actors to engage in processes of social learning, to reexamine old ideas about Self and Other, to denaturalize existing perceptions, and to consider the possibility of redrawing the bounds of moral and political community.

Further, a number of conflict transformation scholars have examined the seminal role that institutions might play in providing this 'innovative space' for bringing former enemies together to facilitate processes of intergroup reconciliation in the transformative moment. For instance, Yaacov Bar-Siman-Tov, a pioneer in this regard, notes that shared societal institutions may be indispensable precursors to the kinds of social learning ultimately necessary to intergroup reconciliation. In essence, Bar-Siman-Tov contends that such institutions can provide a crucial 'first space' for renewed contact, communication and other social exchanges among former enemies, and that these experiences, in turn, can provide the new knowledge needed to trigger the reconciliatory processes that transform identities, beliefs and relationships (2004). More specifically, he highlights how institutions can provide forums for former antagonists to begin to develop new forms of trust, shared norms and values, a sense of collective identification, and a mutual commitment to non-violent interaction—all factors considered integral to intergroup reconciliation and sustainable peace (idem: 67–71).

However, within the conflict transformation literature, it is the body of constructivist scholarship from the field of political science that has developed perhaps the most sophisticated theories to date concerning the role that structures and institutions can play in facilitating reconciliatory processes of social learning. These authors have argued that by fostering growth in social networks of trust and communication, institutions can help former enemies to learn to relate positively to one another and to develop a sense of collective identification. Indeed, as Emmanuel Adler and Michael Barnett note in their foundational work on the formation of peaceful 'security communities' in the international system, "because identities are created and reproduced on the basis of knowledge that people have of themselves and others, learning processes that occur within and are promoted by institutions can lead actors to develop positive reciprocal expectations and thus identify with each other" (1998: 41–42).

For instance, constructivist scholars have highlighted how institutions can help to build non-violent relationships among former enemies by working both directly and indirectly to transform the 'social facts' of collective identities and the hostile patterns of interaction that previously informed intergroup enmity (Wendt 1992: 2000; Cronin 1999). In particular, these authors have noted the importance of institutions as forums in which actors are brought together to engage in increased interaction and communication—two elements considered critical to facilitating the social learning process, as they allow actors to "[re]discover their preferences, to reconceptualize who they are, and to reimagine their social bonds" (Adler and Barnett 1998: 43). In essence, by providing the initial sites for renewed socialization and learning about the Other, institutions can help actors to renew their trust in one another through the experience of more positive interaction, to develop more compatible systems of beliefs and values, and ultimately "to identify with those who were once on the other side of cognitive divides" by fostering a more inclusive sense of collective identity that leads to more peaceful and cooperative relationships (idem: 45).

Similarly, other constructivist authors have stressed the importance of institutions as the "organizational platforms" needed for the articulation, transmission and socialization of the normative structures that inform the 'content' of new identities and set limits on the behaviors governing their relations (Adler and Barnett 1998; Finnemore and Sikkink 1998; Keck and Sikkink 1998; Sikkink 2011). In this way, beyond serving as a focal point around which a new sense of common identity and attachment can coalesce, institutions can also help to disseminate new sets of moral values and ethical rules among members of the burgeoning community. In so doing, institutions draw upon their accumulated reserves of authority and legitimacy in an attempt to encourage the emergence of a new normative culture, using their structures to pressure and persuade actors to challenge their existing beliefs and to internalize new moral values and related behaviors (Adler and Barnett 1998: 42; Finnemore and Sikkink 1998: 912).

While, to date, constructivist scholars have reserved such theories for tracking social learning between actors at the international level, a cross-fertilization of the insights derived from this work could allow the transitional justice literature to better theorize the role played by transitional institutions in facilitating processes of reconciliation in deeply divided socie-ties.[11] Transitional justice institutions tend to attract tremendous public attention in post-conflict environments as potent symbols of social breaks with divisive past violence. As Ruti Teitel argues, a central contribution of all such institutions is their ability to mark a fundamental "normative shift" in post-conflict societies by condemning the fear, divisiveness and injustice that characterized past violence and promoting a reconstituted sense of collective rights and responsibilities that cuts across racial, ethnic and religious lines (Teitel 2002: 225). Further, these institutions are often explicitly tasked by transitional authorities with creating more reconciled societies based on the values of democracy, human rights and shared commitment to the rule of law and the non-violent resolution of future conflict (Teitel 2002; Annan 2004). Transitional justice institutions may therefore also be uniquely positioned to promote social learning following the transformative moment that accompa-nies the end of widespread violence in divided societies, as they can provide the initial forum for bringing former enemies together to confront the legacies of past violence and to reconsider the nature of their relations (Aiken 2009).[12]

To date, the insights of conflict transformation scholars about the seminal roles of identities and institutions in building more peaceable relations among enemies have yet to be comprehensively employed in examining the relation-ship between transitional justice and reconciliation.[13] I argue, however, that applying this transformative logic to the environments of societies rebuilding in the wake of mass intergroup violence provides a vital entry point for theorizing how transitional justice institutions might work towards the identity change required for reconciliation and the stabilization of peace. Indeed, I contend that transitional justice mechanisms may be of crucial importance to reconciliation efforts in such contexts, as their structures can encourage the kinds of socialization and social learning enabling ethnonational groups to alter antagonistic identifications and to develop a more inclusive sense of collective identity characterized by amity and peaceable relations. In particular, I suggest that the psychosocial processes of social learning that these institutions promote are the 'linchpin' for redefining divisive identities and transforming relationships from ones of conflict and hostility to those of friendship and cooperation.

To be clear, this is not to make the overly ambitious claim that transitional justice institutions are a 'magic bullet' that can foster lasting intergroup reconciliation in and of themselves. Reconciliation is an ongoing and multi-faceted process likely to require other elements operating outside of the limited timelines and mandates covered by formal transitional justice strategies. Rather, I argue that these institutions, if properly designed, can serve as catalysts of social learning through which former enemies can come to reimagine the nature of their relations and obligations to one another, and through this reimagining, can begin to create the conditions necessary for reconciliation and positive peace. This still leaves questions, however, as to how exactly these institutions can contribute to transforming entrenched hostilities in divided societies and to building the more inclusive conceptions of collective identity and moral community linked to reconciliation. These questions are taken up in the following chapter, which introduces an innovative 'social learning model' that theorizes the causal relationship between intergroup reconciliation and transitional justice.

Notes

1   See the work of William Sumner (1906) for a foundational discussion of ethnocentrism. While Henri Tajfel's (1978) 'Minimal Group Paradigm' has shown that the simple act of categorization tends to entail preferential treatment of the ingroup, this does not necessarily lead to a corresponding increase in conflict or competition with the outgroup.

2   Notably, this reflects recent constructivist theory in international relations, which holds that relations between states are not necessarily conflictual, but rather exist on a fluid continuum of possible relationships including friendship, rivalry and enmity dependent upon the nature of their identifications and past social interactions (Wendt 1992; 1994; 2000; 2003; Risse-Kappen 1996; Adler and Barnett 1998; Algappa 1998; Hopf 1998).

3   This is echoed in Thomas Eriksen's conception of 'identity politics' from social psychology (2001: 42–43).

4   Robert Putnam emphasizes the distinction between forms of social capital that 'bond' homogenous groups together by means of exclusivity, and more inclusive forms of social capital that 'bridge' ties between identity groups. In societies deficient in 'bridging' social capital, groups lack the trust or desire to work towards shared goals through mutual collaboration (Putnam 2000: 22).

5   As Herbert Kelman has argued, "social psychological evidence suggests that [protracted and intractable identity conflicts] can change, and historical evidence shows that they do change" (Kelman 1997: 222–223).

6   Notably, the five-part model of reconciliation outlined here combining social, psychological and structural factors shares a number of common points with a similar model developed by Brandon Hamber and Grainne Kelly (2005).

7 This reflects findings from the 'Common Ingroup Identity Model' from recent studies in social psychology that illustrate the strong link between the formation of such 'superordinate' identities and the creation of more positive perceptions and relations between previously antagonistic groups (Gaertner 1994; Gaertner and Dovidio 2000; Brewer and Gaertner 2001).

8 Notably, the formation of collective identification through social learning is also considered to be a central element required for the creation of sustainable peace between international actors by constructivist scholars in international relations (Wendt 1992; 1994; 2000; Adler and Barnett 1998; Cronin 1999).

9 'Transitional justice' can be considered either broadly or narrowly. Broadly, it includes the full range of interlinked processes and mechanisms used domestically and/or by the international community to address the legacies of past human rights violations and violence within a country and to promote the goals of accountability and reconciliation. Narrowly, it refers only to the formal institutions used in these larger strategies, such as trials, tribunals or truth commissions. The approach taken here is in line with broader interpretations, focusing on how wider justice strategies, and not just formal institutions, might be designed to facilitate social learning mechanisms (although formal or 'centralized' institutions will likely form the central element of any wider strategy). On this distinction between 'broad' and 'narrow' interpretations, see Roht-Arriaza (2006: 12) and Aiken (2010).

10 Herbert Kelman suggests a degree of 'strategic optimism' for being able to transform identities and overcome intractable conflicts in divided societies as "social psychological evidence suggests that they can change, and historical evidence shows that they do change" (Kelman 1997: 222–223).

11 Some early work in line with this cross-fertilization does exist (Jesse and Williams 2005), examining how international institutions might help to ameliorate ethnonational conflict in divided societies through the creation of more common identifications.

12 The hypothesis that transitional justice institutions might act as such "catalysts for reconciliation" in post-conflict societies has also been advanced by Beth Rushton (2006: 138).

13 That said, some conflict transformation scholars have begun early work on examining the role of transitional justice institutions as part of broader processes of reconciliation and sustainable peace (Staub and Bar-Tal 2003; Bar-Tal and Bennink 2004; Kriesberg 2004; Jeong 2005; Staub 2006; Oberschall 2007; Aiken 2008).

Chapter 3

A social learning model of transitional justice

Having explored insights from the conflict transformation literature examining the crucial role of identity in divided societies, this chapter turns to outlining a new 'social learning model' of the causal relationship between transitional justice and intergroup reconciliation. In short, the chapter argues that transitional justice institutions capable of promoting reconciliation in divided societies will need to advance three key broad types of social learning: instrumental, socioemotional and distributive. These broader categories are in turn linked to five specific social learning mechanisms that are considered to be the necessary, if not sufficient, interventions required of any transitional justice strategy capable of advancing processes of social learning and intergroup reconciliation in divided societies, namely positive contact, transformative dialogue, truth, justice and the amelioration of material inequalities. This chapter concludes by summarizing the main aspects of this social learning model and offering some preliminary thoughts as to the implications of this framework for understanding the connections between transitional justice and reconciliation in divided societies.

Social learning and transitional justice

The effort to design a theoretical framework capable of tracing the complex causal chains linking institutions of transitional justice to the psychosocial processes of reconciliation in divided societies involves three distinct components. First, it must attend to insights derived from recent work by conflict transformation scholars as to the unique barriers to intergroup reconciliation in divided post-conflict societies that social learning processes must address if they are to be effective in altering antagonistic identities and the relationships between them. Second, it requires an operationalization of the specific social learning processes necessary to identity transformation and intergroup reconciliation. This work must combine the structural-institutional focus of current transitional justice studies with the more sophisticated psychosocial theories of social learning and identity politics developed in the conflict transformation literature. Finally, such a model should also consider how the particular design of transitional justice institutions and the strategies by which they are conducted might serve to impede or impel these particular mechanisms of social learning and, in so doing, either detract from or contribute to a society's potential for reconciliation and sustainable peace.

That said, we must first determine what forms of social learning are needed for reconciliation in divided societies and, more specifically, what specific roles transitional justice strategies might play in advancing this learning. While the constructivist literature offers a useful starting point for theorizing the causal effects of institutions on the formation of collective identities, it often falls short of clearly accounting for the operative social and cognitive mechanisms of social learning processes and of delineating the ways in which different institutional designs might mediate these mechanisms. As Jefferey Checkel notes in his recent critique of current constructivist theory, many authors fail to operationalize the psychosocial 'micromechanics' behind processes of social learning, particularly in terms of specifying the conditions under which learning will be most effective and outlining the specific ways in which actors' "interests and identities are shaped through and during interaction" with institutions (Checkel 2001: 561).

However, within conflict transformation scholarship, the field of social psychology has advanced perhaps the farthest in exploring the specific kinds of social learning required for reconciliation in divided societies, and it therefore provides a useful starting point for this study's investigations. A recent 'state of the art' collection of social psychological work suggests that intergroup reconciliation ultimately requires the promotion of three distinct processes of social learning in post-conflict environments. The first of these processes, *instrumental learning*, refers to strategies designed to engage actors in sustained cooperative interaction—interaction that allows former antagonists to begin to transform their relationships with one another and to "gradually learn to replace enmity with trust and negative with positive perceptions of the Other" (Nadler et al. 2008: 6). *Socioemotional learning*, on the other hand, involves interventions designed to directly confront the emotional and perceptual legacies of past conflict as a means of breaking down obstacles to reconciliation caused by existing feelings of victimization, guilt, distrust and fear between groups (ibid: 5).

These two processes of social learning are distinct from one another both in the interventions required for their development and in their temporal contexts. As Arie Nadler and Nurit Shnabel illustrate, "socioemotional reconciliation is focused on the past of the conflict and asserts that the key to a reconciled future lies in a constructive confrontation with the painful past [whereas] efforts of instrumental reconciliation are focused on the present and are based on the premise that ongoing cooperation between the adversaries in the present will result in a reconciled future" (Nadler and Shnabel 2008: 44). However, these types of social learning are highly interdependent: the trust and cooperation built through instrumental learning provide the basis for a successful engagement with the past, while acts of socioemotional learning help societies to overcome the emotional and psychological barriers to interaction related to past violence that otherwise militate against the development of more positive intergroup relations.[1]

Finally, it is also clear that the relative ability of socioemotional and instrumental initiatives to contribute to intergroup reconciliation is heavily mediated by related aspects of *distributive learning*—sustained attempts to reduce structural and material inequalities and limit perceptions of inequitable power relations between former antagonists. As Arie Nadler and his colleagues argue, alongside instrumental and socioemotional social learning, "the move to peaceful intergroup relations hinges on ensuring that the adversarial groups perceive equality of opportunities to procure material and social resources" (Nadler et al. 2008: 10). Accordingly, this study asserts that a combination of all three of these broader social learning processes will ultimately be required for a society deeply divided by legacies of intrastate violence to be reintegrated and successfully reconciled.

To date, though, existing studies in transitional justice have tended to focus almost exclusively on socioemotional learning—that is, how different justice institutions or mechanisms can contribute to reconciliation by providing elements of truth and justice to address past abuses. While these efforts remain vitally important, insights from the conflict transformation literature suggest that such initiatives will necessarily need to follow, or work in tandem with, longer-term interventions designed to promote intergroup interaction and distributive equality if they are ultimately going to successfully build reconciliation and sustainable peace in divided societies. In unpacking the relationship between transitional justice and reconciliation, what is therefore needed is a broader interpretation of transitional justice itself, one that considers how instrumental and distributive aims can be incorporated within or alongside the institutions and mechanisms that seek to provide accountability for past atrocities. In essence, this reinterpretation suggests that the relative success of any transitional justice strategy in contributing to intergroup reconciliation will depend on its ability to promote instrumental and distributive processes of social learning alongside socioemotional interventions. At the very least, transitional justice mechanisms must be designed to work in tandem with other ongoing societal efforts to rebuild trust, cooperation and intergroup equality between former enemies.

Nevertheless, while the distinction between instrumental, socioemotional and distributive learning processes offers a point of entry to investigating the link between transitional justice and reconciliation, this work still falls short of operationalizing the specific mechanisms required to promote these types of social learning. This operationalization is a crucial part of considering how transitional justice institutions and the strategies they employ can best advance mechanisms of social learning and most effectively contribute to intergroup reconciliation and sustainable peace in divided societies. To fill this gap, this study draws on a synthesis of insights from conflict transformation and transitional justice theorists and practitioners, highlighting five specific learning mechanisms that emerge as points of consensus in the scholarship as necessary, if not sufficient, elements required for reconciliation. These five elements include positive contact, transformative dialogue, truth, justice and the amelioration of intergroup inequalities. I argue that the capacity of transitional justice interventions to facilitate reconciliation in divided societies depends, in large part, upon whether the strategies and institutions these interventions employ can engender instrumental, socio-emotional and distributive learning by way of these five interrelated and mutually supporting mechanisms.

es operationalized mechanism

Instrumental learning

The first mode of social learning, instrumental learning, refers to rebuilding relationships and fostering less antagonistic perceptions between formerly divided groups. Renewed positive interaction and communication across group boundaries is the first, and perhaps most crucial, mechanism of social learning necessary for intergroup reconciliation. However, a review of the literature indicates that an increase in the quantity of intergroup inter-actions, while important, simply does not prove a potent enough challenge to the polarized identifications and entrenched animosities formed by past conflict. What matters most, scholars suggest, is the nature and quality of the interactions that take place and the societal context in which these interactions occur.

Positive intergroup contact

The argument that increased contact can lead to better relations among groups in conflict is the central assertion underlying the longstanding 'Contact Hypothesis' in social psychology. At root, this theory holds that an increase in positive intergroup contact can have a reliably independent effect on improving intergroup relations, as this contact directly reduces prejudice, challenges stereotypes and misperceptions, and can break down rigidified perceptions of the Other as a monolithic and inherently hostile group (Allport 1954; Hewstone and Brown 1986; Pettigrew 1998; Hewstone and Greenland; Brewer 2001; Stephan and Stephan 2001). Similarly, positive contact is often the primary way in which former enemies can come to understand one another's perspectives and to develop the shared sense of empathy necessary to restoring an equitable moral community in the wake of mass violence (Kenworthy et al. 2005; Staub and Bar-Tal 2003; Staub 2006). In effect, such encounters serve as the vital first step in processes of rehumaniz-ation, means by which enemies begin to see members of the 'Other' as people entitled to the same rights and protections as the Self, and to challenge the 'reversal of morality' that legitimized the use of violence in the past and could threaten to do so again if left unaddressed (Moses 1990; Kelman 1999; Staub 2001; Stephan and Stephan 2001; Halpern and Weinstein 2004; Kruger 2006).

Within the conflict transformation literature, this kind of positive contact is directly linked to reconciliatory social learning, as it is held to be fundamentally important to the formation of more inclusive collective identities among former antagonists. The work of social psychologist Samuel Gaertner and his colleagues on the 'Common Ingroup Identity Model' shows how the experience of positive contact can help to "transform members' cognitive representations of their memberships from separate groups to one more inclusive group . . . [essentially] from 'us' and 'them' to a more inclusive 'we'" in which positive feelings, equal moral standards and cooperative behavior prevail (Gaertner et al. 1994: 22; Gaertner and Dovidio 2000; Brewer and Gaertner 2001). Similarly, related insights from sociology's Symbolic Interactionism School (SIS) suggest that the experience of relating in new ways through sustained positive interaction and contact can foster the kinds of social learning required for the development of a more inclusive, cooperative and peaceable sense of collective identity (Mead 1934; Blumer 1969).[2] As Alexander Wendt illustrates:

> By showing others through cooperative acts that one expects them to be cooperators too, one changes the intersubjective knowledge in terms of which their identities are defined . . . . By teaching others and themselves to cooperate . . . actors are simultaneously learning to *identify* with each other—to see themselves as a "we" bound by certain norms.
>
> (1994: 390)

For these reasons, the promotion of positive intergroup contact is now considered by many conflict transformation scholars to be an essential mechanism of social learning and reconciliation in deeply divided societies (Foster and Finchilescu 1986; Ryan 1995; 2007; Hughes and Carmichael 1998; Hewstone et al. 2005; Gibson 2004). Moreover, beyond its own independent role in helping to overcome existing intergroup divisions and hostility, the restoration of contact is also widely recognized as a primary process upon which many other elements necessary for reconciliation rely (Staub 2006: 887). For instance, the opportunity for transformative intergroup dialogue is intrinsically dependent on renewed interaction between groups. Further, a renewal of positive contact is an essential starting point for the development of mutual trust between former enemies following the end of violence. Indeed, the formation of lasting trust necessarily requires a history of positive reciprocal interaction that allows actors to develop reasonable expectations of one another's future behavior—patterns that depend on the initial renewal of contact across group boundaries (Adler and Barnett 1998; Bar-Siman-Tov 2004).

However, to have a beneficial impact on reconciliation, contact must occur under certain conditions and in conducive contexts. More specifically, work on the Contact Hypothesis highlights that in order to facilitate social learning, positive intergroup contact must be of a non-adversarial quality, must take place between groups afforded equal status in society, must ideally be conducted over an extended period of time, and must be undertaken in the pursuit of cooperative or superordinate goals which actively aim to transform group divides. Additionally, to be most effective, such contact should take place in a societal context marked by supportive institutional structures, the agreement of relevant authorities, and a broader normative climate conducive to improved intergroup relations (Hewstone and Brown 1986; Kenworthy et al. 2005). Even outside of these optimal conditions, however, scholars have indicated the potential benefits of even relatively brief or indirect positive contact across group boundaries, suggesting that these efforts can have 'ripple effects' that can spread throughout a group (Hewstone et al. 2005; Stephan and Stephan 2001). That said, more recent studies also indicate that group identity should remain salient during such periods of contact in order for reductions in prejudice and stereotype to be generalized across all members of a group, rather than being limited to the specific and possibly exceptional individuals engaged in particular interactions (Brewer and Gaertner 2001; Hewstone et al. 2005).

Therefore, it is crucially important that transitional justice institutions incorporate mechanisms of positive contact into their strategies in order to help promote the processes of social learning required for reconciliation. In particular, the strategies employed by these institutions should ideally allow for periods of direct or indirect interpersonal encounter between former enemies during which as many of the conditional and contextual conditions for positive contact as possible can be met. Notably, the literature also suggests that justice strategies should avoid overly individualizing or downplaying the collective dimensions of the conflicts for which they are accountable, ensuring that the benefits of positive contact can be widely felt throughout both groups. This observation is particularly salient in responding to cases of mass violence, as given the scope of such violence, it is often impossible to include all former participants in the justice process and 'representative' examples or cases must necessarily be selected (Minow 1998; Imbleau 2004; Kerr and Mobekk 2007).[3]

It is equally imperative that transitional justice strategies seek to create a relatively supportive or at least neutral environment in which such encounters can take place, as contact that is adversarial, threatening or initiated under conditions of high anxiety is extremely unlikely to reduce prejudice and negative stereotypes and may in fact even serve to reinforce biases (Stephan and Stephan 2001; Kenworthy et al. 2005; Tausch et al. 2007). Additionally, if the interactions that these strategies produce among former enemies are predominantly adversarial instead of cooperative, it is doubtful whether this contact will be conducive to building mutual trust, rehumanizing the Other, and patterning the kind of relations upon which a more collective sense of identity can be based. Finally, to satisfy the 'equal status' requirement needed for positive contact, transitional justice strategies may need to ensure that they also in some way seek to address severe intergroup disparities in socioeconomic or sociopolitical status—disparities often tied to past conflict—either before or in tandem with provisions for encounter. Indeed, several studies have shown that in societies where such disparities align with group cleavages, the potential for meaningful intergroup contact remains severely limited, and where it does occur, it has very little lasting impact on changing existing identities or beliefs (Foster and Finchilescu 1986; Ruane and Todd 1996; Stephan and Stephan 2001).

Transformative dialogue

As important as positive contact might be for providing a basis for social learning, it is clear that simple contact, while significant, is only a first step towards meaningful reconciliation. What is of equal importance is the content of such interaction and, in particular, whether it can ultimately provide the basis for meaningful and transformative dialogue across group boundaries. The breakdown of meaningful intergroup interaction over the course of conflict limits opportunities for dialogue and understanding and provides an environment in which biases, misconceptions and cognitive distortions about Self and Other can flourish (Coleman 2002; Maoz 2004; Oberschall 2007). Accordingly, a renewal of 'bridging' communication among former enemies in the post-conflict environment is frequently cited in the conflict transformation literature as a key mechanism of social learning (Rothman 1997; Abu-Nimer 2001; Fisher 2001; Ropers 2004; Jeong 2005; Ellis 2006).

These authors recognize the crucial importance of intergroup dialogue to the processes of 'identity negotiation' needed for reconciliation in the aftermath of protracted identity conflicts. In effect, they hold intergroup dialogue to be a necessary mechanism by which groups can begin to dissolve the rigidified, monolithic and ethnocentric perceptions about the Other that informed past conflict, and as a way for former enemies to transform these understandings and to construct more inclusive and more peaceable conceptions of their identities (Lewin 1948; Northrup 1989; Abu-Nimer et al. 2001; Kelman 1999; 2001; 2004; 2008; Hermann 2004). As Adler and Barnett explain, while an increase in the quantity of intergroup interaction may be important for expanding the boundaries of moral and political community, the kind of learning about the Other gained through *quality* communication is essential to building the sense of shared identification necessary to reconciliation. Sustained positive contact can eventually "enable a group to think together, to see together, and to act together" (1998: 7; Linklater 1998: 79).

Similarly, other conflict transformation scholars highlight the importance of intergroup dialogue for social learning in divided societies as it can challenge the negative perceptions of the Other developed over the course of past violence. Jay Rothman, for instance, notes the particular need for engaging former enemies in transformative processes of "reflexive dialogue" in order to soften seemingly intractable identity conflicts by allowing the Self to begin viewing the Other as a valid partner for future cooperation. He argues that reconciliation in such contexts relies on the creation of opportunities for renewed communication in which prior combatants are able to reframe their understandings of their own and each other's identities. Rothman suggests that this kind of communication fosters 'we-feeling' and empathy—a sense of similarity between Self and Other in terms of basic values and needs (Rothman 1997: 234). Similarly, Donald Ellis (2006: 138) and others have argued in favor of "transformative communication" in the wake of intractable conflict to "widen the circle of identity inclusion," reduce entrenched biases and prejudice, and promote the kind of "moral growth" that replaces practices of delegitimization with feelings of empathy and a mutual recognition of the Other's humanity (Stephan and Stephan 2001; Staub 2001). Finally, other scholars such as Lewis Mehl-Madrona (2006: 297) and Tamar Hermann (2004: 58) have argued that a precondition for reconciliation is "the need to open channels, or space, for direct and candid communication between the protagonists," or the creation of a "conversational" or "dialogical space" in which former enemies are brought together and given the opportunity to critically reassess the images they hold of one another and the nature of their shared relationship.

Empirically, these assertions have been largely borne out by authors testing the impact of 'Interactive Conflict Resolution' strategies, 'dialogue groups,' and 'problem-solving workshops'—all programs that have achieved some success in advancing social learning by bringing together small former enemies to engage in processes of sustained dialogue with one another (Montville 1990; Rothman 1997; Abu-Nimer et al. 2001; Kelman 1999; 2001; 2004; 2008; Abu-Nimer 2001; Fisher 2001; Ropers 2004). However, as with positive contact, there are conditions and contexts in which reflexive dialogue is most likely to be effective in promoting reconciliatory social learning. Again, studies suggest that communication should ideally take place among equal-status participants, in supportive environments marked by limited threat or anxiety, in contexts where group identity remains salient, in pursuit of a shared goal to overcome group divides, and over extended periods of time (Stephan and Stephan 2001; Ellis 2006). In particular, the quality of communication is considered especially significant, because if the dialogue is antagonistic or adversarial, it will likely not work to positively transform existing identities and expectations. This suggests the importance of supportive inbuilt forums in transitional justice strategies for encouraging reconciliatory forms of communication. Indeed, dialogue processes between recent enemies should be carefully mediated and monitored—what Ellis refers to as "controlled communication"—and it is therefore critical to design strategies around providing opportunities for these appropriately facilitated interpersonal encounters (2006: 143, 165). Further, the recognition that communication must occur over a sustained period of time suggests that transitional justice strategies should secure opportunities for ongoing dialogue as opposed to more limited 'one-off' exchanges. As Norbert Ropers argues in his meta-analysis of dialogue strategies in divided societies, to ensure the stability of future peace, it is of utmost importance to establish the longer-term institutional structures required to facilitate enduring and self-sustaining processes of intergroup communication (2004: 186).

Finally, it is also evident that in order to effect the broader societal changes necessary for lasting reconciliation, the dialogue processes promoted by transitional justice strategies cannot be limited to interpersonal interactions between a small number of individuals. Instead, transitional justice strategies will likely require sequential or simultaneous institutional interventions to promote transformative dialogue throughout the target society, including in local communities, between elites, and at the broader regional or national level (Lederach 1997; 1998; Kaufman 2001; 2006; Stover and Weinstein 2004). In particular, several scholars have noted the importance of using public institutions such as educational systems and radio, print and television media as forums for members of divided groups to be brought together and encouraged to hear, often for the first time, one another's perspectives and stories regarding past abuses (Staub 2006; Chapman 2009; Hamber 2009). As the social psychologist Ervin Staub illustrates, the awareness and the discussions linked to this kind of 'societal dialogue' about the past are often critical to reconciliation after mass violence, as they can help to alter antagonistic identifications and to restore the understanding and empathy ultimately needed to rehumanize the other:

> As the members of each group describe the pain and suffering of their group at the hands of the other, they can begin to open up to the pain of the other. They can grieve for themselves, for the other, and assume responsibility for their share in the historical antagonism and violence.
>
> (Staub 1989: 255)

Indeed, several scholars (Minow 1998; Gibson 2004; Rushton 2006; Chapman 2009) within the field of transitional justice have noted the ability of transitional justice institutions to serve as facilitators of societal dialogue and to provide a crucial "source of public education and socialization" through their "capacity to reach out to, inform, or influence the population" during the transformative post-conflict moment (Chapman 2009: 159). However, in order to encourage reconciliatory learning through this kind of societal dialogue, transitional justice strategies must incorporate ways to reach out to, inform and engage the wider local population in their work (Kerr and Mobekk 2007: 180). As Beth Rushton has noted, in so doing, transitional justice strategies can encourage broader forms of instrumental learning that extend beyond the limited number of interpersonal encounters that can realistically be facilitated during more formalized justice procedures, and can therefore act as catalysts for wider societal reconciliation (2006: 138).

Socioemotional learning

While contact and dialogue remain vital to social learning, it has also been recognized that reconciliation necessarily requires addressing the history of past violence among former enemies. Indeed, the ways in which transitional authorities choose to acknowledge and provide accountability for past violence are themselves crucial to social learning processes in divided societies. In particular, most scholars agree that the achievement of reconciliation and sustainable peace in the aftermath of conflict requires an element of 'justice' that formally recognizes the wrongs committed during past violence and seeks in some way to acknowledge and repair the injustices done to the principal victims. Further, the literature widely recognizes the importance of creating an officially accepted and mutually agreed-upon 'truth' about what took place between former antagonists. This kind of shared narrative limits the ability of either side to appropriate past conflict as the basis of myth, propaganda or discriminatory history that might spark a future return to violence.

Justice

The provision of justice as a central component of social learning processes in societies divided by histories of mass violence has been recognized by many scholars working within the fields of both conflict transformation and transitional justice as a necessary, if not sufficient, condition for intergroup reconciliation and sustainable peace (Fletcher and Weinstein 2002; Montville 1990; Lederach 1998; Minow 1998; Lerche 2000; Biggar 2001; Rigby 2001; Oberschall 2007; Huyse and Salter 2008). Several prominent authors in these fields have argued that justice is inextricably linked with the potential for peace in the post-conflict environment, noting that in the long journey towards reconciliation between former enemies, "the passage from negative to positive peace runs through justice" (Miall et al. 2000: 208). In particular, many of these scholars warn against the inherent dangers of permitting impunity for past violence in divided societies, as victims have shown little inclination to simply 'forgive and forget,' and such grievances can provide fertile ground for future returns to conflict (Minow 1998). As Nigel Biggar argues, a sense of injustice tends to fester among victims if left unaddressed, and this "help[s] to infect future generations with an indiscriminate hatred of the perpetrators and their descendants—and also with an endemic mistrust of the state that, having failed in its duty to vindicate victims past, seems ready to tolerate the injury of victims future" (2001: 8). Ignoring injustice, as Biggar notes, makes for an unstable relationship among former enemies that is "liable to explode and rupture the half-forgetful present with the unfinished business of the past" (ibid.).

While many debates exist within the literature as to which type of justice is most effective and as to what form justice institutions should take (particularly surrounding the relative merits of 'restorative and 'retributive' approaches), there is nonetheless agreement about the need for transitional authorities both to hold perpetrators responsible for their crimes and to acknowledge and reduce the sense of injustice felt by those victimized by past violence (Kriesberg 2001; 2004; Exline et al. 2003; Huyse 2003; Goldstone 2004; Ross 2004). At the same time, scholars also recognize that the kind of justice employed in transitional societies must necessarily be 'partial,' effectively forgoing the total retribution of unrestrained revenge in favor of more tempered forms of accountability that will neither reinforce existing divisions nor contribute to the cycle of injury and counter-injury between antagonists (Lederach 1998; Rosenblum 2002; Huyse 2003; Long and Brecke 2003). To paraphrase legal scholar Martha Minow, in order to encourage social learning and reconciliation in the wake of mass violence, justice must walk a path between the opposing poles of vengeance and impunity—a path that acknowledges the wrongness of the harm done to victims, assigns responsibility to perpetrators for their actions, and recognizes the need to work towards repairing past injustices (Minow 1998).

The provision of justice for both victims and perpetrators has been shown to have an independent effect as a social learning mechanism capable of promoting the kind of reconciliation needed for sustainable peace in divided societies (Rigby 2001; Fletcher and Weinstein 2002; Teitel 2002; Long and Brecke 2003; Stover and Weinstein 2004; Gibson 2004). Indeed, acknowledging injustices done to victims and holding perpetrators accountable for their crimes are processes that symbolize a shift in the normative ethos of post-conflict societies and that work to delegitimize violence against the Other (Teitel 2002; Ross 2004; Chinapen and Vernon 2006). In this capacity, justice can serve as a critical bridge between a society's divisive past and its more inclusive future, signaling an expansion of the boundaries of moral and political community and an extension of equal rights and protections to all individuals (Lerche 2000; Mani 2001; 2002; Teitel 2002).

By indicating that the use of force will no longer be permitted as a means of resolving conflict between groups, justice also provides expectations of more cooperative intergroup relations in the future and a minimal foundation on which mutual trust might be built (Jeong 2005; Santa-Barbara 2007).

Moreover, by directly acknowledging the injustice of past violence, justice strategies can also begin to reduce feelings of victimization and animosity that could otherwise threaten to reignite conflict (Minow 2002). Additionally, several scholars have noted that the recognition of dignity and basic moral worth afforded by processes of justice may be vital to victims' healing and can therefore influence their future willingness to engage in reconciliation with the Other (Lederach 1998; Minow 1998; Biggar 2001; Staub 2001; 2006; Staub and Bar-Tal 2003; Bar-Tal and Bennink 2004; Jeong 2005). As Howard Zehr has argued in his seminal work on the philosophy of justice,

> an experience of justice is so basic that without it, healing may be well impossible. . . . Victims need assurance that what happened to them was wrong, unfair, undeserved . . . [t]hey need to be heard and affirmed . . . victims need to know that steps are being taken to rectify the wrong and to reduce the opportunities for it to occur.
>
> (1990: 28)

Such contributions explain why the 'justice' component of transitional justice is crucial to reconciliation outside of its capacity to facilitate other aspects of social learning. However, it should be noted that highlighting the independent effects of justice doesn't mean ruling out the beneficial impact of justice on other mechanisms of social learning. For example, by signaling the advent of a new community in which all individuals are to be accorded the same moral worth and political rights, justice in the post-conflict environment can also help to create the supportive normative climate and the recognition of equal status between groups needed to reinitiate positive contact and communication. Further, the mistrust and unhealed feelings of victimization and animosity tied to continued injustice strongly militate against the formation of a more inclusive and peaceable sense of collective identity (Mani 2002).

Truth

Aside from the experience of justice, it has been widely posited that coming to terms with the past also requires some form of historical inquiry that can record the 'truth.' Truth is understood here as a mutually accepted (or at least mutually tolerable) shared understanding between former antagonists about past events—the kind of understanding necessary for post-conflict societies to achieve reconciliation and sustainable peace (Hayner 1994; 2002; Lederach 1998; Minow 1998; Kiss 2000; Lerche 2000; Hamber 2002; Freeman and Hayner 2003; Imbleau 2004; Kriesberg 2004; DeLaet 2006; Llewellyn 2006; Mendez 2006; Braham 2007; Aiken 2008; Kelman 2008). Indeed, as Tristan Anne Borer notes, within the transitional justice literature there now exists a "near unanimity among most scholars, as well as practitioners, that societies coming out of periods of violence must in some way examine, acknowledge and account for violence committed by various groups in order to move forward" (2006: 4). For the most part, these authors discount the simplistic argument that building a factual record of the past can itself bring about more peaceful relations (the assumption that 'revealing is healing'), suggesting instead that truth recovery processes, while necessary for reconciliation, cannot facilitate healing on their own and are only one required element of broader post-conflict peacebuilding strategies (Adam and Moodley 2005: 128). Further, scholars acknowledge that the truth uncovered by transitional interventions in the wake of mass violence will likely never be factually complete or all-encompassing, and at best will provide a selective 'small-t' or "representative truth" of the causes and scope of past atrocity and the roles played by former enemies (Stanley 2002; Imbleau 2004; Rushton 2006).

Nonetheless, truth is vital to reconciliation; in particular, it proves essential to securing sustainable peace by "narrow[ing] the range of permissible lies" that can be appropriated in the future to reignite conflict (Ignatieff 1998: 174). However, as Borer herself indicates, the causal connection between truth and reconciliation remains largely unexplained by transitional justice scholars (2006). While a strong correlation between the two has been evidenced, explanations of this connection have been based largely on anecdotal evidence with very few sustained theoretical or empirical studies as support (Hamber 2001; Rushton 2006; Braham 2007). In particular, little attention has been given to how truth recovery processes can contribute positively to the more social and psychosocial components of intergroup reconciliation—an oversight that is likely due to the limited dialogue between the transitional justice literature and the related body of conflict transformation scholarship that centrally highlights the importance of social learning.

In synthesizing this scholarship, I argue that the establishment of 'truth' in the post-conflict environment contributes to social learning by helping to overcome antagonistic belief systems formed through the experience of past violence. Such beliefs, if left unaddressed, not only risk recidivist violence but also block the formation of a more positive sense of collective identification. Notably, in his studies of protracted and intractable conflict in divided societies, the social psychologist Daniel Bar-Tal writes extensively about the dynamics surrounding the formation of such divisive belief systems, suggesting that

> [o]ver the years, groups involved in conflict selectively form collective memories about the conflict. One the one hand, they focus mainly on the other side's responsibility for the outbreak and continuation of the conflict and its misdeeds, violence and atrocities; on the other hand, they concentrate on their own self-justification, self-righteousness, glorification, and victimization.
>
> (2003: 78)

These biased collective memories, in turn, are actively institutionalized and maintained by groups over the course of conflict, socialized through cultural and political channels and transmitted to future generations. They eventually come to color all aspects of intergroup relations and become a central component of group identity in divided societies (ibid.).

In deeply divided societies, therefore, former enemies are likely to have widely divergent views about the 'truth' of past events, as each group bases its interpretations upon its own inevitably oppositional and exclusionary collective memories. These beliefs—the sense that the actions of the Self are legitimate and noble, while those of the Other are unwarranted and unjust— work to maintain an oversimplified understanding of ingroup/outgroup relations, casting all members of the enemy group as responsible for the evils of past conflict and therefore turning them into legitimate targets for future violence (Azar 1990; Minow 2002; Bar-Tal 2003; Cairns and Roe 2003; Devine-Wright 2003). Further, beliefs about the Self's undue victimization may be used to justify a return to conflict in retaliation for violence committed against one's own group. Psychologist John Mack has dubbed this process the "egoism of victimization," suggesting that the perpetuation of these polarized narratives effectively ensures that fear, threat and negative stereotypes continue to persist among groups. Left unchallenged, these biased beliefs can preclude social learning and intergroup reconciliation by limiting the kinds of contact and communication needed to develop trust and mutual empathy, effectively "stand[ing] rigidly in the way of new information that might provide a correcting view to the prevailing group dichotomization" (Mack 1990: 124).

Accordingly, I contend that the most important aspect of transitional justice institutions' efforts to establish a truthful accounting of the past is their ability to facilitate social learning through a critical reexamination of the biased myths, narratives and collective memories tied to perceptions of past violence. This reconsideration can open the door to more positive collective identifications and cooperative relations among former enemies. As Herbert Kelman contends, "confronting history and coming to terms with the truth is an essential component of any reconciliation effort," noting that "the reexamination of historical narratives and the reevaluation of national myths—on both sides of a conflict—are valuable contributions to such an effort" (Kelman 2004: 123). This assertion is reinforced by a recent comparative survey of reconciliation in post-conflict societies carried out by William Long and Peter Brecke, which found that those countries most successful in achieving sustainable peace invariably pursued processes of public truth-telling that acknowledged the mutual complicity of all parties involved and actively challenged misperceptions of the past. Consequently, Long and Brecke argue that truth-telling processes can provide a crucial step towards reconciliation by disseminating new information—information needed by former enemies to transcend their own preoccupations with victimization and to "begin a process of redefinition of identity of the [O]ther from enemy to potential partner in a negotiated settlement and common new future" (2003: 149). Therefore, while a comprehensive accounting of the past cannot itself achieve reconciliation, truth-telling is nonetheless vital to social learning as it "plays a critical, perhaps indispensible role in the process of national reconciliation [by] contribut[ing] directly and indirectly to the redefinition of identity" (idem: 69).

Institutions of transitional justice are often essential to this process of reconciliation, as they serve as the initial forums for the establishment of truth in divided societies, providing the mechanisms for developing a new 'official' shared understanding of the past—an understanding that can't be appropriated by any one group (Kiss 2000). One such mechanism is the creation of a written account of past conflict. As such, most truth commissions employed to date have been mandated to discover, clarify and formally compose an official historical record of periods of past violence (Hayner 1994; 2000; 2002). However, for this new understanding of the past to be widely accepted and to thereby contribute to intergroup reconciliation, these institutions and the truth they produce must be viewed as legitimate by all parties involved in past conflict. It is therefore essential to include all groups in the process of gathering the truth and shaping the historical record to avoid the perception that the new narrative represents the biased viewpoint of the victors—a perception that would only further entrench division and feelings of victimization (Imbleau 2004). In fact, there is evidence to suggest that in divided societies it is not truth per se, but the "moderating truth" that comes from mutual acknowledgment of complicity in past abuses, that is the essential ingredient in dismantling the 'egoism of victimization' and altering understandings of the Other as an essentially evil and intractable foe (Gibson 2004: 329). Truth, understood in this sense, is therefore an integral component of social learning associated with the ongoing negotiation of identity needed for reconciliation in divided societies, as it helps both to soften feelings of antagonism and to transform hostile relationships between former enemies rigidified by the memories of past violence (Rushton 2006).

Distributive learning

However, it is clear that the social learning required for reconciliation cannot be limited to changes in social interactions, cognitive perceptions or understandings of the past. Many conflict transformation scholars assert that these psychosocial transformations must be matched by the learning processes that arise through concrete material and structural changes in the day-to-day lives of individuals in post-conflict societies (Azar 1990; Miall et al. 2000; Abu-Nimer et al. 2001; Staub and Bar-Tal 2003; Bar-Tal and Bennink 2004; Kriesberg 2004; Miall 2004; Jeong 2005). Severe challenges to basic human needs, the experience of living under difficult conditions, and, in particular, acute inequalities in the distribution of economic wealth, social status or access to political power are all factors around which protracted and intractable identity conflicts can coalesce (Staub 1989; 2000; 2006; Azar 1990; Amstutz 2005). Further, the overt physical violence of conflict in divided societies is often underpinned by even deeper forms of 'structural violence,' efforts by one identity group to use the state apparatus to repress the Other and thereby to entrench severe imbalances in socioeconomic or sociopolitical power (Galtung 1969; 1985; 2001). These structural inequalities may stand in the way of more cooperative relations and significant changes to the politics of identity between groups even when a formal peace agreement brings active violence to a close. As Johan Galtung has argued throughout his influential career in Peace Studies, fostering reconciliation and sustainable peace between former enemies requires the pursuit of a 'double goal': the initial conditions for negative peace brought about by the end of physical violence must be established, and a more positive peace addressing the deeper structural violence underlying the conflict should then be initiated (1969: 183).

The amelioration of structural and material inequalities

There is strong evidence from the conflict transformation literature to suggest that the amelioration of material inequalities is a necessary mechanism of social learning involved in altering antagonistic identifications and relations in divided societies. For instance, Joseph Ruane and Jennifer Todd note that structural and economic imbalances are themselves constitutive of divided identities, and that they help to create a self-reinforcing system of conflict by encouraging greater levels of both ingroup solidarity and outgroup differentiation (1996: 5–6, 12–13). Ruane and Todd's study also indicates that the continued presence of inequality can limit the potential for perceptual and ideological changes regarding the Other even when myths and biased understandings of the past are directly challenged by new information. In other words, the daily lived realities of relative deprivation effectively preclude a group's revision of its status as a continually victimized party and therefore obviate against any changes in the belief that its members are justified in the future use of retaliatory violence (ibid.: 207). For reconciliation and sustainable peace to occur, the insights of these and other related scholars suggest that attention must be paid to dismantling not only the polarized system of social and psychological relationships after conflict, but also the related system of dominance, dependence and inequality that reinforces and reproduces these polarizations (Azar 1990; Ryan 1995; 2007; Cairns and Darby 1998; Lerche 2000; Fahey et al. 2006; Shirlow and Murtagh 2006). Indeed, the work of psychologists Ervin Staub and Daniel Bar-Tal stresses the importance of combining psychological transformations with real changes in the socioeconomic conditions of groups, arguing that "when conflict is already entrenched and groups have inflicted violence on each other, psychological changes are required for overcoming hostility. But without structural changes, psychological changes may not be possible to bring about or maintain" (2003: 731).

As previously noted, the transformative potential of the key social learning mechanisms of contact and communication is greatly restricted when these interactions take place under conditions of material inequality. At a basic level, the opportunities for such encounters are often limited in a society divided by severe structural differences, as the places in which group members live, work and socialize are directly mediated by socioeconomic status. Moreover, where interactions do occur, these structural divisions may be so wide that the contact between members of different groups remains cursory and superficial, resulting in relationships that can be "contiguous yet utterly remote" (Foster and Finchilescu 1986: 125). In a series of social psychological studies carried out by Nicole Tausch and her colleagues, perceptions of inequalities in relative group status were found to be both a strong predictor and a mediator of the transformative potential of intergroup contact. In effect, those who perceived themselves to be of lower status were far less likely to seek to engage in meaningful contact, and when contact did occur, it often led to feelings of increased anxiety and threat and had little positive effect on breaking down existing stereotypes or reducing established prejudices (Tausch et al. 2007). Ultimately, as a result of intergroup inequality, other necessary facets of social learning such as mutual trust, empathy, and a more inclusive sense of moral and political community can remain underdeveloped.

This suggests that in order to successfully facilitate processes of social learning and intergroup reconciliation, some effort to reduce structural and material inequalities must likely be incorporated into transitional justice strategies in divided societies. Indeed, in recent years, transitional justice scholars have increasingly recognized that distributive or 'restitutive' reforms are an essential part of broader post-conflict peacebuilding work (Simpson 1997; Mani 2001; 2002; 2008; Villa-Vicencio 2006; Arbour 2007; Rigby 2001; Miller 2008; Lambourne 2009; Muvingi 2009; Aiken 2010). That said, it is highly unrealistic to expect that transitional justice institutions will, in and of themselves, be able to effect this kind of broader societal change—such a task is often simply beyond the limited budgets, mandates and timelines accorded these institutions. However, as key catalysts of social learning in the transformative post-conflict moment, transitional justice interventions must, at a minimum, at least signal a commitment to a general improvement in the material conditions experienced by former antagonists.

There are two particular ways in which justice institutions might facilitate distributive learning by way of this 'symbolic' approach. The first is to include provisions for some form of reparations program or material compensation for those worst impacted by past violence or for those who experienced severe socioeconomic and sociopolitical disadvantage under previous systems of repression. While the sheer scale of mass violence realistically means that such compensation can likely only ever be emblematic, reparations nevertheless remain an important way in which transitional authorities can acknowledge the injustice of past disparities and indicate their commitment to establishing more equitable future relations (Rigby 2001; Villa-Vicencio 2001; 2006; Stanley 2002; Hamber and Wilson 2003; Vandeginste 2003; DeGreiff 2006; Elster 2006; Guembe 2006; Sharpe 2007). As Brandon Hamber and Richard Wilson argue, while the limited material gains of reparations may certainly be of some help to the most disadvantaged, this kind of compensation is perhaps most important in its symbolic ability to mark a clear normative break with the inequalities of the past (2003: 4). Hamber and Wilson do note, however, that such endeavors can be fraught, as determining which groups or individuals might be eligible recipients of compensation is always a challenge. They also suggest that reparations will need to be part of a broader series of justice initiatives and reforms to avoid being stigmatized as a 'payoff' or 'blood money' offered in lieu of real social change (idem: 14).

Second, transitional justice institutions might be designed to work in tandem with or alongside broader structural and material reforms as part of a package of initiatives undertaken by transitional authorities to address legacies of past abuses. Similarly, justice strategies might make recommendations or suggest binding reforms for transitional societies to carry out after the formal justice mechanisms themselves have completed their work (Hayner 2002). In either case, such an approach can help signal to former antagonists that alongside the instrumental and socioemotional initiatives associated with transitional justice, more forward-looking and longer-term efforts are also being undertaken to correct existing structural and material imbalances. There is evidence within the transitional justice literature that such broader distributive reforms may be essential to curtailing further abuses and may help to directly promote processes of healing and reconciliation among former enemies (Stanley 2002; Mani 2002; Lambourne 2009; Aiken 2010). However, as Elizabeth Stanley warns, if these distributional or developmental policies are not actually carried out, they run a high risk of making all transitional justice efforts appear 'toothless' and illegitimate, greatly damaging their ability to contribute to broader societal transformation and reconciliation (2002: 11).

Permissive conditions

In addition to these five key social learning mechanisms, it is important to highlight at least two additional precipitating or permissive conditions that may enable transitional justice strategies to effectively promote social learning and reconciliation in divided societies. While a deeper investigation of these permissive structural factors remains beyond the scope of this study, and while these factors are therefore bracketed in its examination of the causal relationship between transitional justice and intergroup reconciliation, it is important to note that the presence of negative peace and the existence of supportive elites or leadership might themselves be important first steps for successful transitional justice interventions in divided societies.

The existence of a negative peace

As discussed in Chapter 2, due to the self-reinforcing nature of identity-based conflict, it is likely that that the ability of transitional justice institutions to contribute to social learning will be most effective during the 'transformative moment' that follows the end of widespread violence between groups (Väyrynen 1999; Coleman 2002; Eder et al. 2002; Wilmer 2002). The end of overt intergroup violence brings with it the initial possibility of allowing former antagonists to begin challenging and potentially transforming the hostile relationships and identifications that perpetuated past conflict. As Ho-Won Jeong has noted,

> [r]econciliation and reconstruction designed to transform intercommunal relationships can take place in the absence of active violence. The control of violence at interpersonal and intercommunal levels is thus a prerequisite to establishing a constructive relationship.
>
> (2005: 4)

This is not to say that the mechanisms of instrumental, socioemotional and distributive learning are impossible in the midst of violence or that they do not have a potentially important role to play in limiting conflict. Indeed, elements of each of these types of social learning could also have great utility as conflict resolution tools that could be used to help to move divided societies towards the initial cessation of widespread violence. However, given the deeply polarizing effect that violence has been shown to have on groups in divided societies, it remains highly unlikely that the deeper transformation of identities and relationships associated with social learning and intergroup reconciliation will be possible without the prior existence of at least a state of negative peace between antagonists.

The presence of conducive elites or entrepreneurs

Second, while this study's model focuses almost exclusively on how the processes and mechanisms of transitional justice institutions can contribute to social learning, it is crucial to underscore that these institutions do not themselves have independent agency. To be sure, the initial creation of these institutions as well as their subsequent structures, procedures and goals all depend on the actions and interests of key domestic or international actors. While not discounting the central part played by local 'bottom-up' actors, the role played by domestic leaders, elites or international actors is crucially important in facilitating (or at least not actively impeding) a social and political climate conducive to addressing past human rights abuses in divided societies. At a minimum, this requires a commitment by these actors to take advantage of the opportunity offered by the transformative moment after the establishment of negative peace to break the cycle of violence that has hitherto conditioned relations between communal groups. A large body of literature has examined the part that ethnic activists, sectarian leaders and other domestic 'spoilers' can play in derailing transitional justice initiatives and undermining broader attempts at post-conflict peacebuilding (Gross-Stein 2002; Kaufman 2006; Kerr and Mobekk 2007). Conversely, elites and other powerful leaders within post-conflict societies also have the potential to act as influential political or normative 'entrepreneurs' who can lend much-needed legitimacy to transitional justice efforts and can support the creation of new societal relations based on a mutual respect for human rights and a culture of non-violence (Finnemore and Sikkink 1998; 2001; Keck and Sikkink 1998; Sikkink 2011). These entrepreneurs may therefore prove integral to social learning both by attracting or coercing others to engage with the processes and mechanisms of transitional justice institutions and by modeling a commitment to reconciliation between former antagonists (Adler and Barnett 1998: 39).

A social learning model of transitional justice

Building on an interdisciplinary synthesis of recent scholarship from conflict transformation and transitional justice, this study offers a new framework with which to begin theorizing the causal relationship between institutions of transitional justice and intergroup reconciliation in divided societies. The central contention of the model developed here is that this connection is heavily mediated by social learning; in other words, that transitional justice strategies will be successful in promoting reconciliation to the extent that they are able to facilitate changes in the antagonistic identities and hostile systems of relations between former enemies developed during past violence. Having already considered the various discrete elements of the social learning model, a basic illustration of the proposed causal processes at work is detailed in Figure 3.1.

To review, this model holds the reconciliatory potential of transitional justice strategies to be dependent on their ability to promote five key social learning mechanisms between former enemies: positive contact, transformative dialogue, the promotion of truth, the provision of justice, and the amelioration of structural inequalities. In turn, these mechanisms advance the aspects of instrumental, socioemotional and distributive processes of social learning ultimately required to transform the hostile divisions between Self and Other and to facilitate intergroup reconciliation. This new reconciliatory relationship forms the necessary basis for sustainable peace among former enemies, and is marked by the presence of mutual trust, respect

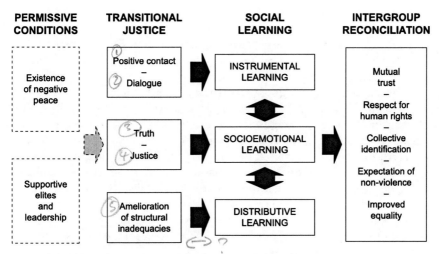

Figure 3.1 A social learning model of transitional justice

for human rights, a more inclusive sense of collective identification, a reduction in structural disparities, and an expectation that future conflicts will be settled by means short of violence.

To be clear, it remains highly unlikely that all of these mechanisms of social learning will be extant in every transitional justice strategy. Where they do exist, they will more likely appear in gradients rather than being simply present or absent. In addition, it is likely that various post-conflict societies will have different relative needs for instrumental, socioemotional and distributive learning processes. It may therefore be more useful to think of these processes on a continuum, and to acknowledge that each may be promoted by different institutional strategies to a greater or lesser degree. Indeed, the highly individuated nature of context, culture, and each society's unique requirements for justice in the post-conflict environment suggests that no one 'best' model is ever likely to be beneficial or even practicable across all societies.

This social learning model therefore recognizes the need for context-dependent strategies, leaving open the possibility that these processes of social learning might be promoted by a range of different justice strategies, be they truth commission, trial or indigenous approach. However, it remains crucially important that the strategy employed be one that suits the exigencies of the society in which it is undertaken in order to be considered legitimate by the populations it seeks to reconcile. This contextual legitimacy may be key to an institution's ability to encourage former enemies to participate in its structures and to prompt individuals to accept, and eventually internalize, the kinds of social learning about the Other ultimately needed for reconciliation and sustainable peace (Stover and Weinstein 2004; Roht-Arriaza 2006; Kerr and Mobekk 2007).

This is not to say, however, that the study of transitional justice is all relative or that all institutions are created equal in their ability to contribute to intergroup reconciliation—indeed, this model suggests that individual institutions must be designed with the question of how best to promote positive processes of social learning in particular contexts in mind. It is, after all, the institutional strategies themselves that draw people together and engage the politics of identity through social learning, so while no one approach can ever be universally applicable, institutional design remains of great importance to efforts at reconciliation. Again, however, the argument forwarded here is that transitional justice debates should move away from questions of whether any one type or model of institutional approach is intrinsically better than another, and towards an examination of the ways in which different approaches might serve to impede or impel the processes of social learning necessary to intergroup reconciliation.

In the following chapters, the utility of the social learning framework developed here is tested against the two very different approaches to transitional justice employed in the deeply divided societies of Northern Ireland and South Africa following those countries' transitions away from conflict during the 1990s. In so doing, these chapters seek to explore the impact that Northern Ireland's 'decentralized' approach to transitional justice and South Africa's Truth and Reconciliation Commission have had on catalyzing the instrumental, socioemotional and distributive learning processes identified in the framework as being crucial to advancing intergroup reconciliation. In addition to providing a basis for testing this new social learning model of transitional justice, it is hoped that observations drawn from these two cases may point the way towards future 'best practices' that could help to guide policy regarding the design of future transitional interventions in deeply divided societies.

Notes

1   Nadler and Shnabel suggest a 'two-staged process' of reconciliation in which instrumental learning paves the way for a second stage of socioemotional learning (2008: 45). However, while not explicitly stated in their work, it is clear that this interdependence functions more as a two-way street, as they also illustrate how the presence of feelings of victimization and injustice can lead to social, moral and emotional distancing—all of which can significantly impede instrumental learning.

2   While two distinct schools of thought, recent studies have shown that SIT and SIS may in fact be complementary (Cronin 1999). SIT emphasizes the psychological aspects of the constitution/categorization of identity that accompanies group membership, while SIS focuses more on changes to group identifications

that occur via processes of social interaction and from the symbolic meaning assigned to particular situations.

3   Here one can think of the decisions by international tribunals such as the ICTY or ICTR to prosecute only those 'most responsible' for past crimes, or, conversely, the decisions made by many truth commissions to focus only on a representative fraction of cases in their proceedings.

Chapter 4

Transitional justice in Northern Ireland and South Africa

Having outlined the new social learning model of the relationship between transitional justice and intergroup reconciliation, this chapter introduces the case studies of Northern Ireland and South Africa. Both of these countries have been deeply divided by past histories of violence and gross human rights abuses carried out between antagonistic identity groups. While not discounting the crucial role played by the British government and security forces, the sectarian violence of Northern Ireland's 'Troubles' was largely carried out between domestic communities of nationalists/Catholics and unionists/ Protestants in addition to agents of the British state. In South Africa, during the struggle to bring an end to the institutionalized discrimination of apartheid, conflict followed clearly defined categories of racial identity. Most centrally, this conflict involved acts of mass repression and violence committed between members of the ruling white minority and the majority population of black South Africans. However, despite histories of protracted (and seemingly intractable) conflict, during the 1990s, both of these countries engaged in negotiated peace processes that brought an end to large-scale intergroup violence. Following the end of violence, Northern Ireland and South Africa employed very different transitional justice strategies to deal with the legacy of past abuses as part of their efforts to promote post-conflict reconciliation and sustainable peace. Northern Ireland's 'decentralized' transitional justice approach has combined a range of civil society interventions with discrete government initiatives to address the country's history of violence. Conversely, in South Africa, the transitional justice strategy employed to come to terms with apartheid-era abuses has centered primarily on the innovative South African Truth and Reconciliation Commission (TRC) implemented by the South African government.

Northern Ireland

For much of the last century, Northern Ireland has been the very archetype of a deeply divided society, with communities of (largely Roman Catholic) Irish 'nationalists' locked in a protracted and seemingly intractable territorial conflict with both local (largely Protestant) pro-British 'unionists' and the security forces of the British state. The historical roots of these divisions and the patterns of national and religious conflict that followed are often traced as far back as the sixteenth and seventeenth centuries. During this time, a period known as 'The Plantation of Ulster,' armies of the English Crown successfully occupied large areas of the island of Ireland and established colonies of Protestant settlers brought over from England and Scotland to live in the Northern province of Ulster.

However, the more modern genesis of the conflict in Northern Ireland began in 1921 with the signing of the Anglo-Irish Treaty. This act effectively partitioned the island of Ireland into two separate states and brought an end to the Irish War of Independence, which had seen militant nationalists or 'Republicans' and the Irish Republican Army (IRA) wage a protracted guerilla campaign against British rule, targeting British police and army forces who responded with declarations of martial law, troop reinforcements and violent reprisals against both the IRA and members of the Catholic civilian population.[1] In the South, a new sovereign Republic or 'Irish Free State' was founded as a state to be governed by its majority Irish Catholic population. In the North, the state of Northern Ireland—encompassing most of the historical territory of the province of Ulster—was created, allowing the Protestant majority residing there to opt to remain within the United Kingdom.

Acceptance of the Treaty (and with it, acquiescence to the partition of the island of Ireland) deeply divided the Republican movement, leading to a civil war between pro- and anti- treaty factions that was fought until the mid-1920s.[2] This conflict was particularly vicious in Northern Ireland, where, given the close proximity of Catholics and Protestants living together, violence took on a much more sectarian flavor. The vast majority of the more than 500 killed during the war were targeted by militant members of the 'Other' community or by British security forces in a series of retaliatory acts of vengeance (English 2003; Lynch 2006). This period of strife was largely brought to an end between 1923 and 1925 with the defeat of the anti-treaty movement, the evacuation of the British Army from the South, and the solidification of the boundary delineating the British-controlled region of Northern Ireland from the newly established Irish Free State.

Unlike the new Irish Free State to the South, Protestants remained the clear majority in Northern Ireland, albeit alongside a substantial Catholic minority. As a result, following partition, Northern Ireland was governed by an unbroken succession of unionist leadership between 1922 and 1972. During this time, the Protestant majority used its numerical advantage to establish control over the devolved Northern Ireland government and to institute a program of "systematically organized domination" and discrimination against what was viewed as a potentially subversive Catholic minority (O'Leary and McGarry 1993: 110–139; Knox and Quirk 2000). Politically, unionist dominance during this period was ensured by the widespread use of biased electoral laws and gerrymandering practices at both local and state levels, practices that left nationalists largely disenfranchised from the exercise of real legislative or executive power (Darby 1995). Unionists also maintained control over the judiciary and policing forces, whose members were almost exclusively drawn from within the Protestant community. Many of these administrators also retained strong ties with unionist political parties and the Protestant Orange Order (Darby 1976). Socioeconomic discrimination manifested itself in unequal access to employment, housing and education on the basis of religion, leading to severe disparities between Protestant and Catholic communities in terms of their relative levels of unemployment, income and living conditions (Cairns and Darby 1998: 755).

As a result, during this period, existing divisions based on religious, political and economic status between nationalists/Catholics and unionists/ Protestants only became more acute within the new state of Northern Ireland. These disparities meant that nationalists and unionists led increasingly segregated existences, often living, learning, working and socializing in separate spaces (Shirlow and Murtagh 2006). Combined with the continued anger and frustration of the Catholic population over the discriminatory policies of the unionist government, this separation exacerbated feelings of prejudice, distrust and outright hostility between the two communities (Fitzduff and O'Hagan 2009). In particular, members of the Catholic minority increasingly came to view the unionist-dominated governments of Northern Ireland as fundamentally illegitimate and unjust, leading to small-scale acts of violence being carried out by more militant Republican elements against state security forces and infrastructure.

An increase in relative levels of affluence during the 1950s and 1960s eventually led to the formation of a Catholic civil rights movement in Northern Ireland. This movement included the Northern Ireland Civil Rights Association (NIACRA), which began to aggressively lobby for greater equality in the areas of voting rights, housing, employment and policing services. In 1968, a civil rights march in the city of Derry was violently broken up by members of the police force, the Royal Ulster Constabulary (RUC), leaving many of the marchers seriously injured. Television coverage of the incident sparked international indignation, and touched off three days of serious rioting in Derry between Catholic residents and members of the RUC. In August 1969, these skirmishes culminated in several days of sustained rioting known as 'The Battle of the Bogside,' during which eight were killed, hundreds injured, and more than 2,000 families displaced from their homes. The rioting was only brought to a close when the Government of Northern Ireland (GNI) requested that the British Army intercede to help restore order: a move that at the time was warmly welcomed by nationalists who sought protection against what they perceived as attacks by the unionist-dominated policing services.

Despite subsequent movements by the British government to initiate a range of reforms designed to address the core demands of the civil rights movement, communal segregation and polarization only intensified between 1969 and 1971 as riots, sectarian shootings and bombings grew in number (Ruane and Todd 1996; Cairns and Darby 1998). The turbulence of this time also led to the formation of illegal paramilitary organizations that, citing the inadequacy of the protection offered by security forces, took up arms in defense of their respective communities. In 1966 the Ulster Volunteer Force (UVF) was formed, an organization of armed Protestant 'Loyalists' who dedicated themselves to the violent destruction of the 'Republican threat' and the protection of Northern Ireland's union with the UK. Similarly, a more militant strand of the IRA known as the 'Provisional IRA' (PIRA) was formed under the mandate to defend nationalist communities from Loyalist attack and to end British rule in Northern Ireland through armed struggle. This period also saw the rise of more polarized political parties in nationalist and unionist communities. Under the leadership of Gerry Adams, the Republican Sinn Féin (SF) emerged as the political wing of the newly re-formed PIRA in 1970 and began to win support at the expense of the more moderate Social Democratic and Labour Party (SDLP). Similarly, the radical Democratic Unionist Party (DUP) was formed under Reverend Ian Paisley in 1973, drawing support away from the more moderate Ulster Unionist Party (UUP).

In August 1971, the British government passed a policy of 'Internment' allowing members of the Army and the RUC to arrest and detain suspected paramilitaries without trial. A series of Internment raids in nationalist areas erased any remaining goodwill between these communities and the British Army, which was, like the RUC, increasingly perceived as a partisan extension of the unionist government (Darby 1995). The days following the Internment raids saw a large upswing in violence during which 17 people were killed and thousands of families living in 'mixed' nationalist/unionist neighbourhoods were burned out or otherwise forced to flee their homes (Shirlow 2001; Shirlow and Murtagh 2006). On January 30th, 1972, a planned civil rights march in Derry organized against Internment ended in tragedy when a unit of the British Army fired upon the protesters, killing 14 civilians and wounding 13 others. This incident, which became known as 'Bloody Sunday,' further galvanized members of the nationalist community and prompted many youths to join Republican paramilitary groups (Hegarty 2002). It also led to a major increase in acts of armed sectarian violence between nationalist and unionist communities and against members of the security forces (Fay et al. 2001; Sutton 2010).[3] In response to this violence, the British government reimposed a policy of 'Direct Rule' under the British Secretary of State for Northern Ireland, effectively marking the beginning of a period of intense sectarian conflict known as 'the Troubles' that lasted for nearly three decades.

The 'Troubles'

The sectarian violence of the Troubles, which gripped Northern Ireland between the early 1970s and the late 1990s, largely took the form of a three-cornered fight between armed Republican and Loyalist paramilitary groups and the security forces of the British state. For their part, Republican para-militaries viewed themselves as being engaged in a 'Long War' to free themselves from the rule of British occupiers, and undertook a protracted shooting and bombing campaign against military, economic and political targets both within Northern Ireland and in England itself (Coogan 1995). At the same time, given that the policing and security forces of Northern Ireland were widely perceived as being deeply biased in favor of unionists, Republicans also cast themselves as the armed protectors and internal police of the national-ist community, employing intimidation, beatings and 'punishment' kill-ings to self-regulate criminal activity (Knox and Monaghan 2002). Similarly, Loyalists viewed themselves as the last line of defense for the Protestant com-munity and for Unionism itself against a Republican onslaught. Accordingly, they responded with attacks on Republican paramilitaries and political activ-ists, though the vast majority of their attacks simply targeted civilians belonging to the wider nationalist community (Sutton 2010).[4] For its part, the British government maintained that it remained a neutral arbiter throughout the violence of the Troubles, seeking to uphold law and order in Northern Ireland and to protect the country from the 'criminal' and 'terrorist' actions of the PIRA and other paramilitary organizations. However, there is now ample evidence to suggest that in some cases members of the state secu-rity forces actively colluded with Loyalist paramilitaries over the course of the conflict, resulting in the killings not only of Republican activists but also of a number of nationalist civilians (Cassel et al. 2006).

During the years of the Troubles, an estimated 3,526 individuals were killed and 47,541 more were injured. This included the victims of the approximately 36,923 shootings and 16,209 bombings that occurred over the nearly three decades of the conflict (Sutton 2010). Initial violence spawned numerous cycles of 'tit for tat' or revenge killings that targeted political figures and armed members of opposing factions. Notably, however, the overwhelming majority of those victimized by the violence were unarmed nationalist and unionist civilians either caught in the crossfire or deliberately targeted by paramilitary organizations for their communal affiliations (Fitzduff 2002). Indeed, recent accountings of the conflict have shown that 1,844 civilians lost their lives during the conflict, with 1,101 of these identi-fied as belonging to the Catholic community, 572 as Protestants, and 171 as being from outside of Northern Ireland. The other major targets of violence during the Troubles were British security forces (including the army and policing services), of whom 1,105 were killed, the vast majority at the hands of Republican paramilitary organizations (Sutton 2010).

However, by the end of the 1980s, the strain of living with the constant threat of shootings and bombings had taken its toll on Northern Ireland's population, and a growing 'war-weariness' among both nationalist and unionist communities precipitated a major decrease in civilian support for paramilitary and political violence (Byrne 1995). At the same time, a recognition started to emerge among the major political parties involved in Northern Ireland's national struggle that the use of violence was no longer an effective means of advancing their political aims, whether they be continued union with the UK or the establishment of a united Ireland. The conflict's chief combatants also seemed to realize that the war in Northern Ireland could not be won by strength of arms alone, leading SF to increasingly prioritize use of the 'ballot box over the Armalite' and the British government to declare in 1989 that it no longer had a 'selfish or strategic' interest in Northern Ireland and would be open to considering political talks with Republicans if violence was ended.[5]

As a result, a lengthy peace process began in the early 1990s following a series of secret talks among nationalist, unionist and British politicians, along with leaders of the principal paramilitary organizations (Smyth 1997). By 1994, large-scale political violence was brought to an end when Loyalist and Republican paramilitaries declared a ceasefire in the wake of a spike in internecine violence that left many dead. Multi-party peace talks began in earnest in 1996, but soon stalled when faced with contentious issues such as the decommissioning of paramilitary weapons, proposed reforms of the policing services, the release of political prisoners, and, most importantly, questions about how Northern Ireland might best be governed in the future (Fitzduff 2002). In the interim, several major bombing attacks were carried out by the PIRA against targets in Britain before it rejoined the other major paramilitary organizations in their ceasefire in July 1997.

On April 10th, 1998, all the major parties involved in the Northern Ireland conflict (including the main paramilitary bodies, SF, the DUP, and the governments of Britain and Ireland) signed the Good Friday Agreement or Belfast Agreement (BFA). In effect, the BFA was a peace treaty that sought to bring an end to the political conflicts of the Troubles, including a commitment by all of its signatories to use "exclusively peaceful and democratic means" to contest the national question in Northern Ireland in the future. It also included provisions for the establishment of a 'power-sharing' government in Northern Ireland though an Assembly with devolved legislative powers, an agreement to release paramilitary prisoners and decommission paramilitary arms, guidelines for extensive policing reforms, and a constitutional guarantee that the national status of Northern Ireland could only ever be changed following a majority vote of its citizenry.

In May 1998, the BFA was approved by successful referendums in both Northern Ireland and the Irish Republic and was officially adopted on December 2nd, 1999, effectively bringing an end to the widespread sectarian violence of the Troubles.[6] However, continued tensions between nationalist and unionist communities surrounding the perennially contentious issues of police service reform and arms decommissioning effectively deadlocked the new Northern Ireland government on a number of occasions between 2000 and 2007, during which British rule was temporarily reinstated through the Northern Ireland Office. Talks between SF, the DUP and the British and Irish governments eventually culminated in the landmark 2006 'St. Andrews Agreement' and the resumption of a stable power-sharing government in May 2007 led by the DUP's Ian Paisley (as First Minister) and SF's Martin McGuinness (as Deputy Minister).[7]

Decentralized transitional justice in Northern Ireland

At first glance, with fewer than four thousand killed over nearly three decades, the scale of the sectarian violence of the Troubles appears relatively minor when compared to other contemporary cases of intercommunal conflict, including the horrors perpetrated in Rwanda and the Former Yugoslavia. However, given the small geographical size and population of Northern Ireland (currently under two million), the Troubles nevertheless had a devastating impact on societal cohesion in the country. A recent study has suggested that nearly one in every thirty people in Northern Ireland was at some point directly affected by a personal loss during the Troubles, either through friendship networks or familial relations (Fay et al. 2001). Further, as O'Leary and McGarry note, the experience of this protracted violence helped to solidify dichotomous and antagonistic relationships between nationalist and unionist communities, cementing "legacies of hatred, suspicion, and distrust" (1993: 278). The impact of violence on communal relations was further compounded by the deep sense of victimization felt within nationalist communities at having been historically marginalized under a system of socioeconomic and political discrimination by a unionist majority (ibid.). As a result, even after the signing of its formal peace agreement, Northern Ireland has remained a deeply divided society, marked by a polarized political system, high levels of residential, social and educational segregation, and feelings of prejudice, fear and resentment between nationalist and unionist communities (Shirlow 2001).

Viewed through the lens of transitional justice, the post-conflict experience of Northern Ireland appears in many ways anomalous. Unlike many transitional societies, even during the height of the violence of the Troubles, Northern Ireland remained a functional Western liberal democracy with an intact legal system, police force and judiciary centralized under the British government. As a result, numerous investigations, arrests and imprisonments of those found responsible for Troubles-era violence were already being carried out under British law over the course of the conflict instead of being deferred until after the peace process (Campbell and Ni-Aolain 2002). Moreover, while

Northern Ireland did undergo a 'transition' from conflict to peace with the signing of the BFA, it did not go through a corresponding change in government or constitutional status. Aside from the addition of the new power-sharing Assembly in Northern Ireland, the system of devolved governance under British rule and the main institutions of government have remained largely intact following the Agreement.

Most notably, however, Northern Ireland is unique because, unlike other divided societies that transitioned away from legacies of mass violence in the 1990s, its peace process was not accompanied by the formation of a formal or 'centralized' transitional justice institution, such as a tribunal or truth commission, to address the legacy of abuses related to past violence. In part, this was due to the fact that Britain maintained sole jurisdiction over past abuses given its continued rule over Northern Ireland. Given the long-held official view that the acts of violence committed by paramilitary organizations during the Troubles were acts of 'ordinary' criminals rather than being political or potentially 'extraordinary' in nature, the position of the British government has traditionally been that such crimes can and should be dealt with internally through the criminal justice system rather than by a specialized transitional justice intervention. Ultimately, however, the lack of a centralized transitional justice institution in Northern Ireland should be understood as a direct result of the political context in which the Belfast Agreement itself was situated.

Indeed, in many ways, the Agreement was a pragmatic choice by unionist and nationalist political leaders—made in concert with the leadership of the main Republican and Loyalist paramilitary organizations and the British and Irish governments—to negotiate an end to violence but to nonetheless continue their struggle for the national identity of Northern Ireland by political means. In effect, even after the peace process, the seminal question of nationalism and the future constitutional status of Northern Ireland that underpinned the conflict remained unresolved, with the BFA signifying very different things for the state's two main communities. For unionists, the Agreement was viewed as enshrining a final constitutional protection that would prevent a potential reunification with the Irish Republic without their express consent. For nationalists, the Agreement was seen as yet another stepping stone towards the larger goal of the eventual reunification of Ireland and the end of British rule. Therefore, while an agreement was reached as to the necessity of peace in Northern Ireland through the BFA, no consensus has ever been formed regarding the past, particularly regarding the morality (or otherwise) of the use of violence by any one side during the Troubles to advance their nationalist goals (Hamber 2002: 93).

Accordingly, since issues surrounding responsibility and victimization remain major points of division between the communities in Northern Ireland, these issues were left largely unresolved in the 'fault-neutral' framework of the Belfast Agreement. While the BFA indicates a general regret for the Troubles' 'legacy of suffering' and underscores a future commitment to using "exclusively democratic and peaceful means of resolving differences on political issues," nowhere does it attempt to assign any kind of moral responsibility for the violence of the past (GNI 1998). Although this decision helped to stabilize the peace process and ensured an end to political conflict, it nevertheless effectively ruled out the use of a centralized transitional justice mechanism mandated to investigate past abuses. In essence, because of the continued existence of zero-sum perceptions of who was 'right' and who was 'wrong' in employing violence during the Troubles, no single transitional justice strategy has thus far been able to be employed without being perceived as biased or sectarian.

However, evidence suggests that some progress is being made in transforming the hostile mindsets and antagonistic attitudes that have long characterized intergroup relations in Northern Ireland—changes that likely account, in no small part, for a marked decline in levels of intercommunity violence in recent years (Devine et al. 2011). While no official centralized trial, tribunal or truth commission process has ever been employed by national or international actors in Northern Ireland to provide accountability for the violence of the Troubles, many of the positive gains that have been made towards intergroup reconciliation do appear to be linked to a uniquely 'decentralized' program of transitional justice that has emerged in the years following the Agreement (Aiken 2010). Instead of following any single transitional justice strategy, this decentralized approach has included a widespread network of 'bottom-up' community-based programs designed to encourage positive cross-community interactions and improve existing relations between divided nationalist and unionist communities. These attempts to rebuild community relations have come alongside a 'piecemeal' approach to addressing the past undertaken by a disparate array of discrete governmental and civil society initiatives that have sought to develop 'truth' and 'justice' in various ways (Bell 2002; Aiken 2010). Finally, these efforts have all taken place against the backdrop of a series of broader equality and equity reforms undertaken by the British and Northern Ireland governments to address the legacy of structural and material inequalities between Catholics and Protestants. In the following chapters, the various aspects of this decentralized justice strategy are considered, with a particular focus on detailing the contributions they have made to advancing intergroup reconciliation in Northern Ireland by promoting instrumental, socioemotional and distributive social learning.

South Africa

The system of apartheid ('separateness' in Afrikaans) was formally established in South Africa under legislation passed by the party of the white minority, the National Party (NP), in 1948. Building on the history of racial discrimination already long established by the British under the system of Pass Laws established during the nineteenth and early twentieth centuries that greatly curtailed the rights and mobility of black South Africans, apartheid effectively sought to extend an official policy of racial separation into every aspect of South African life. Under apartheid law, South African society was formally divided into four racial identity groups—'black,' 'white,' 'colored,' and 'Indian'—and each adult South African was forced to carry an identity card at all times specifying his or her inclusion in one of these groups. Membership in these categories prescribed differential access to social, political and economic rights, and was used as the basis for limiting interracial contact and socialization under a segregationist agenda of 'petty apartheid.' In 1949, the Prohibition of Mixed Marriages Act effectively outlawed marriage between persons identified as belonging to different races, while the Immorality Act of 1950 rendered interracial sexual relations a punishable criminal offense. In an effort to further curtail cross-racial socializing, the Reservation of Separate Amenities Act of 1953 used these classifications to prohibit members of different races from accessing the same amenities, segregating public restaurants, hospitals, beaches, pools and restrooms with government signs clearly demarcating which facilities were reserved for which race. The Bantu Education Act, also introduced in 1953, created a separate—and greatly inferior—system of education for black South Africans, eventually leading to the development of separate universities for Indians, coloreds, blacks and whites. During the 1950s, legislation was also designed to formalize a system of racial discrimination in the workplace, ensuring the placement of whites (and, to a lesser extent, Indians) in professional or management positions and the relegation of blacks to the most menial and undesirable labor. As Hanif Vally, Strategy Advisor for the South African Foundation for Human Rights and Former Chief Legal Advisor for the TRC explains, under apartheid,

> society was defined by your racial identity. You had special laws that defined your racial identity and from that flowed all your rights in society. Which hospital you went to, which train you used, which station you used, which bus you used, which school you went to, where you were buried. Social engineering to its extreme—everything was defined by race. And of course there [were] gross inequalities in terms of facilities made available.
>
> (Interview: July 6th, 2008)

These racial categories were also used as the foundation for a broader structural policy of geographical and political separation in South Africa, often referred to as 'grand apartheid.' The cornerstone of this policy was the Group Areas Act of 1950, which effectively partitioned South Africa into a number of separate geographical zones allotted to different racial groups, while also making it compulsory for each race to live in these designated areas. Further, under the Bantu Authorities Act of 1951, black 'homelands' or 'Bantustans' were created outside of South Africa's major urban centers, effectively setting aside less than one-quarter of all the country's land for the majority black population while reserving the rest (including some of the most fertile and desirable areas) for the minority white and Indian populations. This policy, combined with additional legislation that removed blacks and coloreds from the voters' rolls, both further entrenched racial segregation and ensured that whites would remain the demographic majority and would retain dominant political and economic control of South Africa. Under the Homelands system, blacks were legally stripped of their South African citizenship and were instead made nominal citizens of one of ten self-governing and nominally independent Bantustan 'nations.' The Bantustans were divided among South Africa's eight major black ethnic groups and had their own health, education and public services. This system prevented black South Africans from living in the 'white' cities in which they worked, instead granting them temporary work permits as 'foreign' laborers and subjecting them to arrest and detention if caught without a valid work pass. This meant that many black families were divided, as the men had to live in cramped hostel settlements set aside in the cities in which they worked, while the rest of their families lived in informal settlements or 'townships' that were often many miles distant.

Between the 1950s and 1980s, these policies also led to an aggressive program of 'resettlement' by the government that forcibly removed black, Indian and colored populations from designated white areas in Johannesburg, Cape Town, Pretoria and Durban and transferred them to planned communities away from South Africa's urban centers. This physical resettlement, along with the social segregation enforced under petty apartheid, meant that race divided South African society not only in a legal sense, but also in cultural, economic, geographical and political ways. As Dr. Alex Boraine, Former Deputy Chair of the South African Truth and Reconciliation Commission (TRC) and Co-Founder of the International Center for Transitional Justice (ICTJ) notes, "apartheid succeeded so well in separating people," creating a "very real" racial schism across South African society (interview: June 16th, 2008).

However, the discriminatory policies of apartheid also fostered a significant internal resistance movement within South Africa. This resistance was linked to the growing power of the predominantly black African National Congress (ANC) party, which, in the early 1950s, began to lead acts of mass civil disobedience in a series of strikes, protests and boycotts. To combat this perceived threat, in 1950, federal authorities adopted the Suppression of Communism Act, legislation that gave the government broad latitude to take action against any group aiming "at bringing about any political, industrial, social, or economic change within the Union by the promotion of disturbance or disorder" (1950). Under this legislation, the police and security forces of the apartheid state began responding to internal resistance with increased levels of violence and brutality. On March 21st, 1960, a peaceful protest against the Pass Law system led by the Pan Africanist Congress (PAC) ended in bloodshed when police in armored vehicles fired into the crowds, killing 69 people in what would later be known as the 'Sharpeville Massacre.' In the wake of widespread protests following Sharpeville, the government declared a state of emergency, during which it detained over 18,000 people suspected of plotting against the state. Shortly thereafter, the ANC and PAC were banned as political organizations and forced into exile, with both organizations consequently adopting more militant stances. In response, under the leadership of individuals including Nelson Mandela, the ANC formed the Umkhonto we Sizwe (MK) as its military arm and began carrying out acts of sabotage against state structures.

In June 1976, a peaceful uprising led by students in the Johannesburg suburb of Soweto against the Bantu education system again ended in violence when police and the military fired on the protestors, killing hundreds and wounding many more. In 1977, Steve Biko, leader of the emerging Black Consciousness Movement, was taken into custody by police and killed while being held in detention. Security measures by the state only tightened further during the 1980s. Under President P.W. Botha, numerous states of emergency were declared by the government between 1985 and 1989, giving the police and military unprecedented latitude in their actions against anti-apartheid organizations and leading to an increase in the use of tactics such as abductions, torture, physical violence and detention without trial. The state also exercised extensive media censorship throughout the period in order to try and control the public response to these measures. The armed wings of the ANC and PAC liberation movements consequently continued their campaigns of violence against the state, bombing public areas and state institutions and killing both government officials and civilians. Outbreaks of intracommunity violence among black South Africans also became more common as those suspected of collaborating with the government were beaten and killed. Some of the most vicious outbreaks of violence occurred in the late 1980s and early 1990s between supporters of the ANC and those of their political rival, the Zulu-dominated Inkatha Freedom Party (IFP) led by Mangosuthu Buthelezi—a conflict widely believed to have been actively promoted by a 'third force' working on behalf of the apartheid security forces (Ellis 1998).

However, with the apartheid system coming under increased scrutiny both internally and internationally, the position of the government became untenable. In 1990, the National Party, under the new leadership of F.W. de Klerk, began a series of reforms and negotiations to bring the apartheid system to an end. Many of the most discriminatory laws of the apartheid state were repealed, and the thirty-year ban on the political parties of the liberation movement, including the ANC, the PAC and the South African Communist Party (SACP), was finally lifted. In February 1990, Nelson Mandela was released from prison and negotiations began in earnest between the ANC and the NP to begin a transition to multi-racial democracy in South Africa. In spite of these gains, some of the most extensive violence of the apartheid era occurred during this period, with extensive bloodshed continuing between the ANC and the IFP. A number of acts of interracial violence also occurred during this time. Right-wing Afrikaners assassinated the charismatic leader of the SACP, Chris Hani. The military wing of the PAC, the Azanian People's Liberation Army (APLA), launched an attack on a white church in Cape Town in 1993, killing eleven and wounding nearly sixty more in what became known as the 'St. James Massacre.'

However, despite the persistence of violence, negotiations continued, and in 1993 a new Interim Constitution of 'National Unity and Reconciliation' was agreed upon between the NP and ANC in the hopes of creating "a historic bridge between the past of a deeply divided society characterized by strife, conflict, untold suffering and injustice, and a future founded on the recognition of human rights, democracy and peaceful co-existence and development opportunities for all South Africans" (GSA 1994). Democratic elections were subsequently held in April 1994, during which the votes of nearly twenty million South Africans firmly established the ANC as the majority party in a new multi-racial government of National Unity under the leadership of President Mandela. As President from 1994 to 1999, Mandela presided over South Africa's 'transformative moment' and played a crucial role in setting the magnanimous and reconciliatory tone that marked the post-apartheid period.[8]

However, despite South Africa's relatively peaceful transition to democracy, the racial divisions entrenched for nearly six decades under the apartheid system left a country riven by deep societal cleavages. As Audrey Chapman and Hugo van der Merwe argue, the effects of nearly fifty years of institutionalized racism under the apartheid system proved devastating for social cohesion in South Africa, as "in an effort to divide and conquer, apartheid political policies manipulated and reinforced divisions among and within various South African racial and political groups . . . [leaving] a legacy of deep social divisions, psychological scars, and distrust between groups" (Chapman and van der Merwe 2008b: 6). These divides were further compounded by the presence of deep structural and distributive imbalances between racial groups in areas such as income, housing, employment and education—all the result of decades of discrimination under apartheid legislation. This meant that, despite the transition to a multi-racial democracy, the majority of black South Africans still largely continued to live in the same impoverished conditions and geographically distant 'township' settlements that they had occupied under apartheid. Further, much disagreement lingered between white and black South Africans concerning the 'justness' of the political violence that had brought an end to apartheid. A number of whites still held the view that the state had been defending them from the terrorist tactics of the insurgent Communist threat posed by the ANC, while for most black South Africans the liberation struggle was a 'just war' fought against the morally corrupt and inherently racist system of apartheid (Gibson 2004: 157–158).

Truth and reconciliation in South Africa

The South African Truth and Reconciliation Commission was a direct product of the negotiated settlement that brought an end to apartheid-era violence in South Africa. As the transition to multi-racial democracy in South Africa followed neither an outright victory for the apartheid government nor for the ANC and the other liberation movements, it was instead the end result of a gradually—and quite tenuously—negotiated peace settlement. To help protect the stability of the nascent peace process and to prevent any party from being provoked into a return to violence, an amnesty clause was included in the 'postamble' of the new 1993 Interim Constitution. This provision mandated that an amnesty would be "granted in respect of acts, omissions and offences associated with political objectives and committed in the course of the conflicts of the past" for all those who may have violated human rights during apartheid-era violence, including members of both the government security forces and the liberation movements (GSA 1994). As Howard Varney, Director of the Truth Seeking Program for the ICTJ and former member Head of the TRC's Investigation Unit notes, this conditional amnesty provision was an essential means of protecting South Africa's peaceful transition towards democracy:

> In the early 90s when the negotiations were happening, there's no doubt that the country was in a fragile place. . . . We were teetering on the brink. So the conditional amnesty was a tool by which those involved in activities that could scuttle the whole process could use it as an escape route, a safety valve . . . it helped to keep people engaged in the peace process, in the transition . . . to help us cross this historic bridge from the violent past to the peaceful democratic future.
>
> (Interview: June 24th, 2008)

Taking this constitutionally protected amnesty provision as a starting point, considerable consultation then followed to determine the shape of South Africa's transitional justice process, including a series of public hearings and discussions with local civil society leaders and international non-governmental organizations. In the end, due largely to sustained pressure from human rights organizations and the influence of the recently concluded Chilean National Commission for Truth and Reconciliation, it was decided that the conditional amnesty provision would be incorporated into a centralized national truth commission framework. While most truth commissions tend to deemphasize criminal prosecutions to some degree in favor of a focus on truth recovery, a defining characteristic of the TRC was the extent to which it associated itself with principles of restorative justice. Indeed, as opposed to the retributive approach traditionally employed in trials or international tribunals, in which the primary aim is to secure prosecution and punishment for individual perpetrators of past abuses, from its conception the TRC embraced an alternative philosophy that was "concerned not so much with punishment as with correcting imbalances, restoring broken relationships—with healing, harmony, and reconciliation" (TRC 1998: vol. 1, ch. 1, para. 36).

The TRC's adoption of a restorative justice approach emphasizing the promotion of interracial reconciliation can be understood, at least in part, as a pragmatic decision: the TRC was bound by the Interim Constitution to grant amnesty to perpetrators, so it could never have pursued a program of unrestricted prosecutions. As one observer suggests, the creation of the South African TRC was first and foremost born out of a creative political compromise, "an invention of necessity in response to the political constraints and opportunities of the time" (Chapman and van der Merwe 2008b: 13). However, the Commission's restorative mandate was also heavily influenced by Mandela's calls for interracial reconciliation and by the Judeo-Christian theology of its Chair, Desmond Tutu, who consistently highlighted the importance of interpersonal reconciliation, confession and forgiveness in his vision for the TRC. It was also strongly reflective of traditional African values of *ubuntu* or 'humaneness,' a philosophy that envisions crime as a threat primarily to the interconnected web of relationships that bind all individuals together in a harmonious society. Accordingly, in lieu of punishment, *ubuntu* instead emphasizes the need to shift from confrontation to conciliation and to seek ways in which to rebuild damaged relationships and restore a common respect for human life by bringing together all members of the community affected by the crimes of the past in the justice process. Finally, the restorative principles adopted by the TRC echoed the broader commitment by Mandela's new South African government to addressing the past in a way that sought to overcome past divisiveness and to promote a new sense of national reconciliation, emphasizing "a need for understanding but not for vengeance, a need for reparation but not for retaliation, a need for ubuntu but not for victimization" (GSA 1995).

The structure and mandate of the South African TRC were outlined in the Promotion of National Unity and Reconciliation Act ('the Act'), which was adopted with the full support of President Mandela on December 15th, 1995. Under this Act, the TRC was tasked with the overall objective of establishing "as complete a picture as possible of the causes, nature and extent of the gross violations of human rights" committed between March 1960 and May 1994, "including the antecedents, circumstances, factors and context of such violations, as well as the perspectives of the victims and the motives and perspectives of the persons responsible for the commission of the violations, by conducting investigations and holding hearings" and of "compiling a report providing as comprehensive an account as possible of the activities and findings of the Commission" (ibid.).

Alongside these truth recovery functions, in line with its restorative ethos, the TRC was also explicitly charged with contributing to the promotion of 'national unity and reconciliation' by using its proceedings to help "transcend the divisions and strife of the past, which generated gross human rights violations . . . and [their] legacy of hatred, fear, guilt, and revenge" (GSA 1994). In this way, the Commission was to aid the process of interracial reconciliation by serving as an historic 'bridge' to a new society based on a common respect for the moral worth of all South Africans "irrespective of colour, race, class, belief, or sex," thereby helping to counter the "dehumanizing past" of the violence and institutionalized racism that characterized apartheid (TRC 1998: vol. 1, ch. 4, para. 43). This goal was most visibly embraced by the Commission's Chairman, Desmond Tutu, who championed the role of the TRC in the creation of a 'rainbow nation' in which citizens of all colors would be reconciled within the single rainbow of the new South African society (Tutu 2000).

To assist with reaching these ambitious objectives, the empowering Act of the TRC endowed the Commission with unprecedented powers of search, seizure and subpoena, as well as a comprehensive witness protection program. Given a delineated operational timeframe of roughly two-and-a-half years between mid-1995 and 1998, the TRC was also provided with the largest professional staff and greatest financial resources of any truth commission undertaken to date, with a complement of nearly 400 staff members, several dedicated offices throughout the country, and a total operating budget of over $50 million USD. To head the Commission, 17 Commissioners were appointed by President Mandela following a public nomination and selection process, including the charismatic and influential Anglican Archbishop Desmond Tutu as Chair and Alex Boraine, a former President of the South African Methodist Church and respected South African Parliamentarian, as Deputy Chair.

Structurally, the TRC worked by way of three main interconnected committees, each responsible for the fulfillment of a different aspect of the Commission's twin goals of truth seeking and reconciliation. The first of these, the Human Rights Violations Committee (HRVC), was charged with "establishing and making known the fate or whereabouts of victims" and "restoring the human and civil dignity of such victims by granting them an opportunity to relate their own accounts of the violations of which they are the victims" (GSA 1995). This included the collection of nearly 22,000 statements from those who came forward to identify themselves as the victims of past human rights abuses, with slightly fewer than 2,000 of these individuals being given the opportunity to provide their testimony publicly in a series of 80 community hearings held in townships, small towns and urban centers throughout the country. These hearings each lasted between one and three days, and were designed to provide a public forum for the victims of apartheid violence to recount their stories of past abuse to a sympathetic and supportive panel of Commissioners. These public hearing events drew large local audiences and intense media coverage in newspapers, on radio and on television both within South Africa and around the world (Thiessen 2008: 202).

Second, the TRC's Amnesty Committee (AC) was assigned the task of processing and facilitating the granting of the conditional amnesties mandated under the constitution to those individual perpetrators of gross human rights violations who made "full disclosure of all the relevant facts relating to acts associated with a political objective" committed between 1960 and 1994 (GSA 1995). The incorporation of these individual amnesties in the truth-recovery process was a unique innovation of the TRC. As opposed to the 'blanket amnesties' associated with previous truth commission models employed in Latin America, amnesties under the TRC were conditional, and were granted only to those who fully disclosed their involvement in past crimes, were able to prove a political motivation for their actions, could show 'proportionality' between the act and the political objective sought, and were willing to appear in quasi-judicial public hearings to answer questions from Committee members. Overall, over 7,000 individuals applied for amnesty through the AC; 5,143 of these applicants were refused outright for not meeting the 'conditional' criteria of the amnesty provision, and 1,973 of them were granted a public hearing process. Of those given a public hearing, 1,167 were granted amnesty while 806 were eventually denied (Chapman and van der Merwe 2008b). Like the HRVC's work, the AC hearings also drew heavy public interest and were subject to extensive coverage by national and international media.

Third, the Reparations and Rehabilitation Committee (RRC) was tasked with designing and making recommendations to the President about the "measures that should be taken with regard to the granting of reparations to victims or the taking of other measures aimed at rehabilitating and restoring the human and civil dignity of victims" (GSA 1995). Notably, it was decided that the reparations and related measures envisioned under the TRC would only apply to a 'closed list' of those 22,000 'official' victims who had both suffered an individual gross human rights abuse and filed a certified victim's statement with the HRVC before December 1997. As one of the RRC Commissioners has noted, this limited definition of victims eligible for reparations under the TRC effectively excluded "millions of South Africans who, while they may not have suffered a gross violation of human rights under apartheid, nevertheless suffered the daily violation of living under apartheid" (Orr 2000: 243). After much deliberation, the RRC ultimately recommended a financial compensation package of approximately

R120,000 for each of the registered victims to be paid out over a six-year period, in addition to a wide range of health, educational, housing and other support services. However, after a series of delays, victims ultimately received only a small interim payment of R3,000 and, over five years after the completion of the TRC's work, a single one-time payment of R30,000 (equivalent to roughly $4,000 USD at the time) (Chapman and van der Merwe 2008b: 286).

These Committees were also supplemented by the work of a dedicated Investigations Unit and a Research Department. The Investigation Unit was charged with the substantial dual task of trying to corroborate the accuracy of victim statements made to the HRVC and of reviewing the veracity of claims made to the Amnesty Committee to ensure truthful and accurate 'full disclosure' in exchange for amnesty. The Research Department, on the other hand, sought to provide a broader historical background of the abuses committed under apartheid. In addition to these structures, the TRC also held a series of six public institutional hearings focused on key sectors of the previous regime—including the legal system, the health sector, business and labor, and the media—to examine their possible involvement in broader patterns of human rights violations under the apartheid system. Additional 'special hearings' were held on topics considered to be of particular importance to understanding key facets of apartheid-era violence, including the policies of political parties, compulsory military service, the use of chemical and biological weapons against opponents of the government, and the impact of violence on women and youth. Finally, specialized hearings were also held to address the involvement of specific individuals in past violence, including, most notably, Winnie Madikizela-Mandela (the former wife of Nelson Mandela). Overall, these public hearings represented another key expansion of the TRC on past truth commission models, in that they tried to sketch a more systemic picture of apartheid's structural abuses to complement the focus of the HRVC and AC on individual human rights violations.

The main work of the TRC concluded in October 1998, resulting in the publication of a 3,500-page five-volume Final Report of its key findings.[9] Initial reactions to the TRC and its Final Report among South Africa's primary political parties were mixed. While the TRC was praised by President Mandela as having "contributed to the work in progress of laying the foundation of the edifice of reconciliation," the ANC party nonetheless sought a court injunction to block the release of the Final Report, citing numerous inaccuracies in its portrayal of the ANC's complicity in human rights violations during its liberation struggle (BBC News, October 30th, 1998). For its part, the NP made numerous assertions of unfair bias by the TRC in favor of the ANC, and many of its senior figures—including former President P.W. Botha, one of the principal architects of the apartheid system—refused to engage with the process entirely. While the NP did not take legal action against the Commission's Final Report, its former leader, F.W. de Klerk, was able to secure an out-of-court settlement that forced the TRC to 'black out' sections of its Final Report detailing adverse findings against him. Finally, Buthelezi and the IFP remained consistently opposed to the TRC from its inception, discouraging its supporters from participating and attacking the Commission as being deeply biased against their organization.[10]

Nevertheless, as the government's main avenue for addressing the gross human rights violations that had occurred under apartheid, the work of the TRC is now widely considered by both national and international actors to have made a crucial contribution to processes of reconciliation in the 'transformative moment' marking South Africa's historic transition from apartheid rule. While certainly not without its critics, the TRC is often credited with having helped both to protect against the renewal of violence in the wake of South Africa's transition and to promote improved interracial relations and a new sense of national unity (Minow 1998; Hayner 2002; Amstutz 2005; Gibson 2004). As a result of these perceived successes, many other countries undergoing a similar period of transition have since turned to the unique truth commission structure of the South African TRC and employed it as a model for their own transitional justice strategies (Graybill and Lanegran 2004). However, as a number of scholars have noted, understandings as to how or why the TRC may have been causally linked to increased reconciliation remain largely unspecified and undertheorized (Braham 2007; Aiken 2008; Chapman and van der Merwe 2008b; Chapman 2009). In an effort to address this gap, the following chapters consider the contributions that the Commission made to interracial reconciliation in post-apartheid South Africa, with a particular focus on assessing the role it has played in promoting crucial forms of instrumental, distributional and socioemotional forms of social learning.

Notes

1 A particularly egregious exchange occurred on November 21st, 1920, when a coordinated IRA attack causing the deaths of 14 British agents led to British security forces opening fire on a crowd at a Gaelic football match in Dublin, killing 14 Irish civilians in an incident subsequently dubbed 'Bloody Sunday' (Dolan 2006).
2 More than 500 were killed during this period, including more than 300 Catholic civilians, 35 members of the IRA, nearly 200 Protestant civilians and 80 members of British Security Forces (English 2003: 39–40; Lynch 2006: 67, 227).
3 In the three years prior to Bloody Sunday, 213 people were killed as a result of sectarian violence, while in the three months directly following Bloody Sunday, more than 400 were killed.
4 Loyalist paramilitary groups were responsible for 870 civilian deaths during the conflict, more than any other armed organization. Of these deaths, 727 were from the nationalist community (Sutton 2010).

5 In fact, a secret research document of the British Military known as the 'Glover Report' had concluded by the early 1980s that the IRA was unlikely to be defeated militarily (Cronin 1980).

6 The last major act of Troubles-era violence occurred in August 1998 when the Real IRA (RIRA), a dissident Republican paramilitary group opposed to the peace process, exploded a bomb in the town of Omagh. This led to the deaths of 29 Catholic, Protestant and international victims and the serious wounding of over 200 civilians. Fortunately, the attack was roundly condemned by both nationalist and unionist communities and only served to galvanize support for the peace process.

7 Full powers in relation to policing and criminal justice have since been transferred to the Assembly as of April 12th, 2010.

8 One illustrative instance of this was Mandela's encouragement of black South Africans to support the 'Springboks' rugby team—long a symbol of white dominance—in the 1995 Rugby World Cup. Following the Springboks' victory, Mandela appeared in a Springbok jersey to present the trophy to the white Afrikaner team captain, Francois Pienaar. This was widely viewed as a major symbolic step in the interracial reconciliation between white and black South Africans (Farquharson and Marjoribanks 2003).

9 Upon the completion of the Amnesty Commission's work in 2001, a sixth volume was added to the report in 2003.

10 Upon the release of the report, these assertions intensified, and a series of court challenges eventually led to an out-of-court settlement leading to changes to the wording of the Report's dealings with the IFP.

Chapter 5

Instrumental learning

Instrumental learning refers to those social and cognitive processes of identity negotiation necessary to reconciliation that are derived from engaging former antagonists in sustained cooperative interaction. This kind of interaction allows groups to begin to transform existing negative perceptions of and antagonistic relationships with the Other. As discussed in the social learning model outlined in Chapter 3, instrumental learning depends on the promotion of two key learning mechanisms. First, as insights from the long-standing 'contact hypothesis' in social psychology suggest, instrumental learning requires strategies designed to promote positive contact across community boundaries. Indeed, a substantial body of experimental and real-world research has evidenced the independent effect of positive intercommunity contact on challenging negative stereotypes and misperceptions, reducing prejudice, and in aiding in the development of a more inclusive sense of shared identification—all factors considered essential for reconciliation and sustainable peace in divided societies. Second, the content and context of such interaction is important, particularly in terms of whether it can serve to foster deeper exchange in the form of transformative intercommunal dialogue. This kind of intergroup dialogue is held to be a key mechanism of instrumental learning, as it can enable groups to begin to transform the rigidified and hostile perceptions about the Other that informed past conflict. This step, in turn, allows for greater recognition of shared values and needs, the development of mutual trust, and the broadening of intercommunal empathy to include a reciprocal recognition of basic humanity and moral worth.

By critically examining the very different transitional justice strategies adopted in the post-conflict environments of Northern Ireland and South Africa, this chapter considers the ability of each country's strategy to contribute to instrumental learning by promoting positive contact and transformative dialogue. In Northern Ireland, attempts to encourage instrumental learning have largely centered on efforts to improve 'community relations' between nationalist and unionist populations. A variety of such initiatives have been undertaken by both governmental and civil society actors as part of the country's broader 'decentralized' transitional justice strategy. In

South Africa, instrumental learning has largely been associated with the TRC's efforts to clear space for interracial encounter and to promote societal dialogue about the past between black and white South Africans. This chapter considers both cases in turn in order to explore and assess the causal relationship between transitional justice, instrumental learning and intergroup reconciliation.

Instrumental learning in Northern Ireland

As previously discussed, living with the constant threat of conflict over the course of the Troubles proved devastating to social cohesion between nationalist and unionist communities in Northern Ireland. For instance, following the outbreak of the Troubles in the late 1960s, stark patterns of residential and physical segregation began to develop in Northern Ireland's cities and towns. 'Mixed' neighborhoods of nationalists and unionists became increasingly rare, particularly in working-class urban areas in Derry and Belfast where families were either forced out of their homes or left voluntarily for fear of violence. By the beginning of the peace process in the early 1990s, it is estimated that fully 70 percent of the population of Northern Ireland had come to live in completely segregated 'single-identity' communities (Shirlow 2001: 60).

An extensive system of territorial demarcation consisting of flags, curb paintings and murals developed over time to further delineate the geographical boundaries of these communities, resulting in the carving up of urban areas into psychological 'chill zones' where members of the Other community feared to tread (Shirlow and Murtagh 2006: 9; Hughes et al. 2007: 36). The most proximate of these segregated neighborhoods often became the most starkly divided, with high-tension 'interface' zones developing between nationalist and unionist enclaves. These interface areas were virtual no-man's lands, with entire streets of housing abandoned for fear of violence. Perhaps the starkest signs of these divisions were the numerous 'peace walls'—reinforced barrier fences standing up to 25 feet high—constructed in the cities of Derry and Belfast to separate the most violence-prone communities living in interface areas (Goldie and Ruddy 2010). The most extreme segregation in the country was concentrated in deprived lower-class urban areas, while more affluent middle-class areas were more likely to be mixed and integrated (Shirlow 2001).

This physical separation was matched by patterns of social segregation, which have long been prominent in Northern Ireland. For example, evidence from the annual Northern Ireland Life and Times (NILT) survey collected in 2000 showed that even shortly after the conclusion of the peace process 60 percent of all Catholics and 77 percent of Protestants reported that 'all' or 'most' of their friends belonged to their own religion (ARK 2001). Where cross-community friendships did develop, these relationships often only functioned so long as certain difficult or potentially divisive topics such as politics or religion were never mentioned (Trew 1986: 93–106; Cairns and Hewstone 2002). Moreover, there is now a large body of literature that discusses the informal system of 'telling' that emerged in Northern Ireland throughout the Troubles, meaning that one's affiliation as nationalist or unionist could effectively be 'read' by others through symbolic identifiers such as surname, school, accent, place of birth or support of a particular sporting team. As Mari Fitzduff illustrates, informal interactions across community lines were therefore often "limited by an instinctual treating of the Other as different—one of them," with the result that meetings were "circumscribed by a caution that . . . usually prevents any honest and open dialogue, particularly about issues that are pertinent to the conflict" (Fitzduff 2002: 31).

Similarly, as a result of the Troubles more intimate relationships also remained exceedingly rare, with 'mixed' marriages between communities comprising less than 10 percent of all marriages in Northern Ireland as of 2003 (Niens et al. 2003: 123–140). Furthermore, in one survey fully half of all adult respondents polled following the peace process indicated that while growing up they had no friends from outside their religious community before the age of 15 (Hughes et al. 2007). In large part, this was due to a highly segregated education system in which children in Northern Ireland almost exclusively attended single-identity denominational schools through- out both their elementary and secondary years (Hewstone et al. 2005: 8). As Ray Mullan, Director of Communications for the Northern Ireland Com- munity Relations Council, has noted, these extensive patterns of physical and social segregation meant that many in Northern Ireland continued to "grow up their entire lives here in silos . . . they go to separate schools, they live in separate areas, they go to separate churches, so they have a separate world that they live in, and that is an Orange [Protestant/unionist] or a Green [Catholic/ nationalist] world" (interview: April 21st, 2008). This discussion of the pervasiveness of segregation in Northern Ireland is echoed by Mari Fitzduff, who illustrates that

> [t]his overall situation [in Northern Ireland] means that it is quite possible for a substantial number of people, particularly those within working-class urban areas or in rural areas, to study, live, work, and socialize almost completely, for most of their lives, within their own community and not develop close or sustained relationships with someone from another community.
>
> (2002: 7)

Perhaps most troubling, such segregation creates a 'cyclical and inter- dependent' relationship, reinforcing the existing prejudices, stereotypes and fears about the Other community underpinning the violence of the Troubles

(Hughes et al. 2007: 36). Studies suggest that even after the formal peace process, the widespread lack of opportunity for more positive encounters across communal lines in Northern Ireland continued to limit the dissemination of new information capable of challenging existing attitudes and mindsets developed during the Troubles. Further, when contact did occur, such as in public shops, in the workplace, or in more mixed middle-class neighborhoods, research has shown that often the majority of these interactions were exceedingly polite or "superficially courteous," and are therefore "not of a degree to alter suspicions or change stereotypes" (Hewstone et al. 2005: 8).

As Miles Hewstone and his colleagues illustrate, in this way, entrenched patterns of physical and social segregation developed during the Troubles served to maintain existing psychological divisions between nationalist and unionist communities by "fostering mutual ignorance, suspicion and distrust and by maintaining prejudice and negative stereotypes" that prevent against the chance for social learning and reconciliation (Hewstone et al. 2008b). This is a point echoed by Dr. Pete Shirlow of the University of Belfast, who suggests that despite the positive steps that were taken towards the signing of the Belfast Agreement, "negative attitudes and hostility directed toward the 'Other' community remain[ed] a feature [of Northern Ireland] . . . especially in the areas affected most by violence." As a result, he notes that relationships between the two communities were often characterized by continued animosity "marked around a mixture of fear, misunderstanding and the attachment of negative characteristics" to one another (Shirlow 2001: 67). In fact, there is now evidence to suggest that the perpetuation of such antagonisms in highly segregated interface areas has been responsible, in large part, for the 'low-intensity' sectarian violence between nationalist and unionist communities that has continued following the BFA in the form of youth-led rioting, fighting and property damage (Hansson 2005).

(Re)building 'community relations' in Northern Ireland

In recognition of the role that continued communal divisions can play in motivating and sustaining conflict, efforts have been under way at various levels of society in Northern Ireland to reopen space for positive contact and dialogue across community lines. In the 1970s and 1980s, such efforts were largely limited to the small-scale attempts of community groups, religious organizations and non-governmental peace organizations to try to rebuild trust, cooperation, understanding and better relations at local levels. However, with the development of the peace process in the early 1990s, a full-scale program involving government, civil society and grassroots actors emerged under a coordinated mandate to improve 'community relations' between nationalists and unionists.

For the most part, this community relations strategy has relied on an effective division of labor for addressing intercommunal divisions. The

Government of Northern Ireland (GNI) has taken on the 'top-down' tasks of delineating an inclusive policy agenda and providing the social and political leadership and the necessary resources to sustain effective contact, dialogue and development initiatives in local communities across Northern Ireland. The actual on-the-ground work of promoting instrumental learning has thus largely been left to local governments and a vibrant grassroots community and voluntary sector. These actors tend to carry a great deal of legitimacy within their own communities and they have evidenced high levels of success in identifying and adapting the broader community relations agenda of the GNI to the needs of local populations. This 'bottom-up' work has in turn been facilitated by the coordination of a highly trained, well-funded and professionalized civil society sector that administers and monitors targeted funding for community-based reconciliation initiatives on behalf of the Northern Ireland government and a range of international and regional donors. Overall, this approach to rebuilding community relations in Northern Ireland has resulted in a streamlined flow of funding, training and oversight, all of which are designed to 'trickle down' to support a network of instrumental learning initiatives at local levels.

Government interventions

In 1987, the Secretary of State for Northern Ireland established the Community Relations Unit (CRU) under the Northern Ireland Office (NIO), which was charged with "bringing the two sides of the community towards greater understanding" in an effort to support and stabilize the emerging peace process (Hughes and Knox 1997: 330).[1] The CRU was created to help prioritize attempts to address and reduce communal divisions in Northern Ireland, as well as to ensure that these issues remained a focal point of all future government initiatives. In this capacity, the CRU formulated policy strategies, provided advice to government ministers, and undertook research to identify and evaluate existing efforts already under way to repair existing communal divisions between nationalists and unionists.

However, the fact that the NIO was tied to the British government meant that it was not viewed as an impartial actor, a fact that greatly restricted its ability to engage directly in the work of intercommunity reconciliation. Accordingly, the CRU focused instead on promoting various local initiatives and providing funding to improve their community relations efforts. While extensive grassroots reconciliatory work was already being carried out by an array of independent civil society organizations and local community actors during the violence of the Troubles, much of this work was chronically underfunded and operated on an uncoordinated ad hoc basis.[2] Unfortunately, the 'scattershot' nature of these efforts limited the overall impact of individual organizations' attempts to improve existing intercommunity relations (Frazer and Fitzduff 1994). The CRU aimed to address this problem by providing funding and support for projects that pursued a common mandate focused on the renewal of contact and dialogue between divided communities. This mandate was based on the assumption that increasing opportunities for positive interactions between nationalist and unionists would ultimately encourage greater mutual understanding and improve cross-community relations (Knox and Hughes 1996).

One of the first major investments made by the CRU in this community relations project was undertaken at the level of local government. In July 1989, all 26 of Northern Ireland's District Councils were invited by the CRU to take part in a Community Relations Programme (DCCRP). In essence, the DCCRP made Councils eligible to receive core funding from the CRU to support local projects in their districts that were specifically designed to increase cross-community interaction. This involved the appointment of dedicated Community Relations Officers (CROs) to each District Council to ensure that sensitivity to improved community relations was reflected in all local government policy and to administer small 'seed grants' that redistributed government funding to local community and voluntary organizations engaged in the promotion of cross-community contact and dialogue (Knox and Hughes 1996).

In 2000, following the signing of the BFA, the powers of the CRU were transferred from the NIO to the Office of the First Minister and Deputy First Minister (OFMDFM) under the newly devolved Assembly. After a period of extensive consultation with academics, civil society representatives and local communities, in 2005 the CRU launched a new 'Policy and Strategic Framework for Good Relations' entitled *A Shared Future*. This document set out a series of "practical steps and actions, based on common fundamental principles" which were to be "coordinated across government and throughout civic society to ensure an effective and coherent response to sectarian and racial intimidation with the aim of rebuilding relationships rooted in mutual recognition and trust" (CRU 2005: 7). In particular, *A Shared Future* aimed to strengthen and streamline the government's existing mandate to support programs that sought to combat sectarianism, encourage mutual understanding, and develop a greater sense of shared identity through the promotion of cross-community contact and dialogue. These strategies were further incentivized among non-governmental organizations and local community actors by the allocation of targeted grant funds for local projects that demonstrated a "worthwhile and cost-effective contribution to increasing cross-community contact and cooperation and enhancing mutual respect, understanding, and appreciation of cultural diversity" (ibid.).[3]

Civil society initiatives

At the level of civil society, the CRU also recognized a need to create an independent organization at arm's length from the government to avoid alienating any segments of society and to add legitimacy to its work. The Community Relations Council (CRC) was therefore formed in 1990 as an independent company and registered organization to work as a unified regional body to support efforts by local organizations to improve community relations across Northern Ireland. In many ways, the CRC was designed to act as a 'mezzo-level' or intermediary organization between government and the community/voluntary sector, serving as a gatekeeper for government funding and oversight of local community relations projects.[4] In this capacity, the CRC would help to administer government funds by distributing small grants to local community organizations, provide these groups with training and research on 'best practices' in community relations work, and serve as an advisory body for government agencies and commercial institutions dealing with issues of sectarian division.

In addition, a wide range of local community organizations engaging in mediation, peace-building and socioeconomic development work also emerged in Northern Ireland over the course of the Troubles and the ensuing peace process. Broadly speaking, these have taken the form both of programs operated primarily within and on behalf of a single community (often referred to as 'single-identity' work) and of non-partisan initiatives involving both communities in addressing issues of common concern ('cross-community' work). In 2001, over 130 registered organizations were working on various kinds of cross-community initiatives—a number that has increased in recent years as opportunities for grant funding have multiplied through the CRU, CRC and DCCRP. These include individual groups engaged in development projects aimed at regenerating local communities as well as programs designed to provide innovative ways to encourage cross-community contact and dialogue. They also involve larger 'peace-building partnership' networks of multiple organizations, which have developed in urban centers such as Derry and Belfast and have created opportunities for sharing resources, strategies and best practices for effective community relations work.[5]

While the sheer number of these organizations prevents a complete review of their work, one prominent example is the Glencree Centre for Peace and Reconciliation ('Glencree'). Founded in 1974, Glencree is a highly regarded non-profit organization committed to finding non-violent ways to encourage reconciliation within and between communities. Through a small core of highly trained staff and volunteers, the organization has sought to provide the space for carefully mediated cross-community contact and dialogue. These encounters have included work with political elites in 'Political Dialogue Workshops,' with former paramilitaries, police and British security forces in its 'Ex-Combatants Programme,' and also with individual victims of violence from Britain, the Republic of Ireland and Northern Ireland in its 'LIVE Programme' (Murphy and Adair 2004). The central aim of all of these initiatives is to provide an inclusive forum where members of different communities are able to meet, exchange views, build relationships, and address issues over a series of repeated encounters. These encounters, extending over several sessions, take the form of recurring conferences, workshops and extended residential stays at Glencree's Conference Centre, which is located in a relatively 'neutral' venue across the border in County Wicklow in the Irish Republic. In addition to these encounter programs, Glencree also operates a series of certified training workshops aimed at teaching civil society and the grassroots community skills in negotiation, mediation, conflict transformation and reconciliation to help them in their own work.

One other prominent example of a local 'bottom-up' program that has worked to improve relations by bringing members of divided communities together in networks of interaction, trust and dialogue is the non-governmental Belfast Interface Project (BIP). The BIP was originally established in 1995 with a small professional staff and a mandate to identify the major issues of concern to conflict-prone interface communities and to consult with civil society and the local community and voluntary sectors to come up with ways to address these issues. As of 2008, the BIP's work extended to an executive membership committee made up of 45 community organizations engaged in development and reconciliation work in interface areas and to over 600 individual members drawn from both nationalist and unionist communities. With this network, BIP facilitates exploratory contact and dialogue between interface communities and transfers good practices between organizations working in these areas through intercommunity conferences and small grant programs. Beyond these efforts, the BIP has also contributed to a number of practical interventions that have helped to significantly reduce interface tensions and increase the mediative capacity of local communities. One of the most successful of these interventions has been the creation of a mobile phone calling network between local community leaders on both sides of an interface area that has been used to effectively defuse potential tensions and prevent 'anti-social behavior' from spilling over into violence (Goldie and Ruddy 2010).

Finally, it should be noted that Northern Ireland has benefited from a wealth of external funding—both regional and international—supporting local initiatives aimed at improving intercommunity relations through contact and dialogue. Much of this funding has come through the EU's Programme for Peace and Reconcilition (PEACE) which, since 1995, has provided over €2 billion to support reconciliation efforts in Northern Ireland.[6] While a small fraction of these monies have taken the form of direct grants to local community organizations, most often funds have been disbursed through intermediary funding bodies (IFBs) that work to support grassroots initiatives by overseeing small grant programs within the community and voluntary sectors. These bodies include organizations like the CRU, CRC and DCCRP, as well a range of other 'mezzo-level' civil society organizations, such as the Community Foundation for Northern Ireland and the International Fund for Ireland. While operating as independent entities with distinct mandates, the goals of these organizations have nevertheless tended to run in parallel with those of the *Shared Future* policy of the Northern Ireland government in their focus on promoting new opportunities for cross-community interaction. As a result, local community organizations have often been able to cobble together an extensive array of funding from a variety of governmental and non-governmental sources to support programs aimed at promoting instrumental learning in Northern Ireland.

Education initiatives

One other area of work in line with the broader aims of Northern Ireland's community relations agenda that deserves special attention is that of integrated education. Since Partition in 1921, Northern Ireland has seen extraordinarily high levels of educational segregation. Even following the peace process, most schoolchildren have continued to attend denominational primary and secondary schools that are predominantly either Catholic or Protestant. Indeed, estimates from as late as 2008 suggest that 95 percent of all students in Northern Ireland are enrolled at essentially 'single-identity' institutions that offer little opportunity for interaction with members of the Other community (LaMarche 2008). In the 1970s, research began to highlight the potentially detrimental effects that this deep level of educational segregation could have on relations between the two communities, suggesting that such an arrangement served to perpetuate negative intergroup attitudes and to engender mistrust, suspicion and prejudice in future generations (Darby et al. 1977; Murray 1985; Gallagher 1995; Abbott et al. 1998; McGlynn et al. 2004; Hayes et al. 2007). Accordingly, it has been made increasingly clear that the future improvement of community relations necessarily requires more opportunities for cross-community interaction and understanding in Northern Ireland's schools.

One significant advance in this regard was made by a series of targeted reforms of the existing curriculum initiated by the GNI. Following the Education Reform (Northern Ireland) Order of 1989, in 1990 the Department of Education for Northern Ireland introduced a major program of educational reform and a compulsory set of common curricular initiatives designed to promote a greater 'culture of tolerance' in the school system (Hamber et al. 2009). These initiatives included notable programs such as 'Education for Mutual Understanding' and 'Cultural Heritage' that were introduced to help children learn to "respect themselves and others" and "to know about and understand what is shared as well as what is different about their cultural traditions" (Knox and Hughes 1996: 85).

However, for the most part, these changes to the curriculum were simply overlaid on the existing segregated school system. In other words, while these programs were applied in both Catholic and Protestant schools, actual inter-school or cross-community contact and dialogue, while recommended, were not compulsory components of these initiatives and therefore occurred infrequently. Accordingly, while these programs had a beneficial impact on helping students develop a better understanding of the other community's cultural background, their ability to effect deeper changes in the attitudes, beliefs and relationships between members of the two communities was relatively limited (Smith and Dunn 1990; McGlynn et al. 2004).

Nonetheless, along with these curriculum changes, a more 'bottom-up' movement for integrated cross-community schools also began in the late 1970s, largely through the advocacy of a campaigning group of parents known as All Children Together (ACT). In 1981, the work of ACT led to the creation of Northern Ireland's first integrated school, Lagan College, in the city of Belfast. In 1989, the Northern Ireland Council for Integrated Education (NICIE), a voluntary non-governmental organization, was established to help coordinate efforts to develop and promote integrated education. In 1991, a charitable trust, the Integrated Education Fund, was also founded with money from the Northern Ireland government, the EU and various international donor organizations to provide financial support for the creation of new integrated schools. As of 2008, there were 61 integrated schools in Northern Ireland, comprising 20 secondary schools and 41 primary schools with an estimated enrollment of just under 20,000 students.[7]

These integrated schools take as their mission "the bringing together in one school of pupils, staff and governors, in roughly equal numbers, from Protestant, Catholic, other faiths and no faith backgrounds . . . [as a way of] bringing children up to live as adults in a pluralist society, recognizing what they hold in common as well as what separates them, and accepting both" (NICIE n.d.).[8] In addition to providing a 'mixed' environment in which children from both communities are brought together on a daily basis to interact in the classroom and during extra-curricular activities, these integrated schools also include special training programs to prepare instructors to teach in cross-community settings, as well as a curriculum program that includes opportunities for facilitated conversations about potentially contentious aspects of Northern Ireland's different cultural traditions and its history of sectarian conflict. As former NICIE CEO Michael Wardlow stresses, it is this combination of cross-community contact, specialized teacher training and a "willingness to take risks and talk about sectarianism" within the integrated school system that can aid processes of intergroup reconciliation by bringing children to challenge their existing stereotypes and prejudices (interview: April 21st, 2008).

Assessing instrumental learning in Northern Ireland

The sheer variety of organizations and initiatives aimed at fostering intercommunity contact and dialogue in Northern Ireland makes it difficult to provide an assessment of each individual program's contribution to instrumental learning. Nonetheless, a 2008 study carried out by researchers from the University of Ulster and Queen's University Belfast provides substantial evidence to suggest that the strategy of increasing levels of intercommunity interaction through the integrated 'community relations' approach has had a positive effect on promoting more reconciled relations between nationalists and unionists. In particular, this study shows that increased contact has been highly effective in building levels of cross-community tolerance, trust, friendship, understanding and positive affect, while at the same time reducing perceptions of intergroup threat, anxiety, bias and prejudice (Hewstone et al. 2008a).[9] The study also correlates the increase in cross-community contact supported by the community relations strategy with declines in both polarized perceptions of community identity and support for political violence. Accordingly, as its authors note, this study "provides the most compelling data yet from Northern Ireland . . . that cross community contact *is* effective, and has an impact on multiple measures of community relations [and] that contact has a *causal* or *longitudinal* effect on attitudes, hence it should be central to policies aimed at improving community relations" (ibid.: 8).

In addition, there is evidence from another 2008 study conducted by Professor Orla Muldoon and her colleagues from the University of Limerick to suggest that the positive contact and dialogue associated with community relations programs are responsible, at least in part, for a growing trend of individuals in Northern Ireland adopting group identities that are less oppositional than traditional nationalist/unionist or Protestant/Catholic divides (Muldoon et al. 2008). For instance, while 59 percent of respondents continued to identify themselves with one of the two traditional communal identity groups, 30 percent of respondents indicated that they "implicitly rejected the traditional communal divisions in Northern Ireland" (ibid.). Furthermore, nearly one-third of Protestants and Catholics described themselves as being equally British and Irish in their identity and indicated that they did not view these nationalities as mutually exclusive. Perhaps most promisingly, while 37 percent continued to identify primarily as British nationals and 26 percent as Irish, more than one-quarter of the population (29 percent) surveyed described themselves first and foremost as belonging to a more inclusive 'Northern Irish' identity group—a number that has increased over 10 percent since 1999 (ibid.).

These findings are supported by other contemporary studies that have drawn on similar longitudinal survey data to evaluate the impact of youth engagement in cross-community programs aimed at promoting instrumental learning in Northern Ireland. Indeed, these studies similarly reveal that among youths, participation in such programs has led to more positive perceptions of the 'Other,' significantly greater support for religious mixing and intercommunity friendships, and a marked decline in negative feelings towards members of the other community (Schubotz and Robinson 2006;

Schubotz and McCartan 2008).[10] Accordingly, as noted social psychologist Miles Hewstone and his colleagues contend, the focus on renewing intergroup contact and dialogue adopted by Northern Ireland's community relations strategy "would seem to be not only useful, but necessary, for building a new society in Northern Ireland, one that is no longer deeply divided, sectarian, and split along lines of identity, but a mixed, tolerant polity with emerging forms of cross-cutting identities" (Hewstone et al. 2008a: 219).

To be sure, in line with the aims of the government's *Shared Future* policy for improving community relations, the people of Northern Ireland themselves appear to have increasingly come to recognize that reconciliation and sustainable peace likely depend on increasing opportunities for inter-communal interaction. For instance, data collected by the NILT survey in 2010 shows that fully 88 percent of all respondents in Northern Ireland believe that "better relations between Protestants and Catholics will only come about through more mixing of the two communities," a figure that has increased by 9 percent since the 2005 introduction of the *Shared Future* strategy (ARK 2011). In addition, the vast majority of those polled indicated in the same survey that they were in favor of greater levels of intercommunal mixing than they currently experience in almost every aspect of their daily lives, including where they live (86 percent), work (88 percent), engage in leisure activities (88 percent) and go to school (85 percent)—all numbers that have increased since the adoption of Northern Ireland's community relations strategy (ibid.; Devine et al. 2011). Furthermore, when asked in 2007 whether the "government is actively encouraging shared communities where people of all backgrounds can live, work, learn, and play together" the vast majority (73 percent) of respondents gave the government a 'passing grade' in assessing its accomplishments to date (ARK 2008).[11]

This argument also appears to be borne out by recent studies that have examined the impact of integrated education on instrumental learning. While integrated schools still only make up about 5 percent of the total education system in Northern Ireland, a growing body of research suggests that these schools have had a very positive effect on instrumental learning for the students involved. For instance, in a 2004 study of former students from the integrated education system, 93 percent of students surveyed indicated that these schools had a significant positive impact on their lives by engendering a greater level of respect for cultural diversity and building a greater sense of trust around future cross-community interactions. In addition, participation in integrated education also correlates with a marked increase in the number of lasting friendships maintained across communal lines in adult life, as well as a greater willingness to marry those belonging to the other community (McGlynn et al. 2004). A more recent study from 2007 appears to corroborate these findings, indicating that those who attended integrated schools exhibit reduced levels of prejudice, less divisive and sectarian political views, and much less polarized perceptions of religious and national identities (Hayes et al. 2007). In both studies, these improvements were directly linked to the provision of positive intergroup contact and to a curriculum that encouraged students in, rather than avoided, dialogue about controversial and divisive issues.

These findings also dovetail with perceptions of the importance of integrated education for improving community relations held by the broader population in Northern Ireland. In an independent assessment survey carried out by social research agency Millward Brown Ulster in May 2008, over 84 percent of respondents from both communities indicated that they believed integrated education to be 'important' for peace and reconciliation in Northern Ireland. Tellingly, 85 percent also believed the experience of integrated education to be pivotal in promoting mutual respect and understanding between nationalist and unionist communities as well as in developing a shared and improved future for Northern Ireland as a whole (Milward Brown Ulster 2008).

However, while Northern Ireland's strategy of promoting intercommunity contact and dialogue appears to have had a positive effect on community relations, it is also clear that not all of these initiatives have been equally effective in promoting the kinds of instrumental learning necessary for intergroup reconciliation. Recent evaluations of 'best practices' in community relations work by both governmental agencies and independent actors have offered several insights into the most productive instrumental initiatives that have been employed in Northern Ireland to date (Knox 1994; Knox and Hughes 1996; Hughes and Knox 1997; Knox and Quirk 2000; Good Relations Unit 2006). First, these evaluations make it clear that the most effective programs for promoting instrumental learning in Northern Ireland have provided opportunities for carefully mediated, structured and long-term intercommunity interactions within a safe and egalitarian setting. On the other hand, short-term or 'one-off' programs that bring people from different communities together to engage in brief periods of shared activity with minimal follow-up have had little benefit in improving relations, and have occasionally even had adverse effects on instrumental learning by serving to confirm existing prejudices or stereotypes about the Other (Hughes and Knox 1997). Such programs have included well-intentioned initiatives such as 'Intercultural Excursions,' where youths from hardline nationalist and unionist neighborhoods are taken on holiday together abroad, as well as other high-profile community relations events such as dramas, fairs or concerts designed to create enjoyable venues for intercommunity interaction. While these programs do encourage brief moments of positive encounter and may even produce a small number of interpersonal friendships, ultimately they have been shown to provide little in the way of lasting cognitive or attitudinal change as participants are simply reintroduced to existing divisions and prejudices upon returning to their segregated communities (Knox and Hughes 1996). As Michael

Doherty, Director of the Peace and Reconciliation Group (PRG) in Derry cautions,

> contact work that's short term can be very, very ineffective. What contact work in short periods of time does, in my view, is actually reinforces old prejudices. That you meet them for a short while from the other side and they begin to act out from the other side in the way you had always thought they had acted out. And you begin to hear: "that's the way they do behave" and so you reinforce the prejudice. And you don't get a chance to work alongside them or do anything else to then help reduce that prejudice again. So for me contact work is only effective if it's long term. And that is over a longer period of time. Because you've got to take into consideration that these people are asked to go back into their own camps again to be reinforced again by their people about how the Other is.
>
> (Interview: February 14th, 2008)

Second, many of the most successful instrumental learning programs have involved community members coming together in common purpose to work towards a shared superordinate goal that neither community would be able to achieve on its own (Fitzduff 2002; Good Relations Unit 2006). Most often these programs combine elements of intergroup contact and dialogue with community development work—for instance, having members of local nationalist and unionist communities work together to clean up and revitalize a shared interface area that fell into disrepair during the Troubles. As Professor Christine Bell, Director of the Transitional Justice Institute, illustrates, "if you just get people together for the sake of having contact, I don't think it's terribly effective. The more you can engage people in joint projects or in some place where they're negotiating some of the difficult issues around community safety, attacks on each other, or equality and poverty issues in the area the more you can build positive relations" (interview: February 13th, 2008).

Third, those community relations programs that appear to have most effectively promoted instrumental learning are those that have not shied away from engaging individuals in sustained dialogue surrounding the controversial issues underlying communal prejudice and division (Knox and Hughes 1996; Fitzduff 2002; Good Relations Unit 2006). This was a point raised by Sue Divin, CRO for the Derry City Council District, an area in which some of the worst violence of the Troubles occurred and in which deep divides continue to mark relations between nationalists and unionists. Divin argues that the most effective

> community relations work will not duck the issues in whatever form, whether it's using arts, cultural events, workshops . . . whatever vehicle you take, when you get people together you've got to be looking at the

issues and challenging their mindsets. And if you're not doing that, you're not going to change the mindsets and things that need to be changed.

(Interview: February 10th, 2008)

Indeed, many of those experts interviewed in Northern Ireland stressed the powerfully transformative effect that renewed contact can have on building intercommunal empathy and challenging entrenched prejudices, stereotypes and fears about the Other when combined with opportunities for engaging in safe and sustained dialogue processes. In Northern Ireland, many of these dialogue processes have taken the form of carefully mediated 'storytelling' forums in which a small number of nationalists and unionists are brought together to recount their personal experiences of past conflict and to hear those of others. Based on his extensive work in promoting dialogue between ex-combatants, victims and civilians at the Glencree Centre for Peace and Reconciliation, Wilhelm Verwoerd notes that such processes may be essential to instrumental learning as they allow people "a chance to look beyond their political narratives and political stereotypes, to individualize and humanize the Other." As he explains, the experience of dialogue helps to get

> people who were in deep conflict actually to a point where they are willing to look beyond those crude stereotypes, get through the initial anger and mistrust and emotional baggage and get to a point where there's a willingness to be in the same place, and a willingness to move beyond that.[12]

(Interview: April 29th, 2008)

In addition, as Michael Doherty contends, experience from Northern Ireland suggests that storytelling and similar forms of intercommunal dialogue can lead not only to a greater willingness to reconcile in the present but also to a more nuanced and empathetic understanding of the past. As he suggests, storytelling provides an opportunity to

> look at each other and hear each other's stories [and to go] away with a completely different mindset about the Other . . . You do not destroy people's real feelings about what they say happened to them, but you go away with a better understanding as to why some things actually happened, looking at the cause, the impact of the other party's actions, and the impact it had on the other party.

(Interview: February 14th, 2008)

However, past evidence would also suggest that it is important to build towards these more difficult encounters through incremental levels of engagement. Both the quantity of contact and the quality of interaction (in terms of being able to deal successfully with increasingly difficult issues) should increase over time, with each meeting building on the trust, respect and confidence developed over the last. Therefore, while the promotion of positive cross-community interaction remains the ultimate aim of community relations policy in Northern Ireland, research on best practices suggests that this goal may need to be pursued in sequential fashion (Fitzduff 2002; Good Relations Unit 2006). For instance, in cases where communities have had little or no past experience of positive relations with one another, efforts should begin with 'single-identity work' in which members engage in programs within their own communities to build the levels of confidence necessary to initiate fruitful engagements with the Other. This internal work has been recognized as a first step towards reducing existing feelings of fear, insecurity and anxiety that might otherwise prevent the experience of cross-community contact from promoting positive instrumental learning (Tausch et al. 2007). A number of experts interviewed discussed the need for such incremental and sequential encounters, including Michael Doherty of the PRG in Derry, who underscored that

> preparatory work is needed to do community relations work . . . communities need to look inwardly at themselves to give them the confidence to even think about engaging with the other side . . . . They need to look at where they're coming from as a way . . . of leading into community relations work and as a means of allaying some of the fears that are out there.
>
> (Interview: February 14th, 2008)

Importantly, however, this kind of single-identity work is ultimately insufficient for overcoming relational divisions and prejudices and so is widely considered to be of use only as a stepping stone towards more extensive cross-community engagement (Hewstone et al. 2008a; Hewstone et al. 2008b).

Nonetheless, taken as a whole this analysis suggests that there is now evidence to suggest that many positive gains for instrumental learning and intercommunity reconciliation have been made through the community relations strategy adopted in Northern Ireland, particularly when opportunities are provided to allow for sustained processes of positive cross-community contact and dialogue.

Instrumental learning in South Africa

From its inception, one of the principal aims of apartheid legislation was to limit opportunities for meaningful interracial interaction in nearly every aspect of daily life in South Africa by forcing members of different races to live, work and socialize apart. As a result, while extensive contact did occur between racial groups during the apartheid era, for the most part such interactions were limited to the hierarchical relationships that developed in the workplace between laborers, domestic workers and their more affluent white employers. Between white and black South Africans, in particular, these encounters were heavily mediated by great imbalances in socioeconomic and political power and allowed only for largely superficial relationships that were "contiguous, yet utterly remote" (Foster and Finchilescu 1986: 125). As Professor Deborah Posel, Director of the Wits Institute for Social and Economic Research (WISER) at the University of the Witwatersrand describes, under apartheid, South Africa faced an all-encompassing system of "interlocking segregation and interlocking racism" that prevented against meaningful forms of interracial contact and communication. As she notes, "not only did white and black South Africans live apart, they traveled on separate trains and buses, they went to separate cinemas, they shopped in separate shopping centers, and in the workplace there were hierarchies of authority that put white people on top and black people on the bottom" (interview: July 3rd, 2008).

Accordingly, while little reliable empirical survey data of apartheid-era attitudes exists, it is widely recognized that by limiting meaningful interracial interaction, the apartheid system largely precluded the possibility of developing crucial bonds of mutual trust, respect, understanding and empathy between racial communities. In particular, interracial relationships between black and white South Africans remained highly polarized, characterized at best by mistrust and misunderstanding and at worst by hostility, prejudice and pervasive feelings of fear and threat. Indeed, as William Gibson has illustrated, prior to the transition from apartheid in South Africa, "both black and whites most likely understood and trusted each other very little, rarely integrated, held vicious stereotypes about each other, and disliked and were highly threatened by those of other races" (Gibson 2004: 158).

Perhaps most tellingly, several expert interviewees stressed the powerful dehumanizing effect that apartheid's overlapping elements of physical, social and psychological separation had on the ways in which many South Africans came to perceive members of other races. For instance, interviewees note that for many whites, black South Africans were considered to be 'less human' or 'less civilized' than their white counterparts and were therefore correspondingly seen as less deserving of empathy or equal treatment. For instance, Sarah Crawford-Brown of the University of Cape Town, a former counselor with the Trauma Centre for Victims of Violence and Torture, argues that under apartheid, the common tendency for whites to "see in racial stereotypes" meant that many often "didn't see [blacks] as real people" (interview: June 26th, 2008). Similarly, Deon Snyman, a Reverend in the Dutch Reformed Church and Operations Director of South Africa's Restitution Foundation, observes that "one of the big problems within the apartheid system was that people did not really get the opportunity to know each other as human beings, and as equals. .... in a certain sense, we were very close but very far from each other" (interview: June 26th, 2008).

These physical and psychological divides were only further exacerbated by the growing levels of violence and repression that accompanied the latter years of apartheid as the predominantly black liberation movement intensified its armed struggle against the government's predominantly white security forces. Moreover, the exponential increase in violent crime that emerged in South Africa during the 1980s and 1990s was also widely credited with aggravating interracial division and mistrust. While crime statistics show that the vast majority of violent criminal activity was concentrated in predominantly homogenous black areas of South Africa, many whites nonetheless came to perceive themselves as the primary targets of black criminal violence (Hamber 1999). Driven both by fear and the reality of increasing levels of violence, South Africa's predominantly white middle-class suburbs became increasingly separated and segregated, with their residents living in gated communities or private homes fortified by high walls, razor wire, high-tech alarm systems and private security guards.

In light of apartheid's legacy of racial division and segregation, finding innovative ways to increase the quantity and quality of interracial interaction has consistently been identified as a necessary, if not sufficient, condition for the promotion of instrumental learning and reconciliation in post-apartheid South Africa. Indeed, as Professor James Gibson asserts, given the highly divided nature of apartheid-era South Africa, interracial reconciliation in the post-apartheid period requires that "people come to interact with each other more (the breakdown of barriers across races) and communicate more, acts that in turn lead to greater understanding and perhaps acceptance and result in the appreciation and exaltation of the value of racial diversity" (Gibson 2004). This sentiment is echoed by Hugo van der Merwe of the Center for the Study of Violence and Reconciliation (CSVR), who has stressed the importance of finding ways to increase positive forms of interracial interaction as a means of 'rehumanizing' members of other racial groups in post-apartheid South Africa. Van der Merwe suggests that "there's a lot of value in an environment where there's been such artificial separation in the past that just the fact of contact allows [one] to see some commonalities, to recognize a basic humanity—it counts for a lot" (interview: June 16th, 2008). In a similar vein, Dr. Garth Stevens of the University of Witwatersrand argues that, while certainly not a panacea that can in and of itself reverse the damage of apartheid's racial segregation, a renewal of positive interaction across racial lines is nonetheless "going to be critical" to the transformation of antagonistic mindsets and the reparation of interracial relationships (interview: July 2nd, 2008). Accordingly, he asserts that in order to encourage the kind of instrumental learning between racial groups ultimately required for reconciliation in post-apartheid South Africa, "one should create spaces for increased integration, for increased contact, so people can start engaging in ways that allow people to start understanding other people's perspectives, their different worldviews, [and their] different histories" (ibid.).

However, it is also clear that interracial contact itself is not always enough to overcome prejudice, and that contact may sometimes even reinforce bias as it often did under apartheid. Therefore, it is widely recognized that reconciliation in post-apartheid South Africa ultimately requires not only greater levels of simple interracial exposure, but also opportunities for members of different racial groups to engage in open and meaningful dialogue with one another about the impact of apartheid-era violence on their lives and the divisive influence of apartheid's policies on interracial relations. Indeed, in the 2007 Survey Report of the Institute for Justice and Reconciliation's (IJR) South African Reconciliation Barometer (SARB) study, it was recognized that "frank and open dialogue about [South Africa's] racial legacy is an irreplaceable determinant of, but also an important indicator for, national reconciliation" (Hofmeyr 2007: 28).

A number of expert interviewees in South Africa have also cited the crucial importance of creating new arenas for dialogue in which members of different racial groups can be brought together to listen to one another's experiences and to be exposed to different perspectives as a path towards better mutual understanding and rehumanization. For instance, Glenda Wildschut, a former TRC Commissioner, contends that the experience of positive encounter, coupled with opportunities for meaningful dialogue with those on the other side of racial divides, remains a key requirement for building a new sense of interracial understanding and reconciliation in post-apartheid South Africa. Accordingly, she argues that even following South Africa's transition to democracy, there continues to be a very real need "to bring people from diverse communities together, so they are able—in a very safe space—to hear each other's stories" (interview: June 25th, 2008). Similarly, as Vincent Williams, Director of the Cape Town Democracy Centre of the Institute for Democracy in South Africa (IDASA) has argued, aside from simply increasing interracial contact, the movement towards reconciliation and sustainable peace in South Africa

> has to find expression in the way people think about each other and the way in which they relate to each other. And in order to do that, you have to create opportunities for dialogue, you have to put the tough issues on the table . . . [and] talk about issues of difference. Because unless we do that we're going to push things under the carpet and not deal with them and it's going to come back and bite us.
>
> (Interview: June 22nd, 2008)

As the primary institution tasked with promoting reconciliation during South Africa's transition from apartheid, it is important to assess the ways in which the TRC itself was able to facilitate instrumental learning between black and white South Africans. Accordingly, the TRC's efforts to encourage positive contact and transformative dialogue will now be considered in turn, with particular attention being paid to the role that each of these elements has played in advancing instrumental learning and interracial reconciliation.

Encounter and interracial contact in the South African TRC

The early emphasis placed by the Commission on limiting retribution in favor of bringing together victims and perpetrators as participants in its conditional amnesty and public hearing processes has led some in the field of transitional justice to label the TRC the "most developed model of a restorative justice truth-telling mechanism to date" (Llewellyn 2006: 98). Nonetheless, despite the Commission's restorative mandate, in actual fact it appears to have provided very few opportunities for victims and perpetrators to come directly together in positive encounter with one another.

At the most basic level, this seems to be attributable to the structural design of the TRC, a design that largely kept separate the processes by which victims and perpetrators engaged with the Commission. For the majority of victims, their interactions with the TRC were limited to the statements and testimonies they made under the auspices of the HRVC. Similarly, all matters related to perpetrators were dealt with by the AC. This meant that while both victims and perpetrators could come forward to relate accounts of their involvement in apartheid-era violence, for the most part they did so in discrete and distant environments. This distance was further compounded by the fact that the hearings for the HRVC and AC were held not only in separate geographic locations, but also at different times; the AC hearings only began after the work of the HRVC had already been completed. Ultimately, as Jennifer Llewellyn notes, the "separation of processes" under the TRC greatly "reduced opportunities for face-to-face encounters between the parties involved" and therefore may have limited the instrumental learning that could result from such exchanges (ibid.).

However, one opportunity for meaningful encounter was provided through the AC hearings. While the primary aim of the AC was to hear perpetrators' accounts of their past transgressions and decide upon their eligibility for amnesty, it was also mandated to notify any victims who were identified in these accounts and to provide them with the opportunity to be present at the hearings and to provide their own explanations of past events. This gave victims a formal space in the hearings process, allowing them to submit evidence, to provide statements to the Committee detailing the human rights violations that occurred, and even to directly challenge the versions of events put forward by perpetrators. By including both victims and perpetrators in the amnesty process, the AC hearings therefore created at least a minimal opportunity for mediated interaction and dialogue about the past—elements considered critical to instrumental learning. Indeed, in a study conducted by the CSVR of perpetrators who came forward to participate in the hearings, the vast majority indicated that they wanted to meet with those victimized by their crimes, and that the possibility of speaking with victims directly and securing their understanding was a vital aspect of their own reconciliation process (Abrahamsen and van der Merwe 2005: 9). Similarly, a study of victims involved in the amnesty process showed that a majority also expressed a desire for interaction with their perpetrator and a belief that such dialogue was necessary for their own personal healing and reconciliation (Phakathi and van der Merwe 2008).

Unfortunately, in practice, a number of factors appear to have largely prevented the potential for positive encounter offered by the amnesty hearings. First, as in the HRVC proceedings, fewer than two thousand of the more than seven thousand perpetrators who applied for amnesty were actually given the opportunity to have their cases heard publicly and to have any kind of interaction with victims. Second, even in those public hearings that did occur, a lack of adequate resources often prevented the AC from being able to locate victims in time to inform them of the pending case. This meant that victims simply were not present in a large number of the cases considered by the AC (Ernest 2004). Third, it should be noted that statistically, the opportunity for instrumental learning through meaningful encounter across racial lines remained somewhat limited in these processes, as a majority of both victims (73 percent) and perpetrators (58 percent) who took part in the AC proceedings were black, with most public hearings (60.5 percent) involving both black applicants and victims (Abrahamsen and van der Merwe 2005: 119).

In addition, even when victims were able to attend the AC hearings, they often did not find an environment conducive to positive interracial interaction. As the quasi-legal structures of the AC hearings tended to take the form of courtroom proceedings, victims and perpetrators were typically not allowed to engage in direct interpersonal dialogue and instead had their interactions framed by lawyers acting as their representatives. In addition, the highly legalistic nature of the amnesty hearings also meant that the interactions that did take place often had a competitive rather than a conciliatory tone, with both victims and perpetrators being faced with antagonistic cross-examination by legal counsel. Aside from limiting opportunities for direct interracial dialogue, this also severely limited the ability for victims and perpetrators to give full and open accountings of their experiences of past violence (Chapman and van der Merwe 2008a: 271).

Taken together, these restrictions appear to have been a source of frustration for victims and perpetrators alike, many of whom had indicated a strong desire to meet directly with the other party and had expected the amnesty process to provide a space conducive to more restorative and reconciliatory encounter (Abrahamsen and van der Merwe 2005: 9). As a result, the failure of the AC process to truly promote positive interracial interaction between victims and perpetrators was one of the TRC's most substantial missed opportunities for encouraging instrumental learning. Indeed, as Chapman and van der Merwe detail,

> the amnesty processes, the one place where the TRC managed to get both sides to the same venue, did not create an environment where survivors and perpetrators could engage in a restorative justice process as they understood it . . . [thus] the amnesty process—where probably the most space existed for dialogue—was not seen as contributing to reconciliation among survivors [and] research shows that even amnesty applicants were disappointed that the TRC did not manage to create a more effective space for dialogue between applicants, their victims, and their communities.
>
> (2008a: 271)

Nonetheless, while the formal structures of the Commission may have provided few opportunities for meaningful interracial encounter, a number of victims nonetheless still voiced a strong desire to meet directly with perpetrators outside of the formal structures of the TRC process (Kiss 2000: 72). On a number of occasions following a victim's testimony in the HRVC, when asked by Commissioners whether or not they would be interested in meeting with those who perpetrated crimes against them, a substantial number indicated their willingness to do so. Similarly, many victims who participated in the amnesty hearings also expressed a desire to meet and talk with perpetrators outside of the legal auspices of the AC to help them gain a greater understanding of perpetrators' motivations (Phakathi and van der Merwe 2008: 131–132). Interestingly, this appears to have been met by a similar desire among some—though certainly not all—of those perpetrators who applied for amnesty for further interaction with their victims, with many perpetrators expressing the belief that "the amnesty process did not provide adequate space for this [dialogue]" (ibid.).

In a very small number of cases in which the identities of both parties were known and each had indicated a desire to meet, Commission members working outside of the official TRC process did sometimes work to facilitate opportunities for more informal encounters between victims and perpetrators (Llewellyn 2006: 99). Interestingly, when these informal encounters did occur, there is substantial anecdotal evidence to show that they often led to remarkable displays of generosity and understanding on the part of both victims and perpetrators (van der Merwe 2001a: 96; Phakathi and van der Merwe 2008: 138). One such example recorded in the TRC's Final Report surrounds the 'Trust Feed Massacre' of 1998, an incident in which Captain Brian Mitchell, a white Station Commander at the local police station, collaborated with members of the IFP in an attack on a rival political organization that ultimately resulted in the deaths of eleven black civilians, six of whom were women and children. After being sentenced to life imprisonment, Captain Mitchell applied for and was granted amnesty through the AC in 1997, during which he expressed remorse, asked for forgiveness, and pledged to help rebuild the Trust Feed community he had damaged. Through the facilitation of the TRC, a meeting was arranged between Captain Mitchell and the Trust Feed community in which "the community was given enough time to express its feelings and ask direct, clarifying questions of Captain Mitchell who was also given an opportunity to express his feelings and ask for forgiveness" (TRC 1998: vol. 5, ch. 9, para. 78). This was followed by a process of mediation in which it was discussed how Captain Mitchell might best help to repair the harm he had done to the Trust Feed community. While the meeting was very emotional, it was nonetheless by all accounts predominantly characterized by goodwill and a willingness to work towards rebuilding relationships on all sides, with plans for future meetings made between parties to continue the "long process of reconciliation" (TRC 1998: vol. 5, ch. 9, para. 80). Unfortunately, however, while several expert interviewees cited examples of informal meetings such as those at Trust Feed that seemed to lead to genuine interracial reconciliation between victims and perpetrators, due to their ad hoc nature, these opportunities remained few and far between and applied only to a handful of exceptional cases (Llewellyn 2006; Chapman and van der Merwe 2008a).

Nonetheless, based on the perceived success of these informal initiatives, a number of prominent reconciliation-oriented civil society organizations in South Africa attempted to create a more structured framework to expand the process of mediated victim-perpetrator encounters. The idea was that these organizations would seek to build on the small number of existing ad hoc encounters facilitated alongside the TRC and would develop them into a more sustainable mediation program that could extend beyond the relatively limited timeframe of the Commission. Unfortunately, as Phakathi and van der Merwe note, this initiative largely failed "to get off the ground" due to a lack of interest and support from the TRC, as well as a widespread reluctance among amnesty applicants' lawyers to allow their clients' participation for fear it might unfairly prejudice their ongoing cases in the Commission's AC hearings (2008: 139).

Societal dialogue and the South African TRC

While opportunities for direct interracial encounter remained relatively minimal throughout the TRC process, there is some evidence to suggest that the Commission may nonetheless have been able to contribute to instrumental learning among South Africans in a more indirect way. Indeed, one of the most important innovations of the TRC in relation to previous truth commissions was the degree to which its hearings were made open, transparent and accessible to the public (Hayner 2000; 2002; Kiss 2000; Gibson 2004; Thiessen 2008). This approach related to one of the central aims of the Commission, which was to use the public hearings to promote national unity and reconciliation by engaging the broader South African public in "interaction, discussion, and debate" throughout the process of truth recovery (TRC 1998: vol. 1, ch. 5, para. 40). As the TRC's Final Report notes, by making the hearings process open to the public, its goal was

> to try to transcend the divisions of the past by listening carefully to the complex motives and perspectives of all those involved. It made a conscious effort to provide an environment in which all possible views could be considered and weighted, one against the other. People from all walks of life were invited to participate in the process . . . [and] the public was engaged through open hearings and the media.
>
> (ibid.)

As previously discussed, over the course of the TRC's mandate, the personal accounts and findings provided in its public hearing processes all received extensive attention in South Africa's print, radio and television media and were widely followed by South Africans of all races in addition to a great many international observers.[13] In this way, the public hearings afforded millions of ordinary South Africans—black, white and otherwise—who could not participate directly in the Commission's proceedings a chance to nonetheless engage with its work. As Audrey Chapman and Hugo van der Merwe recount, "the individual stories and media images arising from the TRC hearings turned the process of dealing with the past into a visceral experience which all South Africans across the board could (or had to) engage" (2008b: 279). Accordingly, the highly public nature of the TRC hearings effectively enabled the Commission

> to reach out on a daily basis to large numbers of people inside and outside South Africa, and to confront them with vivid images on their television screens or on the front pages of their newspapers. People saw, for example, a former security police officer demonstrating his torture techniques. They saw weeping men and women asking for the truth about their loved ones . . . [and this] helped generate public debate on central aspects of South Africa's past and to raise the level of historical awareness.
>
> (TRC 1998: vol. 1, ch. 5, para. 5)

Therefore, while the TRC's opportunities for direct interracial encounter may have remained limited, coverage of its proceedings nevertheless provided a crucial forum for members of different racial groups to engage in a 'societal dialogue' about the past with one another.[14] For many South Africans emerging from apartheid, this was the first opportunity they had ever been given to listen to the stories, perspectives and motivations of individuals who had historically existed on the other side of racial and political divides (Minow 1998). As such, the shared experience of engaging with coverage of the TRC's public hearings helped to create a dialogical space for instrumental learning in South African society. In this space, individuals could begin to critically reassess the preconceived perceptions and prejudices they may have held about other racial groups and, in so doing, to lay the groundwork for more positive future interracial relationships. As Charles Villa-Vicencio, former Director of Research for the TRC has noted, by creating space for this kind of societal dialogue in the transformative moment of South Africa's transition from apartheid, the public process of the TRC helped to provide "the initial public step in the process of South Africans getting to know one another after generations of isolation, exploitation, estrangement and mutual suspicion" (2000a: 206).

Among those experts interviewed, a consensus emerged that the opportunity for societal dialogue fostered by the TRC's public hearings may have been one of the Commission's most important contributions to instrumental learning and interracial reconciliation in post-apartheid South Africa. For instance, several interviewees highlighted the powerful effect that exposure to the personal testimonies of victims had on 'humanizing' members of other racial groups by building a new sense of empathy across racial lines regarding the suffering caused by past human rights abuses. For instance, according to Madeleine Fullard, current Head of the National Prosecuting Authority's Missing Persons Task Team and former Senior National Researcher with the TRC illustrates, under apartheid,

> white people hardly encountered black people at a human level, they encountered them as units of labor, as domestic workers, as gardeners. Literally alien beings. . . . And suddenly [through the TRC] you have this forum created where black people are speaking about their experiences in their lives and it's a kind of humanizing process . . . It's an insight into the experience of the Other, however fleeting. Just to see a man crying on the TV screen about his experience of torture . . . It has a humanizing component . . . It's at a human level that it has an impact.
>
> (Interview: July 8th, 2008)

Indeed, the Commission itself recognized the 'humanizing' aspect of the TRC's public processes as a crucial contribution to interracial reconciliation in South Africa, noting in its *Final Report* that

> [m]any people who witnessed the accounts of victims were confronted, for the first time, with the human face of unknown or silenced victims

from the past. The public victims hearings vividly portrayed the fact that not only . . . was there a disrespect of human rights in the abstract, but the very dignity and 'personhood' of individual human beings were centrally violated.

(TRC 1998: vol. 1, ch. 5, para. 90)

Similarly, other interviewees highlighted the importance of hearing the stories and perspectives of those who testified before the TRC for challenging entrenched racial stereotypes, and for thereby helping South Africans of different races to begin to view each other as more fully realized individuals. In particular, the fact that the public hearings included testimonies from black and white South Africans who had been both victims and perpetrators during the struggle over apartheid helped to break down existing prejudices that 'all blacks' or 'all whites' were to be feared or mistrusted. As Tlhoki Mofokeng, Acting Chair of the Khulumani Support Group for Victims in South Africa describes, during the TRC "the nation was listening and hearing" to coverage of the public hearings, and "for a number of blacks who saw white as white or white is the same—it basically disappeared because they saw humanity in that aspect, that there's other human beings who are more human than being white or being black" (interview: July 1st, 2008).

Furthermore, by bringing to the fore contentious issues related to human rights abuses under apartheid, the public hearings of the TRC also served as an important catalyst for South Africans of different racial groups to begin engaging independently in their own processes of dialogue with one another about the past. As Howard Varney, a former member of the TRC's Investigative Unit and now Director of the Truth-Seeking Program for the ICTJ recounts, during the TRC's timeframe, the public hearings provided a focal point around which critical dialogue about past violence and issues of race could began to coalesce in South African society. As Varney further explains,

It was the public nature of the inquiries that really managed to involve a big section of the South African society. We became involved in the daily debates that were going on. . . . It was always on the radio, always in the press, almost on a daily basis . . . I think it's still true to say that the TRC played quite a key role in South Africa's transition because it engaged with the wider public in confronting the past. Of course, not all the engagement was necessarily positive, but still, the fact that people *were* engaging was what this process was all about.

(Interview: June 24th, 2008)

In essence, by breaking the silence about South Africa's history of human rights abuses and antagonistic racial relations, the public hearings helped to bring these formerly taboo subjects into open conversation among South Africans. At the very least, this provided South Africans with the opportunity for instrumental learning about the Other by creating an environment in which people were able to critically address difficult issues in both public debate and private conversation. As TRC Commissioner Mary Burton observes, during the public hearings, "things were said that had remained unspoken, and they were now in the public domain and had to be taken into account by everybody ... [and] that led to better relationships" (interview: June 23rd, 2008). This point is echoed by Dr. Fanie du Toit, Director of the non-governmental IJR, who contends that perhaps one of the most important contributions of the TRC's public hearings was their ability to initiate broader conversations that exposed and challenged antagonistic perceptions of the past, in effect "playing a role as a dialogue platform in society where a new kind of discourse could be formed" (interview: June 18th, 2008). Similarly, Vincent Williams of IDASA confirms the profound impact that the TRC process had on encouraging dialogue about interracial relations throughout South Africa in the wake of the transition from apartheid, arguing that

> [a]ll things considered, [its public nature] was probably the most important aspect of the TRC. It was a nation having to confront itself through the stories of particular groups and individuals. So when I sit at home at night and watch TV—and it was broadcast on TV, on radio— there was no way you could actually avoid knowing what was going on. And the fact that as a nation we had to confront that past history was, I think, critically important for reconciliation [and] an important stepping stone for the entire nation. . . . In some ways, even if that was all that had happened I think that would have been important.
>
> (Interview: June 22nd, 2008)

Taken together, these observations suggest that the opportunities for societal dialogue and engagement provided by the TRC aided processes of instrumental learning by softening the rigidified perceptions of racial identity that had been formed under apartheid and by helping to lay the foundation for more reconciled relationships in the future. Indeed, as James Gibson argues in his highly regarded 2004 study of the impact of the TRC on interracial reconciliation in South Africa, the societal dialogue enabled by public engagement with the Commission's work appears to have been a vital first step towards transforming the "cognitive dogmatism" surrounding racial identities formed during the apartheid era (2004: 159). In particular, Gibson contends that by serving as a site of "social persuasion" in which black and white South Africans were exposed to critical new information about one another, the TRC was able to introduce an element of "cognitive dissonance" that directly challenged highly polarized and antagonistic existing understandings of racial identity. In this way, the information conveyed by the public process of the TRC appears to have played an important role as an "engine for change in racial attitudes" between black and white South Africans, "getting people to rethink their attitudes . . . and stimulating South Africans to re-evaluate their understandings of race and racial conflict" (ibid.).

Indeed, there is some evidence to suggest that the instrumental learning associated with the Commission's ability to foster societal dialogue has led to new considerations of racial identity that are far less monolithic and oppositional. Given the extent to which racial division was institutionalized during the apartheid era, it is perhaps not surprising that both black and white South Africans have continued to self-identify with race as their primary marker of group identity following South Africa's transition (Gibson 2004: 54). Interestingly, however, a much wider attachment to a broader and more inclusive 'South African' national identity among both blacks and whites also coincided directly with the work of the TRC. By comparing survey results collected in 1996 (when the TRC was just beginning) and 2001 (when the Commission's work was drawing to a close), Gibson shows that the number of both black and white respondents claiming 'South African' as either a primary or secondary label of self-identification grew markedly. Among blacks, this margin increased from 35.2 percent in 1996 to 47.8 percent in 2001, while for whites it grew from 53 to 62.9 percent in the same period (Gibson 2004: 55). Further, the vast majority of both black and white respondents identifying as 'South African' asserted that this sense of shared national identity was "very important to them" and that they were "proud to call themselves South African" (idem: 56).

Perhaps just as importantly, Gibson's work also reveals that this growing sense of shared national identity has not come at the expense of zero-sum tension with existing racial identities; rather, the two identity types have come to coexist "simultaneously and without apparent conflict" (idem: 59). While it is difficult to establish a direct causal relationship, the strong correlation between the timing of the work of the Commission and the rise in adherence to a more inclusive South African identity would seem to suggest that, at least in part, the instrumental learning promoted by the TRC helped to lay the groundwork for Tutu's conception of a more reconciled 'Rainbow Nation' in which distinct racial identities coexisted peaceably under the banner of a shared sense of South African nationalism. Indeed, as Gibson concludes, "to the extent that reconciliation implies that all South Africans express some degree of allegiance to the country, this data indicates a fairly high level of reconciliation" (idem: 56).

However, while the societal dialogue facilitated by the public nature of the TRC process provided an important means of instrumental learning in South Africa, its effects on interracial reconciliation were also limited by several factors. First, although the extensive media coverage of the TRC hearings did manage to reach much of the population, there were still millions— particularly in South Africa's poorer black townships—effectively left out of the societal dialogue process because of illiteracy and a lack of ready access to radios and television sets.[15] At the same time, white South Africans who didn't want to engage with the TRC could always simply tune out by switching off the television or turning the dial on the radio. As Natalie Jaynes, a Project Leader with South Africa's IJR, notes, "You could just not buy the newspapers or even if you had the newspaper, turn the page, just ignore it, change radio stations, not watch the news. Whatever it is there were ways of ignoring it and many people did for whatever reason" (interview: June 18th, 2008). This was reflected in the fact that white South Africans consistently registered a lower interest in the TRC proceedings than their black counterparts, a trend that intensified over time as many white South Africans grew increasingly uncomfortable with the revelations emerging from the Commission's public hearings.[16]

Further, the degree to which the beneficial effects of instrumental learning associated with societal dialogue can extend beyond the relatively limited timeframe of the Commission's work remains unclear. While the TRC received extensive media coverage in its earliest years (particularly during the highly publicized HRVC hearings), this attention began to wane somewhat towards the end of its mandated timeframe (Thiessen 2008). This seems a particularly important point, as research on the relationship between dialogue and instrumental learning suggests that building intergroup reconciliation ultimately requires sustained conversation. While survey evidence shows that many South Africans have remained very interested in continuing this societal dialogue through other forums such as current affairs programs, live public debates, and the broadcasting of public events, to date the South African government has created few of these kinds of opportunities following the conclusion of the TRC.[17] Further, while the vicarious societal dialogue process initiated by the TRC appears to have had a positive impact on the attitudes and mindsets of those who tuned in to the proceedings, this kind of instrumental learning may not prove sustainable unless followed by a corresponding increase in opportunities for sustained interracial encounters.

To be sure, the need for targeted follow-up interventions designed to increase contact and dialogue between members of different racial groups remains evident in the wake of the Commission's work. Data collected from the IJR's annual SARB survey as recently as 2010 shows that only 38 percent of all South African respondents indicate that they 'always' or 'often' speak to members of different races over the course of a typical weekday (Lefko-Everett et al. 2010: 34). In addition, a further 42 percent indicated that they 'rarely' or 'never' spoke to people belonging to different racial groups in their daily lives (idem: 34). Tellingly, of this number, only 30 percent of South Africans showed a desire to talk with people from other racial groups more often than they do at present (ibid.).

In exploring whether South Africans have started to form deeper social relationships across racial lines, results from the same survey indicate that only 21 percent of South Africans 'often' or 'always' socialize with members of other racial groups, while fully 60 percent report that they 'rarely' or 'never' do so (ibid.). In a similar vein, when asked about whether they would approve of future integration, nearly one-third of South African respondents (33 percent) indicated that they would disapprove of sharing their neighborhood with a member of the Other group (idem: 35). Further, nearly half (47 percent) of those surveyed responded that they would disapprove of a close relative marrying someone from the other group. Similarly, 43 percent indicated that they could not imagine themselves belonging to a political party made up predominantly of members of another racial group (ibid.).

This lack of interaction appears to directly correlate with the continued presence of mistrust and misunderstanding between racial groups in contemporary South Africa. For instance, 62 percent of South Africans surveyed responded that they still found it difficult to understand the 'customs and ways' of racial groups other than their own (ibid.). Moreover, over one-third (35 percent) of all respondents indicated that they still considered people belonging to racial groups other than their own as inherently 'untrustworthy.' Notably, more than half (51 percent) of white respondents indicated that they found black South Africans 'most difficult' to associate with, while the same number of black South Africans similarly indicated that they found it most difficult to associate with white people (idem: 36).

Continued mistrust, misunderstanding and social distance between racial groups in South Africa also appears to have ensured that when interracial interaction does occur, most often it does not enable meaningful or potentially transformative dialogue about race and racial relations. Indeed, when questioned as to whether they would be willing to openly discuss such issues with members of other racial groups, survey results from 2011 show that 36 percent of South Africans would 'never' feel comfortable sharing their 'true thoughts' about race (Lefko-Everett et al. 2011: 31). Of this number, approximately one-third (33 percent) indicated they would never do so in a public place like school or work (ibid.). Overall, as Vincent Williams of IDASA notes when reflecting on the racial divisions that continue to plague South Africa following the completion of the TRC's work,

[a]s in the past, there's a lot of suspicion, a lot of prejudices, a lot of stereotyping that was going on and I think those continue to govern the relations between different races . . . black people still tend to have very stereotypical pictures of who and what whites are and similarly whites will have very stereotypical images and those define the parameters of how people relate . . . [Their interactions] are very much characterized by not dealing with issues—not hostile, not showing animosity—but not addressing the problems in South African society. People are just living past each other.

(Interview: June 22nd, 2008)

The relationship between low levels of interracial interaction and continued prejudice appears to be a cyclical one: little opportunity for contact and communication means little chance to challenge stereotypes and prejudicial mindsets, while mistrust and misunderstanding in turn limit the desire or willingness to build new interracial relationships. The self-fulfilling nature of this cycle has manifested itself perhaps most clearly in the patterns of 'self-segregation' or 'informal segregation' that continue to divide racial groups even in the absence of the apartheid laws that originally kept them apart. Studies have shown that segregated patterns of socialization remain prominent in South Africa following the transition, including in what would seem to be highly integrated spaces such as 'nonracial' student residences on university campuses or urban restaurants and clubs (Foster 2005). This point was echoed by many of the experts interviewed in South Africa, including Michele Ruiters of the non-governmental Institute for Global Development, who notes that the persistence of racial divides continues to make socialization— particularly outside of the workplace—very difficult: "In the workplace you find that people do mix, but it's extremely superficial. You don't find social mixing. If you go to any bar in South Africa, you won't find a very mixed group of people hanging out together" (interview: July 10th, 2008).

However, these continued patterns of 'informal segregation' were most strikingly illuminated in a 2005 study by Kevin Durrheim and John Dixon that investigated the extent of informal contact between members of different racial groups by looking at patterns of socialization on South Africa's beaches. Beaches are a favored leisure spot for members of all races, but they were clearly demarcated and segregated by race under the laws of apartheid. Durrheim and Dixon found that nearly ten years after the formal end of apartheid, when members of different racial groups went to the beach, they still chose to sit in separate areas and would even get up and move farther away if members of a different race came within close proximity (2005). This process is illustrated by Don Foster, Professor of Psychology at the University of Cape Town, who explains that

> [o]nce upon a time the whole beach was white, now it's opened up—and the point of this is important because there's no rules governing this anymore, the apartheid rules are gone—but this informal segregation continues at astonishingly high levels . . . As black people come onto the beaches, the whites and the Indians disappear. Everyone sits under their own umbrella and that space is still 99.9 percent racialized. Whites sit with whites, Indians sit with Indians, coloreds with coloreds, blacks with blacks—certain parts of the beach become resegregated.
>
> (Interview: June 24th, 2008)

Accordingly, as Foster contends, despite the new opportunities for interracial contact and communication provided in many of these seemingly 'mixed' areas in post-apartheid South Africa, people of different racial backgrounds still tend to "gather in little areas of their own making," with the result that "the degree of everyday contact between and among these still racialized groups is just about zero" (ibid.).

The role of civil society: encounter and dialogue after the TRC

These observations underscore the need for longer-term efforts to continue the unfinished work of the Commission in addressing the spatial, social and psychological legacies of apartheid's divided past in order to prolong the process of instrumental learning and to improve race relations in contemporary South Africa. In this regard, it is important to note that from its inception, the TRC was always intended to be the beginning, rather than the end, of a range of initiatives required to move South African society towards interracial reconciliation following its transition (Villa-Vicencio 2000a: 199). To this end, a small network of civil society organizations has emerged in South Africa following the end of the TRC's mandate with the express aim of carrying forward the reconciliatory goals of the Commission by facilitating carefully mediated encounters between formerly divided South Africans.

Such groups include the highly regarded 'Institute for Healing of Memories' (IHOM), led by Father Michael Lapsley, a white South African and anti-apartheid activist who himself became the victim of apartheid-era violence when he lost both hands and the use of an eye after receiving a parcel bomb from South African security forces. The IHOM originally emerged alongside the TRC as a parallel forum for South Africans of different racial backgrounds to meet with one another to tell their personal stories and have them acknowledged by others in a safe and supportive environment. By engaging South Africans in this kind of dialogue, the IHOM sought to "facilitate reconciliation between the racial groups and to heal psychological wounds [thereby] making it possible for individuals to contribute effectively towards the reconstruction of South Africa" (IHOM 2011). Following the formal TRC process, the IHOM has continued to provide a range of storytelling and dialogue workshops for small groups of South Africans designed to build a "growing empathy with the experience of others." Ultimately, the IHOM hopes to contribute to "a transformation of the relationships between people of different ethnic groups [and] races" by using these encounters to directly challenge the "[a]ttitudes and prejudices that have developed out of anger and hatred between groups that can lead to ongoing conflict and spiraling violence" (ibid.).

In a similar fashion, the Centre for the Study of Violence and Reconciliation (CSVR), a non-governmental research organization based out of Johannesburg, has been running an 'Ex-Combatants Reintegration and Restorative Justice

Project' since 2004. This project seeks to provide mediated spaces for further dialogue between ex-combatants and victims of human rights abuses. It expands on work from an earlier 'Victim–Offender Mediation' pilot project initiated by the CSVR in 2002 that brought together perpetrators and their victims (including South Africans from multiple racial groups). These programs were born out of surveys conducted with victims and perpetrators who participated in the TRC's amnesty process and later identified the need for further direct dialogue as a means of helping with healing, reconciliation and community reintegration of ex-combatants (CSVR 2011).[18] Additionally, a small number of independent faith-based community groups have engaged in similar forms of dialogue work, and a handful of professional groups such as the Centre for Conflict Resolution (CCR) at the University of Cape Town have focused on using skills training, mediation services and workshops to bring parties together in dialogue encounters to help resolve racial or community conflicts (CCR 2012).

Internal and external evaluations of several of these projects suggest that they have indeed had a positive impact on instrumental learning for the majority of their members, with participants evidencing a greater understanding of the Other's perspective, improved attitudes towards the Other and a greater willingness to reconcile (Ramirez-Barat and van der Merwe 2005; Greenbaum 2006; Niyodusenga and Karakashian 2008).[19] For example, evaluations of the IHOM workshops show that participants were "able to open to the experience of people different from themselves," and that many "reported a change in attitude towards people of other racial groups, and some were prepared to take a step towards forgiveness and reconciliation" (Niyodusenga and Karakashian 2008: 4). Similarly, assessments of the CSVR's Victim–Offender Mediation project note that the project's work "helped to rebuild a bridge of mutual understanding" between victims and offenders and showed a potential for "assisting with transformation" between parties from different racial backgrounds "by providing the opportunity for people to challenge stereotypes and learn to know each other as people rather than political or racial opponents" (Ramirez-Barat and van der Merwe 2005).

Many of the experts interviewed in South Africa were also extremely positive in their individual assessments of the impact that civil society organizations' dialogue workshops have had on ongoing processes of instrumental learning and reconciliation following the TRC. As Vincent Williams of IDASA contends, in many respects, the work of these organizations has facilitated the crucially important processes of direct interpersonal encounter and dialogue that ideally "should have happened at the time of the [TRC] hearings." As a result, Williams notes that these civil society efforts

> are really beginning to achieve the kind of reconciliation that was envisaged, where people are actually sitting down and talking about

what had happened, engaging in some kind of dialogue, and they are emerging out of that with a much stronger sense of what they have in common and what they need to do collectively for reconciliation. . . . It was left to others to subsequently pick up where the TRC left off to try and achieve real reconciliation in that sense.

(Interview: June 22nd, 2008)

Similarly, other interviewees stressed the critical part that these efforts play in enabling individuals from different racial groups to come together in reconciliatory dialogue, especially considering that South Africa's continued physical, social and economic separation would likely not allow these individuals to do so in the course of their daily lives. As former TRC Commissioner Glenda Wildschut argues, the kinds of dialogue workshops facilitated by groups such as the IHOM remain crucial in a post-TRC South Africa as they "create a moment where people have an opportunity to begin a conversation of reconciliation, to begin a conversation about healing the divisions between communities and individuals" (interview: June 25th, 2008). Accordingly, while Wildschut indicates that the TRC may have played an important role in initiating a broader process of societal dialogue about race in post-apartheid South Africa, she underscores the need for this reconciliatory momentum to be consolidated and extended by encouraging ongoing interpersonal encounters, where South Africans

are able—in a very safe space—to hear each other's stories . . . allowing people to be able to see the story of the Other, through a personal account, not through hearsay or a story that is read somewhere . . . there's this personal contact and I think that's been the power of the workshops—encounter with a real person, and hearing the person's story, whatever that may be.

(ibid.)

Nevertheless, despite these positive assessments, the number of mediated encounters that have been facilitated by such dialogue workshops following the TRC remains very small, with only a handful of civil society organizations actively engaging in these initiatives across South Africa. This seems attributable, at least in part, to the lack of funding and support for reconciliation initiatives from Thabo Mbeki's ANC government, which came to power following the conclusion of the TRC. Mbeki himself, who never appeared to be a wholehearted supporter of the Commission's findings, seemed to largely consider the question of reconciliation settled following the TRC's work and therefore deemphasized support for government and civil society programs aimed at instrumental learning in favor of focusing on socioeconomic reforms (Chapman and van der Merwe 2008c: 298). Organizations engaged in the work of instrumental learning in South Africa therefore had to remain self-supporting or to rely on funding assistance provided by foreign governments, private foundations and non-governmental organizations. As a result, while South Africa is home to a thriving civil society sector, only a very small proportion of this sector (including groups like the IJR, CSVR, IHOM and CCR) has been able to remain focused on programs designed to promote opportunities for social learning through interracial contact and dialogue. Given the limited scale of these initiatives and the relatively large population and geographical size of South Africa, it seems likely that the ability of this work to have a broader impact on instrumental learning and reconciliation in South African society, aside from its effects on the small number of individuals who have been able to participate directly in these programs, will remain minimal.

Notes

1   The CRU was originally established as the 'Central Community Relations Unit' in 1987, but in 2000, this was shortened to the CRU when the body was relocated under the new devolved Assembly. For simplicity's sake, this body will simply be referred to as the CRU throughout.
2   By 1985 it is estimated that there were already approximately 86 independent non-governmental 'peace groups' dedicated to removing sources of tension and conflict between the two communities (Frazer and Fitzduff 1994).
3   It should be noted that since the resumption of the devolved Northern Ireland Assembly in 2007, the official *Shared Future* policy introduced under direct rule is due to be replaced by a new community relations policy framework by the OFMDFM. This framework, entitled *Cohesion, Sharing, and Integration*, has been released for public consultation and has led to considerable debate and discussion (Devine et al. 2011). That said, during this interim period, many of the actions of the devolved government have continued to follow the original *Shared Future* policy.
4   While legally an independent non-governmental organization with its own executive board and mandate, the CRC might more accurately be categorized as a 'quango' or quasi-NGO, as the majority of its funding is provided directly by the CRU and the OFMDFM.
5   One example of such a partnership would include 'The Junction' in the city of Derry, which, in addition to running its own educational and reconciliatory programming, works as a central hub for collaboration with other non-governmental organizations such as The Peace and Reconciliation Group, The Holywell Trust and St. Columb's Park House and as an informal liaison with the local CROs.
6   This has come through three interrelated funding programs, PEACE I (1995–1999), PEACE II (2000–2006) and PEACE III (2007–2013).
7   Integrated schools are created in two ways. One is the establishment of a new school with an integrated curriculum and enrolment. The second is a process whereby 'single-identity' schools are 'transformed' into integrated schools by adopting these same criteria.

8 In practice this means that integrated schools are required to have at a maximum a 60/40 split in enrolment, mixed teachers and a 'culturally respectful' curriculum (NICIR n.d.).

9 This highly regarded study brought together several academic experts to outline the relationship between contact and reconciliation in Northern Ireland, with data derived primarily from survey questionnaires posed to 404 respondents in a longitudinal study conducted between 2006 and 2007.

10 These reports draw on data supplied by the Northern Ireland Life and Times Survey (NILT), which has recorded the attitudes, values and beliefs of the adult population in Northern Ireland on social issues since 1998, as well as the Young Life and Times Survey which has monitored attitudes to community relations among 16-year-olds across Northern Ireland since 2003.

11 On a scale of 1 to 10, 70 percent gave the government a score of 5 or higher on its efforts in this regard as compared to 27 percent who indicated a score of 4 or lower.

12 This is a point echoed by Dr. Brandon Hamber, Director of the International Conflict Research Institute (INCORE) at the University of Ulster, who notes, "I think that storytelling more than anything else has a humanizing effect . . . I think what happens is you begin to hear more of the human side of people, things they've struggled with . . . it humanizes the way you look at other people" (interview: February 14th, 2008).

13 Survey evidence from 2000 reveals that public interest in and awareness of the TRC's activities remained relatively high throughout its mandate, with only 11 percent of black and 12 percent of white respondents claiming to know 'little' or 'nothing' about the work of the TRC (Thiessen 2008: 201).

14 This is reflective of the *TRC Report's* own recognition of the need to establish a 'social' or 'dialogue' truth in the hopes of contributing to national unity and reconciliation by involving the public as participants in the TRC process (1998: Vol. 1, Ch. 5, Para. 40).

15 This was a point raised by Piers Pigou, Director of the South African History Archive (SAHA) at the University of the Witwatersrand and former member of the TRC's Investigative Unit: "Love it or hate it, you couldn't ignore [the TRC], it was there in your face everywhere you turned. That's presupposing you had access to television and radio of course, or other media which of course a significant portion of the population doesn't have" (interview: July 1st, 2008).

16 For instance, white television viewers of the TRC *Special Report* coverage on the SABC remained at roughly 4.1 percent between 1996 and 1998, while African TV owners had a viewership of 13.7 percent. Towards the end of the Commission, these numbers had further dropped from an average viewership of 7 percent to less than 3 percent (Thiessen 2008: 202).

17 Data collected through the IJR's 2003 SARB survey of South African opinion shows that "the overwhelming majority (78 percent) of South Africans believe the government should require both the print and broadcast media to provide citizens with more opportunities for engaging in meaningful dialogue" surrounding "issues pertinent to the reconciliation process" (Lombard 2003: 51).

18 While the dialogue projects run through CSVR tend to focus primarily on community reintegration following so-called 'black on black violence,' they have also involved the promotion of interracial reconciliation between victims and perpetrators (Ramirez-Barat and van der Merwe 2005).

19 These findings are derived largely from external assessments carried out by the CSVR and IHOM, respectively, which included interviews and questionnaires posed to participants to gauge changes in their attitudes and perceptions that may have occurred as a result of their participation in these programs.

Chapter 6

Socioemotional learning

Conflict transformation and transitional justice scholars agree on the crucial importance of interventions promoting socioemotional learning in divided societies. Such interventions are designed to confront the emotional and perceptual legacies of past conflict in order to break down potential obstacles to reconciliation caused by existing feelings of victimization, guilt, distrust and fear between groups. The provision of justice is central to such efforts, requiring transitional authorities to counter perceptions of impunity for past human rights abuses by acknowledging those victimized by violence and by assigning some form of accountability to perpetrators. In this way, the provision of justice can also contribute to social leaning by symbolizing a shift in the normative ethos that once legitimized the use of violence between former antagonists, and can therefore serve as a vital bridge between a society's divisive past and a more inclusive and peaceable future. Alongside justice, socioemotional learning also requires some aspect of historical investigation capable of establishing the 'truth'—understood as a mutually accepted or at least mutually tolerable shared understanding capable of countering the highly biased collective memories and narratives of past abuses between former enemies. Left unaddressed, such antagonistic belief systems have been shown to directly impede the development of more cooperative relations and sustainable peace in deeply divided societies.

This chapter examines the contributions made to processes of socio-emotional learning by both truth and justice as provided by the transitional justice strategies adopted in Northern Ireland and South Africa. Northern Ireland's decentralized transitional justice program has taken a 'piecemeal' approach to socioemotional learning, combining a range of discrete government initiatives with numerous independent efforts to address the past undertaken by non-governmental organizations and the local community and voluntary sector. Such efforts have included a variety of programs designed to facilitate victim acknowledgment, prisoner reintegration, and local truth recovery, along with a series of legal investigations by governmental actors designed to begin addressing the unresolved legacies of Northern Ireland's Troubles. In South Africa, on the other hand, efforts to promote socioemotional learning have come almost exclusively out of the much more unified TRC process. First of all, the Commission centrally emphasized the importance of attempts to establish an accurate historical record of apartheid-era abuses through its public hearings and research and investigative units. The TRC also endeavored to deliver a degree of 'restorative justice' in an effort to repair relationships and build national unity in the wake of South Africa's transition by providing a forum for the public acknowledgment of victims and offering a unique—and highly controversial—conditional amnesty provision to those who perpetrated human rights abuses during apartheid.

Socioemotional learning in Northern Ireland

By the mid-1990s, the major parties to the Troubles in Northern Ireland recognized that violence was no longer an effective means of moving their respective agendas forward. In many ways, the Belfast Agreement (BFA) was therefore a pragmatic choice by unionists, nationalists, the British government, and key paramilitary organizations—an effort to negotiate an end to overt violence but to continue their struggles by more peaceable political means. As a result, while an agreement was reached regarding the necessity of peace in Northern Ireland, no corresponding consensus was ever reached regarding ultimate responsibility for the violence of the past. In the interest of maintaining the stability of the peace process and protecting the 'fault-neutral' framework of the BFA, the highly contentious issue of accountability was left largely untouched and unresolved.

As a result, nationalist and unionist communities have remained deeply divided in their views of who the 'real' victims and perpetrators of past conflict are, thereby placing very different demands on what might be required to satisfy calls for 'truth' and 'justice' in a post-conflict Northern Ireland. For instance, most nationalists view themselves as having been victimized by an illegitimate and repressive state and made the targets of unjust violence carried out by its security forces and Loyalist paramilitaries. Correspondingly, most Republicans (and many nationalists) interpret the historical use of violence by the IRA against the British state and security forces or in defense of nationalist communities as a justifiable act of 'freedom fighters.' For these individuals, 'truth' requires a greater recognition of the involvement of the British state in the conflict, including an acknowledgment of its collusion with Loyalist paramilitaries in the killing of nationalist civilians. On the other hand, unionists tend to view themselves as the victims of past violence at the hands of seditious nationalist rioters and Republican 'terrorists' who acted in flagrant disregard for the laws of the state. They consequently interpret the steps taken by security forces against the nationalist population as appropriate responses to criminal acts, and see 'justice' as securing criminal prosecution and imprisonment for these crimes. For its part, the British government has continued to position itself as an impartial arbiter forced to mediate a two-sided sectarian conflict, a role that in the past occasionally mandated the use of harsh tactics in response to the violent criminal activities and terrorist acts undertaken against the state.

Notably, these deeply divided interpretations of responsibility for past violence persist despite the existence of a remarkable body of factual evidence about the injuries and deaths that occurred during the Troubles. Independent, non-partisan databases like the Conflict Archive on the Internet (CAIN) located at the International Conflict Research Institute (INCORE) have archived the precise names, times, dates and circumstances surrounding nearly every conflict-related death from 1969 onwards (CAIN 2012). In this sense, the broader factual 'truth' regarding culpability for deaths is already largely known, with details readily available as to which organizations were responsible for specific deaths even if individual perpetrators remain anonymous.[1]

Nonetheless, despite the availability of this wealth of information, there still remains no broader agreement between the communities about why people were killed or whether the use of violence was somehow justified. Accordingly, because of the perpetuation of zero-sum perceptions of who was 'right' and who was 'wrong' during the Troubles, no single institution has been able to attempt to provide 'truth' or 'justice' for the past without being perceived as potentially biased or sectarian. These ongoing difficulties have effectively prevented against the development of a centralized transitional justice institution such as a tribunal or truth commission to address the past in Northern Ireland. Instead, the country has seen a much more decentralized and 'piecemeal' approach to truth recovery and to justice, with various projects being undertaken by an array of governmental, non-governmental and local community actors. While space does not permit a full accounting of these initiatives, a number of the most prominent of these measures are considered here in turn, alongside an assessment of this piecemeal strategy's ability to contribute to socioemotional learning and intergroup reconciliation between nationalist and unionist communities.[2]

Victim support and acknowledgemnt

During the negotiations leading up to the BFA, the Government of Northern Ireland (GNI) recognized that a sustainable peace would centrally require acknowledging and addressing the needs of those victimized by past violence. Accordingly, in 1997 a Victims' Commission was created under the leadership of Sir Kenneth Bloomfield by the British Secretary of State for Northern Ireland, which was tasked with "look[ing] into possible ways to recognize the pain and suffering felt by victims of violence arising from the troubles of the last 30 years" (Bloomfield 1998: 8). After a period of extensive consultation with civil society and local communities, a final report entitled *We Will Remember Them* (known more commonly as 'The Bloomfield Report') was released by the Commission in April 1998. The Report recommended, among other provisions, increased access by victims to financial compensation, trauma counseling and targeted social services, the establishment of non-partisan victim memorials, and the creation of a standing ombudsman charged with representing victims' concerns to the government (ibid.).

The crucial importance of addressing the needs of victims was further reinforced by the BFA, whose signatories recognized that it would be "essential to acknowledge and address the suffering of the victims of violence as a necessary element of reconciliation" (GNI 1998). As a result, in June 1998 a Victims' Liaison Unit (VLU) and a specialized Victims' Minister were created within the Northern Ireland Office to take on the task of coordinating future government policy in response to victims' concerns. Their work included establishing schemes to distribute core government funding to local community support groups for victims and survivors. It also involved providing financial support for the Northern Ireland Memorial Fund (NIMF) and the Community Foundation for Northern Ireland (CFNI), independent charitable organizations established as Intermediary Funding Bodies (IFBs) to administer and monitor small grant assistance to victims, their families, and their caregivers as part of a broader effort "to promote peace and reconciliation by demonstrating recognition of the needs of victims and survivors as an important part of the healing process in Northern Ireland" (NIMF 2012).

Further, following the reestablishment of the devolved Northern Ireland Assembly in 2000, a dedicated Victims' Unit was created within the Office of the First Minister and Deputy First Minister (OFMDFM) to oversee a government-wide policy for addressing victims' needs. This policy mandate, entitled *Reshape, Rebuild, Achieve*, was designed to "deliver practical help and services to the surviving physically and psychologically injured of violent, conflict-related incidents and those close relatives or partners who care for them" (Victims Unit 2002). This assistance included a targeted range of initiatives that addressed the particular needs of victims and their families in the areas of health, education, housing and employment. *Reshape, Rebuild, Achieve* also introduced additional funding to be distributed to individual victims and victims' groups through small grants administered via IFBs, including the 'Victims Survivors Development Scheme' and 'Victim Survivors Core Funding Scheme' under the Community Relations Council (CRC).

More recently, in 2008 the OFMDFM created a Commission for Victims and Survivors (CSVNI) to consult with and act as a permanent ombudsman for victims, to review the adequacy of existing victim-related law and policy, and to serve as a general source of advice for government with regard to best practices in moving forward. In 2009, a Victims and Survivors Forum was created, a consultative body of approximately thirty representatives drawn from government, the voluntary sector and both nationalist and unionist community organizations involved in victims' work designed to provide advice and information on behalf of victims to the CSVNI. In April 2012, a new independent Victims and Survivors Service was introduced by the Northern Ireland Executive as a centralized body providing access to government grant funding for individual victims and victims' groups. In total, between 1998 and 2008, the Government of Northern Ireland invested over £20 million in victims' initiatives, with more recent announcements indicating that this funding increased to £36 million between 2009 and 2012 (OFMDFM 2008). Notably, these investments have been supplemented with extensive funding for victims' issues through the estimated £2 billion provided by the European Union's PEACE program for Northern Ireland.

This review evidences a consistent approach to victims' issues in Northern Ireland following the Belfast Agreement, illustrating a largely 'bottom-up' strategy for providing victim services. While the Government of Northern Ireland has taken the lead in setting the overall policy agenda, it has done so following extensive consultation with both individual victims and non-governmental victims' organizations. Indeed, though the GNI and the EU have provided considerable funding for victims' services, for the most part these funds have been channeled through IFBs in order to support a wide range of community-based victims' organizations which themselves carry out the vast majority of the 'on-the-ground' work. These organizations include 'single-identity' victims' groups that work almost exclusively with members of one community, such as the nationalist Relatives for Justice (RFJ) or the unionist Families Acting for Innocent Relatives (FAIR), as well as 'cross-community' groups like the highly-regarded WAVE Trauma Centre that have provided localized services to all victims of the conflict in Northern Ireland since the early 1990s.

Overall, assessments of the funding, support and service delivery that have been provided to victims in Northern Ireland following the BFA have been quite positive. One independent evaluation of Northern Ireland's bottom-up approach to addressing victims' issues found that it "has been instrumental in helping establish and sustain a wide cross-section of work in the areas of victims" and that, "overall, the groups are engaged in a wide variety of activities which are beneficial to victims" (Clio 2002: i). A similar external assessment carried out by Deloitte in 2001 found that the decision by the GNI "to filter funding to the grass roots organizations . . . facilitated the victims sector in providing a range of services . . . [that were] identified as having assisted individual victims" (Deloitte 2001: 5). Furthermore, the same Deloitte study also found that the increased opportunities for funding provided by institutions such as the VLU, Victims' Unit, and the NIMF "ha[ve] increased awareness of victims related issues and resulted in an increased range of services to victims which are accessible at a local level" (ibid.).

In addition, nearly all those experts interviewed in Northern Ireland indicated that the acknowledgment of and assistance paid to victims have been crucial in aiding individual healing as well as in facilitating the broader process of societal reconciliation. As Professor Brandon Hamber of the International Conflict Research Institute (INCORE) at the University of Ulster argues, the support provided by the "sophisticated service-delivery system" developed in Northern Ireland after the BFA has been one of the "major fundamental components" in helping victims to come to terms with the past (interview: February 14th, 2008). Similarly, Dr. Matthew Cannon, CEO of the Irish Peace Institute at the University of Limerick, notes that the focus on victims and the support provided by both government and local community programs form the "cornerstone" of much broader efforts to help communities move toward improved relations and reconciliation after the Troubles (interview: April 14th, 2008).

That said, despite the high level of sustained funding and the extensive support services provided by government, NGOs and the community/voluntary sector, issues surrounding victims continue to serve as points of communal division due to widely divergent, and often antagonistic, perceptions of past violence. Indeed, the issue of who should be considered a 'legitimate' victim of the conflict in Northern Ireland remains highly politicized, with many expert interviewees such as Dr. Pete Shirlow of Queen's University Belfast noting that victimhood is consistently appropriated as a "political football" or a tool for politicians to use against the Other community, while victims themselves are often squeezed "like a grape in a vice" between the competing narratives of nationalists and unionists seeking to assign blame for the violence of the past (interview: April 24th, 2008). For instance, several prominent nationalist victims' organizations such as the RFJ have taken issue with the findings of the Bloomfield Report, arguing that it prioritizes the victims of paramilitary violence while downplaying attention to those victimized by the actions of the police and security forces (PFC 1999). More broadly, many nationalists believe that the GNI has established an implicit 'hierarchy of victims' under which 'innocent' unionists and state security forces are considered to be more deserving of support, while Republican 'terrorists' and those guilty by association in the nationalist community are less so (Hamber 1998; Lundy and McGovern 2001). Similarly, there are many within the unionist community who do not believe that former paramilitary combatants should be considered 'victims,' as they "feel that 'real' victims had no choice over life, death or injury, whereas perpetrators had the choice whether or not to take part in premeditated acts of violence" (NIHRC 2003).

Indeed, the high degree of continued communal polarization over issues of victimhood remains clearly evident in survey data collected by the Northern Ireland Life and Times (NILT) survey as recently as 2004.[3] For instance, when asked whether they thought 'support for victims' was an important element of dealing with the legacy of the Troubles, a vast majority of both Catholics (92 percent) and Protestants (85 percent) indicated that they considered this provision to be 'fairly' or 'very' important. However, when asked whether 'all those people who were killed or injured as a result of the conflict matter equally no matter whether they were paramilitaries or members of the security forces,' more than twice as many Catholics (69 percent) as Protestants (33 percent) indicated that they 'agreed' or 'strongly agreed' (ARK 2005). Notably, a similar disparity exists between the communities in response to the question of whether 'all those people who were bereaved as a result of the conflict should be treated equally,' with 81 percent of Catholics as compared to 54 percent of Protestants indicating they 'agreed' or 'strongly agreed' when asked (ibid.).

Prisoner release and reintegration

Alongside the attention paid to victims, the Belfast Agreement included provisions to address the perpetrators of past violence in the form of an early release program for those who had been imprisoned for their involvement in the Troubles. Under the framework of the BFA, over 450 'qualifying' prisoners—largely ex-combatants from Republican and Loyalist paramilitary organizations—were to be released by the British and Irish governments within two years of its signing. This was widely recognized as being a necessary condition for getting potential paramilitary 'spoilers' on board with the BFA and a requirement for moving the peace process forward. Notably, while this release did significantly cut short the term of incarceration for many prisoners, it was not a blanket amnesty process, as its provisions were limited to members of those paramilitary organizations engaged in ceasefires at the time, did not expunge the record of conviction, and only released prisoners on conditional licenses that could be revoked if an individual engaged in further criminal activity.

The decision to release prisoners under the BFA was also accompanied by a specific clause requiring the British and Irish governments to "provide support both prior to and after release, including assistance directed towards availing of employment opportunities, re-training and/or re-skilling, and further education" (GNI 1998). Much like the support provided to victims, this assistance has largely taken the form of direct funding grants administered to non-governmental and local community organizations by IFBs such as the CFNI on behalf of core funders including the GNI and the EU. In the period between 1995 and 2003, financial support for community-based organizations aiding prisoner reintegration totaled over £9.2 million. This included funding for 61 community groups and a further 29 projects involving working with politically motivated prisoners and their families to secure provisions of education, skills training, financial and welfare advice, housing and accommodation, and counseling services (McEvoy 1998: 1572). These projects are led by the work of the independent Northern Ireland Association for the Care and Resettlement of Offenders (NIACRO), a group that acts as one of the primary 'umbrella' organizations and advocacy groups for ex-prisoner issues.

On the whole, these programs appear to have met with a good deal of success, with only 20 of the 450 political prisoners released having had their licenses revoked for reengaging in violence or criminal activity in the ten years following the signing of the BFA (McEvoy and Shirlow 2008). Further, there is also significant evidence that ex-paramilitaries played a key role in preventing outbreaks of future violence both during and after the peace process by using their legitimacy within their own communities to help to 'sell' the BFA and diffuse sectarian tensions surrounding its passage. As Mike Ritchie, Director of the non-governmental Committee on the Administration of Justice (CAJ) illustrates,

> the importance of ex-prisoners in terms of selling the Agreement in local communities was pretty significant. . . . On the Republican side, the IRA and Sinn Féin were taking very, very controversial decisions and the people who sold those decisions in local communities were people who had been released, the ex-prisoners . . . they were basically interpreting politics to people on the ground. And when there were problems and difficulties in local areas it was ex-prisoners that people turned to. . . . On the Loyalist side, they gradually became more important in relations to interface work, riots and violence at the interfaces . . . when there came to be networks to try and tamp things down, it was Loyalist ex-prisoners who were to the fore in relation to that. And I think they have really been in advance of their communities in advancing dialogue and trying to bring about more peaceable ways of resolving problems.
>
> (Interview: April 21st, 2008)

While many former combatants have found it difficult to secure regular employment due to a lack of higher education and prior criminal convictions, through retraining in conflict resolution, mediation and dialogue skills, they have found new work with grassroots peace-building organizations. This has provided many paramilitary ex-combatants with a new sense of purpose and a means to secure an income outside of criminal activity following the peace process. However, just as importantly, it has also allowed community organizations to draw upon the huge amount of legitimacy and credibility that paramilitaries carry in their own communities and to channel this towards more positive reconciliatory efforts (Knox and Monaghan 2002).

Indeed, the work of Kieran McEvoy and Pete Shirlow from Queen's University Belfast shows that a surprising number of paramilitary ex-prisoners have become proactively engaged in important reconciliation initiatives at local levels. In particular, ex-prisoners have shown a great propensity for working with youth to reduce sectarian mindsets and 'anti-social' violence, as many young people tend to look up to former combatants as heroes or 'hard men' whose words and actions carry significant weight. The incorporation of ex-combatants into peace-building has also had a powerful symbolic effect, as people have been able to witness those who once advocated the use of violence to secure political ends put down their weapons and become proponents for nonviolence, reconciliation and respecting the rule of law (McEvoy-Levy 2001; McEvoy and Shirlow 2008). In this way, as McEvoy illustrates, following the peace process in Northern Ireland, ex-combatants have become crucial leaders in processes of grassroots conflict transformation and reconciliation:

> If you understand violence, you've inflicted violence, and quite often for ex-combatants, you've been on the receiving end of violence, you bring a significant amount of credibility if you're saying violence isn't the way forward. It's not a nice liberal do-gooder middle-class academic or clerical figure who is making the argument. It's an ex-combatant who may have killed people, who may have directly lost members of their family, and who understands violence who is saying that violence isn't the way forward. That's a very powerful message that brings a significant moral credibility to it.
>
> (Interview: April 17th, 2008)

This is a point underscored by Dr. Matthew Cannon of the Irish Peace Institute, who contends that "some of the best reconciliation work is being done by ex-prisoners. . . . Those who experienced the worst of [the violence], some of those people can be, and are, excellent community relations workers" (interview: April 14th, 2008).

One prominent way in which ex-prisoners have become involved in grassroots reconciliation efforts is through 'restorative justice' initiatives. Based on projects led by former Republican and Loyalist combatants and funded largely by NIACRO and Atlantic Philanthropies (an international grant-making endowment), these highly-regarded programs now operate within both nationalist and unionist communities. Initiatives like the nationalist Community Restorative Justice Ireland (CRJI) and the Loyalist Northern Ireland Alternatives (NIA) and Greater Shankill Alternatives focus on efforts to replace the Troubles' 'informal' system of violent internal policing with lawful and non-violent solutions based on dialogue, victim–offender mediation, community service and a greater willingness to work in partnership with statutory agencies such as the Police Service of Northern Ireland (PSNI). Most often, interventions for perpetrators of minor crimes include apologies and agreements to desist, compensation for damages, or agreements to participate in community service or personal development programs (Knox and Monaghan 2002).

Evidence suggests that these programs have enjoyed a good deal of success to date, being widely accepted among local populations, serving as efficient checks on paramilitary 'punishment' violence such as 'kneecappings,' shootings and beatings, and contributing to a significant overall decline in violent criminal activity in the neighborhoods they serve. Indeed, in the period between 1999 and 2005, paramilitaries were involved in more than 1,800 recorded 'punishment' shootings and assaults. However, as one evaluation report shows, following interventions from CRJI and NIA, potential paramilitary punishments dropped by 82 percent and 71 percent respectively, while beatings and shootings had nearly stopped altogether in restorative justice project areas by 2005 (Mika 2006). Moreover, the strong liaisons that many of these restorative justice initiatives have established with the PSNI have also played important symbolic roles in helping to rebuild public perceptions of the legitimacy of Northern Ireland's policing services within nationalist communities (McEvoy and Eriksson 2006: 321–327).

Regardless, the decision to release paramilitary prisoners has been highly controversial, with reactions largely remaining polarized between nationalist and unionist communities, particularly among those who were directly or indirectly victimized by past paramilitary violence. As Christine Bell, Director of the Transitional Justice Institute of the University of Ulster has argued, while without the release of paramilitary prisoners "there wouldn't have been a peace process and there wouldn't have been an Agreement," this provision nonetheless "divided unionists and nationalists like a hammer, like an axe down the middle" (interview: February 13th, 2008). As McEvoy illustrates, for the unionist population, whose leadership denied the political nature of the Troubles and portrayed the conflict as "an extended crime wave committed by men of violence for their own gain," the release of paramilitary prisoners—Republican or Loyalist—was for the most part viewed as a "travesty" and a "sacrifice of justice" (interview: April 17th, 2008). On the other hand, the nationalist community, whose leaders had long narrated the conflict as a political struggle against an unjust state, has evidenced a much greater willingness to countenance the early release of Republican prisoners and to reintegrate ex-combatants into their communities. In a poll conducted in 2000 by the NILT survey, 63 percent of Catholics indicated either a neutral position or direct support for the release of prisoners under the Agreement, a position matched by only 17 percent of Protestant respondents. Furthermore, fully 76 percent of Protestants claimed that they still either 'opposed' or 'strongly opposed' the decision, a position shared by only 29 percent of Catholics (ARK 2001). Accordingly, this suggests that, much like initiatives surrounding victim support, programs for ex-prisoners and ex-combatants continue to serve as points of communal division as a result of widely divergent (and often antagonistic) perceptions of past conflict.

Public inquiries

Alongside support for victims and ex-prisoners, several legal initiatives have been attempted by the British government and the GNI following the BFA to begin to address the unresolved legacy of Northern Ireland's past and to provide measures of 'truth' and 'justice' to its citizens. Absent a more centralized process like a tribunal or truth commission, in the main these initiatives have involved a series of discrete investigations into prominent deaths stemming from Troubles-era violence. In particular, many of these investigations have taken the form of independent public inquiries undertaken by the British government under the Tribunals of Inquiry (Evidence) Act of 1921.

By far the most prominent of these initiatives has been the 'Bloody Sunday Inquiry' (BSI), a tribunal of inquiry opened by British Prime Minister Tony Blair in 1998 to investigate the shooting deaths of fourteen Catholic civilians by soldiers of the British Army in the city of Derry on January 30th, 1972— one of the single most deadly incidents of violence that occurred during the Troubles. Blair's decision was prompted by long-standing grassroots action undertaken by the Bloody Sunday Campaign, a group led by relatives of those killed and injured on Bloody Sunday that sought to reopen an investigation into the incident in the wake of the highly controversial 1972 Widgery Inquiry. Under the direction of then Lord Chief Justice Widgery, the Inquiry had summarily exonerated British security forces of any wrongdoing and suggested that the victims may themselves have been aggressors, or at the very least were supporting attacks by armed 'gunmen and bombers' against the soldiers. However, these findings were almost immediately challenged, with many commentators raising concerns that the Inquiry's findings had been marred by bias and faulty forensics, and had disregarded the testimony of a number of civilian eyewitnesses that suggested the victims were unarmed and were not posing a threat to the soldiers when they were killed (Government of Ireland 1997; Hegarty 2002; Mullan 2007).

Taken together, the events of Bloody Sunday and the subsequent Widgery Inquiry proved to be incredibly detrimental to community relations in Northern Ireland. In fact, these events are widely considered to have been a 'watershed' moment in the Troubles that led directly to a major upswing in armed sectarian violence and attacks against policing and security forces (Ni Aolain 2000).[4] As Angela Hegarty has noted, for many in the nationalist community, the events of Bloody Sunday and the perceived 'whitewash' of the Widgery Inquiry that followed entrenched feelings of injustice and further deepened a sense of distrust of and alienation from the British state and security forces (2002: 1165). Conversely, for those in the unionist community, Widgery's findings simply reinforced the 'official version' of Bloody Sunday propagated by the British government and military, which held that the soldiers had acted with just cause in defending themselves against attacks from nationalist and Republican 'gunmen and bombers.'

The new BSI began its work in 1998, overseen by an international tribunal of judges drawn from the Commonwealth and chaired by Lord Mark Saville of Newdigate. Between 2000 and 2004, the BSI interviewed and received statements from over 2,500 individuals. Of this number, more than 900 were called before the Inquiry to provide oral testimony, including the victims' families, experts, eyewitnesses and the British soldiers implicated in the fatal shootings. This was supplemented by the Inquiry's collection of a large amount of multimedia evidence, including 13 volumes of photographs, 121 audiotapes and 110 videotapes. Following several years of delay, this information was ultimately compiled into an extensive final report (totaling more than five thousand pages in length) detailing the BSI's key findings and conclusions and submitted to the Secretary of State for Northern Ireland in March 2010. The total cost of the Inquiry has been estimated at over £200 million, making the BSI the largest single public inquiry ever undertaken to date by the British government.

Based upon the evidence collected, the BSI's final report ultimately concluded that the shootings on Bloody Sunday were the result of "soldiers opening fire unjustifiably." The report therefore held that the "immediate responsibility for the deaths and injuries on Bloody Sunday lies with those members of Support Company whose unjustifiable firing was the cause of those deaths and injuries" sustained by victims (Saville et al. 2010: ch. 4, para. 1). Further, the Report is unequivocal in its exoneration of the civilian victims who were killed and wounded, ultimately finding that none of the victims was "armed with a firearm . . . or bomb of any description" or "posing any threat of causing danger of serious injury" to the British soldiers when they were shot (Saville et al. 2010: ch. 3, para. 70). Indeed, in several instances, the Tribunal found that statements made by soldiers before the Inquiry alleging that they had fired at gunmen and bombers involved contradictory claims or assertions understood at the time by the soldiers themselves to be false or "knowingly untrue" (idem: ch. 3, paras. 101–113).

The Final Report of the BSI was officially released to the public on June 15th, 2010, accompanied by a public statement by Conservative Prime Minister David Cameron. In his statement, Cameron came out in full support of the Inquiry's findings, noting that "the conclusions of this report are absolutely clear. There is no doubt, there is nothing equivocal, there are no ambiguities. What happened on Bloody Sunday was both unjustified and unjustifiable. It was wrong." Further, after acknowledging in his statement the responsibility of the British Army for the events of Bloody Sunday and the grief of the families of those killed, Cameron went on to issue a formal apology, stating that he was "deeply sorry" on behalf of the British government for those affected by the violence of that day (BBC News, June 15th, 2010b).

Evidence from a 2012 study shows that the BSI's work has served to advance several crucial aspects of both truth and justice in addressing the divisive legacy of Bloody Sunday. Perhaps most importantly, the BSI's findings and Cameron's apology have provided a crucial source of official acknowledgment that those killed and wounded on Bloody Sunday were innocent—the single most important goal in terms of justice sought by the families of victims who campaigned for the new Inquiry (Aiken 2012: 25). In addition, for many in the broader nationalist community, the Inquiry is widely viewed as having gone a long way towards addressing and repairing the deep sense of injustice that resulted from the Bloody Sunday shootings and the subsequent biases of Widgery (idem: 26). Further, the BSI's findings, combined with Cameron's unequivocal support and apology, have largely replaced long-standing and conflicting communal perceptions of the events of Bloody Sunday with a mutually accepted truth recognizing the innocence of victims and wrongdoing on the part of the soldiers involved (idem: 19).

Nevertheless, following the release of the BSI's Report a number of critics within the nationalist community have raised concerns that the Inquiry's investigations were biased in favor of limiting the legal exposure of the British state. For instance, many have criticized the BSI for failing to situate its investigation in the context of broader patterns of killings and alleged wrongdoings by the British state and security forces during the Troubles, and for neglecting to move 'up the ladder of command' beyond the soldiers directly involved to investigate the potential complicity of senior British political and military officials, thereby allowing Bloody Sunday to be portrayed as an isolated incident in which a rogue army squad simply 'ran amok' on the day in question (Aiken 2012: 20). Such critiques were further exacerbated by decisions taken by the British government to allow state funds to be used to provide legal counsel for the implicated soldiers and to permit them to testify anonymously, while at the same time subjecting civilian witnesses (including victims and family members) to "highly adversarial" or even "brutal" cross-examination by barristers representing the soldiers (Hegarty 2002: 212). In addition, many of the family members of those killed and wounded have decried the fact that to date there has been very little 'real' justice in the form of accountability resulting from the Inquiry's findings, given the fact that there have not yet been any prosecutions announced of the soldiers implicated in the shootings (Aiken 2012: 28).

Conversely, while now largely recognizing that the Bloody Sunday shootings were unjustified, some unionist leaders have raised questions as to why so much time and money has been expended on investigating this single incident while many other similarly deadly cases involving the killing of unionist civilians or members of the policing and security forces by Republican paramilitaries remain unresolved. As a result, many have claimed that the truth created by the Bloody Sunday Inquiry has reinforced the view that nationalist victims of state violence are more deserving of attention than individuals from other groups who were killed during the violence of the Troubles (idem: 20).[5] The continued divisiveness of this perceived inequality in dealing with the past was perhaps most clearly evident in the strong reaction voiced by Jim Allister, leader of the Traditional Unionist Voice Party, who, upon the public release of the BSI's Report, stated that my primary thoughts today are with the thousands of innocent victims of the IRA who have never had justice, nor benefitted from any inquiry into why their loved ones died. Thus today's jamboree over the [BSI] report throws into very sharp relief the unacceptable and perverse hierarchy of victims which the preferential treatment of "Bloody Sunday" has created.

(BBC News, June 15th, 2010a)

However, despite these limitations there is early evidence to suggest that the release of the Inquiry's findings and the subsequent apology by David Cameron have helped to promote aspects of socioemotional learning between nationalist and unionist communities (Aiken 2012). In effect, by helping to provide elements of both truth and justice, the BSI appears to have helped to put to rest one of the Troubles' most contentious events—one that had long stood in the way of improved relations between the two communities, both within the city of Derry and across broader Northern Ireland (idem: 31). As Pat McArt, who edited a prominent local newspaper in Derry for almost a quarter of a century, reflected in January 2012, "Bloody Sunday was a massive poison on the city. You could feel it. Now there's a different atmosphere. The whole cultural and social thing is moving on" (McKittrick 2012).

Alongside the BSI, there have also been other attempts at employing the legal inquiry model to investigate high-profile cases of violence related to Northern Ireland's Troubles. For instance, under an agreement worked out between the British and Irish governments in the Weston Park talks of 2001, Canadian Judge Peter Cory was tasked with carrying out an independent investigation to consider the possibility of security force collusion in several 'marquee' murders committed during the Troubles (Cory 2003). These cases included the killings of nationalist solicitors Rosemary Nelson and Pat Finucane by Loyalist paramilitary organizations, the death of Robert Hamill after an attack by a Loyalist mob, and the death of Loyalist Volunteer Force (LVF) leader Billy Wright, who was murdered inside Northern Ireland's infamous Maze prison by jailed members of the INLA (Irish National Liberation Army) in 1997. Ultimately, Judge Cory recommended that the British government should immediately launch fully independent public inquiries into each of these cases.

However, in the wake of Judge Cory's investigation, the British government passed the Inquiries Act 2005, which ceded control over the scope of all future inquiries in Northern Ireland to the executive of the British government. In effect, this granted government ministers powers to limit judicial purview, restrict public access, allow evidence to be given in secret, and end any ongoing inquiry at a time of their choosing. As Cory himself has argued, this Act "makes a meaningful inquiry impossible" by eliminating its independent and public nature and by granting the British minister in charge "the authority to thwart the efforts of the inquiry at every step" (PFC 2005). This move has been further condemned by the human rights advocacy group Amnesty International, who have charged that

> [t]he Inquiries Act 2005 undermines the rule of law, the separation of powers and human rights protection. It cannot be the foundation for an effective, independent, impartial or thorough judicial inquiry in serious allegations of human rights violations. Nor would it provide for public scrutiny of all the relevant evidence.
>
> (2005: 1)

Nevertheless, in 2005 the British government opened an inquiry into the death of Billy Wright. The Wright Inquiry, which cost an estimated £30 million, concluded in 2010 and found that while major failings in prison security were apparent, there was no evidence of collusion between authorities and members of the INLA, a Republican paramilitary organization (MacLean et al. 2010). The public inquiry into the Nelson murder was delayed until April of 2008. The Nelson Inquiry's report was ultimately released in May 2011 and similarly found no evidence of collusion by state security forces or the GNI leading directly to her death, though it did note that some members of the RUC had actively made abusive remarks about Nelson and that state agencies had been negligent in their efforts to protect her (Morland et al. 2011). Beset by similar delays, the Hamill inquiry did not begin until January 2009 and, at the time of writing, has yet to release a final report of its findings. Finally, in October 2011, Prime Minister Cameron announced that despite a commitment made in 2004 by the Northern Ireland Secretary of State to hold an inquiry into the death of Pat Finucane, under the new Inquiries Act, his government had effectively decided to disallow a public inquiry. Instead, it was decided that existing case files would be submitted for review by a Queen's Counsel appointed by the government—a move that has greatly upset and disappointed the Finucane family and other members of the nationalist community (BBC News, October 11th, 2011).

Overall, while this more recent series of public inquiries into past events has been able to provide an element of 'truth' by offering new insight into some of the Troubles' most contentious murder cases, critics of the Inquiries Act have identified potential issues with independence and impartiality in cases where members of the British state and security forces might be implicated. For instance, Angela Hegarty has illustrated that, given the British government's role as an active combatant in the Troubles, public inquiries that remain under its control cannot be expected to be unbiased mechanisms capable of securing truth and justice for past violence. As she details, to date public inquiries have resulted in very few actual prosecutions of security force or government actors for Troubles-era violence, with evidence suggesting that in Northern Ireland, public inquiries have frequently been employed "not as a tool to find truth and establish accountability for human rights violations, but as a way of deflecting criticism and avoiding blame" by the British state (2002: 49).

Regardless, at the time of writing it appears that further public inquiries by the British government into Troubles-era deaths are unlikely. Following the conclusion of the Bloody Sunday Inquiry in 2010, which faced criticism for its lengthy duration and high cost, Owen Paterson, the Secretary of State for Northern Ireland, made it clear that the Cameron government would no longer be turning to public inquiries to address the legacy of conflict in Northern Ireland. As Paterson stated in October 2011, "experience has shown that public inquiries into the events of the Troubles take many years and can be subject to prolonged litigation which delays the truth emerging." As a result, he argued, "the Prime Minister and I do not believe that more costly and open-ended inquiries are the right way to deal with Northern Ireland's past" (BBC News, October 12th, 2011).

Police enquiries

However, legal investigations into the violence of the Troubles have not been limited to public inquiries. They have also included a range of initiatives led by different branches of the policing services, many of which have focused on issues of potential policing and security force collusion with paramilitaries during the conflict. Between 1989 and 2003, three police enquiries led by John Stevens, Deputy Commissioner of the Metropolitan Police, were commissioned by the British government. All three explored allegations of collaboration between police and security forces and Loyalist paramilitaries surrounding a series of conflict-related deaths spanning from 1987 to 1989. The investigations undertaken during the Stevens Enquiry were massive in scope, involving the documentation of some 9,256 statements, the collection of over 10,000 documents, and the seizure of over 15,000 evidentiary exhibits. In April 2003, parts of the Enquiry's final report were publicly released, revealing that members of both the British Army and the RUC had colluded with UDA Loyalist paramilitaries, and that this collusion had led to the targeted killings of nationalists, including the solicitor Pat Finucane (Stevens 2003). In total, these investigations cost close to £100 million and culminated in the arrest and conviction of well over 100 individuals.

In addition to the Stevens Enquiry, under the Police (Northern Ireland) Act of 1998, the Office of the Police Ombudsman for Northern Ireland (OPONI) also retains the power to initiate independent investigations in the public's interest in response to allegations of police misconduct, including in historical cases of reportedly 'grave or exceptional' abuse. In 2003, the Ombudsman at the time, Nuala O'Loan, used this power to open an investigation into allegations of RUC collusion in the murders of several individuals carried out during the 1990s, including that of Protestant Raymond McCord Jr. This investigation led to the release of a final report in

2007 that found, among other things, evidence of extensive RUC collusion with members of the Loyalist Ulster Volunteer Force (UVF) paramilitary group that contributed directly to the deaths of a number of both nationalist and unionist civilians (O'Loan 2007).

Notably, however, both the Stevens and O'Loan enquiries report having been met with severe institutional intransigence and obfuscation on the part of former members of the RUC and the British Army, who at times engaged in the suppression or destruction of evidence. Furthermore, while these investigations have resulted in some arrests, those indicted have almost exclusively been paramilitaries or civilians employed as 'agents' by 'handlers' in the security forces, while former RUC officers, British soldiers and senior officials implicated in these organizations have largely escaped prosecution. Indeed, as an independent international panel that examined cases of alleged collusion in sectarian violence concluded in 2006 after its own extensive investigation,

> There is compelling evidence that officers of the British State—in particular, RUC officers and UDR [Ulster Defence Regiment] members and their agents—were involved in sectarian murders of Catholics. There is credible evidence that their activities were known and supported, tacitly and in some cases explicitly, by some of their RUC and UDR superiors and, to some extent, by some British intelligence and army officers. Despite this knowledge, appropriate criminal investigations and prosecutions of these murders were not conducted, even in the face of evidence amounting to probable cause for arrest.
>
> (Cassel et al. 2006: 58)

Accordingly, while these enquiries may have helped to uncover some elements of 'truth' regarding security force and paramilitary collusion in wrongful deaths during the Troubles, the translation of this truth into 'justice' in the form of criminal prosecution—particularly for agents of the British state—has to date remained greatly limited.

Furthermore, there is evidence to suggest that reactions to these enquiries have largely served to reinforce, rather than reduce, existing divisions between nationalists and unionists. For many nationalists, the enquiries only confirmed long-standing beliefs that collusion occurred during the Troubles and inflamed frustration at the lack of prosecutions for those implicated. For instance, Alex Attwood of the Social Democratic and Labour Party (SDLP) has publicly demanded in the wake of the Ombudsman's Report that "those involved in any of this—be they agents or officers or anyone else—should face the full consequences for their actions, including prosecution" (BBC News, January 22nd, 2007). More extreme unionists, on the other hand, have tended to portray the findings as 'Republican propaganda' and the enquiries themselves as 'witchhunts' undertaken against members of the security forces who were simply 'doing their jobs.' As a result, they have largely condemned any plans for future prosecutions. As Jim Spratt of the Democratic Unionist Party (DUP) has argued in his critique of the Ombudsman's 2007 findings, "if this report had had one shred of credible evidence then we could have expected charges against former Police Officers. There are no charges, so the public should draw their own conclusion, the report is clearly based on little fact" (ibid.).

Historical Enquiries Team

In 2005, these ad hoc enquiries into the past were supplemented by the development of a new standing investigations unit under the PSNI called the Historical Enquiries Team (HET). Led by David Cox, a well-respected former member of the London Metropolitan Police Service, and staffed by a team of professional police investigators, the HET has been endowed with a budget of roughly £34 million and a mandate to reopen and review existing records of Troubles-era deaths and to initiate new investigations where evidence might warrant. Notably, this includes all 'unresolved' cases, irrespective of whether the suspected perpetrator was a member of the security forces, a paramilitary or otherwise, meaning that the HET is ultimately responsible for reviewing 2,563 cases surrounding 3,268 deaths. In most instances the HET is expected to carry out these investigations itself, except where reviews reveal evidence of possible police wrongdoing and cases are referred to the Office of the Police Ombudsman of Northern Ireland for investigation. At the time of writing, the HET is proceeding in chronological order through its case investigations, and has reviewed over 830 separate cases to date (PSNI 2012a).

While a legally based policing initiative, from its inception the HET has been avowedly victim- and family-focused in its work, aiming to bring "at least a measure of knowledge and understanding" to the families of those killed during the Troubles (PSNI 2010). To achieve this goal, the HET has worked directly with the families of those killed in an attempt to acknowledge any outstanding issues related to the death in question. Moreover, following case review, the HET provides affected families with a copy of its findings (though most often with the identities of any suspected perpetrators removed due to legal restrictions). Notably, the HET has also endeavored to build ties with prominent NGO groups in Northern Ireland who have acted as intermediaries representing and working on behalf of individual victims. The HET has also developed working engagements with human rights organizations active in Northern Ireland, such as British Irish Rights Watch, the Pat Finucane Centre (PFC) and the Committee on the Administration of Justice (CAJ), which work on behalf of families wishing to have their cases reexamined. As a result of this extensive public outreach, the HET has become widely respected by nationalists and unionists alike for its ability to offer an important source of 'truth' to bereaved families by accumulating factual evidence about the deaths of their loved ones and thereby providing a measure of official acknowledgment of their loss. For example, Professor Kieran McEvoy of Queen's University Belfast praised the "high integrity" of members of the HET and noted that many victims' groups representing victims of state violence had "warm things to say" about the HET's efforts to engage with families (interview: April 17th, 2008).

That said, there are several obstacles that have limited the effectiveness of the HET's work. For instance, an independent report commissioned by the NGO Healing Through Remembering in 2006 found that the likelihood of successful prosecutions resulting from the HET's work is minimal due to the difficulties associated with the degradation of physical and eyewitness evidence in decades-old Troubles-era cases (Boyd and Doran 2006). A number of interviewees such as Mike Ritchie of the CAJ have emphasized this point, noting that the array of evidentiary challenges facing the HET's investigations makes it "highly unlikely or virtually impossible that there [will] ever be prosecutions" in most, if not all, of these historical cases (interview: April 21st, 2008). Indeed, as several prominent observers have noted, despite the HET's continued efforts to pursue prosecutions for Troubles-era cases in Northern Ireland,

> the reality is that as each day passes securing justice becomes less and less likely. . . . In many historic cases witnesses have died, exhibits are no longer credible or have disintegrated over time. The evidence collected in the 1970s, and indeed in more recent times, is highly unlikely to meet modern forensic standards. This is the reality of the situation.
>
> (CGPNI 2008)

Overall, this means that while the HET may be able to uncover the 'truth' about many of these cases, it is highly unlikely to be able to meet the demands for justice (in the form of prosecutions) that are demanded by many victims. This is a significant limitation given the sustained desire for future prosecutions for Troubles-era deaths through the criminal justice system evidenced across both communities in Northern Ireland. Indeed, survey data collected in 2004 shows that 67 percent of all respondents in Northern Ireland indicated that securing more police investigations and prosecutions was 'important' or 'very important' to them in successfully dealing with the past (with only 16 percent indicating they believed this to be 'fairly' or 'very' unimportant) (ARK 2005). Notably, while communities may differ strongly in terms of *whom* they wish to see prosecuted, agreement on the need for further investigations and prosecutions appears to cross group boundaries, being supported by a majority of both Catholics (62 percent) and Protestants (70 percent) (ibid.).

However, evidence would also seem to suggest that when prosecutions have occurred as a result of the HET's investigations into past cases, these cases have for the most part been interpreted through the sectarian lens of the nationalist/unionist divide. At the time of writing, the HET's investigations have led to a total of 72 arrests, 70 of which were related to deaths linked to Loyalist paramilitaries and only two of which were related to Republican crimes. This imbalance is largely due to the fact that 65 of these arrests were linked to Operation Ballast, a single enquiry into murders carried out by the Loyalist UVF located in North Belfast (PSNI 2012a). Nevertheless, many unionists perceive the HET arrests as having unduly targeted their community. As Brian Ervine of the Progressive Unionist Party (PUP) has argued, "the lion's share of [Troubles-era] murders were carried out by the IRA and Republicans. Yet, the lion's share of the people being arrested are Loyalists" (BBC News, June 22nd, 2011). Accordingly, as Ervine contends, the disproportionately higher arrest and conviction rate of Loyalists has been viewed as "treating the working class unionist communities with utter contempt" (Clarke 2011).

Furthermore, a recent report by Patricia Lundy of the University of Ulster has raised serious questions in regard to potential HET bias in cases that might potentially implicate the police and British security forces in Troubles-era deaths. Lundy's report reveals that, along with retired British police, former RUC officers who were active during the Troubles occupy key positions in the HET's directorate and tend to be greatly overrepresented on the HET's investigation team (Lundy 2007: 29).[6] Lundy also points to the fact that a great deal of the funding provided to the HET comes directly from the Northern Ireland Office (NIO), who, as the British government's representative in Northern Ireland, "would not be perceived as a neutral observer by most nationalists" (ibid.). Lundy contends that these structural issues have raised questions about the independence of the HET and the possibility of "a conflict of interest for families seeking answers to questions about the role of the State in the conflict" (idem: 33).

In addition, more recent work by Lundy suggests that British soldiers have received preferential treatment during the interview process as compared to other suspects investigated by the HET, raising major concerns regarding the impartiality of its enquiries into deaths caused by the security forces. Indeed, as her April 2012 report concludes, "there appears to be inequality in treatment where state agencies, in this case the military, are involved, compared to non-state or paramilitary suspects" (Lundy 2012: 8). Therefore, Lundy argues, "I don't believe [the HET] is independent. The research indicates that the interviews with soldiers are not impartial, they are not effective and they are not transparent" (BBC News, April 5th, 2012).

In the wake of Lundy's findings, many within the nationalist community in particular have raised concerns about the HET's ability to objectively investigate the potential criminal responsibility of British security forces in

Troubles-era deaths. This issue has become particularly contentious as, at the time of writing, the HET is reviewing the highly controversial 'Ballymurphy Massacre' in which eleven Catholic civilians were shot and killed by British Army soldiers over a period of three days in Belfast. These murders took place during raids carried out as part of Operation Demetrius, an effort to arrest and imprison individuals suspected of being involved with Republican paramilitaries. As a result, despite the public confidence the HET has been able to establish within the nationalist community, a number of family members of those killed have now called for an independent review of all HET cases dealing with the British Army (ibid.). In addition, perceptions of potential bias in favor of security forces have led Relatives for Justice—the largest nationalists victims' group currently operating in Northern Ireland—to advise its membership to boycott all ongoing HET investigations. Taken as a whole, the limitations on prosecutions combined with concerns raised by both nationalist and unionist communities about the independence of these investigations suggest that while the HET may be able to provide acknowledgment to the families of victims, it likely cannot act as the primary vehicle for either truth recovery or justice in Northern Ireland.

Civil society and local community initiatives

Alongside the range of legal investigations employed by the governments of Britain and Northern Ireland, a number of independent initiatives have been undertaken by non-governmental and local community organizations to explore alternative avenues for addressing the past in Northern Ireland. Chief among these has been the work of the cross-community NGO Healing Through Remembering (HTR). The organization was formed in 2001 by an independent Project Board that included representatives from nationalist and unionist communities, former members of the state security forces, and a number of NGO workers and academics working on ex-prisoners' and victims' issues. From its inception, HTR sought to explore options for truth recovery and remembrance in Northern Ireland by way of promoting the larger goals of individual and intercommunal healing—issues considered too contentious and potentially divisive to be undertaken by a government body. Indeed, under the 2002 *Reshape, Rebuild, Achieve* strategy released by the OFMDFM's Victims Unit, the GNI effectively deferred the "important and sensitive matter" of "seeking views on the development of truth and justice processes for Northern Ireland" to civil society groups like HTR (Victims Unit 2002: 16).

Accordingly, HTR undertook a lengthy consultation process with individuals and organizations across Northern Ireland to determine "how should people remember the events connected with the conflict in and about Northern Ireland and in so doing, individually and collectively contribute to healing the wounds of society" (HTR 2002: iii). On the basis of the submissions received, a 2002 report was produced by HTR and submitted to the GNI that recommended several approaches to dealing with the past. These suggestions included the creation of a Day of Private Reflection, a collective storytelling and archiving project, the building of a permanent memorial or museum, a call for all past combatants to publicly acknowledge their responsibility for past political violence, and the establishment of an independent research team to identify practicable options for a mechanism of inclusive truth recovery and acknowledgment (ibid.).

This initial work led to the establishment of a specialized working subgroup within HTR on Truth Recovery and Acknowledgment, whose membership included representatives from nationalist and unionist communities, members of victims' groups, academics and local community actors, as well as individuals from Loyalist, Republican, military and policing backgrounds. Following a two-year period of research and consultation, in 2004 this group released its own report, entitled *Making Peace With the Past: Options for Truth Recovery Regarding the Conflict in and about Northern Ireland* (McEvoy 2006). This report sought to counter the assumption that a single truth-recovery mechanism would be required—or even feasible—in Northern Ireland given the persistence of deep divisions between communities over perceptions of the past. Instead, the report outlined four separate practical options for truth recovery that might usefully be drawn upon individually or in combination. These included options for internal investigations within security forces and paramilitary organizations, community-based 'bottom-up' truth-recovery initiatives, the creation of an independent truth commission (loosely modeled on the South African TRC) and the establishment of a 'Commission of Historical Clarification' which would attempt to create a broad shared historical narrative of what occurred during the Troubles. However, the report highlights that these potential initiatives would need to operate independently of the state and of any communal political interest, and would have to be able to effectively acknowledge the mutual complicity of all parties involved in past violence. Above all, the report underscores that any future truth recovery processes in Northern Ireland must prioritize the needs of victims and attempt, wherever possible, to seek to repair their losses through acknowledgment, service provision, and compensation (ibid.).

However, it should be noted that much of the widely respected work of HTR, while certainly invaluable for promoting increased dialogue and discussion about the past, has been largely left at the conceptual stage due to continued divides within Northern Ireland and fears that one community might use these processes to appropriate the past for its own ends. To date this has meant that only two of the most 'apolitical' projects suggested by HTR have been put into actual practice in Northern Ireland. This included the creation in 2007 of a 'Day of Private Reflection,' to be held on June 21st of each year to allow people from Northern Ireland, Great Britain and the Republic of Ireland to "acknowledge the deep hurt and pain caused by the conflict, to reflect on our own attitudes, on what more we might have done or still do, and to make a personal commitment that such loss should never be allowed to happen again" (HTR 2012). More recently, HTR also undertook a two-year project in conjunction with Queen's University Belfast to document existing public and private collections of conflict-related artifacts in Northern Ireland (arms, equipment, flags, clothing, audio/visual recordings, photographs and printed materials) and to make them available through an online database.

Local community initiatives

At a more local level, several unofficial 'grassroots' truth recovery efforts have also emerged organically to fill the gap left by the absence of a formalized transitional justice mechanism and the continued distrust of state-led initiatives dealing with the past. These have tended to be 'single-identity' projects taking place within local communities of nationalists or unionists which are already largely in agreement about responsibility for past violence.

Perhaps the most prominent example of these initiatives has been the Ardoyne Commemoration Project (ACP). The ACP was created in 1998 within the small nationalist community of Ardoyne in North Belfast as a response to the perceived 'hierarchy of victims' that many nationalists believed was being perpetuated by the GNI's existing victims' policies. Indeed, from its inception, the ACP's guiding ethos was 'the equality of victims,' with no one from the Ardoyne community being excluded from the collective memory being established "because of their religious or political beliefs, the circumstances of their death, or the agency responsible for it" (Lundy and McGovern 2002: 2). Accordingly, the ACP sought to fulfill a desire among community members to acknowledge and commemorate their victims in an effort "to set the record straight" as a "counter to state-sanctioned forgetting" (Lundy and McGovern 2002: 2). In this capacity, the ACP worked to collect over 300 oral interviews with members of the Ardoyne community over a period of four years, ultimately recording the stories of the 99 individuals killed over the course of the Troubles within that neighborhood. Local ownership and participation was considered essential to the success of the project, with each of the 300 interviewees retaining ultimate editorial control over his/her statements. In 2002, these testimonies were published in a volume edited by Patricia Lundy and Mark McGovern entitled *Ardoyne: The Untold Truth*, a copy of which was then distributed to all of those who had participated in the process.

Evaluations show that participation in the ACP provided community members with an important source of acknowledgment and recognition for the losses suffered during the Troubles, with many participants reporting that the project helped them to overcome the 'denial of truth' about events in Ardoyne that they felt dominated official state accounts (Lundy and

McGovern 2005: x). Others reported that the act of storytelling itself was a very therapeutic experience, noting that the existence of a forum in which people were willing to listen to the accounts of victims was important for their own healing (ibid.). In particular, many participants noted that the ACP had helped to open space for community dialogue and debate about the past and had broken the "culture of silence" that surrounded previously "taboo" subjects within the community, such as the role played by Republicans in the internal violence that resulted in the deaths of many nationalists in Ardoyne during the Troubles. This newfound openness was held to have played a vital role in reducing continued intracommunity tensions and in "stimulating self-reflection and shifting long-held viewpoints" about the past (ibid.).

Further, Patricia Lundy suggests that the ACP may also have helped to build a greater willingness among participants to engage in future cross-community truth-recovery projects with unionists and representatives of the British security forces. Indeed, Lundy contends that the successes of local single-identity projects such as the ACP evidence the importance of 'sequencing' truth recovery efforts in a highly politicized context like Northern Ireland, with intracommunal truth recovery being the first necessary 'building block' for people to develop the sense of self-confidence, security and receptiveness necessary to grapple with the much more contentious issues surrounding cross-community truth-telling. As she argues, "it's about timing, it's about people getting to a particular level where they can deal with things—and that's the learning process, I think. You cannot just throw people in with all of those emotions and possibly anger to talk about such contentious and sensitive issues without being exposed to that at some level before" (interview: April 22nd, 2008). Accordingly, Lundy suggests that grassroots truth-recovery processes like the ACP demonstrate a need to consider a 'staged' approach that begins with smaller, more localized intracommunity processes before expanding outwards to deal with the much more difficult and divisive issues associated with cross-community efforts.

However, while local initiatives like the ACP have an important role to play in divided societies like Northern Ireland where there may be competing visions of the past, it is also recognized that they will likely be insufficient in and of themselves to meet the broader societal demands for truth and justice necessary for reconciliation. As Lundy and McGovern note, community-level organizations will by definition be limited in their ability to gain new information from statutory agencies outside the community, to obtain official recognition or compensation for victims, or to pursue any form of legal accountability for those implicated in their findings (2005: xii). Accordingly, they suggest that local truth-recovery efforts should be considered only one component of a larger 'parallel process' of multiple initiatives to be employed within divided societies by way of sufficiently addressing the past (ibid.).

Furthermore, it is recognized that the competing truths that might emerge from a series of hermetic processes among local communities must ultimately themselves be reconciled with one another to some degree to allow for a broader process of socioemotional learning and reconciliation. In essence, the creation of single-identity truths among nationalists and unionists, while important, must eventually pave the way to a shared cross-community acknowledgment of the past if the goal is to move beyond existing divisions. Indeed, as Lundy and McGovern contend, for Northern Ireland, "reconciliation is impossible in the absence of such a truth-telling process when a section of the population can continue to deny that the state ever acted wrongly whilst another section feels their suffering has never been acknowledged" (2001: 30).

Assessing socioemotional learning in Northern Ireland

From the preceding review of Northern Ireland's piecemeal approach to addressing the past, it is clear that some aspects of socioemotional learning have been forwarded by the range of discrete initiatives undertaken by government, NGOs and the local community/voluntary sector. However, it is equally evident that there still exists no agreement in Northern Ireland as to the moral responsibility of state and non-state actors for past violence, or as to which actors should legitimately be assigned the roles of victim, perpetrator or innocent bystander. As a result, the past is still typically perceived through the zero-sum lens of existing communal divides, meaning that more comprehensive attempts to advance truth and justice for past abuses have been met with mistrust, suspicion and fear. These obstructions have, in turn, greatly impeded opportunities for the kinds of inclusive socioemotional learning that are ultimately needed to advance intergroup reconciliation in Northern Ireland.

Indeed, as Nadler and Shnabel have warned, this is a common danger in post-conflict societies where no clear agreement exists as to responsibility for past violence, and where all actors view themselves as the only 'true' victims of conflict. As they illustrate,

> under these conditions of 'double victimhood' processes of socioemotional learning are more difficult. Since both parties view themselves as the victims they regard the other as the perpetrator who is responsible for . . . admitting responsibility for past wrongdoings. This is likely to lead to an impasse and an inability to move forward with socioemotional social learning.
>
> (Nadler and Shnabel 2008: 39)

In Northern Ireland, the stalemate over addressing the past caused by this sense of mutual victimization has only been further exacerbated by the inclusion of the British state and security forces as a third 'victimized' party—a party that, with few exceptions, has been extremely hesitant to publicly admit to any wrongful culpability for the violence of the Troubles.

This continued barrier to socioemotional learning is perhaps most evident in reactions to a recent effort initiated on behalf of the British government to replace Northern Ireland's piecemeal strategy for dealing with the past with a more centralized intervention. In 2007, the Secretary for Northern Ireland announced the formation of an 'Independent Consultative Group on the Past' (CGPNI) which was mandated "to consult across the community on how Northern Ireland society can best approach the legacy of the events of the past 40 years" and "to make recommendations, as appropriate, on any steps that might be taken to support Northern Ireland society in building a shared future not overshadowed by the events of the past" (CGPNI 2009: 22). To cement its credentials as an impartial body, the CGPNI included an array of representatives from nationalist, unionist and British communities in addition to international advisors. Following its creation, the CGPNI embarked on a major review of the existing ad hoc mechanisms for addressing the past as well as an extensive eighteen-month consultation process in Northern Ireland, the Irish Republic and Great Britain. Building on this foundation, the CGPNI set out to make recommendations for comprehensively confronting the past based on the guiding principle that "the past should be dealt with in a manner which enables society to become more defined by its desire for true and lasting reconciliation rather than by division and mistrust, seeking to promote a shared and reconciled future for all" (idem: 13). These recommendations were released in January 2009 with the publication of the *Report of the Consultative Group on the Past* (ibid.).

Among other initiatives, the Report recommended the creation of an independent 'Legacy Commission' which, loosely following the structures of the South African TRC, would serve to centralize "processes of reconciliation, justice and information recovery" with the "overarching objective of promoting peace and stability in Northern Ireland" (idem: 6). Chaired by an independent International Commission and working under a five-year mandate with a proposed budget of £300 million, this Legacy Commission would effectively take over the examination of historical cases from the OPONI and HET under a new Review and Investigation Unit, engage in a separate process of truth recovery and inquiry into the past through a series of public hearings, and create a Truth Recovery and Thematic Investigations Unit to replace the current use of public inquiry processes to look into issues of concern stemming from past violence.

In conjunction with the CSVNI, the proposed Legacy Commission would also include a Reconciliation Forum that would centralize support services for victims. This Forum would also provide means for commemorating victims by way of a storytelling initiative, the continuation of an annual Day of Reflection and Reconciliation, and the creation of a shared memorial of the conflict. Perhaps most controversially, in an attempt to allay current perceptions of a 'hierarchy of victims,' the report also suggested a one-time 'recognition payment' of £12,000 to the families of all those who died as a result of the conflict regardless of political affiliation or status (whether civilian, paramilitary combatant or member of the policing or security forces) (idem: 21).

However, upon its release the CGPNI's Report was met with controversy, bitter condemnation and angry protests that revealed the continued sense of victimization and deep division surrounding the violence of the past (Burns 2009). This outcry was spearheaded by the vocal reactions of those who lost relatives during the Troubles, many of whom focused their attacks on the plans to treat all victims of the conflict equally in terms of access to proposed reparations. For instance, one unionist woman whose brother, an RUC police officer, was killed in a 1997 Republican paramilitary attack, charged that her brother "was an innocent man defending this whole community. When IRA men died while launching cowardly attacks on this community, they actually received justice. The families of those murderers should not be consoled with a single penny today" (ibid.). Similarly, Peter Robinson, leader of the DUP and current First Minister of Northern Ireland's Assembly, responded to the CGPNI Report by saying that his party has "consistently opposed any equation between the perpetrator of the crimes during the Troubles and the innocent victim," contending that "[t]errorists died carrying out their evil and wicked deeds while innocent men, women, and children were wiped out by merciless gangsters" (ibid.). As a direct result of these reactions, in February 2009, Shaun Woodward, then Secretary of State for Northern Ireland, publicly rejected the implementation of the reparations scheme proposed by the CGPNI, noting that "very clearly the time is not right for a recognition payment" (BBC News, February 25th, 2009).

The continued intractability of the polarized perceptions evidenced in these statements does not bode well for the realization of the CGPNI's recommendations for a more comprehensive or centralized approach to dealing with the past in Northern Ireland in the near future. This difficulty was recognized by Rev. Robin Eames, one of the two co-chairs of the CGPNI, who conceded in the wake of the protests following the report's release that "[m]aybe this gesture, for those outside our group, is too sudden" (Burns 2009). More recently, an Inquiry led by the British Northern Ireland Affairs Committee into the feasibility of implementing the CGP's recommendations produced a report released in December 2009 which concluded that

> [t]he fact that public reaction was so strong is itself evidence of the need to address the deep-rooted divisions that continue to exist within Northern Ireland. The sectional divisiveness of that reaction in itself highlighted the danger that implementing proposals not supported by the two main parts of the community in Northern Ireland would do more harm than good. . . . We have reluctantly concluded that there is

not enough cross-community consensus at present on many of the issues that the Consultative Group raised for the wide-ranging project that it recommended to succeed. . . . Without that, it could not hope effectively to fulfill its mandate of helping to lead Northern Ireland towards reconciliation and a peaceful shared future.

(Ibid.)

As a result, the Committee ultimately determined that due to the fact that "Northern Ireland has not yet reached a consensus on how to move on from its recent past," plans to move forward with the CGPNI's proposals were premature (NIAC 2009).

Overall, these findings suggest that despite the contributions made by the 'piecemeal' array of governmental and non-governmental efforts to provide acknowledgment, accountability and a shared memory of the Troubles, attempts to address the past remain highly divisive in Northern Ireland. As a result, efforts to promote socioemotional learning through truth and justice, on the other hand, appear to have been much less successful to date. In particular, a deep sense of unjust victimization, unresolved arguments about the morality of past violence, and a fear that the Other community might try to appropriate the history of the conflict for its own political agenda continue to impede attempts to deal more comprehensively with the past. These divides continue to serve as barriers to the advancement of social learning and intergroup reconciliation in Northern Ireland.

Socioemotional learning and the South African TRC

As institutions of transitional justice, truth commissions focus primarily on providing a full and official acknowledgment of past abuses "to establish an accurate record of a country's past, clarify uncertain events, and lift the lid of silence and denial from a contentious and painful period of history" (Hayner 2002: 25). The South African TRC was no exception. Indeed, the TRC's primary mandate was to promote elements of both truth and justice in order to address the legacy of abuses committed during the apartheid era and to advance its broader overarching goal of national reconciliation.

At the time of transition, many of the abuses committed during the apartheid era—particularly those carried out by members of the ruling National Party (NP) government and security forces against members of the black majority—remained largely uninvestigated, meaning that most victims had received little in the way of justice in the form of either acknowledgment or accountability. Further, the facts surrounding many of the abuses committed under the apartheid system were shrouded in secrecy and denial, with the result that many family members of those killed, tortured or 'disappeared' were left wondering what had happened to their loved ones and who was ultimately responsible for these crimes. Accordingly, it was widely recognized that in order to begin processes of both individual and national healing following South Africa's transition to democracy, there would be a need both to end impunity for past crimes and to establish "as complete a picture as possible of the causes, nature and extent of the gross violations of human rights" committed during the struggle over apartheid between 1960 and 1994 (GSA 1994).

In addition, the TRC's investigations into past human rights abuses were also considered to be a vital element in countering the divisive interpretations held by black and white South Africans of the abuses committed during apartheid-era violence. For many black South Africans, abuses committed against members of the complicit white minority—both civilians and members of the government and security forces—were viewed as justified components of a liberation struggle carried out to end the institutionalized racism of the apartheid regime. Conversely, many in the white community were constantly exposed to state propaganda that portrayed violent actions undertaken by the government security forces as necessary efforts to protect the country from an insurgent threat posed by 'godless communists' and terrorists within the black majority (TRC 1998: vol 1, ch. 2, para. 56). Perceptions of the past were further complicated by the apartheid government's concerted attempts to promote division, distrust and violence between different ethnic and political factions as part of a broader strategy to "divide and conquer" the majority (Chapman and van der Merwe 2008b: 6). Indeed, in describing the apartheid system, former Deputy TRC Commissioner Alex Boraine explains that "South Africa has come out of a period in which its society was based on lies and deceit . . . [one] in which radio and television were little more than giant propaganda factories producing a packaged product to reinforce oppression and exclusivity" (Boraine 2000: 151).

Accordingly, as Chapman and van der Merwe detail, at the time of South Africa's transition, "the public memory of [the liberation struggle] was (and largely still is) racially divided," with the result that "the causes, nature, and extent of the violence have been deeply contested" (2008b: 7). For this reason, establishing an official, unbiased account of past events was crucial to fulfilling the Commission's broader goal of building national unity and reconciliation, as it offered a potential corrective to interpreting the past in "partisan, selective ways" or through "narrow memories" that might otherwise "all too easily provide the basis for mobilization towards further conflicts" (TRC 1998: vol. 2, ch. 5, para. 51). As Elizabeth Kiss notes, from its outset, the TRC "made a special point" to use its hearings and investigations to help discredit some of the "widely circulated accusations and counteraccusations" that could otherwise "easily provide the basis for mobilization towards further conflicts" following South Africa's transition (2000: 72). By including victims, bystanders, and perpetrators in its truth-recovery and justice processes, the Commission sought to build "an inclusive remembering of painful truths about the past" that could be shared among South Africans of all races, a task ultimately considered "crucial to the creation of national unity and transcending the divisions of the past" (TRC 1998: vol.1, ch. 5, para. 51).

Truth and the TRC process

Several of the TRC's innovations with regard to truth recovery were designed to contribute to this more 'inclusive remembering' of the past. The first of these involved the collection of statements from 21,519 individual victims of apartheid-era violence through the Commission's HRVC (Human Rights Violations Committee). Of this number, a representative number of 1,800 victims drawn from different racial groups were also given the opportunity to testify and provide their accounts publicly through the nearly 100 public victim and community hearings held across South Africa by the HRVC. Second, the unique conditional amnesty provision of the TRC helped to encourage over 7,000 perpetrators—including members of the black liberation movement as well as those who fought against them in the police and security forces of the apartheid government—to provide full accountings of their own past complicity in human rights violations to the Amnesty Committee (AC).

In addition, the Commission's Institutional Hearings offered a window onto the roles played in apartheid-era oppression by several key sectors of South African society, such as business, the media, the legal system and state security forces. Its Special Theme hearings, on the other hand, were designed to build an understanding of some of the broader patterns of the abuses committed under apartheid, such as the impact of violence on children, youth and women, as well as to illuminate the details of several key past events. The Commission's Investigation Unit worked to collect and analyze information in order to corroborate victim and perpetrator statements made before the HRVC and AC. Similarly, its Research Department examined submissions made to the TRC and used existing archival material to help establish a truthful historical picture of patterns of human rights abuses committed under apartheid. Alongside these more investigatory processes, the TRC also created a Register of Reconciliation where bystanders—those neither directly victimized by, nor perpetrators of, apartheid violence—could contribute personal reflections on their own experiences under apartheid. A detailed official summary of the findings from all of these facets of the TRC's truth-recovery efforts was collected and published in the TRC's Final Report in 1998.

Based on the TRC's many truth-recovery efforts, the Commission was able to establish elements of a 'macro' truth detailing the broader patterns of responsibility for apartheid-era abuses in its final report.[7] One of the principal judgments reached in the TRC's Report was an unambiguous condemnation of apartheid as a 'crime against humanity' due to its "enforced system of racial discrimination, separation and repression" (TRC 1998: vol. 1, ch. 2, para. 1). The TRC also made important determinations regarding ultimate responsibility for the range of human rights abuses committed between 1960 and 1994, including widespread killings, abductions, torture and severe ill-treatment of victims. Overall, it found that the former South African state under the National Party (NP) and its security and law-enforcement agencies were responsible for the greatest number of these violations, abuses often carried out under the direct orders of senior politicians and security officials. The TRC also determined the Inkatha Freedom Party (IFP) to be the primary non-state perpetrator of gross human rights violations and the major overall perpetrator of killings on a national scale (most of which targeted supporters of the rival ANC (African National Congress) party), with evidence that the IFP had operated in direct collusion with elements of the apartheid state in many of these actions. Finally, to a lesser extent, the TRC also found the ANC culpable for gross human rights violations carried out in pursuit of its armed liberation struggle, noting, in particular, the crimes that were carried out in ANC camps while in exile and the large numbers of civilians killed by members of its 'MK' military wing (TRC 1998: vol. 5, ch. 6).

Alongside these broader findings, the HRVC and AC's extensive investigations also contributed to establishing a more 'micro'-level truth by helping to uncover previously unknown or undocumented factual evidence about what took place in individual cases of physical human rights violations committed during the apartheid era. For its part, through its statement-gathering and public hearing processes, the HRVC officially recorded the personal stories and accounts of nearly 22,000 victims of apartheid-era violence from all racial backgrounds, leading to the collection of new evidence in more than 30,384 cases of human rights violations.[8] As Fanie du Toit suggests, this provided a "personal truth to victims about what happened to their loved ones," while also building the foundation for a detailed factual record of specific apartheid-era abuses (interview: June 18th, 2008). In addition, as many observers have noted, by combining the 'carrot' of amnesty with the 'stick' of threatened prosecutions for those who didn't participate in its AC process, the TRC was able to gain access to new information from perpetrators that would likely have remained out of reach had a blanket amnesty or adversarial criminal prosecutions been employed (Hayner 2000; Chapman and van der Merwe 2008b). Indeed, as Priscilla Hayner contends, by offering a conditional amnesty in exchange for factual information about past human rights violations, the TRC effectively "turned the amnesty application process into a tool to uncover details of past crimes, making South Africa the first country in the world to hear detailed testimony about crimes from the perpetrators themselves" (Hayner 2000: 36).

However, despite these contributions, there were several significant limitations to both the macro- and micro-level truths that were uncovered by the TRC. For instance, as several observers have noted, the voices of many potentially eligible victims were left out of the HRVC process as many remained unaware of how to apply to participate in the TRC (van der Merwe 2001a). Further, a recent analysis of the HRVC proceedings conducted by Audrey Chapman and Patrick Ball reveals that fully 90 percent of statements contributed to the HRVC were from black South Africans—a significant overrepresentation relative to their percentage of the overall South African population. At the same time, due to the TRC's avowed desire to be even-handed in its approach to recognizing the suffering of all racial groups, white South Africans who provided statements before the HRVC were four times as likely to be asked to appear to testify publicly, a number that may have falsely equated the harms faced by blacks and whites under apartheid. Additionally, evidence shows that some key groups, such as the liberation movements, were grossly underrepresented throughout the HRVC process due to pressure from political leaders who discouraged members from coming forward or a personal reluctance to acknowledge their status as 'victims' of apartheid violence (Chapman and Ball 2008).

At the same time, other critics have noted that the narrow legal focus of the AC on making determinations about individual cases meant that it often neglected to examine the broader context in which abuses occurred, particularly regarding the potential responsibility of more senior political and military figures in the chain of command (Chapman and van der Merwe 2008a). Accordingly, while the AC did provide an avenue for hearing accounts from perpetrators, most key leadership figures from the apartheid government, the ANC and the IFP simply refused to participate in the hearings, meaning that those who did come forward were most often foot soldiers or 'trigger-pullers' who had little knowledge of the broader scope of human rights abuses (Chapman and Ball 2008: 165).[9] As Howard Varney, former Head of the TRC's Investigations Unit, illustrates, "a lot of senior people who knew the truth didn't come forward . . . [w]e didn't see National Party leaders in the form of De Klerk or P.W. Botha coming through and acting like statesmen. Most of the security force and military hierarchy didn't come forward to speak the truth" (interview: June 24th, 2008). Further, other observers have noted that perpetrators belonging to certain groups, including the South African Defence Force, the IFP and the NP, were also significantly underrepresented in the AC process, which may have created a somewhat distorted view of overall political responsibility for past crimes (Ernest 2004).

In addition, the TRCs Investigation Unit, which was given the prodigious task of corroborating both the validity of HRVC victims' statements and the testimony provided by AC applicants, was severely hampered by chronic understaffing, a lack of adequate resources and related managerial and bureaucratic difficulties. As a result, the Unit was ultimately able to review the facts of only a small percentage of the claims made before the AC and so remained limited in its ability to determine whether perpetrators had 'fully disclosed' information about past violations (Chapman and van der Merwe 2008a). The work of the Investigation Unit was further confounded by the wholesale destruction of state documents by the NP government prior to South Africa's transition—an act that eliminated a key source of primary data about the human rights abuses committed under apartheid. As the TRC's Final Report details, "the former government deliberately and systematically destroyed a huge body of state records and documentation in an attempt to remove incriminating evidence and thereby sanitize the history of oppressive rule" (TRC 1998: vol. 1, ch. 8, para. 1). Indeed, Fanie du Toit of the IJR notes that "once the TRC started working, the government shredding machines worked twice as hard," leading to a large-scale destruction of documents that might otherwise have granted access to some crucial aspects of the truth surrounding apartheid-era abuses (interview: June 18th, 2008).

Further, perhaps one of the most significant limitations placed on the TRC's ability to uncover the truth surrounding apartheid-era abuses stemmed from the fact that the Commission's founding Act largely restricted the HRVC and AC to investigating individual cases of physical gross human rights violations such as killing, abduction, torture or severe ill-treatment (GSA 1995). As a number of critics have noted, this narrow focus, while important for helping to establish the 'micro truth' about specific violations, may nonetheless have unintentionally prevented the Commission from engaging with the deeper 'macro truths' about the structural, racial and ideological elements of the apartheid system that ultimately drove such abuses. Accordingly, as Chapman and van der Merwe illustrate, the TRC's tendency to treat the human rights violations it investigated "as discrete events rather than as manifestations of a pattern to accomplish defined objectives" meant that it "often dealt with the institutionalized racism of the apartheid system primarily as background" (2008b: 249). They therefore conclude that despite some of the evidence collected through the TRC's broader Institutional Hearings, in the main, "the Commission failed to link the structural dynamics of the apartheid system to the abuses of the apartheid era." This obscured crucial aspects of the truth about past abuses, as such abuses were considered almost exclusively "as the product of individuals' decisions and actions rather than the intentional outcome of the dynamics of the apartheid system" (idem: 249–250).

It would also appear that there have been some issues with the dissemination of the truths that were uncovered through the Commission's investigations to the general public. While many South Africans were exposed to the public hearings of the TRC by virtue of the extensive media coverage they received, to date very few have ever had access to the volumes of the Commission's final report—the only detailed source of many of its findings. In large part, this is due to the fact that no easily accessible copy of the Report was ever created for widespread consumption aside from the rather ponderous (and very expensive) official multi-volume hardcover set released by the Commission.[10] As a result, many of the findings included in the TRC's Report have remained beyond the reach of most South Africans, for whom they were supposedly intended, and have ironically been read primarily by foreign researchers and academics (Chapman and van der Merwe 2008a). As Madeleine Fullard, a former member of the TRC's Research Unit notes, within South Africa "essentially the TRC Report is invisible . . . you can't really say that the report has had an impact on South African society. I wonder if even one percent of South Africans have ever looked at the TRC Report. . . . I worked on writing sections of it and I can tell you I've never read it from cover to cover and I doubt I ever will [as it's a] vast thing" (interview: July 8th, 2008).

Finally, despite the Commission's contributions to establishing the truth about apartheid-era human rights abuses, there also remains a clear discrepancy among racial groups in terms of how the TRC's efforts to provide a relatively impartial and unbiased account of the past have been perceived. This divide was apparent even before the work of the Commission began, with many whites fearing that the TRC would function as a political tool of the ANC party that could be used to scapegoat members of the white community. In May 1995, just as the TRC was getting under way, 63 percent of whites reported that they doubted the TRC would be able to uncover 'what really happened' with regard to past crimes, while 72 percent of blacks remained confident the TRC would succeed in its goals (HSRC 1995). This view appears to have stayed largely unchanged following the completion of the Commission's work, with survey data from 2000 and 2001 revealing that only 34.5 percent of all white respondents believed that the TRC had done an 'excellent' or 'very good' job in providing a true and unbiased account of the country's history, as compared to 85.1 percent of blacks surveyed (Gibson and Macdonald 2001: 20).

That said, other public opinion polls would seem to indicate that, despite these perceptions of bias, most South Africans do believe that in the end the TRC did largely succeed in uncovering the 'truth' about past abuses. For instance, a 1998 poll showed that half of respondents (both black and white) felt that the Commission had ultimately been successful in its truth-recovery efforts. Of this number, only 5 percent of blacks believed that the TRC had failed in obtaining the 'truth' about past events, though a somewhat larger number (39 percent) of white South Africans felt this was the case (HSRC 1998). Nevertheless, by 2000–2001, over 63 percent of white South African respondents were ready to agree that overall the TRC had done an 'excellent' or 'pretty good job' in helping the families of victims find out what had happened to their loved ones, alongside 88.7 percent of their black counterparts (Gibson and Macdonald 2001: 20).

Socioemotional learning from the TRC's truth

Overall, in spite of these limitations, evidence suggests that the truth-recovery efforts of the TRC have been quite successful in helping to advance socioemotional learning by contributing to the creation of a shared understanding of apartheid-era violence and a common memory of the past that has now been widely accepted across racial groups in South Africa. Survey data collected during James Gibson's 2000–2001 study reveals that following the work of the TRC, an overwhelming majority of both black (94.3 percent) and white (72.9 percent) South Africans indicated that they agreed that apartheid was a 'crime against humanity' that needed to be brought to an end, and that many horrific acts were committed by the government in the name of racial separation (Gibson 2004: 80). Further, findings from the same survey suggest that as a result of the Commission's work, a majority of both black (76.1 percent) and white (73.8 percent) South Africans have accepted that "those struggling for and against apartheid did unforgiveable things," thereby recognizing a degree of mutual complicity among all racial groups for the violence of the past (ibid.).

This shared recognition seems to be directly related to widespread public exposure among South Africans to the stories of victims and perpetrators from both racial groups who came forward to testify at the Commission's public hearings. For whites, hearing the stories of murder, torture and other human rights abuses committed by the police and government security forces made it impossible to deny that gross violations had been committed on behalf of the apartheid state (Minow 1998: 75). Similarly, for many blacks, the TRC findings showed that actions taken on behalf of the liberation struggle were not always just, while also revealing that many innocent whites had also had been unfairly victimized over the course of past violence (ibid.). As a result, it seems that the TRC was ultimately successful in contributing to a mutual acceptance of a more 'balanced truth' surrounding past abuses, a truth that has helped to moderate some of the more polarized views developed throughout the apartheid period. As Gibson illustrates,

> [a]s a result of the revelations of the TRC, many whites seem to have been convinced to abandon the view that those struggling to preserve the apartheid state were noble and that those challenging the state were vile. Many blacks, on the other hand, learned from the TRC that the liberation forces also committed heinous acts, just as they were shown that at least some of the worst abuses of apartheid were associated with rogue individuals. If nothing else, the TRC seems to have laid to rest some of the fictions that each side in the struggle mobilized to defend its positions and legitimacy. The effect of the TRC seems to have been to move blacks and whites closer together in their understandings of the country's past.
>
> (2004: 98–99)

Indeed, these examples of socioemotional learning appear to be directly linked to the findings revealed by the TRC's truth-recovery process, which showed undeniably that atrocities had been committed by members of both groups during the apartheid struggle and directly challenged perceptions that either side was engaged in a wholly 'just war' or was the only party victimized by past conflict. For instance, the TRC hearings managed to convince many black South Africans that not all whites were committed to the cause of racial repression, and that a number of innocent white victims (with, of course, many innocent black victims alongside them) had suffered as a result of the liberation struggle. As Gibson illustrates, in this way "many black South Africans most likely came away from the truth and reconciliation process believing that the struggle against apartheid was indeed a 'just war' but that many unjust and inhumane actions were taken in the name of liberation" (2004: 162).

Likewise, the TRC's findings appear to have contributed to breaking down myths propagated by apartheid-era governments that suggested that the state was acting justly to protect the country against a terrorist insurgency being waged by 'godless communists' within the black majority. In a survey in 2000 and 2001 76.6 percent of whites indicated that they were "unaware of state atrocities against opponents of apartheid" prior to the work of the TRC, with many whites frequently expressing shock when confronted by the stories and images of human rights abuses revealed during the Commission's hearings (Gibson and Macdonald 2001: 29). The truth revealed by the TRC process therefore appears to have opened the space for crucial processes of socio-emotional learning among many white South Africans, as "whites who were attentive to the truth and reconciliation process learned that their side was less than noble in creating and defending apartheid, that they had been duped and lied to by their own leaders, and that the opposition was perhaps less radically evil in its efforts to create a new system in South Africa" (Gibson 2004: 161).

Perhaps most importantly, the shared acceptance of this more moderate truth about the past facilitated by the TRC has led, in turn, to an increase in positive attitudes and perceptions between black and white South Africans in the post-apartheid era. Indeed, Gibson's 2004 study reveals that among white South Africans in particular, exposure to a more balanced truth surrounding apartheid-era violence led to a "substantively significant" and "remarkably strong" increase in the likelihood that individuals would hold more racially reconciled attitudes towards black South Africans, including a decrease in stereotypes, prejudices and existing feelings of intergroup threat and hostility (ibid.: 132). A similar, although somewhat weaker, correlation between acceptance of the TRC's balanced truth and racially reconciled attitudes towards whites was also evidenced among black South Africans (ibid.: 161).[11]

Overall, these findings were echoed by a general consensus among those experts interviewed in South Africa that the TRC's truth-recovery efforts, while by no means perfect, did indeed contribute to a shared understanding of the past and therefore served as a vital source of socioemotional learning and a platform on which future interracial reconciliation could be built. In particular, several indicated that, despite the potential gaps in the 'truth' it collected, the TRC was able to create an official 'big picture' account of the abuses committed during South Africa's apartheid past that is now widely accepted by members of all racial groups. As Howard Varney explains,

> If there's no truth on the table, if people don't know what happened, there's little chance for reconciliation. Knowledge of the basic story, I think, is an essential requirement. The fact is most people have a good idea of what the story is anyways, but it is good to see it in an official form. I think the SATRC report, although it can be criticized, put that basic story down for the official record . . . the truth commission placed what I would call the 'essential truth' on the table, the central story, which was largely correct. There was a lot missing from it . . . but I don't think it's true to say those omissions and shortcomings mean that there was no reconciliation—there was some.
>
> (Interview: June 24th, 2008)

This point was echoed by former TRC Commissioner Mary Burton, who notes that as a result of the TRC's truth-recovery efforts, it is now "impossible to deny that apartheid was a crime against humanity [as] the grand narrative and the broad strokes of this narrative are in place and there is consensus about that. . . . You cannot deny the general parameters of what apartheid was about and what actually happened—that's all in place and that's all official in a sense" (interview: June 23rd, 2008).

Similarly, other interviewees such as Wilhem Verwoerd, a former member of the TRC's Research Unit, contend that the truth assembled by the Commission has been a crucial element in the ongoing process of national reconciliation, as "even though not everything was told, it provide[d] a basis on which we can say we have a shared understanding of what happened in the past. . . . Basically it said to the entire nation, this is where you come from, this is your past, and this should never happen again" (interview: April 29th, 2008). As Brandon Hamber and Richard Wilson have noted, while the broader truth about the past recovered by the TRC may not in itself be sufficient for the creation of national unity in post-apartheid South Africa, it nonetheless has helped to lay the groundwork for a more reconciled future. As they detail, "by having this shared memory of the past, and a common identity as a traumatized people, the country can, at least ideally, move on to a future in which the same mistakes will not be repeated" (2003: 144).

Despite these contributions, there do appear to be limits to the extent of the socioemotional learning facilitated by the TRC's truth-recovery efforts. Indeed, while the TRC appears to have successfully helped to convince many South Africans that apartheid was a crime against humanity and that unconscionable acts were carried out in its defense, the narrow focus of the truth-recovery efforts carried out by the HVRC and AC hearings may nevertheless have inadvertently made it possible for others to dismiss crimes committed by the state's policing and security forces as the rogue behavior of a handful of individual actors rather than the result of the unjust structures of the apartheid system itself. As Charles Villa-Vicencio, former head of the Research Department for the TRC, contends, since the TRC's investigations often didn't follow accountability up the chain of command or seek to establish the broader patterns of abuses committed by the state, "such killers and torturers [were] represented as psychopaths, aberrations, and misfits . . . the 'rotten eggs' among the other disciplined, professional security force members" (2000b: 74).

This contention is clearly reflected in the data collected as part of Gibson's 2000–2001 survey. Gibson's results reveal that even following the work of the TRC, 43.2 percent of white South Africans and 41.1 percent of black South Africans indicated that they agreed that "the abuses of apartheid were due to evil individuals, not state institutions themselves" (2004: 80–81). These findings were echoed by Chapman and van der Merwe, who, based on findings derived from their own more recent 2008 study, conclude that

> [i]t seems very likely that the human rights violations and amnesty hearings, with their focus on survivor statements of individual survivors and amnesty applications by individual perpetrators, deflected blame away from apartheid institutions and the political system and focused it on individuals.
>
> (2008a: 254)

As a result of these limitations, they conclude that "to the extent that the TRC sought to get people to understand that apartheid of the state and its institutions, not of specific individuals, it seems not to have been particularly successful" (ibid.).

Further, and perhaps even more troublingly, Chapman and van der Merwe also highlight that the TRC's tendency to blame individuals and its limited ability to clearly establish the broader structural responsibility of the apartheid system for past human rights violations has allowed many individual white South Africans to avoid "coming to terms with their own complicity in overtly or tacitly supporting the apartheid system and benefitting from its structural inequalities" (ibid.). Survey data collected in 2001 and 2002 following the conclusion of the TRC's substantive work reveals that over half (51 percent) of white South Africans indicated a belief that "despite its abuses, apartheid ideas were good ones," while approximately a third (33.7 percent) still believed that ultimately "the struggle to preserve apartheid was just" (Gibson and Macdonald 2001: 31). Similarly, when surveyed in 1996 during the early stages of the TRC process, 45 percent of white South Africans indicated that they believed that life under apartheid was better than life post-apartheid, with only 14 percent indicating they thought it worse (Gibson and

Gouws 1997: 172–191). Accordingly, as Chapman and van der Merwe illustrate, the perpetuation of a muted sense of accountability among many members of the white community for abuses committed under apartheid may have been "one of the more ironic, unintended consequences of the TRC's rendition of the past" (2008a: 254).

Justice and the TRC process

Due to the conditional amnesty provision included in the 1995 Promotion of National Unity and Reconciliation Act that founded the TRC process, it was clear from the Commission's inception that it would not take criminal prosecution of the perpetrators of apartheid-era human rights violations as the primary aim of its approach to justice. Instead, the TRC sought to pursue a 'third course' of restorative justice that lay somewhere between unrestrained retribution and impunity, a path "concerned not so much with punishment as with correcting imbalances, restoring broken relationships—with healing, harmony, and reconciliation" (TRC 1998: vol. 1, ch. 1, para. 36). In essence, the mandate of the TRC involved a series of trade-offs in which retributive justice in the form of criminal prosecutions remained limited in order to ensure the stability of the nascent peace process and to forward the Commission's more restorative goals of truth recovery, victim acknowledgment and national reconciliation. Nonetheless, many observers both within South Africa and internationally viewed the TRC's decision to grant conditional amnesties to the perpetrators of politically motivated human rights abuses under apartheid as a 'sacrifice of justice' for victims made by the South African government in exchange for political expediency and national stability (Graybill 2002; Gibson 2004; du Bois-Pedain 2007).[12]

However, despite these critiques, evidence shows that to a surprising degree South Africans themselves were willing to countenance granting amnesty to perpetrators who participated in the more restorative aspects of the Commission's truth-recovery and reconciliation processes. For instance, in national public opinion surveys conducted in South Africa in 1996, 49 percent of black respondents (and 39 percent of whites) indicated that they were inclined to support granting amnesty in exchange for perpetrators' proving full disclosure of their involvement in past abuses (Thiessen 2008: 204). Moreover, nearly half (48 percent) of total respondents indicated their belief that perpetrators "should be given amnesty if they come clean and offer to testify to the Truth Commission," while only 28 percent disagreed (idem: 203). At least among black South Africans, this support only grew over the course of the TRC's operation, with 72 percent indicating by 2000–2001 that they approved of the TRC's decision to grant amnesty (Gibson and Macdonald 2001: 6).[13]

At least in part, this willingness to accept limiting prosecutions of perpetrators would appear to be linked to the perception, particularly among black South Africans, that granting amnesty was ultimately necessary to the broader projects of solidifying peace and reconciliation in the transition from apartheid. In a pilot survey conducted by Macdonald in 2000, 62 percent of black South African respondents identified the TRC's conditional amnesty provision as an integral part of South Africa's movement towards national unity and reconciliation, though again a much smaller number (29 percent) of whites appeared to share this belief (Macdonald 2000). Similarly, in Gibson and Macdonald's later 2000–2001 survey, 65 percent of black South Africans (as compared to 18 percent of whites) indicated a belief that the amnesty associated with the TRC was essential to avoiding civil war in South Africa during its transition from white rule to majority rule (Gibson 2004: 267).

Further, it appears that the potential sacrifice of justice linked to the decision to grant amnesties to perpetrators was mitigated to a significant degree by the extensive emphasis placed by the TRC on providing an alternative form of justice by acknowledging the victims of past human rights violations. Indeed, the TRC is recognized as having offered a number of unique opportunities to advance aspects of justice through victim acknowledgment. These included providing victims with a forum to tell their stories publicly through the Commission's HRVC hearings, giving them the option of becoming active participants in the amnesty hearings of their perpetrators through the AC, and including recommendations for services and reparations to help victims begin to rebuild their lives under the umbrella of the TRC's Reparations and Rehabilitation Committee (RRC). Overall, the Commission's extensive focus on victim acknowledgment has led many national and international observers to label the TRC as one of the most 'victim-centered' transitional justice processes to date (Markel 1999; Kiss 2000; Hayner 2002).

Indeed, based on extensive interviews carried out with a cross-section of victims and members of the TRC staff, Phakathi and van der Merwe conclude that for most victims, acknowledgment in the form of an official recognition of their suffering, a truthful account of perpetrator responsibility, and the provision of an adequate program of reparations to meet their most immediate material needs were often considered to be of greater importance for achieving 'justice' surrounding past abuses than the punishment of perpetrators (2008: 135–136). These findings reiterated those of an earlier 1997 study conducted by van der Merwe among black victims in the communities of Duduza and Katorus, where he found that "quite a few [victims] supported the concept of amnesty because of its potential benefits" for achieving more restorative goals surrounding truth recovery, acknowledgment and reconciliation. As he recounts,

> [m]any victims, in fact, were hoping that their perpetrators would apply for amnesty so that the facts of their case would come to light and there would be some prospect for dialogue, apology, or greater public

recognition. Most victims and community leaders accepted restorative justice as an appropriate or even preferable approach in addressing human rights violations.

(van der Merwe 2001b: 98)

Accordingly, while some victims remained adamantly opposed to the conditional amnesty provisions of the TRC throughout its process, evidence suggests that given the measures of justice provided by victim acknowledgment and recognition, most appeared willing to accept amnesties as the 'price that had to be paid' for truth recovery and national reconciliation. For instance, as Chapman and van der Merwe illustrate,

> while the public seems to have recognized the amnesty provision as an injustice, there seems to have been a general recognition that amnesty was the price to pay for democracy: it was a necessary evil . . . survivors were not overwhelmingly opposed to the idea of amnesty. Many survivors apparently hoped that their perpetrators would apply for amnesty . . . where survivors did not know the identity of the perpetrator and were anticipating that new information would be revealed through the amnesty process.
>
> (2008a: 266)

The same trend was reflected in a 2000–2001 public opinion study conducted by Gibson and Macdonald, which found that if victims were allowed to tell their stories in the TRC hearings, were granted apologies by their perpetrators, and, most importantly, were provided with financial compensation by the government, then the number of South Africans who considered granting amnesties to perpetrators to be 'fair' and 'just' increased exponentially. This study further illustrated that while only 7 percent of South African respondents judged amnesty to be fair when no compensation, apology or voice was given to victims, 46 percent of respondents deemed conditional amnesty just when these three conditions were met (Gibson 2002).

Socioemotional learning from the TRC's justice processes

A strong consensus emerged among those experts interviewed in South Africa regarding the crucial importance of the TRC's ability to provide justice by way of victim acknowledgment to advancing processes of personal healing and reconciliation. As Sarah Crawford-Brown, a former counselor with the Trauma Centre for Survivors of Violence and Torture, has argued, when societies have suffered a past history of violence, "survivors need to be acknowledged, and empowered, and need to tell their stories . . . they need acknowledgment, they need the story to be heard, they need the perpetrators and society to know that this has happened and not to forget it" (interview: June 26th, 2008). Similarly, Thloki Mofokeng of the Khulumani Victims Support Group explains that for many black South African victims, the official acknowledgment provided by the TRC process was essential to reducing the sense of injustice caused by the abuses of apartheid. As he contends, "by saying [a human rights violation] was committed, by denouncing that, and by officially recognizing the pain of victims—that official recognition of the pain of all black South Africans—that means a lot, that means something. The official recognition of injustice, that we recognize injustice for all of you, that means something. People feel acknowledged, officially, and recognized, officially" (interview: July 1st, 2008).

Further, others have contended that, for many black South African victims, the official acknowledgment of their suffering provided by the TRC was an important lever for socioemotional learning, as it symbolized a normative shift away from their previous treatment as second-class citizens in South African society. In this way, the TRC's emphasis on the acknowledgment of the wrongs committed against the victims of apartheid-era violence helped to solidify the new status of those victims as equal members of the moral and political community of South Africa (Amstutz 2005: 102–112). As noted South African scholar Tom Lodge illustrates, the TRC

> gave people who testified at the human rights hearings a sense that they were being acknowledged. That their experiences were important, that they were somebodies at last. So it was important in that sense, in helping to reconstitute people as citizens. And of course that happened vicariously as well, affecting a much larger number of people than those who testified because the truth commission projected its activities very effectively, very dramatically through the media.
>
> (Interview: April 15th, 2008)

Unfortunately, however, evidence shows that the initial magnanimity of black South Africans—and of the victim community in particular—towards the TRC's amnesty provision quickly deteriorated when it became apparent that several other aspects of the Commission's 'victim-centered' restorative justice approach would not live up to expectations. Much of this dissatisfaction stemmed from the government's perceived failure to adequately follow through on the TRC's reparations program, which was designed to provide financial compensation to the victims of past human rights abuses. Indeed, as discussed in greater detail in Chapter 7, the reparations paid to victims of past abuses by the South African government amounted to only a fraction of the monies originally proposed by the Commission's RRC, with these reduced amounts only being made available to victims after several years' delay (Walaza 2000; Orr 2000). At the same time, victims watched as those perpetrators who successfully applied for amnesty were immediately released from prison or granted immunity from prosecution. As a number of expert interviewees noted, this disparity left many victims feeling "marginalized," "ignored" or "sacrificed" by a government which appeared to be giving greater value to the needs of perpetrators. As Professor Amanda Gouws of Stellenbosch University recounts, "this wasn't about putting a price to life, this was about a symbolic gesture that you have made sacrifices so we will pay you something. On the other hand, the perpetrators got off scot-free. If you disclosed everything, you got amnesty. . . . What did the victims get? Nothing—many reparations still haven't been paid. . . . People are very, very embittered about that" (interview: June 17th, 2008).

While the TRC only had the power to make recommendations to the President with regard to reparations, as the public face of the reparations process, the Commission nonetheless remained the primary target for the growing sense of anger, frustration and injustice felt by victims at this disparity. For many victims, these feelings appear to have led to the conclusion that, despite its claims to the contrary, the TRC was a perpetrator-centered rather than a victim-centered institution. As Nahli Valji, Senior Researcher with the CSVR in Cape Town, contends, the perceived failures surrounding the Commission's reparations program compounded the existing sense of injustice felt by many victims and may have hindered their willingness to reconcile. As Valji illustrates, "reparations dragged on for years before it was paid, and yet government was quick to move on things that have benefitted perpetrators . . . in terms of reconciliation it left a bad taste in the mouth of a lot of the victims who came forward to participate in the Commission" (interview: June 24th, 2008). Similarly, other studies have shown that victims' frustration at the TRC's lack of delivery in reparations convinced many to withdraw their support for the Commission's restorative justice approach and helped to build new levels of resistance to the amnesty process (Hamber et al. 2000; van der Merwe 2001b).

Recent evidence would also seem to suggest that many victims remained deeply disappointed in the level of 'truth' they ultimately received from perpetrators through the AC process in exchange for the granting of conditional amnesties. Among those perpetrators who did come forward through the AC process, many limited their testimonies so as to reveal only the bare minimum amount of truth surrounding their complicity in past abuses required to meet the 'full disclosure' criterion necessary to receive amnesty, hoping to limit their exposure to further potential legal action (Sarkin 2008). Further, in a number of cases, amnesties were granted to perpetrators who failed to provide specific information surrounding past abuses or whose testimonies contained clear contradictions or conflicting versions of past events (ibid.). Indeed, following the conclusion of the TRC's work, a number of victims reported feeling that the AC process had largely failed to provide them with the justice and acknowledgment they had hoped for by obtaining the 'full truth' from perpetrators. As Phakathi and van der Merwe note, many victims "felt that the process had failed to provide new details that were vitally important to them. Some stated that the stories were not complete; it was not the whole truth. Others thought that the testimony of the applicant was false" (2008: 124).

Perhaps even more damaging for perceptions of justice and socioemotional learning among victims has been the government's marked failure to follow through on criminal prosecutions for those perpetrators who either chose not to take part in the amnesty process or who were refused on the basis of failing to meet the specified amnesty criteria. To be considered eligible for amnesty, perpetrators had to meet a series of fairly stringent qualifying criteria, including the ability to show that their crimes were political in nature and were committed in 'proportion' to stated political objectives, as well as the willingness to provide a full and truthful account of their past crimes to the AC.[14] This meant that all those perpetrators who refused to take part in the Commission's justice process by applying for amnesty through the AC remained susceptible to prosecution for their crimes. Similarly, those who did come forward to the AC but somehow failed to meet the AC's strict criteria for conditional amnesty also remained liable for criminal prosecution. To be sure, it was this 'stick' of threatened prosecution as much as the 'carrot' of the conditional amnesty itself that encouraged many perpetrators to come forward to participate in the TRC's avowedly restorative truth-recovery process (Rigby 2001; Hayner 2002; Goldstone 2004).

However, as previously discussed, very few of those in positions of leadership within the NP, the ANC and the IFP actually came forward to apply for conditional amnesty and to participate in the AC hearings. Nevertheless, the TRC remained fairly lenient in its approach to these figures, very rarely invoking its extensive subpoena powers to compel senior officials to testify or to help build cases for prosecution against them (Pigou 2008). As a result, only relatively low-level 'foot soldiers' who had a need to seek amnesty for fear of being otherwise prosecuted for their crimes came forward. Even of this number, many—particularly among the apartheid-era police and security forces—simply chose not to apply based on a calculated risk that they, like their leaders, would be able to avoid prosecution. Indeed, an analysis of those amnesty applications that received public hearings through the AC reveals that the majority of individuals (between 53 and 61 percent) who applied for amnesty were from ANC-aligned structures (many of whom were already imprisoned under sentences previously enacted by the apartheid government), while applications from members of government security forces (18 to 23 percent) remained well in the minority (Ernest 2004). As Howard Varney, former head of the TRC's Investigation Unit details,

> the fact is that most perpetrators didn't come forward [to the AC]. The vast majority of applicants were in fact serving prisoners who were just taking the chance they could grab an amnesty for whatever they had done. With a couple of notable exceptions, those perpetrators who could

have qualified for amnesty would only come forward if they were aware there was a police docket with certain information that could lead to prosecution, or there was an imminent prosecution.

(Interview: June 24th, 2008)

For the most part, the risks taken by perpetrators in either limiting the accounts they provided to the AC or in avoiding the process completely appear to have paid off due to an apparent lack of desire by the ANC government to pursue prosecutions. While the TRC reportedly handed over nearly 300 cases for possible prosecution to the National Prosecuting Authority (NPA), very few prosecutions have actually been pursued even when sufficient evidence has been available to do so. In fact, of the thousands of potential cases that may have been viable for prosecution, only four cases involving apartheid-era human rights abuses have been heard in court since the close of the TRC in 2001, with only one conviction having been made as of 2008 (Chapman and van der Merwe 2008a: 268). As Chapman and van der Merwe note, overall "to date there has been very little indication of serious government commitment to pursuing further prosecutions against those denied amnesty or those who did not apply for amnesty" (idem: 267).

As several expert interviewees highlight, the failure to follow through on the promise of prosecutions for those perpetrators who didn't receive amnesty deepened the sense of injustice felt by many victims. Howard Varney argues that the failure to carry out these prosecutions amounted to a fundamental betrayal of the "historic bargain" or "national compact" made with victims who were assured a measure of criminal justice if perpetrators failed to participate in the more restorative processes of the TRC. As Varney illustrates,

> If you don't intend to prosecute, you can't imply that you will when you set up a conditional amnesty because that, in effect, is making false promises. Because you're asking victims to buy into a program in which they give up a measure of their rights in the hope that they'll get truth, perhaps together with reparations, but ultimately justice—if you don't get the truth you'll get justice . . . Make these compromises for the sake of crossing this historic bridge, but we will prosecute those who were denied amnesty or those who didn't apply for amnesty—that just simply hasn't happened.
>
> (Interview: June 24th, 2008)

Similarly, Thloki Mofokeng of the Khulumani Support Group details that while many black victims were willing to countenance amnesty in exchange for truth and reconciliation, this was premised on an understanding that those who did not participate would face criminal sanction. Accordingly, as he suggests, the lack of prosecutions has led victims to question the commitment of the government and the TRC to providing justice: "We understand it was a compromised justice, but there was no follow-through. So people felt very, very betrayed. These guys are not only economically still empowered, still very privileged, but have essentially gotten off scot-free" (interview: July 1st, 2008).

Perhaps not surprisingly, given the sense of disappointment felt by many victims surrounding the promised truth, reparations and prosecutions of those who failed to participate in the Commission's conditional amnesty program, more recent evidence reveals that many victims feel that they did not receive the degree of justice they had hoped for from the TRC process. Survey data collected by the CSVR between 2000 and 2002 reveals that an overwhelming majority of the 172 victims interviewed (88 percent) indicated that they did not feel that justice had ultimately been achieved for them through the amnesty process (Sonis and van der Merwe 2004). A similar 2005 study carried out by David Backer based on a survey of 228 victims in Cape Town found that only 28 percent felt that justice had been achieved (Backer 2005: 8).

Perhaps most troubling is the unintended effect this continued sense of injustice may have had on social learning among both victims and the broader South African population. A number of interviewees drew a direct link between the failure to follow through on the promise of prosecutions for apartheid-era perpetrators and the development of a more widespread distrust or disregard for the rule of law in contemporary South Africa. Indeed, many observers have linked this lack of respect for the rule of law with the maintenance of a pervasive 'culture of violence' in South Africa that finds expression in high levels of domestic abuse, xenophobic violence and the fact that the country has maintained one of the highest violent crime rates in the world (Thiessen 2008: 214–215). This was a point underscored by Thloki Mofokeng, who argues that

> [i]f there had been vigorous prosecutions for those who did not come forward to the TRC, victims would have felt the state recognized that what happened to me was evil, and that those who did that to me and those who did not take part in this compromise arrangement, people would have felt that this sense of impunity is prevented, that impunity is not perpetrated. But right now people think that people have got away with all of this, therefore impunity is entrenched in our broader society. You see this in our crime problem, or in people attacking people and knowing that nothing will happen to them—we can trace it back to the fact that people were never prosecuted.
>
> (Interview: July 1st, 2008)

Similarly, Professor Deborah Posel of the Wits Institute for Social and Economic Research at the University of the Witwatersrand (WISER) notes that in addition to the sense of injustice felt by many victims, the dangerous lack of respect for the rule of law that the government's failure to pursue prosecutions modeled for South African society has been damaging to the long-term goals of national unity and reconciliation. As she warns,

> [i]f it turns out there was no bite in the law, then we're at risk of trivializing a large part of that exercise, and not just in terms of the effect it had at the time. The risk with our TRC was that we prioritized reconciliation over punishment with the idea of amnesty. The worst of all worlds would be that this led a society that is not reconciled, and simultaneously that has no respect for the law. Where the assumption is that if you just have to say sorry enough times, or there is just no legitimacy or efficacy attached to the system of law and justice. That's very much the danger in SA at the moment—this is an exceedingly lawless society.
>
> (Interview: July 3rd, 2008)

The perceptions of these interviewees appear to be reflected in findings from Gibson and Macdonald's 2000–2001 survey. These findings suggest that, despite the TRC's attempts to provide accountability for the violence of the past, it has had very little influence in altering the attitudes towards the rule of law among both black and white South Africans that had prevailed under apartheid. As Gibson notes, this means that the TRC has "had limited influence on attitudes towards the rule of law amongst ordinary people in South Africa," with the result that "there are many good reasons for suspecting that the truth and reconciliation process in South Africa actually had the opposite effect than was intended by those who created it" (2004: 192).

However, despite these potential dangers, there appear to be no imminent plans by the government to pursue additional prosecutions for apartheid-era abuses in the near future. Indeed, in 2002, President Thabo Mbeki granted 33 pardons to prisoners who had been accused of committing acts of political violence during the struggle against apartheid on behalf of the ANC and PAC. Notably, this process was widely criticized, as many of those who received pardons were perpetrators who had previously been refused amnesty through the TRC's amnesty process. In addition, the victims and family members involved in these cases were neither informed nor given an opportunity to have input into the pardons process (Varney and Goulding 2012).

Moreover, under a decision made by the government in 2005, a policy was introduced into the NPA that gave those perpetrators who failed to appear before the TRC a "second bite at the amnesty cherry" (Klaaren and Varney 2003). This policy effectively granted the NPA the authority not to pursue charges (or to dismiss existing charges) in all current cases that were retroactively deemed to have met the TRC's original amnesty criteria.

Importantly, too, the NPA was empowered to make these decisions behind closed doors, without the involvement of victims and without releasing any information—besides the final decision about whether or not to grant amnesty—to the general public (Chapman and van der Merwe 2008c: 285). However, in December 2008, this policy was struck down as a result of a successful challenge brought before the High Court in Pretoria initiated by a small group of relatives of victims killed by state security forces under the apartheid system.

Nevertheless, at the time of writing, South African President Jacob Zuma is considering applications made by 149 apartheid-era perpetrators who have applied for 'Special Pardons.' This pardon process was introduced by the Mbeki government in 2007, and was designed to 'promote national reconciliation and unity' by 'completing the unfinished business' of the TRC with regard to political perpetrators who had not been granted amnesty through the Commission's earlier amnesty process. A Reference Group comprised of representatives from each of the main political parties sitting in the South African parliament has been tasked with reviewing pardon applications and making recommendations to the President. To be considered for pardon, applicants are to disclose the truth surrounding their crimes and to show that those crimes were politically motivated. Those being considered for pardon under this scheme include former apartheid-era Police Minister Adriaan Vlok as well as former Police Commissioner Johann van der Merwe. However, many of those who have applied for Special Pardons are perpetrators who committed crimes including serial killings, bombings, kidnappings, armed robberies and arson in the period between 1994 and 1999—well after the deadline had passed on the TRC's original amnesty process and the country had completed its transition to democracy.

These Special Pardons have received heavy criticism from local human rights and legal organizations who consider the pardons process to be "deeply flawed," "unconstitutional" and "acting inconsistently with the values and principles of the Truth and Reconciliation Commission" (SACTJ 2012). In particular, critics have noted that the pardons process has condoned concealing the identities of senior politicians and security officers who were involved in the murders of anti-apartheid activists and, in several cases, has allowed perpetrators to apply for pardons who have clearly failed to provide full disclosure for their crimes (ibid.). In addition, others have highlighted that the pardons process was originally initiated in secret, with victims only being informed regarding cases in which they were involved after an appeal was made by victims' groups and civil society organizations to the Constitutional Court in 2010 (Varney and Gould 2012). As a result of these issues, Howard Varney and Chandre Gould of the South African Institute for Security Studies have charged that "the Special Pardons process undermines the TRC process, entrenches impunity, and is enormously disrespectful of victims and the people of South Africa" (ibid.). Similarly, members of the South African

Coalition for Transitional Justice (SACTJ) have argued that the Special Pardons process violates the rule of law established in post-apartheid South Africa, and by also "denying South Africans the full truth" about past crimes, otherwise "serves to undermine national reconciliation" (SACTJ 2012).

Indeed, the NPA strategy and the more recent attempts at providing pardons to perpetrators by the Mbeki and Zuma governments in the wake of the TRC appear to have deepened the sense of injustice felt by victims of past abuses. Not only do such programs grant perpetrators a second chance at clearing their names, but they also remove several elements considered vital to victims' acceptance of the TRC's conditional amnesty process, including the transparency of the hearings, public admissions of responsibility, and, most importantly, the trading of a perpetrator's full account of the 'truth' in exchange for clemency (Klaaren and Varney 2003). As a result, observers such as Nahla Valji predict that such programs are likely to further hinder reconciliation, as they are viewed as yet another "sell-out point, another betrayal" associated with the "breaking of the social compact" originally made by the government to victims during the TRC process (interview: June 24th, 2008). This contention is confirmed by Thloki Mofokeng, who notes that given the angry reaction among the 50,000 plus member constituency of victims in the Khulumani Support Group, the perceptions of injustice associated with initiatives like the government's NPA prosecution strategy and Special Pardons program are likely to serve as continued impediments to the ongoing process of reconciliation in South Africa:

> Not only did [victims] get inadequate reparations, but now perpetrators that did not come to the TRC will get a second chance. . . . It will have a huge impact on social reconciliation. One has to remember that reconciliation is a process and it can fade away at any point depending on what happens. And things like that can have a huge impact against the gains we've made in terms of reconciliation.
>
> (Interview: July 1st, 2008)

Notably, survey evidence collected as late as 2011 shows a continued desire to fulfill a need for justice regarding apartheid-era abuses among many South Africans, including the demand for further prosecutions of eligible perpetrators and a more satisfactory acknowledgment of victims. This desire appears particularly strong among black South Africans, who suffered most extensively from both the physical abuses carried out by the state's policing and security forces and the broader structural and distributive injustices of the institutionalized racism of apartheid. For instance, only 46 percent of all South Africans indicated in responses to a 2011 SARB survey that they agreed that "the government has done enough to prosecute perpetrators" to date, including 49 percent of white South Africans and 46 percent of blacks when respondents were divided by race (Lefko-Everett et al. 2011). Perhaps most tellingly, however, the same survey reveals that only a very small minority of South Africans back the government's current strategy of granting further pardons to apartheid-era perpetrators, with only 23 percent indicating that they supported the proposal that "those who committed crimes under apartheid and did not confess to the TRC" should be released from prison—a sentiment shared by 33 percent of whites and only 21 percent of blacks polled (ibid.).

At the same time, 37 percent indicated that they still feel that the government has not done enough to support victims who experienced human rights abuses under apartheid (ibid.). Notably, on the issue of victim support, the survey revealed major race-based disparities. Only 22 percent of whites as compared to 39 percent of blacks indicated their belief that the government has provided insufficient support to date for apartheid-era victims (ibid.). Taken together, these findings suggest that the persistent sense of injustice associated with the failure to prosecute those who didn't receive a conditional amnesty and widespread perceptions of a lack of adequate acknowledgment for the victims of apartheid-era abuses will continue to undermine prospects for socioemotional learning and interracial reconciliation in contemporary South Africa.

Notes

1   Of the 3,526 total deaths catalogued between 1969 and 2001, for example, approximately 58 percent of these are attributable to Republican paramilitaries, 29 percent to Loyalist paramilitaries, and 10 percent to British security forces (including the policing services). Moreover, this data reveals distinct patterns in the violence that was carried out between the conflict's principal combatants. Victims of Republican violence were primarily British security forces (53 percent), followed by Protestant civilians (19 percent), Catholic civilians (11 percent), other Republicans (9 percent), civilians from outside Northern Ireland (5 percent) and Loyalist paramilitaries (3 percent). Loyalist victims, on the other hand, were predominantly Catholic civilians (65 percent), followed by Protestant civilians (13 percent), other Loyalist paramilitary members (10 percent) and British security forces (1 percent). Those killed by British security forces were mostly Catholic civilians (44 percent) and Republican paramilitaries (40 percent), followed by a small minority of Protestant civilians (6 percent) and Loyalist paramilitaries (5 percent) (CAIN 2012).

2   I am indebted to Christine Bell for the term 'piecemeal' in referring to Northern Ireland's decentralized approach to transitional justice (2002).

3   Unfortunately, 2004 is the latest date available for NILT data on this question, though the impressions gained by expert interviews in Northern Ireland conducted as late as 2008 suggest that the data reflects current attitudes.

4   Indeed, in the three years prior to Bloody Sunday, 213 people had been killed as a result of the Troubles, while in the three months directly following Bloody Sunday, more than 400 people were killed (Sutton 2010).

5 In particular, unionists often cite the Claudy Bombing allegedly carried out by the IRA in July 1972, which killed nine civilians, or the Kingsmill Massacre in January 1976 during which ten Protestant men were shot and killed by suspected PIRA paramilitaries. While both cases have been the subject of police investigations, neither received attention or resources anywhere near the scale of the BSI and neither has yet resulted in prosecution.

6 Out of a total of 166 staff involved in the 'policing' side of the HET in November 2007, 67 were former RUC officers (Lundy 2007).

7 This useful distinction between 'macro' and 'micro' truths in relation to the TRC's findings is borrowed from Chapman and van der Merwe, who define 'macro truths' as "the assessment of contexts, causes, explanations for, and patterns of human rights violations along with the determination of responsibility for them" as compared to 'micro truths' which seek to establish the "facts of specific events, cases, and people" surrounding individual abuses (2008a: 242).

8 Nevertheless, given the discriminatory racial nature of apartheid and the majority/minority population demographics in South Africa, nearly 90 percent of victim statements made to the HRVC were by black South Africans (Chapman and Ball 2008: 153).

9 Notable exceptions included former National Party Minister of Police Eugene de Kock and Adriaan Vlok, commander of the feared Vlakplaas policing unit that was found responsible for having committed numerous secret killings, tortures and kidnappings on behalf of the apartheid government.

10 More recently, free access to an online edition of the TRC Final Report was made available by the South African government through the Department of Justice website. However, given the lack of affordable high-speed internet access for the majority of the black population living in South Africa, this online version still largely remains out of reach.

11 One potential reason suggested by Gibson for this weaker correlation is that black South Africans, being more exposed to the 'truth' of apartheid injustices and atrocities on a daily basis, did not perceive many of the revelations of the TRC process as entirely new information (Gibson 2004).

12 This view was illustrated most prominently by an unsuccessful challenge brought before the Constitutional Court of South Africa to deny the Commission's power to grant amnesty by a group of victims led by representatives of the family of Steve Biko, the leader of the Black Consciousness movement in South Africa who died while in the custody of apartheid security forces.

13 Notably, however, the percentage of white South Africans who indicated their approval of the granting of amnesties remained largely unchanged at 39 percent (ibid.).

14 Significantly, only 1,167 of the already relatively small pool of 7,000 potential applicants were ultimately successful in securing amnesty through the TRC. However, it should be noted that a substantial number of the original 7,000 amnesty applicants included those currently in jail for having committed crimes that were clearly not political in nature but who nonetheless wanted to take a chance on qualifying for the TRC's amnesty provision. As a result, the proportional number of those who received amnesty for cases under the TRC's remit is somewhat higher than this figure first appears.

Chapter 7

Distributive learning

There is now evidence to suggest that alongside the elements of identity negotiation linked to instrumental and socioemotional learning, intergroup reconciliation in deeply divided societies also requires the kinds of distributive learning associated with real and tangible change in the socioeconomic conditions of former antagonists. Accordingly, distributive learning refers to efforts to transform relations between divided identity groups that are rooted in reducing structural and material inequality and limiting perceptions of inequitable power relations. As outlined in the social learning framework introduced in Chapter 3, processes of distributive learning can be promoted by a range of different mechanisms in post-conflict societies. These mechanisms might include socioeconomic and legislative reforms, provisions of direct reparations or compensation programs for those worst affected by past abuses, and other interventions designed to at least signal a commitment to establishing more equitable relations between divided identity groups.

This chapter explores the ability of the different transitional justice strategies adopted in Northern Ireland and South Africa to contribute to processes of distributive learning and intergroup reconciliation. In Northern Ireland's decentralized transitional justice approach, such interventions have focused largely on governmental initiatives undertaken to address the deep sense of victimization felt in Catholic/nationalist communities at having been historically marginalized under a system of socioeconomic and political discrimination by the Protestant/unionist majority. In South Africa, the TRC process included several related efforts to address the legacy of institutionalized racial discrimination that characterized the apartheid system. Most notably, these efforts included a proposed reparations program for victims and specialized hearings designed to investigate aspects of structural discrimination under apartheid, as well as a number of recommendations made to the South African government for broader reforms included in the Commission's Final Report. These efforts have operated alongside initiatives undertaken by post-transition ANC governments to begin reversing the deep economic, social and political inequalities that benefited white South Africans at the expense of other racial groups—the majority black population in particular—during the era of apartheid.

Distributive learning in Northern Ireland

The history of structural and material inequalities between Catholic and Protestant communities in Ireland has long been recognized as one of the primary motivators of the island's protracted religious and national conflict. Even before partition, the apparatus of the state was used by the Protestant community to discriminate politically, socially and economically against the Catholic majority (Darby 1995). Anger and frustration with this discrimination galvanized Catholic support for the nationalist movement in Ireland, and inequalities have continued to account in no small part for the close overlap between religious identities and political identifications with nationalism or unionism in the North following partition (Gallagher 1957). Indeed, as Joseph Ruane and Jennifer Todd have argued, while religious and national affiliations have been intertwined with one another in Ireland for centuries, ultimately it was only when these identities were used as the basis for structural and material disparities that intercommunal hostility and violence developed (1996: 2–9). At the same time, conflict over inequality and discrimination served to further solidify the salience of communal divides based on these religious and national identifications. As Ruane and Todd illustrate,

> sociocultural and ideological difference alone would not have produced oppositional communities or intense communal conflict. Difference became conflictual and lasting because it was the basis of access to resources and power. . . . Defending or advancing those interests provided the basis for further communal solidarity and ever sharper communal division. Communal division intensified in turn the sense of sociocultural and ideological difference and the interests on which the structure of dominance rested.
>
> (idem: 12–13)

The self-reinforcing dynamic between identity, inequality and conflict only intensified in the period of unionist dominance that followed partition in Northern Ireland. Indeed, the civil rights movement and the subsequent riots that ushered in the Troubles in the late 1960s stemmed from protests by members of the Catholic community against long-standing practices of discrimination in employment and local housing allocation. In fact, the independent Cameron Commission, which was tasked by the Government of Northern Ireland (GNI) with investigating the origins of the 'disturbances' in 1968 and 1969, concluded that a widespread sense of injustice within the Catholic community was a contributing factor to the violence. In particular, the Commission highlighted the "resentment and frustration felt among the Catholic population" related to complaints of discrimination in housing and employment and "the failure to achieve either acceptance on the part of Government of any need to investigate these complaints or to provide and enforce a remedy for them" (GNI 1969a: paras 129, 229).

Data from the 1971 Census in Northern Ireland shows that during this period, Catholics were over two-and-a-half times more likely than Protestants to be unemployed. At the same time, those Catholics who were employed in the private sector were generally relegated to semi-skilled or unskilled labor positions and were underrepresented in senior management positions and professional 'white-collar' jobs (Melaugh 1995). Similarly, evidence shows that Catholics were far less likely to hold senior positions in the civil service or public sector, as these jobs were almost exclusively dominated by Protestants (Gallagher 1957: 213–214). As John Whyte has detailed, in 1971, only 11 percent of senior public servants identified themselves as being Catholic, even though an overall 31.4 percent of the population occupied such positions at the time (1983).

In the area of housing, many complaints centered on the biased practices evidenced in the distribution of public housing allotments by local district councils, the majority of which were under the control of unionist authorities. Such discrimination frequently resulted in housing being allocated to unmarried Protestants or single-child Protestant families at the expense of much larger Catholic families. However, in many cases, these decisions appear to have been made as much to ensure the electoral dominance of unionists in a Council area as for any motivation linked to prejudice. Indeed the Cameron Commission found that "the principal criterion . . . in such cases was not actual need but maintenance of the current political preponderance in the local government area" (GNI 1969a: para. 138). Regardless, data from the same period shows that the net effect of these policies was the likelihood that Catholics lived in more overcrowded homes and had fewer amenities than their Protestant counterparts (Melaugh 1995).

Grievances during the civil rights movement were also registered against deeply biased electoral practices and the widespread use of gerrymandering techniques by unionists following partition. These practices had long limited the ability of those in the Catholic/nationalist community to exercise real legislative or executive power in Northern Ireland (O'Leary and McGarry 1993: 111–139). For instance, shortly after taking power in the period between 1922 and 1923, the unionist government at Stormont radically altered the system for electing representatives to local councils in Northern Ireland, both by removing proportional representation and strategically redrawing electoral boundaries in a way that greatly disadvantaged the electoral powers of the nationalist minority (Gallagher 1957). In addition, while Britain abolished electoral laws that tied voting rights to property ownership in 1945, these laws remained on the books and in fact were strengthened within Northern Ireland. As members of the socioeconomically disadvantaged Catholic/nationalist minority were far more likely to rent than to own their homes, this policy disproportionately favored the pro-unionist vote, particularly in key urban areas such as Belfast and Derry (ibid.: 13). These gerrymandering practices continued throughout much of the twentieth century, with electoral boundaries occasionally being moved when shifting demographics made it likely that nationalists might win in a unionist ward (Buckland 1979: 243–246).[1] As John Darby has argued, these examples of electoral bias resulted in "a consistent and irrefutable pattern of discrimination against Catholics" by Protestant/unionist politicians, a pattern that intensified perceptions among the nationalist minority that the government of Northern Ireland was fundamentally unrepresentative and illegitimate (Darby 1976: 77–78).[2]

Further, for many years, much of the nationalist community deeply distrusted the policing and security forces employed by the state in Northern Ireland. In large part this was due to the fact that, after partition, the main policing force, the Royal Ulster Constabulary (RUC), was disproportionately drawn from the Protestant community. For instance, between 1961 and 1969, the period leading up to the civil rights movement and the beginning of the Troubles, representation of Catholics in the RUC actually dropped from 12 to 11 percent, levels far below the actual proportion of Catholics in the population (Darby 1976: 59). The regular RUC was also supplemented by the 'B-Specials,' an auxiliary paramilitary police unit that was almost exclusively drawn from the unionist community and had many direct links to the Protestant Orange Order in Northern Ireland (GNI 1969a).

As a result of these imbalances, the policing services were viewed by many in the nationalist community as unrepresentative of Catholics (at best) or simply as a coercive wing of the unionist government (at worst). Such perceptions were further reinforced by the authority granted to the RUC by the 1922 Special Powers Act to "take all such steps and issue all such orders as may be necessary for preserving the peace and maintaining order" (GNI 1922: para. 1). These steps included banning public gatherings and potentially seditious publications, arresting and interning suspects without trial, and searching the vehicle or person of any subject that "does any act of such a nature as to be calculated to be prejudicial to the preservation of the peace or maintenance of order in Northern Ireland" (idem: para. 2).

However, evidence shows that between 1922 and 1975, when the Act remained in force, these powers were employed almost exclusively against Republicans and members of the nationalist community despite the existence of violent Loyalist paramilitary groups and the initiation of several large-scale disturbances by members of unionist political parties (Benewick 1974). Indeed, under the British government's policy of internment, employed between 1971 and 1975 to quell growing violence in Northern Ireland, the Special Powers legislation led to the arrest, punishment and detainment without trial of a total of 1,981 internees, 1,874 of whom were drawn from the minority nationalist community (Coogan 1995: 126). This added to the growing sense of resentment felt by the nationalist population and effectively "ensured that the RUC was seen as an instrument of the unionist government" (Hamilton et al. 1995).[3]

Accusations of discrimination were further reinforced by reports that police often did not behave impartially in their treatment of Catholic and Protestant citizens, in addition to allegations of the widespread use of 'bullying' tactics and unnecessary brutality by the police services in dealing with members of the nationalist community. In particular, the B-Specials were often implicated in reports of discriminatory violence and intimidation, turning the group into a by-word for nationalist fear and vitriol (Rowthorn and Wayne 1988: 38). For example, when the 1969 riots in Derry that ultimately ignited the Troubles were investigated, the government's 1969 Cameron Commission found that "a number of policemen were guilty of misconduct which involved assault and battery, malicious damage to property in streets in the predominantly Catholic Bogside area giving reasonable cause for apprehension of personal injury among other innocent inhabitants, and the use of provocative sectarian and political slogans" (GNI 1969a: para. 177). As the Cameron Commission concluded, an unfortunate outcome of these actions "which were directed against Catholic persons and property, was to add weight to the feeling which undoubtedly exists among a certain proportion of the Catholic community that the police are biased in their conflict against Catholic demonstrations and demonstrators" (ibid.). Furthermore, the sense of discrimination felt by the Catholic/nationalist community regarding the enforcement of law and order was compounded by a similar suspicion of the legal system, due primarily to major imbalances which disproportionately favored Protestants in appointments to Northern Ireland's judiciary (Darby 1976; Hillyard 1983).[4]

Distributive reforms in Northern Ireland

Following the violence of the late 1960s, a number of measures were introduced by the GNI during the early 1970s that sought to alleviate the worst of the grievances identified by the civil rights movement. For instance, in 1971, control of public housing allocation was taken away from local authorities and centralized in a new Northern Ireland Housing Executive (NIHE). This body quickly began working to improve the quality of Northern Ireland's public housing and to ensure a fairer system of housing allocation between Catholic and Protestant communities. These interventions appear to have largely depoliticized the issue of housing, with survey data from 1992 showing that both Catholics and Protestants had by that point come to feel equally satisfied with the allocations and services offered by the NIHE (Melaugh 1992).

At the same time, the British government also introduced an aggressive series of reforms to the electoral system in Northern Ireland. These changes included the redrawing of local council boundaries and the appointment of a Boundaries Commissioner to help ensure a more accurate reflection of population distribution and to put an end to practices of gerrymandering. The government also legislated that provisions tying voting rights to house ownership be abolished and reintroduced the proportional representation system of voting. Both of these initiatives substantially increased representation for the minority Catholic/nationalist population. As Mari Fitzduff notes, while minor disputes occasionally arose following these interventions, for the most part the reforms helped to ensure that "the processes of democracy . . . ceased in the main to be a source of contention between the communities" (2002: 21–22).

Some moderate reforms were also made to the policing services following the 1969 release of an investigatory report by the British Hunt Committee, including, most notably, the overall demilitarization of the structure of the RUC and the disbanding of the much-maligned B-Specials in 1970 in recognition of existing perceptions of their partisanship (GNI 1969b). The Police Act of 1970 also freed the RUC from direct political control by the unionist government, establishing a new independent Police Authority for Northern Ireland tasked with maintaining a more representative police force (Hamilton et al. 1995).

However, the extent of these reforms and their impact on community relations remained limited in the face of the outbreak of widespread Troubles-era violence. Plans to demilitarize the RUC were largely dropped due to the increase in violence, making the police the target of renewed suspicion and distrust. Indeed, while the overall size of the RUC had more than doubled by the early 1990s, its percentage of Catholic representation was effectively halved over the same period, falling to under 6 percent (Hamilton et al. 1995). Recently released evidence documents continued patterns of anti-Catholic discrimination throughout the Troubles, including instances of direct police collusion with Loyalist paramilitary organizations that resulted in the deaths of nationalist civilians (O'Loan 2007). During the 1980s, there were also investigations into the unnecessary use of deadly force by the RUC against the nationalist population, with evidence suggesting the existence of a "shoot-to-kill" policy (Hamilton et al. 1995). Furthermore, although the B-Specials had been disbanded, many of its units were simply adopted into a new auxiliary paramilitary policing unit known as the Ulster Defence Regiment (UDR), which itself quickly fell under suspicion of sectarianism and collusion with Loyalist paramilitaries. While some Catholics joined the UDR in its early days, by the late 1980s, Catholic membership had fallen to less than 3 percent (Elliott and Flackes 1989: 396). As a result, during the Troubles, the RUC and UDR lost much of their remaining legitimacy among the nationalist community, with many neighborhoods becoming virtual 'no-go' areas for members of the policing services. These areas were largely taken over by a system of violent 'internal policing' by the IRA and other Republican paramilitary organizations (McEvoy and Mika 2002).

However, additional reforms were made in the area of employment equity, beginning with the 1969 establishment of the Northern Ireland Commissioner for Administration, who was granted the power to investigate complaints of discrimination on the basis of religious or political belief and to promote fairness in public sector job recruitment by local councils. In 1976, the Fair Employment Act was passed by the GNI, which made it unlawful to discriminate in hiring or workplace practices on the grounds of religious or political affiliation and led to the establishment of a Fair Employment Agency (FEA) to investigate complaints of employment discrimination. The introduction of a new Employment Act in 1989 and the establishment of a Fair Employment Commission (FEC) to replace the earlier FEA made these policies even more robust. Notably, these later reforms included a mandatory requirement that companies with more than 25 employees register with the FEC to ensure their workforce's equitable religious composition, as well as new affirmative action policies designed to increase Catholic representation (Fitzduff 2002: 19–29).

Nevertheless, despite these efforts, by the beginning of the peace process in the early 1990s the Catholic community had seen little change in terms of employment equity. For instance, in 1993, unemployment among Catholics remained more than two times higher than among Protestants, while 45 of the top 50 worst unemployment rates in Northern Ireland were located within predominantly Catholic communities (ibid.: 24). These deficits offset significant gains in other areas, such as the public sector, where the use of affirmative action policies meant that Catholics were being hired and promoted at even higher rates than Protestants.

However, in support of the nascent peace process that began taking shape in the early 1990s, the GNI embarked on an even more aggressive agenda designed to alleviate many of the remaining structural inequalities dividing nationalist and unionist communities. This agenda included a new initiative called Targeting Social Need (TSN), which aimed at better focusing government policies and programs on communities—both Catholic and Protestant—showing the highest levels of deprivation, and at strategically granting monies for skills training and community development. In 1992, the government also increased the amount of funding it provided to Catholic schools with an eye to enhancing training in the areas of science and technology and thus facilitating Catholic employment in traditionally underrepresented fields (ibid.: 25). 1994 saw the introduction of the nationwide Policy Appraisal and Fair Treatment (PAFT) initiative, designed to help ensure that equality and equity informed all aspects of government activity, including its legislative and administrative functions as well as its provisions of public services.

Many other major reforms intended to address structural and material inequalities were introduced alongside the Belfast Agreement (BFA) in 1998, apropos of the Agreement's efforts to actively protect human rights and equality in 'Economic, Social and Cultural Issues.' At an institutional level, this led to the establishment of a centralized Equality Commission that assumed responsibility for overseeing all aspects of existing equality legislation. An independent Human Rights Commission was also created to complement the drafting of an inclusive Bill of Rights for Northern Ireland. These initiatives were supplemented by the extensive Fair Employment and Treatment Order introduced in 1998, which rendered it unlawful to discriminate on the basis of religious or political opinion in housing or employment and permitted the use of affirmative action policies to ensure fair participation in the workplace by both Protestants and Catholics.

To guarantee greater equality in terms of political representation in the Government of Northern Ireland, the BFA also established the Northern Ireland Assembly, a consociational power-sharing arrangement to be governed via a devolved legislature from the parliament buildings at Stormont.[5] Under this arrangement, both the executive and ministerial positions were to be shared equally between nationalist and unionist representatives, with the Assembly being led by a First Minister and Deputy First Minister drawn from each of the two communities. To help ensure that key legislative decisions serve the interests of both communities, it was decided that resolutions under the Assembly must receive a minimum of both nationalist and unionist support, allowing each community a mutual veto safeguard against discriminatory legislation. Following the Assembly's inception in 1999, an Equality Unit, a Gender and Sexual Orientation Unit and a Racial Equality Unit were created under the Assembly's Office of the First Minister and Deputy First Minister (OFMDFM) in order to keep equality and equity issues at the forefront of government policy.

Notably, the BFA also mandated that an extensive review of the criminal justice system be undertaken to increase levels of fairness and impartiality and to foster cross-community confidence and support. This resulted in the 2000 release of *The Review of the Criminal Justice System in Northern Ireland*, a report outlining nearly 300 recommendations targeting increased efficiency, impartiality, and accountability, the majority of which took legislative effect under Justice Acts in 2002 and 2003 (GNI 2000). These included changes to the ways in which appointments were made to the judiciary, as well as initiatives to protect the independence of the judicial process.

The BFA also set in motion an Independent Commission on Policing for Northern Ireland (ICPNI), otherwise called the 'Patten Commission' after its Chair, Chris Patten, which was mandated to explore reforms to the highly contentious existing policing services. In particular, the Commission was tasked with ensuring that policing be "fair and impartial [and] free from partisan political control" and able to win the "public confidence and acceptance" of all communities in Northern Ireland (GNI 1998). A final report known as the 'Patten Report' was released in September 1999, and it outlined over 175 recommendations for police reform (ICPNI 1999). The majority of the Patten Commission's suggestions were subsequently adopted with the passage of the Police (Northern Ireland) Acts of 2000 and 2003.

The policing reform measures adopted in Northern Ireland included the appointment of an independent Police Ombudsman to deal with complaints and allegations of misconduct, as well as the creation of a new Policing Board representative of both communities to replace the old Police Authority and to provide an independent source of oversight and accountability. The ethos of the police force was similarly redefined, based on a strict adherence to human rights codes and an emphasis on community policing versus the militarism of the past. At a symbolic level, the name of the police service was changed from the RUC to the Police Service of Northern Ireland (PSNI), and elements of 'Britishness' were removed from both the appearance and operation of the new organization. Perhaps most importantly, a policy of 'positive discrimination' was implemented in order to correct Catholics' historical under-representation in the police service and to increase the legitimacy of the PSNI within nationalist communities (Bayley 2008).

The impact on distributive learning in Northern Ireland

As discussed earlier, it is by now evident that structural and material inequalities played a central role in the violence of the Troubles, and that past disparities have had a major impact on reinforcing divisions and antagonisms between nationalist and unionist communities (Darby 1976, 1995; Ruane and Todd 1996; Cairns and Darby 1998; Fitzduff 2002; Aiken 2010). Moreover, substantial empirical evidence shows a link between levels of unemployment and relative deprivation and willingness to support more radical political parties and engage in acts of sectarian violence (Fitzduff 2002: 22–23; Honaker 2005: 21–22). Indeed, most of the worst Troubles-era violence took place in the poorer working-class areas of major urban centers like Derry and Belfast, and it is in these same areas that symbols of continued sectarian division (such as flags, graffiti and murals) remain most prominent (Shirlow and Murtagh 2006).

Accordingly, those experts interviewed consistently cited the amelioration of structural and material inequalities in Northern Ireland as a pillar of future reconciliation between nationalists and unionists. Most often this distributive work was invoked as the 'minimum foundation' upon which all other post-conflict activities must build. As Ray Mullan, Director of Communications for Northern Ireland's Community Relations Council (CRC) notes, an element of distributive learning is essential to reconciliatory efforts in Northern Ireland because "equity is about justice. You can't have a good community relations environment if one side feels they are being treated unfairly . . . you cannot build a positive environment if one side feels they are getting the short end of the straw. There has to be equity" (interview: April 21st, 2008).

Overall, assessments of the government's wide-ranging initiatives to make Northern Ireland's economic and political structures more equitable have been very positive, with a shared recognition that disparities between the communities—while certainly still present to a reduced degree—no longer represent the major source of division that they once did. As Jennifer Todd, Professor of Political Science at University College Dublin asserts,

> for a long time the conflict from the perspective of nationalists was fed by inequality, and fed by the effects of multiple inequalities. But it seems to me . . . that there's a threshold where groups don't necessarily have to get to strict equality to become satisfied. And nationalists have, for the most part, got to where they can see the possibility of equality and it's simply become pretty much depoliticized.
>
> (Interview: April 28th, 2008)

Similarly, Mari Fitzduff commends the "considerable success" that many of the initiatives designed to introduce greater equality between communities have had in Northern Ireland since the civil rights movement, observing that "[c]omplaints are no longer heard about rigged voting, unfair housing allocations, or unequal educational funding" (2002: 28). As she illustrates,

> the range of initiatives undertaken since 1970 have begun to bear significant fruit, and have substantially changed the capacity of Northern Ireland society to provide for equal opportunities for its citizens, both Catholic and Protestant alike. They also provide for a background of equity in employment, education, health, housing, and social services . . . this is likely to prevent the re-emergence of nationalist violence in the future . . . and will ensure that such issues will not have the capacity to destabilize a society that has been so convulsed by issues of equality in its history.
>
> (idem: 29)

These qualitative assessments also appear to be supported by recent empirical data surveying key aspects of intercommunal equality in contemporary Northern Ireland. For example, employment equality, once a major source of conflict, no longer seems to be a major contributing factor to intercommunal division. Survey data from 2010 shows that as a result of aggressive reform policies, 42 percent of working-age adults employed in Northern Ireland were Catholic while 48 percent were Protestant—an overall difference of only 6 percent (OFMDFM 2011: 6). Further, the same data illustrates that differences in unemployment rates for economically active adults between the communities have decreased substantially since the end of the Troubles. In 2010, the discrepancy was only 3 percent, with Catholics at 9 percent unemployment compared to 6 percent among Protestants (idem: 21).

Measurements also reveal that other aspects of employment equity have undergone similar changes in recent years. For instance, survey data collected in 2007 shows that Catholics are now just as likely as their Protestant counterparts to be selected for promotion to more senior positions and to hold highly skilled professional positions (Equality Commission for Northern Ireland 2008). Historical differences in median hourly wage rates between the communities have largely been repaired, to the extent that in 2010 Catholics actually made more (£9.44) than their Protestant counterparts (£9.11) on average (OFMDFM 2011: 31). Perhaps most tellingly, survey data from 2001 shows that fully 96 percent of Catholics and 94 percent of Protestants indicated that they did not believe that religion led to unfair treatment when applying for a promotion or a better position over the last ten years (ARK 2002). The same survey also found that a vast majority of both Catholics (85 percent) and Protestants (81 percent) did not believe that they had been refused a job for reasons related to their religion.

Relative equality in terms of access to housing in Northern Ireland, historically another key source of division between the two communities, has likewise been improved. Data from 2010 shows that discrepancies in home ownership in Northern Ireland have decreased substantially in recent years, with 75 percent of Protestant households being owner occupied as compared to 68 percent of Catholic households (idem: 8). At the same time, levels of those renting social housing are now almost identical between Protestants (16 percent) and Catholics (17 percent) in Northern Ireland (ibid.).

These findings correlate with changing perceptions between the two communities regarding equal treatment in the area of housing. For example, a 2001 Northern Ireland Life and Times survey shows that the vast majority (71 percent) of total respondents from both communities indicated that Catholics and Protestants now received equal allocation and treatment in their dealings with the NIHE (ARK 2002). Interestingly, of this number, even more Catholics (81 percent) than Protestants (62 percent) surveyed in 2001 felt that the NIHE treated the communities equally when allocating housing. Similarly, an NILT survey conducted in 2003 found that only 40 percent of Catholic respondents felt that Protestants received better treatment in the area of housing—a number that was actually lower than the 52 percent of Protestants who thought that Catholics were now favored in regard to housing (ARK 2004).

Further, despite the long-standing mistrust of the policing services by the nationalist population, there is evidence that the major reforms undertaken following the Patten Commission to increase the community-oriented and non-partisan nature of the PSNI have made significant inroads. For instance, as of July 2012, the composition of the PSNI stood at 67.45 percent Protestant and 30.34 percent Catholic—nearly five times the percentage of Catholic officers before the BFA and slightly beyond the target of 30 percent set by the Patten Commission for 2011 (PSNI 2012b). There are also indications that perceptions of the policing services as a partisan instrument have changed as well. A 2012 survey conducted by the Northern Ireland Policing Board (NIPB) shows that while more Protestants (64 percent) felt that the PSNI did a 'very' or 'fairly' good job in their area, this view was now shared by a majority (54 percent) of the Catholic population (NIPB 2012: 5). In addition, data from the same survey shows that 62 percent of Catholics and 74 percent of Protestants were 'very' or 'fairly' satisfied that "the police treat members of the public fairly in Northern Ireland as a whole" (idem: 6).[6] Perhaps most promisingly, similar levels of Catholic (79 percent) and Protestant (88 percent) respondents surveyed in 2012 indicated a positive degree of confidence that the PSNI could provide a day-to-day policing service for all the people of Northern Ireland regardless of their community affiliation (ibid.). While these figures still reveal a disparity between Catholic and Protestant perceptions of the policing services, they also evidence remarkable progress when compared to the deep mistrust and antipathy previously shown to the RUC by the nationalist community.[7]

However, it is also clear that a reduction in structural and material disparities, while vital to distributive learning in Northern Ireland, has not itself been sufficient to foster intergroup reconciliation between nationalist and unionist communities. More specifically, although the movement towards relative equality has helped to clear the way for developing less divisive relationships between nationalists and unionists, it has not been able to heal the deep physical, social and psychological scars that remain the legacies of past conflict. Indeed, while they are highly salutary of the efforts that have been made to ameliorate inequalities between nationalist and unionist communities, observers such as Ed Cairns and John Darby remain less certain about the capacity of these reforms to overcome the antagonistic attitudes and mindsets formed throughout the Troubles, noting that "the reduction of material disadvantages has not led to a measurable improvement in relationships between the two ethnic and religious communities" (1998: 758).

One result of these continued divisions is that the successes achieved by the government's ambitious agenda to address elements of structural and material equality still tend to be viewed by each community through the 'zero-sum' lens that marked past conflict. While Catholics have grown increasingly optimistic and secure about their status in Northern Irish society due to government reforms, Protestants report feeling threatened and alienated by the recent gains of the nationalist community and perceive these as coming at the expense of their own victimization (Hughes et al. 2003: 4–5). Indeed, data from the 2003 NILT survey reveals major changes surrounding perceptions of equality, with 80 percent of Protestants reporting a belief that Catholics were now being offered superior job opportunities, and 56 percent reporting that in general Catholics were being treated better than were Protestants (ARK 2004). At the same time, a similar majority of Catholics (72 percent) indicated that they believed Protestants were still receiving superior job opportunities, with an additional 41 percent contending that Protestants were being treated better than Catholics overall (ibid.). However, while both communities perceive an advantage being given to the other in key areas of economic equality, neither group appears to perceive itself as the recipient of any kind of preferential treatment, with only 1 percent of Catholics and 8 percent of Protestants indicating a belief that their own group was usually treated better than the other (ibid.).

One costly outcome of these continued zero-sum perspectives surrounding distributive equality has been an extensive duplication of resources in Northern Ireland since the BFA. In essence, any perceived gains made by one community in securing new public facilities, services or development funding must be met by the provision of separate but equal gains for the other community lest the government be charged with bias. This replication of funding and service provisions has proven extremely expensive, with costs to the Northern Ireland government estimated at approximately £1.5 billion a year (BBC News, August 23rd, 2007). Accordingly, while substantial gains have been made in regard to reducing material inequalities in Northern Ireland, it is apparent that the positive effects for community relations have been impeded by continued mistrust and the same zero-sum perceptions of mutual victimization that previously divided nationalists and unionists during the Troubles.

These ongoing divisions are also evident at the political level, where entrenched feelings of suspicion and animosity remain prominent between the political representatives of nationalists and unionists. This political antagonism is reflected by findings from Joanna Hughes and her colleagues, who analyzed trends from survey data on intercommunity relations collected in 2003 and concluded that

> [d]espite strong attention to the promotion of cultural, political, and religious pluralism and to the equality agenda, there is evidence that Northern Ireland has become a more divided society since the Belfast Agreement. There is growing incidence of cross-community tension, hostility and intimidation that reflects a polarized political battlefield focused on starkly drawn identities and incompatible constitutional demands.
>
> (Hughes et al. 2003: 1)

Indeed, the period following the BFA has been one of political radicalization in Northern Ireland, with Sinn Féin (SF) and the Democratic Unionist Party

(DUP) taking the majority of support from their respective nationalist and unionist communities away from the more moderate Social Democratic and Labour Party (SDLP) and Ulster Unionist Party (UUP) that had prevailed in the past. In the 2011 Assembly elections, for instance, the DUP under Peter Robinson won 38 seats and SF under Gerry Adams 29, far more than either the more centrist UUP (16) or SDLP (14). Furthermore, despite the end of political violence and the peaceful sharing of power between SF and the DUP since the Belfast Agreement, the parties' ultimate political aims for Northern Ireland still remain fundamentally unresolved, with SF continuing to press for a united Ireland and the DUP advocating a continued union with the United Kingdom. As a result of this ongoing divide and disagreements surrounding related issues between the majority DUP and SF, the Assembly has been suspended on four occasions since it took power in 1999, with the most recent suspension lasting for several years (October 2002 to May 2007) while governing powers reverted back to the Northern Ireland Office. That said, despite a growth in electoral polarization, since 2007 the Assembly has enjoyed a much greater degree of stability, with elections in May 2011 marking the first Assembly government since the Belfast Agreement to complete a full term.

However, continued evidence of intercommunity polarization is also reflected on a broader societal level in Northern Ireland. While gains in employment equity have facilitated more frequent intercommunal inter-actions in the workplace, the places where people live, go to school, shop and socialize still remain deeply segregated along communal lines, particularly in the most deprived and disadvantaged working-class areas of Northern Ireland's cities (idem: 2–3). As a result, despite growth in overall levels of relative equality following the peace process, the continued deprivation experienced in these highly segregated areas has proven a strong barrier to the kinds of positive intercommunal contact and interaction that could potentially help to improve future community relations between nationalists and unionists. This is an issue emphasized by Professor Paul Arthur of the University of Ulster, who argues that "the more economic deprivation there is, the less likely you're going to get any kind of community understanding. In some of the working-class housing estates, I would say there is no contact whatsoever with people on the other side" (interview: February 13th, 2008). Arthur's point is echoed by Chris O'Halloran of the non-governmental Belfast Interface Project (BIP), who explains that

> [i]t's become clear that there are many young people, particularly low-income young people, who, because they are unskilled, because they have very low incomes, they have very little experience of the Other community . . . which means that their horizons are extremely limited. And of course that's a perfect situation to foment, or to grow, or breed, or develop attitudes and perceptions of other people that may not be true.

Because there's no way of testing those, of finding out they're not true. So with income comes opportunity. Accompanying low income is a lack of opportunity in terms of challenging stereotypes and prejudice about the Other.

(Interview: April 24th, 2008)

Perhaps most troublingly, a number of recent studies have shown that in many of the most violence-prone interface areas that continue to exist between nationalist and unionist communities, there is a strong correlation between levels of social and economic deprivation, communal segregation and distancing, and the presence of antagonistic sectarian attitudes and mindsets (Murtagh 1994; McEvoy-Levy 2001; Jarman 2002, 2004; NISRA 2005; Shirlow and Murtagh 2006). Indeed, despite the substantial gains made towards improving community relations during the peace process, in many of the worst high-tension interface zones in Belfast's urban areas, low-intensity violence has continued relatively unabated since the Belfast Agreement in the form of rioting and other kinds of sectarian 'anti-social' behavior (Jarman 2006; Hughes et al. 2007). Other research suggests that economic deprivation has proven to be a critical factor in sustaining continued encouragement for Republican and Loyalist paramilitary groups, with the greatest levels of community backing, funding and recruitment for these organizations coming from the most disadvantaged interface areas (Byrne 1995; Byrne and Irvin 2001).

The unresolved danger posed to the future of community relations and sustainable peace in Northern Ireland by the continued existence of such chronically disadvantaged zones was highlighted in June 2011. During this period, several days of sustained sectarian rioting involving hundreds of nationalists and unionists—considered by many observers to be among the most violent incidents in Northern Ireland since the end of the Troubles— broke out at the lower Newtownards/Short Strand interface area of East Belfast. This rioting was also accompanied by shooting attacks from suspected dissident Republican and Loyalist paramilitaries targeting the policing services and members of the Other community (BBC News, June 22nd, 2011). In September 2012 sectarian clashes over deeply contentious parading issues resulted in three nights of severe rioting in North Belfast, during which over 60 police officers were injured from sustained brick, stone and petrol bomb attacks (BBC, 5 September, 2012).

In response to the continuation of such incidents, many of those working to transform the dynamics of interface zones have stressed the crucial importance of addressing the high levels of poverty and social and economic disadvantage that undergird sectarian tension and violence in these areas alongside other efforts to improve community relations through inter-communal contact and dialogue. As a recent strategy document by the BIP outlining how to create 'shared spaces' and improve community relations at interface zones argues, economic development remains a necessary "lever for positive change in interface communities" and ultimately "the poverty and exclusion that drives division and competition at or near interfaces must be taken into account if solutions are to be found" (Goldie and Ruddy 2010: 10–11).

Distributive learning and the South African TRC

One of the defining characteristics of the apartheid system was the deep structural and material inequality it entrenched along racial lines, with the starkest disparities evident between the minority white and majority black populations. This inequality extended into nearly every facet of socioeconomic and political life: income, land ownership, access to political power, employment, education and voting rights (Hirshowitza and Orkin 1997). For instance, the system of 'Bantu education' subjected generations of black South Africans to education that was grossly inferior and vastly underfunded compared to that enjoyed by their white counterparts. Group Areas Acts, Land Acts and Pass Laws all limited the areas in which black South Africans could move freely, live and own land. As detailed in the TRC's Final Report, driven by the guiding policy of 'separate development' that underpinned the strategies of 'petty' and 'grand' apartheid, the minority white population effectively "redrew the map of South Africa":

> The wealth, the cities, the mines, parks and the best beaches became part of white South Africa. A meagre thirteen per cent of largely barren land was parceled out in a series of homelands in which African people were forced to live, while the able-bodied were driven to seek a living as migrant labourers in the cities. . . . All over South Africa, public buildings and amenities were divided and sometimes even duplicated according to race group, retaining the best for the white group. . . . Separate meant far from equal and often resulted in no facilities at all for those who were not white.
>
> (TRC 1998: vol. 1, ch. 4, paras 46–47)

Further, Separate Representation Acts effectively disenfranchised black voters from the South African political system, restricting citizenship and voting rights to their assigned Bantustan regions. The apparatuses of the state, including the legislature, judiciary, policing and security forces, were effectively co-opted by the white minority and used to dominate the black majority, as were key elements of business and the media (Dugard 1978; Dyzenhaus 1998). As Chapman and van der Merwe note, the "institutionalized racism, injustice, and violence at the heart of the apartheid system of compulsory racial separation enabled a white minority, amounting to some 13 percent of the population, to monopolize economic and political power and to relegate the black majority, constituting 75 percent of the population, to a subordinated and politically powerless state" (2008b).

Statistics from the apartheid era help to reveal the staggering scale and scope of these inequalities. In 1975, the Gini coefficent of inequality for personal household incomes stood at 0.68, which at the time gave South Africa the dubious distinction of having the highest levels of recorded income inequality in the world (Holden and McGrath 1986). Other studies from the early 1980s reveal that the average per capita income of whites was thirteen times greater than that of black South Africans, while 30 percent of urban black households had incomes well below the poverty line—a figure that rose to over 70 percent in rural areas and the Bantustans (McGrath 1984). The concentration and depth of poverty throughout the black townships under apartheid was striking, with 81 percent of those living in these areas in 1980 subsisting on incomes well below minimal living standards and 13 percent having no measurable income level whatsoever (Simkin 1984). Further, levels of black unemployment in a number of townships during the same period were estimated at nearly 50 percent (Savage 1987: 611).

Living conditions for black South Africans, particularly in the urban townships, were heavily overcrowded, with upwards of a dozen individuals often living in a single room in substandard housing, workers' hostels, and squatter camps (idem: 615–617). These conditions were compounded by widespread inadequate access to basic living necessities such as food, clean water, fuel, health care and sanitation (idem: 605). However, at the same time, whites living in South Africa enjoyed levels of education, employment status, income and services equal to or better than their counterparts in Europe and North America (Treiman 2005: 11).

Not surprisingly, these economic inequalities had an extremely damaging impact on intergroup relations between black and white South Africans. Studies of black South African attitudes during apartheid revealed consistent findings of dissatisfaction, a sense of socioeconomic injustice, and perceptions of deprivation in relation to members of the white minority. These attitudes, in turn, are shown to have engendered widespread feelings of hostility towards whites and to have fostered intergroup mistrust and animosity (Duckitt and Mphuthing 1998: 811).

In addition, as previously discussed, physically and geographically segregated housing limited opportunities for meaningful cross-racial relationships between black and white South Africans and proved the breeding ground for racial stereotypes, prejudices and misunderstandings (Foster and Finchilescu 1986). While some opportunities existed for sustained interracial contact in the workplace, this too was heavily mediated by the hierarchical relationships and unequal power dynamics tied to socioeconomic status, with minimally educated blacks often performing unskilled or semi-skilled labor under the direction of better educated, better paid and more highly skilled white employers who lived and socialized in worlds vastly different than those of their employees (Treiman 2005: 14–18). Overall, the legacy of apartheid was the creation of "a society that was deeply divided between haves and have-nots, a division mainly between whites and blacks" (Chapman and van der Merwe 2008b: 6). Not surprisingly, many of those experts interviewed in South Africa argued that these deeper and more pervasive structural divisions have posed the greatest challenges to post-conflict reconciliation following South Africa's transition, perhaps proving even more significant than the direct impact of physical violence. As Madeleine Fullard, former TRC Senior National Researcher and current Head of the National Prosecuting Authority's Missing Persons Task Team asks,

> [w]hat is the real challenge facing South Africa [post-apartheid]? It's not the fates of what happened to 60,000 political activists. It's addressing the extreme racial inequalities that structure every aspect of life in South Africa . . . because every single black person suffered discrimination and oppression.
>
> (Interview: July 8th, 2008)

As structural and material inequalities based on racial identity served as one of the most pervasive points of division under apartheid, it has been widely recognized by internal and external observers such as Tlhoki Mofokeng of the Khulumani Support Group that "reconciliation will be impossible without economic redistribution, without any material changes in people's lives" (interview: July 1st, 2008). This sentiment is evident in the responses of many black victims of apartheid violence, who indicate that material compensation and improved access to social services such as housing and health care remain the most important factors for their own processes of reconciliation following the transition, even surpassing demands for the criminal prosecution of perpetrators (Colvin 2006: 191). The inherent interrelationship between the alleviation of material inequalities and the achievement of broader goals of social repair, interracial reconciliation and national unity in the post-apartheid era was underscored by the TRC itself in its Final Report, which illustrated that

> [g]ross socio-economic inequalities are the visible legacy of the systematic, institutionalized denial of access to resources and development opportunities on grounds of colour, race and sex. . . . The road to reconciliation, therefore, means both material reconstruction and the restoration of dignity. It involves the redress of gross inequalities and the nurturing of respect for our common humanity. It entails sustainable growth and development of the spirit of *ubuntu*. It implies wide-ranging structural and institutional transformation and the healing of broken human relationships. It demands guarantees that the past will not be

repeated. It requires restitution and the restoration of our humanity—as individuals, as communities and as a nation.

(TRC 1998: vol. 1, ch. 5, para. 25)

However, while the Commission may have recognized the importance of addressing the structural and material inequalities of the past as a central component of South Africa's interracial reconciliation process, under its empowering National Unity and Reconciliation Act, the TRC was only given the very narrow mandate of investigating gross human rights violations that led to physical infringement of the 'bodily integrity' of victims, including "the killing, abduction, torture or severe ill treatment of any person" (GSA 1995). Indeed, the work of all three main branches of the TRC, including the Human Rights Violations Committee (HRVC), the Amnesty Committee (AC) and the Reparations and Rehabilitation Committee (RRC), focused exclusively on individual cases in which direct acts of physical or mental injury were committed over the course of past political conflict (TRC 1998: vol. 1, ch. 4, para 55). As a result, from the TRC's inception, the more systematic repression and pervasive daily suffering that occurred as a result of racial inequality under apartheid remained largely beyond its mandate. While this focus was dictated by the Commission's empowering Act, there is also evidence to suggest that it reflected an early recognition among the Commissioners that the TRC simply would not have the time or resources required to address the deep legacy of structural and material inequalities between racial groups in addition to dealing with individual physical rights abuses. Instead, it was hoped that other initiatives beyond the TRC would ultimately be employed to attend to these issues.[8]

As a result, the relatively narrow focus adopted by the TRC has received a good deal of criticism from scholars and practitioners alike. As former TRC Commissioner Yasmin Sooka has argued, the "fundamental problem" of the Commission may have been its attempt to separate individual rights violations from the broader structural dynamics in which they occurred. As she notes, by so doing, "you're looking at the political crimes which are manifestations of an unjust system, but you don't look at the unjust system itself which is structural in nature" (interview: July 6th, 2008). Indeed, as several critics contend, by focusing attention on the physical abuses committed by the relatively small number of perpetrators who appeared before the Commission, the TRC may have helped to obscure the much more pervasive system of structural oppression in South Africa—a system that daily affected much of the population on social, political, economic and legislative levels (Mamdani 2001).

Further, others have suggested that by concentrating on the individual complicity of perpetrators in the TRC, the Commission may have helped to propagate a perception that sole responsibility for the crimes of the past should be laid at the feet of the small number of 'bad apples' who appeared before the

AC. This is considered particularly problematic in regard to the perceptions of white South Africans, many of whom, studies suggest, were therefore able to assign accountability for the harms caused by apartheid to the seemingly aberrant actions of a handful of police and security force members who admitted to crimes of abduction, murder and torture in their amnesty applications (Valji 2004). However inadvertent, this has hindered processes of distributive learning and interracial reconciliation by allowing for a disavowal of responsibility among those in the broader white community who, while not directly involved in acts of physical violence, may have supported or otherwise indirectly benefited from the structural inequities of apartheid. As Chapman and van der Merwe note, one of the potential side effects of the individualized focus on physical violence adopted by the Commission was that

> it did not require white South Africans to confront their complicity in the abuses that were revealed in the TRC . . . [as] it neglected to portray the privileged position of the white community (wealth, education, etc.) as something that was gained at the expense of other South Africans. Therefore, white South Africans do not see the present socioeconomic inequalities in the country as something they helped create or have a responsibility to redress.
>
> (2008a: 273)

This distancing is reflected in a marked lack of willingness among many white South Africans to feel a personal compulsion to engage in processes of societal restitution or redistribution in the post-apartheid era. As Professor Amanda Gouws of the University of Stellenbosch notes, "many white people would say, why do I have to do this, what do I have to say sorry for, I didn't kill anybody . . . [white] people don't understand that the privilege of having good education, having middle-class parents, all of that, contributed to where you are today" (interview: June 17th, 2008). This attitude is clearly evidenced in responses from a 2000–2001 survey conducted by James Gibson and Helen Macdonald, which showed that even after the work of the TRC, only a minority of whites (38.4 percent) agreed with the view that "in the past whites profited greatly from apartheid and most continue to profit today from the legacy of apartheid" compared to 87.9 percent of black respondents (Gibson and Macdonald 2001: 29). Notably, this same survey reveals that only 10 percent of whites believe that they should be personally involved in paying compensation to black South Africans, while 78.9 percent of blacks believe whites should have a role in doing so (idem: 24). One clear example of this reluctance has been the inability to gain widespread support from within the white community for the 'Home for All Campaign Initiative,' a civil society program begun after the completion of the TRC process that aimed to have white South Africans sign a commitment acknowledging responsibility as beneficiaries of the apartheid system and voluntarily contribute to a

'Development and Reconciliation Fund' to support disadvantaged communities belonging to other racial groups.

The continued lack of recognition of white South Africans of the benefits they enjoyed under the broader 'structural violence' of racial inequality in the apartheid era has also manifested itself in the underwhelming support by many in the white community for broader societal redistribution efforts following South Africa's transition. For instance, in the same year that the TRC released its Final Report, a 1998 Independent Newspapers poll showed that a majority of whites (87 percent) were against the implementation of any kind of affirmative action program in South Africa aimed to reduce address race-based employment imbalances in either the public service or private companies (Thiessen 2008: 213). A second Independent Newspapers poll conducted in 1999 showed that only 8 percent of whites were in favor of redistributive policies proposed by the government such as land reforms and affirmative action policies, compared to 73 percent of black respondents (ibid.). These findings are echoed in the later 2000–2001 survey carried out by Gibson and Macdonald, which revealed that only 38.4 percent of white respondents indicated that they believed victims of apartheid violence should be given special priority for jobs as compared to 82.7 percent of their black counterparts (2001: 27). Further, in the same survey, only 34 percent of whites agreed that individual companies that profited from apartheid ought to be required to pay any form of compensation, and a mere 9.5 percent felt that white farmers (often among the primary beneficiaries of apartheid's land redistribution policies) should be involved in providing restitution to the victims of apartheid (ibid.).

Indeed, a number of observers have noted that even after the work of the TRC, many whites in post-apartheid South Africa have not only opposed policies of redistribution, but have actually tended to perceive attempts by the government to implement affirmative action policies as forms of 'reverse racism' that unfairly victimize the white community (Gutto 2001: 219). As Madeleine Fullard describes:

> You basically have a white generation now, a generation of whites—whether they are young or old—that basically depict themselves as victims. They are the victims . . . [A] racial group that was quite happy to live with the benefits of the most radical or the most extreme affirmative actions—because what was apartheid except the most radical legislated and extreme form of affirmative action [by] ensuring that you got the best share, the best school, the best everything. But the moment there's the least sense of even slight change it's 'we're being victimized.' You look at white unemployment and it's very low, but you get people saying it's impossible for whites to get a job now and it's such a load of nonsense . . . there's this extraordinary sense of white victimization that has developed.
>
> (Interview: July 8th, 2008)

Taken together, the continued reluctance on the part of many white South Africans to recognize the benefits they received as a result of apartheid's system of racial inequality and their corresponding resistance to redistributive policies suggest that the TRC was only able to promote distributive learning to a very limited degree—a constraint that could prove a major barrier to future interracial reconciliation. As former TRC Commission Mary Burton notes, despite the Commission's best efforts, "still white South Africans do not acknowledge their beneficiary status and do not acknowledge they were part of an unjust system and that they did benefit from it. To the extent that doesn't happen, I have my doubts that we can ever say national reconciliation has happened" (interview: June 24th, 2008).

Distributive interventions within the South African TRC

However, while the TRC itself largely lacked the mandate to directly address issues of material inequality, the Commission did nonetheless incorporate some attempts to take on the structural legacies of apartheid alongside its primary focus on investigating individual human rights violations. For instance, the Commission's unique Institutional Hearings helped to shed light on some of the larger structural elements of apartheid society that reinforced racial inequality, investigating the roles played by the health sector, the legal system, media, business, labor and faith communities—all areas under the control of the white minority. Ultimately, however, it would appear that these inquiries were met "primarily with intransigence and obfuscation" from the actors involved and were able to provide little new insight as to how these institutions functioned as part of the broader system of inequity under apartheid (Chapman 2008: 181–182). As a result, it is now widely recognized that, in the end, these hearings led to very little meaningful acknowledgment of responsibility on the part of these institutional actors as to how they had contributed to or benefited from apartheid's structures of racial inequality (ibid.). This was perhaps most clearly reflected in the rejection by members of the predominantly white business community of the TRC's proposal to have those companies identified as having gained the most financially from apartheid-era policies to pay a one-time 'wealth tax' to alleviate poverty and provide services to the neediest black South Africans (Buford and van der Merwe 2004).

However, the TRC was also explicitly tasked with making a number of recommendations to the President regarding institutional, legislative and administrative reforms that should be introduced in the interest of promoting national unity and reconciliation, many of which sought to directly address elements of socioeconomic inequality between racial groups in post-apartheid South Africa. For instance, alongside the aforementioned proposal of a wealth tax on apartheid's key beneficiaries, the TRC also recommended a one-time donation from major businesses equivalent to 1 percent of their overall net worth and the creation of affirmative action and employment equality legislation to help alleviate racial disparities in the workplace (TRC 1998: vol. 5, ch. 8, para. 24). The Commission also proposed that compensation be paid to those who had their land appropriated or lost their businesses as a result of apartheid-era policies. Recommendations for major reforms were suggested to housing services, the media, the prison system, the legal system, the health care system, the security forces and the policing services in order to make these areas more responsive to, and representative of, South Africans of all races. The TRC also recommended that South Africa ratify major international covenants regarding civil, political, economic, social and cultural rights to ensure that future law and government practices operate in line with international human rights standards (idem: vol. 5, ch. 8).

Nevertheless, none of the recommendations suggested by the Commission in its Final Report was ultimately made legally binding on the South African government. As a result, the ANC governments that have come to power post-TRC have to date implemented very few of the recommendations made by the Commission. Indeed, as Chapman and van der Merwe illustrate, following the conclusion of the Commission's work, "[t]he various recommendations contained in the TRC final report have not been taken seriously by the government. Government departments do not refer to them, and there has been no systematic monitoring of their implementation" (2008b: 282).

Reparations through the TRC

Perhaps the most visible aspect of the TRC's work in addressing material inequalities was the emphasis it placed on providing a reparations program for the victims of apartheid violence. Reparations, defined as "any forms of compensation, *ex gratia* payment, restitution, rehabilitation or recognition," feature prominently in the founding Act of the TRC, where they are framed as one of the basic requirements for the promotion of national unity and reconciliation in post-apartheid South Africa (GSA 1995). The centrality of reparations to the work of the TRC was also noted in its Final Report, in which the Commission recognized that "without adequate reparation and rehabilitation measures, there can be no healing or reconciliation" (TRC 1998: vol. 5, ch. 5, para. 2).

Results from Gibson and Macdonald's 2000–2001 survey reveal the importance of reparations to the broader South African population following the transition from apartheid. Fully 91 percent of the majority black South African population surveyed indicated that they supported payment of reparations in the form of direct government compensation for victims of apartheid-era abuses, and of these respondents, 70 percent felt that "national reconciliation requires material compensation for victims of apartheid" (Gibson and Macdonald 2001: 27).[9] The singular importance placed by the black community on reparations was attributable to two interrelated factors.

First, reparations offered one direct way in which the government could begin to address the dire socioeconomic conditions in which many black South Africans found themselves following the end of apartheid. Second, the issue of reparations had become closely bound up with questions of justice, and for many black South Africans it became a way to counterbalance for victims the potential 'justice deficit' caused by the granting of conditional amnesties to perpetrators (Colvin 2006).

Accordingly, alongside the AC and HRVC, the RRC was created as one of the TRC's three central pillars and was tasked with determining which individuals would qualify as victims for the purposes of receiving reparations. The RRC was also mandated with making recommendations to the President as to what these reparations should entail, both in the form of 'urgent interim reparations' and a longer-term reparations program designed to help rehabilitate and restore "the human and civil dignity of victims" (GSA 1995). Over a period of 18 months, the RRC consulted with victims, civil society leaders and local community organizations in an attempt to gauge the extent of harm suffered by victims, assess their needs, and design appropriate recommendations for reparations policies to be included in the TRC's 1998 Final Report. These recommendations included immediate and long-term financial payments to individual victims, programs designed to aid community rehabilitation (including housing, education, health, and social services), the provision of 'symbolic reparations' to aid in commemorating the past (such as memorials, monuments, a day of remembering and the renaming of public facilities), and broader suggestions for institutional reform in South African society. These programs were to receive funding from a special President's Fund comprised of monies from the new South African government and contributions from private and international donors (TRC 1998: vol. 5, ch. 5).

However, from its outset, the reparations program proposed by the RRC faced several limitations. First, it was decided that both the urgent and long-term reparations programs (as well as access to many of the services proposed under the community rehabilitation program) would only be provided to the small number of 'official' victims who registered to give statements through the HRVC. This meant that while the TRC recognized that nearly all non-white South Africans had suffered—and often continued to suffer—under the structural and material inequalities entrenched under apartheid, only those 22,000 registered on the HRVC's closed list of official victims who had endured gross physical human rights violations would be eligible to receive any form of reparations (Walaza 2000; Orr 2000).

Under the Urgent Interim Reparations (UIR) program, roughly 14,000 of this number received a small one-time grant of between R2000 and R7500 (approximately $250 to $1,000 USD per individual) designed to help meet the costs of immediate medical, emotional or economic needs. However, despite the 'urgent' nature of these reparations, they only began to pay out in

June 1998 (with the process largely completed by 2001), resulting in a total payment of roughly R44,000,000 or the equivalent of $5.5 million USD (Orr 2000). Evidence suggests that many victims were highly dissatisfied with the delays experienced in receiving the UIR and the perceived inadequacy of the sums finally dispensed, with a number indicating that this left them feeling even more alienated from the TRC's mission of reconciliation (Colvin 2006: 289). As a result, as Anna Crawford-Pinnerup of the Centre for the Study of Violence and Reconciliation (CSVR) notes in her overall assessment of the impact of the Urgent Interim Reparations program, "UIR has not in and of itself made a meaningful and substantial impact on the lives of recipients and cannot, therefore, be considered a significant or even an adequate attempt at reparations" (2000: 1).

Beyond the UIR payments, the other components of the RRC's reparations program were delayed even further, and were left largely unaddressed by the Mbeki government until 2003. At this time, President Mbeki declared that the government's main focus would be on providing services for community reparations and symbolic reparations rather than direct financial compensation. In particular, he agreed to renew attention to building memorials, changing apartheid-era place names, and establishing a National Day of Prayer and Traditional Sacrifice. However, aside from the creation of a massive 52-hectare 'Freedom Park' memorial to commemorate the liberation struggle (which was finally largely completed in 2011 at an estimated cost of over $50 million USD) and changes to a small number of official place names, to date there has been little forward movement on these initiatives (Walker 2004).

In particular, despite sustained pressure from victim groups such as the Khulumani Support Group and other civil society organizations, no action was taken by the government in regard to the larger 'interim reparation grants' (IRG) recommended by the RRC until late 2003—more than three years after the original payment date suggested by the TRC. Furthermore, in its Final Report, the RRC had recommended annual IRG payments of R17,000 to R23,000 (approximately $2,100 and $2,900 USD respectively) dependent on individual need to be disbursed over a period of six years. However, in April 2003, the government announced that it would instead only provide victims with a single one-time cash grant of R30,000 (approximately $4,000 USD at the time): a fraction of the original, and already conservative, amount recommended by the RRC.

The persistent delays and the failure of the government to follow through on the TRC's recommendations for reparations have been cited by many observers as having severely damaged prospects for interracial reconciliation by serving as a major source of anger for victims from the black community. In particular, a number of observers note that the government's lack of investment in reparations was perceived as a "betrayal of the promise made to victims" that the 'sacrifice of justice' they were asked to make by accepting conditional amnesties for perpetrators would be matched by a government commitment to improving their lives through financial assistance (Walaza 2000: 254). As Madeleine Fullard notes, for many in the victim community this feeling of being ignored by the government led to an intense sense of grievance and even a degree of revictimization, with the result that "[t]he legacy of reparations has spoiled what would [otherwise] have been a positive experience for many victims" with the TRC process (interview: July 8th, 2008). This sentiment is echoed by Professor Piet Meiring, a former TRC Commissioner who himself worked on the RRC, and who suggests that "there's a sense among the victims that they were left in the lurch, that there were many promises made and many expectations in terms of reparations and that all of that did not come true" (interview: July 6th, 2008). Accordingly, even when the final reparations payments were made, they were simply "too little, too late" and so did little to ease victims' grievances or to contribute to the kind of positive distributive learning ultimately required to help build interracial reconciliation (Chapman and van der Merwe 2008c: 286). In the end, as Wendy Orr, a former TRC Commissioner assigned to the RRC argues, the government's failure to follow through on an adequate reparations program ran the risk of undermining the goals of the TRC by raising and then frustrating victims' expectations, ultimately doing more harm than good in regard to building national unity and reconciliation in post-apartheid South Africa (Orr 2000).

Distributive interventions outside the TRC process

Nonetheless, it must be noted that efforts to address the vast racial inequalities facing post-apartheid South Africa have not been limited solely to the work of the TRC. Many observers have speculated that the inattention paid to reparations by the South African government was largely due to a position adopted by post-apartheid ANC administrations that emphasized broader structural reforms (Chapman and van der Merwe 2008c: 289). These reforms began with the adoption of a highly progressive Constitution under President Mandela in 1996. Among other things, this new Constitution sought to remove racial discrimination from public policy and to extend full citizenship and franchise rights to all South Africans. It also enshrined a Bill of Rights containing extensive legal protections for equal treatment, including the protection of socioeconomic rights, regardless of race (GSA 1996).[10]

Alongside these broader political reforms, the government introduced an array of legislative and financial initiatives in an attempt to begin bridging the vast socioeconomic chasms dividing racial groups. In 1994, the government developed the Reconstruction and Development Programme (RDP) as an integrated framework with the goals of stimulating job creation through public works, engaging in redistribution through land reform, and initiating major infrastructure projects in the areas of housing, education and other social services. This was followed by the Growth, Employment, and Redistribution (GEAR) initiative, a broad macroeconomic program that built upon the initiatives of the RDP to increase economic growth and stimulate job creation (Hoogeveen and Ozler 2005).

In addition, under President Mbeki, the government initiated a series of targeted policies that set out to address the extreme levels of poverty and inequalities in access to economic opportunities faced by the majority of black South Africans. The Employment Equity Act put pressure on employers to implement affirmative action practices to ensure the inclusion of blacks and other underrepresented groups in the labor market and to expedite their movement into more highly skilled (and higher-paid) occupations. This was followed by the 2003 Black Economic Empowerment Act (BEE), which introduced a series of state-subsidized policies designed to increase the number of black entrepreneurs and business owners (Seekings and Nattrass 2004).

As a result of the government's interventions, a good deal of progress has been made in improving the lives of the most impoverished South Africans, particularly in terms of their ability to access basic services and provisions such as electricity, water and housing. The political and legal barriers to racial advancement are now a thing of the past, with many more black South Africans having access to better education, holding higher-level positions, and making middle- and upper-class salaries (Hoogeveen and Ozler 2005).

However, recent evidence shows that almost twenty years after transition, South Africa remains a highly inequitable society, with the majority of black South Africans continuing to be severely impoverished. While trends do show a small decrease in the overall numbers of those living in poverty, the extent of that poverty has deepened for many of the most disadvantaged black South Africans (HSRC 2004: 1). Moreover, the number of unemployed black South Africans has actually grown since the end of apartheid, as have overall levels of income inequality within the country.[11] Further, while structural inequalities between racial groups have generally declined during this period, levels of intragroup inequality within the black community have increased at an accelerated rate (van der Berg et al. 2006). Overall, these trends indicate that while life has improved for some black South Africans, many of these gains are attributable to a small percentage of upwardly mobile middle-class individuals or an even smaller subset of black 'super-elites' who have managed to amass sizeable personal fortunes through policies like the BEE. Accordingly, as Professor Garth Stevens of the University of the Witwatersrand notes, "for a large portion of the population, where the majority of the people are still located in townships in South Africa, the majority of those people still remain black, still remain poor" (interview: July 2nd, 2008).

Indeed, the majority of experts interviewed indicated that the lack of any substantive socioeconomic change in the daily lives of most black South Africans presents perhaps the greatest barrier to social learning and intergroup reconciliation in the country. For instance, as Thloki Mofokeng, Acting Chair of the Khulumani Support Group illustrates,

> [f]or the overwhelming majority of [black South Africans] their lives have not changed. They're still unemployed, they're still very marginalized from structures of government and from any kind of decision making forums. So for many there's been no change at all. . . . So a lot of them are very bitter at what the new dispensation has meant to them. They feel marginalized, they feel betrayed, their position has not changed at all.
>
> (Interview: July 1st, 2008)

In a similar fashion, Professor Amanda Gouws of Stellenbosch University details how the continued experience of poverty and inequality for many black South Africans has reinforced feelings of anger and resentment towards white South Africans who appear to continue to benefit from the structures of apartheid in the wake of the country's transition. As she contends,

> part of the problem with reconciliation [in South Africa] is that it lacks that socioeconomic dimension . . . The poor in this country have gotten so much poorer and they get poorer every week . . . So because of that lack of a socioeconomic dimension people feel that their lives have actually gotten worse since 1994 . . . so you blame apartheid, you blame the past. And in that sense there is no reconciliation.
>
> (Interview: June 17th, 2008)

Echoing this point, other interviewees note that the continued existence of stark disparities between the standards of living of black and white South Africans serves as a persistent source of racial animosity in post-apartheid South Africa. For instance, Marcella Naidoo, Director of the well-respected Black Sash non-governmental organization in Cape Town, observes that

> in many ways this [racial] inequality drives tension. Because you drive past a fancy place like Constantia and yes, there's a few black people sprinkled in between, but it's still not a very mixed community . . . And then you have a large majority of black people, very, very poor and very few white people sit in that community. So there's still that divide, and I think that does drive tensions . . . the attitudes change in my view as the structural arrangements change.
>
> (Interview: June 25th, 2008)

That said, perhaps one of the most damaging impacts of apartheid's legacy of structural and material inequalities between black and white South Africans has been its capacity to continually impede opportunities for the kinds of positive interracial interaction that could potentially lead to improved race relations in post-apartheid South Africa. While South Africa's highly progressive equality legislation and affirmative action policies have meant that members of different races are now brought together to mix formally in the workplace during the day, in large part, blacks and whites are still separated in the evening as they return to homes often located in the very same segregated areas to which they were confined during apartheid. The majority of whites continue to return to homes in relatively affluent suburbs while the majority of blacks return to underprivileged townships and informal settlements often located far outside urban centers.

Indeed, as Fanie du Toit, Director of the non-governmental Institute for Justice and Reconciliation (IJR) argues, the spatial segregation enforced by the residual 'geography of apartheid' remains a key barrier to the kinds of contact and socialization that might otherwise help to improve interracial relations. As he notes, in contemporary South Africa, a continued "bane in terms of race relations is that people sleep in different places. Although they work together at nighttime they withdraw into their communities and they are reminded that they are a certain race or not" (interview: June 18th, 2008). Nahla Valji of the CSVR makes a similar observation, indicating that "people are coming out of the traditional spatial and racial geographies and integrating during the day, but they're going back at night. If you look at the townships, they still are largely preserved, largely the way they were twenty years ago" (interview: June 24th, 2008). These points are further echoed by Piers Pigou, Director of the South African History Archive (SAHA), who notes that even post-apartheid many South Africans continue to live in "parallel worlds" and lead "parallel lives" that all too infrequently have the opportunity to intersect in meaningful ways:

> We still live in societies that are essentially separated from one another . . . Go downtown into the centre of Jo'burg at the end of the working day and look who stands in what bus queues: different race groups going back to their different locations. Of course there's some graying of that area, but we still live in our silos—in our community silos, in our racial silos. I'm not saying there isn't cross-over, but we're still siloed, we're still in our racial silos to a large extent here . . . So we're light years away from discovering each other in this country and what our experiences are.
>
> (Interview: July 1st, 2008)

Notable exceptions to these post-transitional patterns of continued racial separation do exist, and are most often to be found among the more affluent and highly educated members of South African society. Data collected in 2007 by South Africa's Reconciliation Barometer Survey (SARB) shows a direct correlation between levels of economic prosperity and interracial contact, suggesting that "as material disposition improves, the higher the likelihood for inter-racial contact becomes" (Hofmeyr 2007: 42). Additionally, survey results from more recent rounds of the SARB conducted in 2011 confirm that average household living standards continue to be one of the most significant predictors of both daily contact and socialization across racial lines, with the result that "people from households with the lowest living standards are least likely to speak or socialize with people of other racial groups, and those in the most affluent households are far more likely to do so" (Lefko-Everett et al. 2011: 30).

These survey findings reflect a common theme mentioned by many expert interviewees, who consistently pointed to increased economic prosperity as a key determinant not only of greater levels of interracial contact, but also of the increased levels of trust and understanding that such interactions bring. There are several ways in which this correlation operates. Perhaps most importantly, interviewees noted that increased levels of prosperity among a growing minority of the black population have enabled these individuals to move into the more affluent (and predominantly white) neighborhoods of South Africa's cities, allowing them to socialize in the same shopping malls, restaurants, bars and leisure centers as their middle- or upper-class white neighbors. This upward mobility has also provided the opportunity for the children of more affluent black families to attend racially mixed schools with their white counterparts—an integration that many interviewees credit with helping to at least begin the process of improving racial relations among the younger post-apartheid generation. As Nahla Valji notes,

> there's a thin layer of black middle class who have integrated in different ways: they can afford to live in Sandton, [an affluent white suburb of Johannesburg], shop in the same shopping malls, buy in to the same activities, and their children can attend the same schools . . . at that level there's a kind of integration that's happened around the commodification and commercialization of middle class . . . [but] at other [economic] levels its been incredibly minimal.
>
> (Interview: June 24th, 2008)

Similarly, interviewees also noted that an increase in economic prosperity tends to go hand in hand with a greater equality of status in the workplace, meaning that more affluent members of different races have the opportunity to interact as equals on a daily basis. This kind of interaction provides a baseline platform on which relationships of trust and friendship can be built. Accordingly, Fanie du Toit, Director of the IJR, contends that "race relations in this country, in the upper bracket, continue to improve and normalize. I mean by that those people who are earning middle to middle-upper-class income who are in the formal sector and they are working together on a daily basis" (interview: June 18th, 2008). This point was also emphasized by Jan Hofmeyr, a political analyst with the IJR's SARB, who illustrates that by and large, we still live in racially dominant neighborhoods where really the only exposure you get to someone who's your age, someone who's your peer is at the workplace. So the opportunity to expand this kind of exposure is closely linked to questions of the economy and those of job creation . . . people get exposed to each other, see they've got the same intellectual capacities.

(Interview: June 23rd, 2008)

Unfortunately, the percentage of black South Africans who have risen to this level of economic prosperity since transition still remains relatively small, leaving the majority of the black population living in the same segregated townships, attending the same separated and underfunded schools, and suffering under the same conditions of poverty as they did during apartheid. Therefore, as Dr. Garth Stevens of the University of the Witwatersrand details, many of the benefits of social learning gained through the increased contact and interaction associated with increased economic prosperity remain very limited in the new South Africa—particularly for the majority of the black population that remains socioeconomically disadvantaged. As Stevens notes,

there's greater levels of integration at the levels of the new middle class, upper class, and the new elites that are emerging in South Africa. At that level I do think you have greater levels of engagement, contact, and trust and friendship. And I do think things have certainly changed for that particular cohort of the population. But for a large part of the population, where the majority of the people are still located in townships in South Africa . . . the majority of those people still remain lacking, still remain poor. . . . For the majority of black people who continue to live in the same situations they did prior to 1994, I have grave doubts they view other racialized communities very differently in South Africa . . . I think there are possibilities [for better relations], but it's for a very particular group in South Africa.

(Interview: July 2nd, 2008)

This point was reiterated by Michele Ruiters of the non-governmental Institute for Global Development in South Africa, who asserts that in terms of race relations, "among ordinary South Africans, I don't think the perceptions have changed at all because they don't have to mix with each other outside, they don't have to mix with each other socially. . . . Low-income communities remain extremely segregated—it's still the old townships [and] there hasn't been much mobility in those areas" (interview: July 10th, 2008).

Overall, these findings suggest that more conciliatory racial relationships will ultimately only be made possible by removing the impediments to social learning that come with a reduction in levels of material inequality and an improvement of the relative standard of living of the black majority in South Africa. Indeed, when asked whether continued economic inequality was an obstacle to reconciliation in post-apartheid South Africa in the 2011 SARB survey, 46 percent of South Africans agreed that reconciliation was 'impossible' while people who were disadvantaged under apartheid continue to be poor, while only 17 percent indicated they felt reconciliation was possible under these circumstances (Lefko-Everett et al. 2011: 31). This sentiment also emerged time and again as a major point of consensus among the experts interviewed in South Africa. For instance, as Marcella Naidoo of the Black Sash contends, "it is economic change that needs to happen, and the sharing in the wealth of this country which I think is going to bring about less of an emphasis on white and black because as long as we have that inequality we don't have reconciliation" (interview: June 25th, 2008). Similarly, former TRC Commissioner Mary Burton emphasizes that despite its many other positive contributions, the Commission's lasting impact on interracial reconciliation will ultimately be curtailed by the ongoing inequalities that continue to divide racial groups in contemporary South Africa. As Burton concludes,

> [i]n the end it all comes down to the huge inequity, the huge disparity between wealthy and poor. And the fact that the wealthy now includes some black people doesn't make a difference, it still means that the vast majority, more than 50 percent of the population, feel themselves to be marginalized, hopeless and angry. And relations will not get better until we deal with that point.
>
> (Interview: June 23rd, 2008)

Notes

1   One example that aroused particular bitterness was the redistribution of the Londonderry County Borough that, at the time of partition, had a substantial and growing Catholic/nationalist minority. However, under the changes to electoral laws passed in 1923, unionists were able to maintain an electoral majority. Years later when Catholics/nationalists appeared to be in the majority, the electoral lines were again redrawn to assure unionist domination (Buckland 1979: 243–246).
2   The Cameron Commission's 1969 report found the existence of severe "electoral imbalances" that favored unionist representatives, concluding "that there can be no doubt that under modern conditions the electoral arrangements [in Northern Ireland] were producing unfair results" (GNI 1969a: paras 136–137).
3   The Cameron Commission report evidences the tendency of the RUC to take the side of unionists when a conflict occurred between Protestant/unionist and Catholic/nationalist demonstrators, asserting that this bias was "undoubted" and "of general application and long standing" (GNI 1969a: para. 181).

4 Notably, by 1969, Catholics only held six of 68 senior judicial appointments, only one of the six Supreme Court judgeships, and one of four County Court judgeships (Corrigan 1969: 28).

5 Notably, earlier efforts at establishing a devolved government at Stormont were attempted between 1973 and 1974 and 1982 and 1986. In both cases, however, the government was quickly abolished in the face of sectarian divides between hardline nationalist and unionist factions.

6 This is reflective of earlier survey data collected in 2001 by the NILT which showed that 55 percent of Catholics and 71 percent of Protestant respondents felt that both communities were "treated equally" by the police (ARK 2002).

7 For instance, the earlier 'Patten Report' released in 1999 showed that while 70 percent of Protestants thought the RUC treated both communities equally, this opinion was shared by only 25–30 percent of the Catholic population (ICPNI 1999: 14).

8 Indeed, as noted in the TRC's Final Report, "in making its own limited contribution, the Commission had to walk a tightrope between too wide and too narrow an interpretation of gross violations of human rights. The Commission would have neither the life span nor the resources to implement a broadly constituted interpretation" (TRC 1998: vol. 1, ch. 4, para. 43). As a result, "the Commission resolved that its mandate was to give attention to gross human rights violations committed as specific acts, resulting in severe physical and/or mental injury, in the course of past political conflict. As such, the focus of its work was not on the effects of laws passed by the apartheid government, nor on general policies of that government or of other organizations, however morally offensive these may have been. This underlines the importance of understanding the Commission as but one of several instruments responsible for transformation and bridge-building in post-apartheid South Africa" (TRC 1998: vol. 1, ch. 4, paras. 43, 55).

9 Notably, however, this sentiment was clearly not widely shared by the minority population of white South Africans, of whom only 20 percent polled in the same survey indicated that they agreed with the need for reparations to achieve reconciliation (Gibson and Macdonald 2001).

10 This built upon the protections already established under the 1993 Interim Constitution that ushered in South Africa's first multiracial election in 1994.

11 In fact, the Gini coefficent of income inequality has actually grown to over .70 since the end of apartheid (van der Berg et al. 2006).

Chapter 8

Conclusion

Social learning and reconciliation in divided societies

The foregoing analyses of Northern Ireland and South Africa suggest that both societies in many ways remain deeply divided along the same lines of collective ethnonational and racial identity that underpinned their histories of conflict. In South Africa, while the system of apartheid was brought to an end with a relatively peaceful transition to multi-racial democracy in 1994, the majority of white and black South Africans continue to live largely separate lives. Similarly, in Northern Ireland, despite the historic signing of the Belfast Agreement in 1998 that brought the Troubles to a close, societal relations continue to largely be defined by oppositional communal identities: nationalist or unionist, Catholic or Protestant. In both countries, while widespread political violence is now largely a thing of the past and groups live in relatively peaceful coexistence, many of the scars of past violence are still visible in continued patterns of physical, social and psychological separation.

It therefore remains clear that in both Northern Ireland and South Africa the process of intergroup reconciliation remains incomplete. That said, put in the context of the deeply entrenched divides and long histories of communal violence in these countries and the relatively short periods of time that have elapsed since their transitions to peace, the gains that have been made towards reconciliation are nonetheless remarkable. Given that these countries are often cited as relative success stories in overcoming intractable social conflict, both South Africa and Northern Ireland serve as cautionary reminders of the fact that post-conflict reconciliation must be understood as a long-term endeavor that can take generations to unfold, and that there are no 'quick fixes' or 'miracle cures' when it comes to repairing relationships between former antagonists in deeply divided societies.

Moreover, as this analysis has shown, in both Northern Ireland and South Africa it would appear that many of the positive gains made in advancing intergroup reconciliation to date are attributable to the different transitional justice interventions that have been employed in each of these countries to address the legacies of past violence. In Northern Ireland, a 'decentralized' approach to transitional justice emerged following the end of the Troubles, one that has combined a uniquely 'piecemeal' strategy for addressing the past with discrete government programs to improve socioeconomic equality and an array of projects led by local community groups and civil society designed to improve community relations from the bottom up. In South Africa, transitional justice took the form of the highly regarded Truth and Reconciliation Commission (TRC), a unique twist on previous truth commission models that deemphasized legal prosecutions and instead provided a conditional amnesty provision for the perpetrators of apartheid-era violence in an effort to promote truth recovery and encourage societal repair.

Social learning and reconciliation in Northern Ireland

A decade on from the Belfast Agreement (BFA), Northern Ireland remains a society deeply divided by the violent legacy of the Troubles. High levels of communal segregation, continued mistrust and misunderstanding between both political elites and members of broader society, and the perpetuation of zero-sum interpretations of the past mean that Northern Ireland's peace is an unsteady one, with many of the challenges of reconciliation yet to be faced. This is perhaps most clearly evident in the continuation of low-intensity violence and rioting at many of the interface areas which divide nationalist and unionist communities in Northern Ireland, as well as a troubling recent resurgence of 'dissident' violence on the part of both Republican and Loyalist paramilitaries. As a recent assessment by Miles Hewstone and colleagues notes, "the country is still in some way far short of the Agreement's vision of an inclusive, stable, and fair society, firmly founded on the achievement of human rights for all" (Hewstone et al. 2008b: 219). To be fair, this should not come as a surprise given that processes of post-conflict reconciliation are best measured on a scale of decades or generations as opposed to years.

That said, there are some positive indications that intergroup relations between members of nationalist and unionist communities are improving, and that antagonistic and hostile perceptions are beginning to be transformed. For instance, barring the recent actions of dissident paramilitary organizations, there appears to now be widespread agreement among both nationalist and unionist communities that the use of violence is no longer a legitimate means to advance their national aims. This has been perhaps most clearly reflected in the surprising stability of the devolved Northern Ireland Assembly that, since 2007, has successfully governed through a power-sharing arrangement under the leadership of long-time political enemies Sinn Féin and the Democratic Unionist Party. In addition, the development of relative levels of equality between Catholic and Protestant populations in key areas of income, employment and housing has now largely removed these long-standing issues as sources of communal division in Northern Ireland. Further, there is now evidence to suggest that a rise in opportunities for more frequent cross-community interaction has led to increased tolerance, trust and understanding as well as a decrease in stereotypes, prejudice and hostility between nationalists and unionists. For many in Northern Ireland, this interaction also seems to have contributed to new perceptions of group identity and intergroup relations that are less polarized and oppositional than in the past. Indeed, in a recent Northern Ireland Life and Times survey conducted in 2010, more than 62 percent of those polled indicated a belief that relations between Protestants and Catholics were better than they were five years ago, an increase of over 37 percent from when this same question was first asked prior to the peace process in 1989 (ARK 2011).[1] Similarly, when asked whether they thought relations would be better in five years' time, more than half (52 percent) indicated they were optimistic and believed they would be better, with 41 percent indicating they believed they would be about the same, and only 5 percent responding that they thought they would be worse (ibid.). Again, this marked a substantial increase from prior to the peace process in 1989, when only 26 percent thought relations would be better in the future (ibid.).

In light of these indications, what role has Northern Ireland's decentralized transitional justice strategy played in encouraging these nascent signs of social learning and intergroup reconciliation? The analysis provided here would suggest that the continued politicization of any attempts to assign responsibility for past conflict, fueled by a seemingly intractable zero-sum perception of victimization between the principal nationalist, unionist and British antagonists has effectively blocked any significant movement forward in socioemotional learning. Accordingly, those 'piecemeal' initiatives that have been employed to date in an attempt to promote truth, justice and acknowledgment in Northern Ireland have been able to provide only partial solutions, as feelings of intercommunal distrust and contradictory inter-pretations of the conflict continue to thwart the development of any kind of larger, more inclusive societal strategy for coming to terms with the past. In short, the politics of memory in Northern Ireland remain starkly divided along the same highly polarized lines of group identity that underpinned past conflict, and there is little real hope for a shared acceptance of moral responsibility or the creation of a more collective memory at any point in the near future.

This divide is perhaps most clearly evidenced by the failure to gain any significant cross-community support for otherwise well-regarded initiatives for addressing the past such as those suggested by Healing Through Remembering (HTR) and the Consultative Group on the Past (CGPNI). As has been discussed, even areas in which Northern Ireland appears to have enjoyed great success, such as the provision of services and support to victims and the reintegration of ex-prisoners, remain points of division between nationalist and unionist communities due to zero-sum perceptions regarding responsibility for past violence. Further, legal mechanisms such as public inquiries and police enquiries have similarly exacerbated communal divides, a problem that underscores the potential limitations of government-controlled initiatives to advance the aims of truth or justice with regard to examining the involvement of the British state and security forces in past violence. Left unresolved, these issues will continue to impede the processes of social learning required to move Northern Ireland away from non-violent coexistence to a deeper, more integrated and ultimately more sustainable state of reconciliation. As Michael Wardlow of NICIE has noted,

> We're not safe yet, we're in truce. We've put the guns down but we've not moved through truth to transformation. We have not yet transformed our country. The risk of going back to guns is still there. . . . We have a fault line [in Northern Ireland] which is sectarianism, and we're afraid to deal with the past because it's too hard and it talks about victims and perpetrators. So what we do is simply put a veneer over that crack and then we build new structures over that veneer that look lovely and we learn how to live in these structures. And then suddenly something happens and I think you're getting something and I'm not and what happens? The fault line starts to rattle. For reconciliation you actually have to go down, you have to deal with the past.
>
> (Interview: April 21st, 2008)

On the other hand, while addressing moral responsibility for the past has remained highly contentious, considerable achievements have nonetheless been made by the Northern Ireland government's aggressive efforts to reduce structural and material inequalities between nationalist and unionist communities. These policies have greatly encouraged distributive social learning in Northern Ireland, and as a result, the types of social, economic and political discrimination that once drove the conflict have been virtually removed as major sources of intercommunal tension in recent years.

However, it is also clear that while these attempts to foster distributive learning have been vitally important to sustaining peace-building efforts, they have not in and of themselves been enough to overcome communal divides or to create more positive intergroup relationships. Indeed, movements towards greater equality continue to be interpreted along sectarian lines, with unionists in particular evidencing a growing sense of victimization in the face of the relative gains made by the nationalist community. Furthermore, continued communal divisions have meant that many of the positive investments made by the government have suffered from an extraordinarily costly 'duplication of resources,' in which gains for one community must be matched by equal—but separate—gains for the other. As Professor Joanne Hughes of Queen's University Belfast argues, this disproves the notion that a basic increase in economic prosperity will dissipate communal divisions in Northern Ireland, suggesting that such gains will only be effective if they go hand in hand with other efforts to improve community relations. As Hughes illustrates,

> If you continue to make economic choices based on decisions made in the past you're just reinforcing divisions. One way of managing the conflict here was to provide duplicate services for each community, but this may have been at the cost of promoting spaces where relationship building could happen. What's hugely important for economic and social progress in the future is that we start to think about the divisions and then layer economic systems into stronger foundations of better relations.
>
> (Interview: April 24th, 2008)

Perhaps the most evident progress towards intergroup reconciliation in Northern Ireland has been made by the promotion of instrumental learning between nationalists and unionists. This has largely been brought about by the sustained program of 'community relations' interventions introduced by the Northern Ireland government, centered on creating opportunities for positive intercommunity contact and dialogue and supported by a wealth of governmental, regional and international funding. The program's success is in part attributable to the fact that, while addressing the past remains a highly divisive issue in Northern Ireland, there seems to be a much greater degree of accord across both political parties and the broader population that establishing a more peaceful future will necessarily involve building better relations between nationalists and unionists. Notably, many of the advancements that have been made under this community relations program appear to be linked to a cohesive 'top-down' and 'bottom-up' policy approach to repairing communal division that has been shared across government, civil society and a thriving local community and voluntary sector, and has received extensive funding support from regional and international donors.

However, while these initiatives have made measurable gains in terms of improving the attitudes and relationships between nationalists and unionists, the continuation of 'low-intensity' violence at interface areas makes it clear that much work remains to be done to overcome the antagonistic mindsets and attitudes of the past. As Eamonn Deane, Director of the nongovernmental Holywell Trust in Derry has noted, oppositional perceptions of identity between these communities remain alive and well despite ongoing efforts to repair community relations:

> We have not come anywhere near the point of people saying, "Look, I have my identity and it is not threatened by yours, my identity is not dependent on being better than you. I am free to celebrate mine and you are free to celebrate yours" . . . We've got nowhere near that. But I think

we're beginning that journey which would have been impossible a few years ago. But it will take time.

(Interview: April 10th, 2008)

Furthermore, it should be noted that there may be an implicit danger in the inherent tendency of much of the ongoing community relations work to portray the problematic of reconciliation in Northern Ireland as one limited simply to improving relationships between local communities of nationalists and unionists. The British state and its security forces were principal actors complicit in the violence of the Troubles, and for many nationalists they remain primary targets of hostility and antagonism. In the end, it remains clear that all actors engaged or implicated in past conflict will need to be intimately involved in any truly successful process of transitional justice and reconciliation in Northern Ireland.

Overall, this analysis suggests that any transitional justice process capable of contributing to lasting intergroup reconciliation and sustainable peace in Northern Ireland will require the promotion of a tripartite combination of distributive, socioemotional and instrumental social learning between former antagonists. As this review of Northern Ireland's current decentralized transitional justice process has evidenced, all three of these forms of social learning are vital to intergroup reconciliation and, just as importantly, are mutually constitutive of and mutually dependent upon one another. For instance, it is highly unlikely that further attempts to address Northern Ireland's past will prove constructive until basic intercommunal trust, empathy and mutual understanding are first developed through ongoing instrumental community relations work. The recent public outcry that accompanied the release of the CGPNI's recommendations for equal reparations and a more centralized 'Legacy Commission' to investigate past violence might then be read as a sign that such initiatives are still premature for Northern Ireland, and that more work may yet need to be done to first repair trust and good relations between communities. Indeed, as Joanne Hughes and her colleagues contend, improved community relations are vital to the future ability to advance socioemotional learning initiatives in Northern Ireland, as "[t]he building blocks of reconciliation such as deconstructing collective memories and reaching an understanding of the 'other's' grievances and trust-building are unlikely to happen in the absence of positive social relationships" (Hughes et al. 2007: 49). Conversely, it seems equally unlikely that truly reconciled community relations will be able to develop without further socioemotional acknowledgment and accountability being provided for those killed during the Troubles and a common recognition by all parties involved that they share some degree of mutual complicity for the losses sustained throughout the conflict. To be sure, deep disagreements over interpretations of the past continue to be one of the primary sources of communal division in present-day Northern Ireland, helping to sustain stereotypes, prejudices and mistrust that militate against more positive interactions.

Indeed, the notion that reconciliation can be achieved in Northern Ireland by focusing on building future relationships while ignoring the divisions of the past was roundly rejected by nearly every expert interviewed as part of this study. The two are intimately intertwined, and history continues to play a major role in dictating both the quality and quantity of present interactions. As Wilhelm Verwoerd of the Glencree Centre has argued, coming to terms with the past may ultimately allow people in Northern Ireland to move beyond 'thin' reconciliation in the sense of simple coexistence to a 'thicker'—and ultimately more sustainable—reconciliation based on inclusivity, trust, and positive relationships. As he suggests,

> Because of the violence, because of the conflict, relationships between people and between groups have been affected and there's mistrust, there's anger, there's animosity, there's hurt, there's trauma . . . You need to find mechanisms to go and address some of these things. And I do think that some kind of a truth mechanism, that's not overly judicialized, but provides space for storytelling, for acknowledgment, for exploring shared responsibility, [and] also finds ways to humanize those that were involved in the actual killing, the using of violence. I see those as important aspects of a stronger, more sustainable notion of cooperative long-term relationships between formerly divided groups. . . . you cannot ignore the emotional dynamics [from the past] existing between groups and between people.
>
> (Interview: April 29th, 2008)

Accordingly, the continued recognition that a deeper interrogation of the past is required in order to move forward towards a more peaceful and integrated future in Northern Ireland suggests that more truth, justice and acknowledgment than have yet been provided by the country's current 'piecemeal' strategy will ultimately be required for intergroup reconciliation—though perhaps not just yet.

There is also a strong consensus that neither the Northern Ireland peace process that resulted in the Belfast and St. Andrews Agreements nor the socioemotional and instrumental attempts at reconciliation that followed would have been possible if widespread distributive inequalities had continued to divide communities in Northern Ireland. As previously mentioned, because structural and material inequalities motivated the civil rights movement that inadvertently began the Troubles and underlay nationalist grievances throughout the conflict, ameliorating these disparities provided a 'minimum baseline' for future reconciliatory efforts. However, despite the relative parity that now exists, it remains likely that reconciliation will require further efforts to improve conditions within some of the most marginalized communities in Northern Ireland, nationalist and unionist alike. Indeed, the most socioeconomically underprivileged areas of Northern Ireland produced the majority of those who took up arms during the Troubles and were worst impacted by its violence, and these same interface neighborhoods today remain the epicenter for the 'low-intensity' youth-led anti-social violence that continues to plague Northern Ireland. These same areas are also those still marked by the starkest symbols of communal division, and, not coincidentally, they remain the largest bases of support for the country's most extreme political parties. In part, this is because the most underprivileged neighborhoods are typically also the most segregated, offering little opportunity for individuals to engage in the kinds of positive interactions across communal lines required to challenge existing antagonisms. In short, while increasing socioeconomic equality will not in and of itself bring about reconciliation in Northern Ireland, it will likely have a large role to play in assisting other ongoing efforts to improve community relations well into the future.

Further, the experience of Northern Ireland would suggest that related efforts to promote distributive and instrumental forms of social learning will require long-term interventions that may be ill-suited to the limited timelines and mandates often afforded formal transitional justice institutions. For instance, rebuilding widespread intergroup trust, interaction and com- munication is a task that might prove particularly unwieldy for formal structures such as trials and truth commissions and could in some cases best be left to the 'bottom-up' work of civil society and local community actors with the necessary financial and political support of government. The integrated education movement and broader community relations strategy adopted in Northern Ireland appear to illustrate the potential strength of such approaches. That said, Northern Ireland has enjoyed many structural advantages that are unlikely to be readily available to most other divided societies emerging from conflict, such as intact liberal democratic governance structures, a highly trained and professionalized civil society, and unprece- dented access to both regional and international sources of funding to support peace-building efforts. Regardless, even though it serves as a 'best case' example in these regards, Northern Ireland nonetheless remains instructive in the insights it offers about the relative merits of a decentralized approach to transitional justice as well as the note of caution it sounds about the inherent difficulties associated with coming to terms with the past in deeply divided societies.

Social learning and reconciliation in South Africa

More than ten years after the completion of the TRC's work, it is clear that South Africa remains a society still seeking to overcome the deep racial divisions entrenched under apartheid. To be sure, given the systematic way that apartheid enforced racial separation, inequality and antagonism in nearly all facets of daily life, it is perhaps unreasonable to expect South Africa, despite its seemingly 'miraculous' peaceful transition to democracy, to have so quickly achieved the goal of racial harmony envisioned in the dream of a 'rainbow nation.' As many observers note, the long-term process of reconciliation required to overcome the social, psychological and economic legacies of apartheid will likely be generations in the making.

However, fifteen years after the inception of multi-racial democracy in South Africa, there are many positive signs of change in the nature of intergroup relations between white and black South Africans that would indicate at least an initial step down the road to greater interracial reconciliation. Most noticeably, while elevated levels of violent crime and recent xenophobic violence remain major issues of concern in contemporary South Africa, the highly racialized political violence that was associated with the apartheid-era liberation struggle is now largely a thing of the past. In addition, there now exists a widespread consensus among South Africans of all racial groups that the system of apartheid itself was fundamentally unjust and that terrible abuses were committed in its name. Further, while the majority of black and white South Africans continue to live lives that are physically and economically separate from one another, new opportunities for socialization and a much greater willingness to engage in meaningful interracial interaction have nevertheless emerged following the end of apartheid. Where this has occurred, there is evidence to suggest that it has led to a greater sense of understanding and empathy between black and white South Africans and a corresponding decrease in negative racial stereotypes and prejudices. To be sure, while South Africa has a long way yet to go in building more positive interracial relations, it nevertheless remains promising that results from a recent 2011 South African Reconciliation Barometer (SARB) survey show that 59 percent of all South Africans indicate they believe the country has made some progress in terms of reconciliation since the end of apartheid, with only 10 percent indicating that they disagreed (Lefko-Everett et al. 2011).[2]

Further, is clear that many South Africans—both black and white—believe the country's TRC was vitally important for advancing processes of reconciliation in South Africa. Indeed, the same 2011 SARB survey reveals that nearly half (47 percent) of all South Africans polled in 2011 agreed that the Commission had succeeded in bringing about reconciliation, with 37 percent indicating that they remained 'uncertain' in their assessment and only 12 percent responding that they disagreed (ibid.). However, in what ways has the South African TRC served to advance processes of interracial reconciliation following the country's historic transition from apartheid? This analysis suggests that one of the greatest successes of the Commission was the extent to which it was able to capture the imaginations of ordinary South Africans, serving as a symbol of both the end of apartheid and the beginnings of a commitment to a more racially reconciled society. This was no doubt facilitated by the support of charismatic leaders such as Archbishop Desmond Tutu and Nelson Mandela for the work of the

Commission, figures who tirelessly committed themselves to—and in fact themselves embodied—moving beyond the abuses of the past in the service of creating a more inclusive and reconciled future for South Africa.

Indeed, for better or worse, as the main institution tasked with addressing issues of the past in South Africa, for many South Africans and international observers the TRC came to encapsulate the transition itself and became the public face of the reconciliation process. This was due in no small part to the openness and transparency of the TRC process, an innovation that led to extensive media coverage of its public hearings processes and rapt attention to its underlying message of reconciliation. Accordingly, one of the greatest strengths of the Commission's work was its ability to serve as a prominent societal platform for instrumental social learning among members of different racial groups. The TRC therefore served as a crucial catalyst for a 'societal dialogue' about the past in South Africa, one that provided an importantly humanizing window onto the perspectives of victims and perpetrators of other races and also helped to spark a broader public debate about the past.

The highly public nature of the TRC also appears to be directly linked to the success it enjoyed in using its focus on truth recovery to help fashion a 'common memory' of the past that offered a crucial starting point for socioemotional learning. While several factors ultimately limited the extent of the factual information the TRC was able to recover, it nonetheless seems to have largely created a widespread consensus among all South Africans that apartheid represented a crime against humanity and that both black and white South Africans were complicit in carrying out gross violations of human rights. In large part, this acceptance stemmed from the Commission's decision to use the public hearings and the amnesty process itself as a way to involve victims, perpetrators and bystanders in the truth-telling process. This helped to create a more inclusive and balanced truth of the past that proved vital to countering many of the myths, misunderstandings and polarized beliefs about members of other racial groups that were pervasive under apartheid—beliefs that otherwise would have presented a significant barrier to future reconciliatory prospects.

However, there is reason to argue that the Commission was far less successful in forwarding other key mechanisms of social learning in its work, failures that appear to have limited or even actively impeded its ability to promote interracial reconciliation. For instance, despite the emphasis placed on embracing a more 'restorative' approach to justice, little room was provided in the TRC process for the kinds of meaningful interpersonal contact and dialogue across group boundaries that are essential to instrumental social learning. While some very positive informal encounters were arranged outside of the official auspices of the Commission, and while attempts have been made by several civil society organizations to carry similar programs forward post-TRC, the relatively small number of these efforts and the lack of support they have received from the government have minimized their broader impact on society. Given the recognized importance of sustained contact and communication for overcoming entrenched prejudices, stereotypes and hostility in divided societies, the TRC's failure to appropriately emphasize dialogue means that it missed a major opportunity to facilitate social learning and interracial reconciliation in South Africa.

Further, it is clear that, for many South Africans, the TRC failed to provide a sense of acknowledgment and justice that sufficiently offset the harms of the past. Many black South Africans and direct victims of abuses under apartheid indicated a surprising willingness to accept the conditional amnesty provision of the TRC as a sacrifice that needed to be made for national unity and reconciliation. However, this was quickly replaced by a sense of anger and betrayal when the government failed to adequately follow through on promises for victim reparations and prosecutions for those perpetrators who did not receive amnesty. For many victims, this meant feeling used and discarded by the supposedly 'victim-centered' Commission, a sentiment that appears to have largely undermined other aspects of social learning provided by the TRC. Moreover, current plans for future amnesties and pardons to be granted to perpetrators behind closed doors have helped to create the sense of impunity and lack of respect for the rule of law that trouble South Africa today.

Finally, and directly linked to the issue of reparations, the Commission appears to have contributed little to aspects of distributive social learning. While many South Africans were the victims of physical violence, far more—particularly among the black population—suffered on a daily basis under the vast structural and material inequalities entrenched by the apartheid system. Indeed, many victims indicated that their willingness to reconcile was less attached to punishing perpetrators than to addressing inequalities that existed between racial groups as a legacy of apartheid. However, for the most part, the Commission neglected to address these broader structural issues, focusing almost exclusively on individualized cases of physical rights abuses and only rarely drawing connections to the broader socioeconomic context in which they occurred.

This limitation appears to have had the unintended consequence of creating a record of the 'truth' that obscured the complicity of most white South Africans in indirectly supporting and benefitting from the inequities of apartheid—a potentially dangerous limit to the socioemotional learning that the TRC was able to produce. One outcome of this constraint was a marked resistance among the white community to any government attempts at redistribution or affirmative action post-TRC, and a growing sense of having been unfairly victimized by the ANC government. While it is unrealistic to expect the TRC by itself to have fully addressed the vast inequalities of apartheid given its limited timeline and resources, it is readily apparent that the continued existence of racial inequality remains a constant source of tension in post-apartheid South Africa, as well as a major barrier to social learning and interracial reconciliation.

In assessing the overall impact of the TRC on interracial relations, several common themes emerge. First, it is clear that perceptions of the Commission's work—and by extension, its potential influence on the social learning of South Africans—remain strongly divided along the same racial and political lines that existed in South Africa under apartheid. This is reflected in the disparate reactions between white and black South Africans to nearly every aspect of the TRC, including the acceptability of amnesty, the need for reparations and compensation, and the overall validity of the 'truth' that the Commission was able to glean. In large part, these racial divides reflect the entrenched fear and mistrust felt by many in the white community towards the very idea of a TRC process well before the substantive work of the Commission began. Indeed, while a survey conducted by the Institute for Democracy in South Africa (IDASA) in August 1994 revealed that 60 percent of all South Africans favored the establishment of a Commission to investigate human rights abuses, this sentiment was shared by 65 percent of black respondents but only 39 percent of whites (IDASA 1994). Similarly, other survey data collected in 1992 shows that 83 percent of white South African respondents disagreed with the notion that any attempts should be made to punish perpetrators of past injustice, while 74 percent of blacks demanded that "whites who harmed blacks during apartheid" should be held accountable (Schlemmer 1992).

Following the conclusion of the TRC's work, these same divisions have stayed largely in place and appear to have influenced perceptions of the Commission's overall impact on interracial reconciliation. While public opinion surveys conducted by the South African Human Sciences Research Council (HSRC) in 1998 showed that the majority (57 percent) of South Africans evaluated the work of the TRC as having been 'good for the country,' attitudes towards the Commission were revealed to be sharply divergent among black and white respondents (Thiessen 2008: 197). Indeed, this same survey showed that while 72 percent of black South Africans indicated they believed that the TRC had been a 'good or very good' thing for South Africa, most white respondents (55 percent) instead charged that the commission had been 'very bad' for the country (ibid.). Similarly, when asked directly about the TRC's contribution to reconciliation in 1998, surveys show that 56 percent of blacks believed strongly that the Commission had contributed to peace and reconciliation in South Africa, while 54 percent of whites maintained that it had failed to promote reconciliation (idem: 208).

These findings were reflected in a more recent 2000 survey carried out by Helen Macdonald, which, while finding that most South Africans (67 percent) believed that "the TRC initiative was important for building a united South African nation," also showed that this sentiment was held by a minority of whites (29 percent) as compared to a majority (77 percent) of blacks (Macdonald 2000). Similarly, a 2000–2001 survey conducted by Gibson and Macdonald showed that 76 percent of black South Africans strongly believed that the TRC had made a contribution to national unity and reconciliation, while only 37 percent of white respondents indicated a similar view (2001: 3). Taken together, these findings from South Africa help to underscore the seminal importance of group identity in the transitional justice processes of divided societies and, in particular, the substantial impact that identity can have on the nature of the relationships between these institutions and intergroup reconciliation.

Further, this analysis of the TRC's contribution to interracial reconciliation in South Africa also underscores the fact that socioemotional, distributive and instrumental forms of social learning are deeply interrelated, with success or failure in one area directly impacting the reconciliatory potential of another. One clear example of this is the intimate relationship of distributive social learning to the potential for reconciliation derived from the Commission's efforts at forwarding both truth and justice. For instance, many black victims appeared to be willing to accept the potential 'sacrifice of justice' represented by the TRC's amnesty provision if they received forms of financial compensation and access to social services. Indeed, for many victims, positive perceptions of 'justice' having been served often relied more on personal acknowledgment and the amelioration of material inequalities than on the punishment and incarceration of perpetrators. Conversely, the lengthy delays and inadequate payments that ultimately marred the reparations process only seem to have exacerbated the sense of injustice felt by many victims, and have therefore directly impaired the positive impact of this process on reconciliation. At the same time, the highly individualized 'truth' produced by the Commission's near-exclusive focus on acts of physical violence appears to have led to a disavowal of responsibility among many in the white community for the benefits they received under the systematic racial inequalities of apartheid. As a result, most whites have remained consistently opposed to redistributive efforts such as compensation, affirmative action and land reform programs that would potentially lessen the inequalities of the black majority, viewing these interventions as examples of unjust victimization by the ANC government. Accordingly, in considering how the TRC may have contributed to changing the attitudes, identities and beliefs of white and black South Africans in service of interracial reconciliation, this study clearly underscores that the interrelationship of all three types of social learning must be taken into account.

Finally, there is little doubt that in the 'transformative moment' of South Africa's transition to multi-racial democracy, the Commission marked a clear break with the violence and inequitable moral order of apartheid. The innovative hearings of the TRC and the rapt public attention they received indicate that one of the Commission's greatest successes was its ability to capture the South African imagination. In this respect, perhaps more than any other transitional justice mechanism employed to date, the TRC offered a powerful platform for social learning. At the same time, however, it must be noted that much of the TRC's work was confined to a relatively short two-year period, and even in that brief time much of the initial enthusiasm for the Commission shown by the public and South Africa's political parties began to wane. Given the scholarly consensus that post-conflict reconciliation is necessarily a long-term endeavor, this raises questions about the sustainability of the social learning processes initiated by the TRC. Put differently, while the aspects of social learning engendered by the TRC may have been a crucial first step on South Africa's long road to interracial reconciliation, this analysis suggests that sustaining this momentum will ultimately require ongoing efforts beyond the work of the Commission itself.

Perhaps the most significant impediment to the TRC's ability to effect long-term interracial reconciliation has been the consistent lack of follow-up and follow-through on the initiatives it introduced—a failure that is evident across all the processes of social learning deemed essential to transforming intergroup relationships. In some cases, this seems to be the result of oversights made by the Commission itself, but much more often it appears to be attributable to the marked lack of interest shown by subsequent ANC governments in carrying on the legacy of the Commission's work. For instance, while the Commission did support a small number of informal encounters between victims and perpetrators during its mandate, it neglected to take advantage of the opportunity to work with civil society organizations so that these kinds of reconciliatory encounters could be continued and expanded post-TRC. This problem was compounded by the lack of government funding and support for the ad hoc encounters initiated by reconciliation-oriented NGOs, and consequently the overall impact of these encounters has remained fairly minimal.

Taken together, these findings suggest that advancing prospects for interracial reconciliation post-TRC will necessarily depend on finding new and innovative ways to increase instrumental social learning in South African society. Given the self-fulfilling nature of racial segregation and the array of structural and psychosocial factors that continue to perpetuate this segregation in contemporary South Africa, it is likely that some form of external intervention will be required to initiate these processes. The interventions already under way from civil society organizations such as the Centre for the Study of Violence and Reconciliation (CSVR) and the Institute for the Healing of Memories (IHOM) provide one pre-existing model for how these interventions might be structured. Nonetheless, to have any kind of sustainable impact at a broader societal level, the scale of these interventions must necessarily be greatly expanded. However, this kind of expansion would require a significant investment of funds and resources from the current ANC government, one that historically has shown little interest in such 'bottom-up' peace-building efforts following the TRC.

In addition, it remains highly unlikely that any such interventions will meet with success unless greater headway is made by the government in addressing issues of distributive social learning and ameliorating the pervasive socioeconomic and structural divides that continue to keep racial groups apart and reinforce perceptions of difference. That said, with the vast inequalities that need to be overcome and the intransigence of many in the white community regarding early attempts at redistributive policies, this remains an accomplishment far easier said than done. Moreover, it is clear that previous policies such as Black Economic Empowerment (BEE) that have developed a small subset of black 'super-elites' in South African society are not the answer in this regard. Instead, in order to move forward, efforts must be made to find ways to bring the majority black population into greater parity with the members of the white minority and, in so doing, to both alleviate the continued sense of injustice that these continued inequalities foster and create new opportunities for positive interracial interaction and reconciliatory social learning.

At the same time, additional work remains to be done in countering the perceptions of impunity that continue to serve as a source of tension between racial groups in South Africa despite the TRC's attempts to provide socioemotional learning through truth and justice. The first key step in this process is following through on the promise to prosecute those who did not receive conditional amnesty for the abuses they committed during the struggle over apartheid. Failure to do so, combined with current plans to give perpetrators a 'second bite at the amnesty cherry,' will otherwise run the risk of perpetuating a disrespect for the rule of law and support for a continued culture of violence in post-apartheid South Africa.

Further, despite the significant gains made by the TRC's truth-recovery efforts in shedding light on individual cases of physical abuse during apartheid, additional efforts are still required to highlight the impact that broader patterns of structural violence had on the daily lives of black South Africans, as well as the benefits that these inequalities provided—and continue to provide—for the white minority. This would appear to be a key corrective to the sense of unjust victimization that continues to characterize white reactions to current government attempts to extend greater material equality to the poorest black South Africans. In the end, it is clear that there is still a long journey ahead to achieve the dream of a truly reconciled 'rainbow nation' in South Africa. However, as this analysis has suggested, the creation of long-term, sustainable interventions designed to meet South Africa's continued need for instrumental, socioemotional and distributive social learning will ultimately provide the crucial next step on the road to interracial reconciliation.

Social learning and reconciliation in divided societies

The findings presented in this study appear to confirm the hypothesis presented in much of the existing literature on transitional justice that transitional interventions are indeed crucial to helping deeply divided societies come to terms with their violent pasts and are therefore vital components of post-conflict reconciliation processes. In both cases under study there is strong counterfactual evidence to suggest that the absence of transitional justice mechanisms would at best have impeded the development of more positive relationships, and at worst would perhaps have served as the basis for renewed cycles of violence. Furthermore, while it remains difficult to distinguish the specific impact of transitional justice processes from the 'noise' of other societal factors accompanying post-conflict transitions, in both Northern Ireland and South Africa extensive evidence has been presented detailing the positive—and sometimes the negative—impact that these interventions have had on intergroup reconciliation. Such findings are important in and of themselves, and would seem to support the growing consensus that transitional justice interventions are a necessary, if not sufficient, component of broader reconciliation efforts in deeply divided societies.

More importantly, this analysis provides valuable new insights into *how* exactly it is that transitional justice interventions might contribute to processes of intergroup reconciliation in divided societies. Indeed, the primary aim of this research has been to shed new light on the causal mechanisms linking transitional justice interventions to reconciliation—in effect, to provide an early first effort to peer into the 'black box' surrounding this relationship. To this end, one major contribution of this analysis has been to lend substantial support to the underlying supposition that, at least in deeply divided societies, the ability of transitional justice strategies to contribute to intergroup reconciliation is heavily influenced by the politics of identity. As this study has shown, this relationship appears to work in two main ways. First, the work of transitional justice strategies will be deeply affected by the current state of intercommunal relations in the environment in which these strategies operate, and will likely be directly impacted by the relative levels of trust, understanding and empathy that exist between groups divided by past abuses. Where these groups remain deeply polarized and where their relationships are characterized by mutual mistrust, prejudice and hostility, efforts to address the past will be much more difficult. This is perhaps most clearly evidenced by the current impasse over coming to terms with the past in Northern Ireland, an impasse that has effectively blocked ongoing efforts by government and civil society to more deeply interrogate the violence of the Troubles.

At the same time, it would seem that transitional justice strategies can themselves have a reciprocal influence on transforming the nature of communal identities and their interrelationships in post-conflict societies and, by extension, on advancing processes of intergroup reconciliation. For instance, the example of South Africa shows how the TRC's use of a public truth-recovery process has helped to create a more inclusive collective memory of the past. This, in turn, seems to have led to a decrease in intergroup prejudices, stereotypes and hostilities between black and white South Africans.

In both cases under study, the evidence provided would seem to strongly suggest that the causal chain linking transitional justice to increased reconciliation is ultimately forged in the crucible of identity. Recognition of this level of reciprocity between identity and transitional justice is perhaps not surprising, given the inherently collectivized nature of the violence to which transitional strategies are called to respond. Nonetheless, when considering the impact of justice interventions on post-conflict reconciliation in divided societies, to date the role played by identity has been largely overlooked within the existing transitional justice literature. However, this study illustrates the importance of opening new channels of scholarly dialogue between transitional justice and the related disciplines of peace and conflict studies, political science and social psychology—all fields that have made significant efforts to study of the dynamics of identity, conflict transformation and intergroup reconciliation. While this study represents only an early 'first cut' at bridging insights between these disciplines, it nevertheless highlights the importance of engaging in future study examining the nexus between identity, transitional justice and reconciliation in divided societies.

Furthermore, drawing on a wealth of existing survey data as well as new information collected through a wide range of expert interviews in South Africa and Northern Ireland, this analysis finds highly suggestive evidence in support of the proposed hypothesis that the causal relationship between transitional justice and increased intergroup reconciliation is mediated by the ability of transitional interventions to promote positive social learning among divided groups in the 'transformative moment' of their transitions away from past conflict. This analysis also points toward a strong correlation between the ability of these transitional justice interventions to serve as platforms for instrumental, socioemotional and distributive forms of social learning in their societies and the relative contributions that they can make to ongoing processes of intergroup reconciliation. More specifically, in Northern Ireland and South Africa, these findings have indicated that the transitional justice mechanisms employed in each country have been successful in contributing to reconciliation to the extent to which they have been able to catalyze each of the five key social learning mechanisms identified in the theoretical framework proposed in Chapter 3: namely, positive intergroup contact, transformative dialogue, truth, justice and the amelioration of structural and material inequalities. Put simply, in both countries, where the transitional justice processes were successful in promoting each of these social learning mechanisms, it appears that reconciliation also improved. Conversely, where they were inadequate or otherwise failed in fostering social learning, reconciliation appears to have been impeded.

Overall, these insights also suggest that transitional justice mechanisms capable of promoting reconciliation in divided societies will likely ultimately need to foster a combination of distributive, instrumental and socioemotional reconciliation. This holds the promise of being a key contribution to the broader field of transitional justice where the majority of scholarship to date has focused almost exclusively on how these mechanisms might contribute to post-conflict peace-building and reconciliation by promoting what has here been referred to as socioemotional learning—in other words, by fostering aspects of 'truth' and 'justice.' However, the findings of this study, which point towards an inherent interrelationship between instrumental, distributive and socioemotional reconciliation, suggest that transitional justice strategies will be most successful in advancing intergroup reconciliation if they not only work towards the familiar goals of 'truth' and 'justice,' but also help to facilitate—or at least work in tandem with—other societal efforts to promote contact, dialogue and the amelioration of material inequalities.

Insights for 'best practices' in transitional justice

Perhaps most importantly, this study's evidence indicating the importance of these three processes of social learning to intergroup reconciliation in deeply divided societies can provide insight into crucial questions regarding 'best practices' in the design of future transitional justice interventions. For instance, recognition of the interrelationship between instrumental, distributive and socioemotional learning raises an interesting point regarding the potential importance of 'sequencing' for transitional justice interventions in deeply divided post-conflict societies. As the experience of Northern Ireland would seem to suggest, to be most effective in the promotion of intergroup reconciliation, attempts to provide acknowledgment and accountability for the past may need to be delayed until at least a minimal level of progress towards distributive and instrumental social learning has been reached, particularly in those societies where there as yet exists no agreed-upon consensus as to the status of victims and perpetrators. Similarly, in South Africa, the initial positive impact of truth and acknowledgment appears to have been largely undermined in the long term, as these contributions emerged in a context in which very little distributive or instrumental learning had occurred. Notably, these findings warn against the imposition of transitional justice strategies that would seek to assign accountability for past violence too soon in post-conflict societies, as in some cases this might prove counterproductive or even dangerous for nascent reconciliation efforts. This runs in direct opposition to the predominant human rights-based approach to transitional justice rooted in international law that currently requires an immediate response by national or international actors to provide criminal accountability for gross human rights violations in the wake of intrastate violence—clearly a source of unresolved tension between the demands of international justice and national reconciliation that remains to be addressed.

Second, to date, scholarship within the field of transitional justice has largely been driven by a series of comparative debates over which institutional model or approach to transitional justice is best able to achieve the twin goals of ending impunity and promoting reconciliation in post-conflict societies emerging from histories of gross human rights abuses. These arguments have included debates over whether it is better to employ 'restorative' or 'retributive' approaches to justice, the relative utility of truth commissions versus trials, whether these mechanisms should be located at local, national or international levels, and whether formal Western legal approaches to justice are more or less productive than culturally specific 'traditional' or 'indigenous' local responses (Roht-Arriaza 2006). Paradoxically, at the same time, perhaps the one universally agreed-upon consensus in the field is that there will never be any kind of a 'one-size-fits-all' mechanism that can be applied with equal success in all cases, tied to the recognition that the needs of each society in terms of transitional justice will always depend on the exigencies of its specific context (Kerr and Mobekk 2007). This widespread recognition of the need for context-dependent strategies brings into question the utility of the existing institutional approach to analyzing transitional justice interventions. Essentially, if we know that each society will require its own unique approach to transitional justice, it appears unwise to focus efforts on debating the supremacy of any one 'type' of transitional justice strategy.

In this way, the social learning model outlined in this study may offer transitional justice scholars the unique opportunity to move beyond the traditional comparative debates about institutional design. Indeed, the insights gained from this analysis suggest that debating whether one type of institution is intrinsically 'better' than another seems less important than asking whether the processes employed by each strategy serve to impede or impel the kinds of social learning and the subsequent transformations of mindsets and relationships that are ultimately necessary for intergroup reconciliation in deeply divided societies. Accordingly, by refocusing our attentions from structure to process and concentrating on what these institutions *do* rather than what they *are*, the social learning model introduced here offers a potential new avenue for assessing transitional justice interventions based on their relative ability to foster instrumental, socioemotional and distributive processes of social learning. While this study has been limited to studying the impacts on social learning of a particular truth commission and a more decentralized approach to transitional justice, this same model could just as easily be applied to assess the utility of any existing transitional justice intervention in contributing to reconciliation in a divided society—be it restorative or retributive, trial or truth commission, or undertaken by local, national or international actors.

Therefore, the social learning model outlined here could offer a new and innovative way in which to think about 'best practices' in the design of future transitional justice interventions—one that could readily be employed across a variety of different contexts. In essence, the analysis presented here suggests that, at least in the case of deeply divided societies, primary attention must be paid to ensuring that the design of any transitional justice intervention is conducive to catalyzing the three critical categories of social learning that have been discussed. However, because the emphasis here is on ensuring that these processes occur, this leaves open the possibility that the structures required to achieve these types of social learning could take entirely different forms in each country in which they are applied. Put another way, while activating these social learning processes is identified as a 'common denominator' that should direct best transitional justice practices across all divided societies, how each society goes about fostering each of these processes remains entirely context-specific and can be achieved in a variety of ways. Therefore, while this social learning model sets out shared goals that all transitional justice interventions interested in fostering reconciliation in divided societies might work towards, it nonetheless rejects the notion that there ever might be a single mechanism that can effectively achieve these goals across every society.

There are several reasons why this much more flexible reconsideration of best practices based on process as opposed to structure would be a key step forward in the field of transitional justice. First, it recognizes that the needs of each society with regard to achieving instrumental, socioemotional and distributive social learning will differ depending on the nature of the past abuses that occurred, the scale and scope of the violence that transpired, the presence or absence of distributive inequalities, and the current state of intergroup relations when a transitional justice intervention is employed. Indeed, while this study suggests that these three types of social learning must eventually be targeted for reconciliation to occur, the degree to which each of these needs will be present—and therefore the degree to which they will have to be fostered by a transitional justice mechanism—will always be context-specific. For these reasons, simply arguing that one type of institution, be it trial or truth commission, should be a common response to all instances of abuse may actually prove to be counterproductive to achieving the goal of reconciliation. What this social learning model offers instead is a set of common guidelines against which the needs of any particular society can be assessed on a case-by-case basis, providing the information necessary to tailor an appropriate transitional justice intervention to the contours and contexts of each country's process of reconciliation.

Second, at a more micro level, there has also been a growing recognition among transitional justice scholars that many of the aspects identified here as being crucial to social learning, such as justice, might be fulfilled through very different means depending on the cultural contexts of the societies in which they are employed. This has been most clearly illustrated in ongoing debates about whether Western conceptions of criminal justice based on prosecution and punishment should be utilized in non-Western societies, or whether more locally accepted 'indigenous' or 'traditional' approaches might ultimately be more effective in satisfying the needs of justice and reconciliation in these regions (Huyse and Salter 2008). However, the social learning model suggests that either of these approaches might be equally valid ways to fulfill the elements of acknowledgment and accountability tied to the provision of justice needed for socioemotional learning.

Instead, what seems more important is that the majority of those in the society view the approach to justice employed as an appropriate and legitimate response to countering the injustices of past abuse. This sense of legitimacy will ultimately make any mechanism more conducive to fostering the kind of transformative social learning ultimately required for reconciliation. For example, as this study illustrates, despite the controversial amnesty provision included in South Africa's TRC, evidence suggests that many black South Africans were willing (at least initially) to accept a more 'restorative' approach to justice in line with Christian theology and African conceptions of *ubuntu* that emphasized reparation, reintegration and repair over prosecution and punishment. That said, societies such as Northern Ireland that have long been governed by Western legal traditions will likely tend to view justice as requiring the structures of criminal law. Again, however, the emphasis on process adopted by the social learning model highlights the importance of using whichever approach to justice is most suitable to a particular cultural context, and warns against the tendency to suggest the primacy of any one structural approach—be it restorative or retributive—in every post-conflict situation.

Third, this reconceptualization of best practices based on the processes of social learning could also be an important corrective to the traditionally narrow focus in the transitional justice literature on more centralized institutional mechanisms such as trials, tribunals or truth commissions used to provide accountability for past violence. As the case of Northern Ireland seems to demonstrate, many of the most crucial processes of social learning might be carried out through more 'decentralized' initiatives undertaken by government, civil society and local community actors outside of these more formalized structures. Furthermore, Northern Ireland's experience also suggests that there may in fact be certain components of social learning, particularly instrumental and distributive, that stand to benefit from widespread and sustained interventions that might be impossible to incorporate within the limited timelines, mandates and structures often made available to 'centralized' transitional justice mechanisms.

At the very least, this analysis points to the fact that these formal transitional justice structures may often have to work in tandem with other ongoing efforts if they are going to make positive and lasting contributions to social learning and reconciliation in divided societies. This seems particularly evident in the case of South Africa, in which efforts undertaken by the TRC to promote truth and justice during its brief period of operation appear to have been undermined by the lack of attention paid to initiating instrumental and distributive reforms at a broader societal level outside the confines of the Commission's mandate. In any case, the findings of this study suggest the need for a much broader definition of transitional justice: one that moves beyond comparative debates over existing institutional structures and considers a much broader range of processes and mechanisms that might help divided societies move towards post-conflict reconciliation.

Fourth, and in direct relation, in both Northern Ireland and South Africa it is evident that some of the most positive effects on social learning and reconciliation produced by their transitional justice approaches have come from long-term and sustained interventions. For instance, the strength of Northern Ireland's community relations policy is its ability to mobilize grass-roots and civil society organizations to create frequent and ongoing opportunities for cross-community interaction in service of instrumental learning. Conversely, when similar efforts were attempted that relied on cursory or 'one-off' encounters between nationalist and unionist communities, their impact on social learning—and by extension, on intergroup reconciliation—appeared negligible.

Similarly, while the highly public, and highly publicized, forums of the TRC hearings provided a crucial space to begin a process of social learning through societal dialogue in South Africa, their reconciliatory impact was blunted by a distinct lack of effort by the government to promote further avenues for ongoing contact and dialogue following the Commission's close. Similarly, the government has largely neglected to follow through on its implicit vow to prosecute those who did not qualify for conditional amnesties and its promise to provide reparations in an adequate and timely fashion to the victims registered with the TRC. The same could be said of the truth that was revealed by the Commission's work: while many South Africans were exposed to the TRC's findings over the course of its operation, no structures were in place to continue these truth-recovery efforts or to disseminate these findings after its completion. Furthermore, in both countries, distributive social learning only appears to have been successful when lasting and widespread structural and material reforms were initiated to ameliorate inequalities—measures now largely in place in Northern Ireland but still sadly lacking in South Africa.

In terms of best practices, these findings would seem to strongly caution against approaches to transitional justice that hope to achieve substantial advances in reconciliation exclusively within the span of the several years mandated to most formal justice mechanisms directly following a society's transition away from conflict. Notably, however, this continues to be the predominant assumption underlying many of the most popular institutional mechanisms of transitional justice, including trials, international tribunals, truth commissions, and indeed even many indigenous or 'hybrid' justice interventions. Regardless, as this study has suggested, social learning and reconciliation are dynamic processes that do not move in linear ways and that may ebb or even reverse themselves over time if continued efforts are not undertaken to foster their growth. Furthermore, the process of reconciliation in deeply divided societies is itself widely considered to be a long-term endeavor that could take decades or even generations to achieve following the end of widespread violence. Accordingly, it may be naive, and perhaps dangerous, to assume that any transitional justice mechanism, no matter how thoughtfully designed or well funded, can make a significant contribution to this process if its interventions are limited to the span of a few years.

Avenues for future research

While this study is an important first step towards specifying the relationship between transitional justice and reconciliation and shedding light on the crucial role that identity can play in this relationship, further research remains to be done. Significant evidence has been provided to indicate that the proposed social learning model is the key link in the causal chain between transitional justice and reconciliation; however, at this stage, findings remain largely suggestive as opposed to definitive. It is clear that more work—both qualitative and quantitative—will be needed to clearly separate the distinct causal effects of transitional justice interventions from the wide range of other factors at work in post-conflict societies that might impact their potential for reconciliation.

In particular, it is highly likely that the theoretical model will need to be further refined in order to draw out the nuances of the causal linkages underlying the relationship between transitional justice and reconciliation, as well as to identify other crucial causal mechanisms that may have been overlooked in this study's emphasis on social learning. At least in part, this kind of refinement could be initiated by looking to alternative theories that might plausibly explain these causal linkages and then testing these theories against one another to assess their validity against the observations drawn in a kind of 'three-cornered fight' (Hall 2008: 7). This would help both to increase confidence in the inferences drawn from the social learning model, and to eliminate the oversight of other key variables through any potential confirmation bias.

In addition, the presence of conducive elites, entrepreneurs and other powerful societal actors are bracketed in the current model as a crucial 'precipitating condition' for transitional justice strategies that will be capable of promoting the kinds of social learning required for intergroup reconciliation. However, in all likelihood, the interrelationship between these actors and the ability of transitional justice strategies to catalyze social learning is much more complex, involving a series of dynamic interaction effects that are not fully captured in the current framework, which focuses less on individual agency and more on the institutional impact of the processes and mechanisms employed by transitional justice on intergroup reconciliation.

For example, in the case of South Africa, it is evident that much of the legitimacy afforded the TRC came from the support of charismatic individuals such as Nelson Mandela and Desmond Tutu, who lent their moral authority both to the transitional process and to creating a broader climate within post-apartheid South African society conducive to the ideals of interracial reconciliation. Had Mandela, and perhaps Tutu to a lesser degree, not been present or not embraced and embodied the message of reconciliation that captured the imagination of South Africans, would the more restorative aims of the TRC have been as widely accepted or as capable of achieving limited successes in promoting social learning and reconciliation? While this is an unknowable counterfactual, it seems unlikely. Conversely, it would appear that the lack of support for the TRC process by the Mbeki government, evidenced by the administration's failure to follow up with the reconciliatory projects it began, had a deleterious effect on prospects for social learning even years after the Commission completed its work. Similarly, it is unlikely that attempts to address the past through Northern Ireland's decentralized transitional justice strategy would have had a significant impact—or even been possible—without the involvement of key figures such as Gerry Adams and Ian Paisley that ultimately allowed the peace process and a new power-sharing government to move forward. Accordingly, more work remains to be done to investigate the nexus of powerful individual agents, transitional justice, social learning and intergroup reconciliation.

Finally, it is clear that the social learning model must ultimately be tested against a much larger universe of cases before it will be possible to speak conclusively about the broader applicability of this model beyond the 'small-n' study of the cases of Northern Ireland and South Africa examined here. In this regard, it is hoped that this analysis will only be the first of many examining the importance of identity and social learning to the relationship between transitional justice and intergroup reconciliation in divided societies, and that other scholars will be able to take up aspects of the much larger project initiated here. In particular, the cases of both Northern Ireland and South Africa largely downplayed criminal prosecutions in the transitional justice interventions that they employed. However, it should be noted that retributive interventions focused on prosecution and punishment remain the normative response in transitional justice, with domestic trials and international courts such as the International Criminal Court often being the first option considered by individual states and the international community alike to provide accountability for gross human rights violations. For this reason, it will be crucially important in future research to extend the scope of the analysis begun here to investigate the contributions to social learning and reconciliation that these judicially oriented interventions might provide.

However, the preliminary findings provided by the current study would seem to suggest that transitional justice interventions limited to securing criminal prosecution will ultimately not prove conducive to fostering the kinds of social learning required for intergroup reconciliation and sustainable peace. In large part, this is due to the fact that as transitional justice interventions, criminal prosecutions tend to be very narrow in scope, focused almost exclusively on securing legal verdicts of guilt for the perpetrators of past abuses. To be sure, the prosecution and punishment of perpetrators can powerfully fulfill the need for justice through acknowledgment and accountability in post-conflict societies, and may also help to establish a measure of the truth surrounding past events through the evidence collected during criminal proceedings. However, this tends to be the extent of these interventions' goals, meaning that there is very little—if any—attention paid to advancing components of instrumental or distributive learning.

Indeed, the singular focus of criminal justice on proving the individual guilt of perpetrators may often come at the expense of addressing the broader structural and material frameworks present in post-conflict societies, and it provides little space for interventions such as reparations programs that could serve as short-term attempts to repair and redress distributive issues (Lambourne 2009). Furthermore, as opposed to providing a forum in which to bring former enemies together in positive contact and dialogue, the interactions that take place between victims and perpetrators in criminal prosecutions are instead often antagonistic and heavily mediated by the presence of legal counsel (Minow 1998; Amstutz 2005). Accordingly, as Rama Mani has argued, "the adversarial and confrontational nature of trials is considered inimical to reconciliation or reintegration after conflict . . . [because they] tend to harden divisive and hostile feelings between offender and victim" and "reify the homogeneity of each group and the insurmountable difference between the two groups" (Mani 2002: 99–100).

In addition, it may be the case that the justice and truth that retributive mechanisms such as trials provide are not especially conducive to social learning. For example, while criminal prosecution may acknowledge the harm done to victims, assign clear responsibility to perpetrators, and thereby ease the sense of injustice caused by past abuses, the end result is the removal of offenders from society through incarceration or, in some cases, death. As a result, not only do trials risk bringing already divided groups into yet another antagonistic interaction, but even if they are successful in their mandates, they can also foreclose future opportunities for instrumental learning by bringing together former enemies to challenge their existing mindsets or to change the nature of their relationships with one another. This may be particularly dangerous in cases such as Rwanda in which large segments of society were complicit in past abuses, and in which the strictures of criminal justice could demand the potential removal of hundreds of thousands from future reintegration and reconciliation processes.

In terms of truth, the legalistic imperative of trials for due process and the protection of the rights of the accused may overlook the potential for societal repair stemming from full victim disclosure in favor of skeptical cross-examination by defense counsels—a strategy that further marginalizes the narratives of those already most affected by past violence (Hayner 2002). Also, the inherently adversarial system of Western criminal justice might further reduce the potential for meaningful challenges to biased myths and memories, as perpetrators are encouraged to withhold their testimony in order to escape the harsher punishments that might result from full admissions of guilt (Minow 1998). Finally, it should also be noted that the temporal mandate of criminal justice institutions effectively comes to an end following the sentencing of perpetrators, with few provisions, if any, for long-term engagement or follow-up. This strategy runs directly counter to the sustained work that is often crucial to developing intergroup reconciliation and sustainable peace in divided societies.

For these reasons, this study's preliminary findings suggest that purely retributive interventions might not often be the most appropriate choices in the post-conflict environments of deeply divided societies if the ultimate goals are social learning and reconciliation. Indeed, findings from an extensive earlier project conducted by Eric Stover, Harvey Weinstein and other members of the Berkeley Human Rights Center on the contributions of criminal justice to post-conflict reconciliation in the divided societies of Bosnia and Rwanda support this assertion. Their examination of the experiences of these countries would seem to suggest that "there is no direct link" between criminal trials and reconciliation, and they note that "in fact, we found criminal trials—and especially those of local perpetrators—often divided small multi-ethnic communities by causing further suspicion and fear [while] survivors rarely, if ever, connected retributive justice with reconciliation" (Stover and Weinstein 2004: 323).

However, this is not to suggest that criminal justice mechanisms such as domestic trials and international tribunals should be avoided as transitional justice interventions or that they have no role to play in fostering post-conflict reconciliation. Indeed, as previously discussed, for many societies Western traditions of criminal justice are often perceived by victims to be the only legitimate avenue for 'true' justice for past abuses, and in such societies they can make a strong contribution to reestablishing the rule of law and to signaling a shift away from a culture of violence to a culture of mutual respect for human rights. Instead, the findings in this study suggest that such retributive mechanisms, if utilized as the sole societal response to past human rights violations, may themselves be unable to foster the various kinds of social learning ultimately needed to achieve intergroup reconciliation in deeply divided societies.

While more research remains to be done, this may prove to be a crucially important finding, since criminal justice mechanisms still tend to be the 'baseline' transitional response of both domestic and international actors to gross human rights abuses, often with the assumption that such interventions will be sufficient in and of themselves to enable societies to move on from past violence towards sustainable peace (Kerr and Mobekk 2007). In many ways, this is reflective of the emerging movement within both scholarly and policy transitional justice circles that recognizes the need for a greater level of 'hybridity' or a 'mixing' of approaches in order to reach the aim of reconciliation, as well as the need to include distributive and reintegrative efforts alongside formal justice structures (Roht-Arriaza and Mariezcurrena 2006; Lambourne 2009). Indeed, the evidence presented in this analysis would seem to indicate that to achieve the goal of reconciliation, such retributive approaches would likely need to work in tandem with more restorative or reparative interventions that seek to heal damaged relationships and to address the broader structural and material inequalities that often underlie past abuses in divided societies. Ultimately, having provided an important initial exploration of the causal processes connecting identity, transitional justice and post-conflict reconciliation, it is hoped that insights derived from the social learning model developed in this study might be used to guide future explorations into best practices for transitional justice in deeply divided societies.

Notes

1 Notably, of those surveyed, only 3 percent indicated that they felt they were worse (ARK 2011).
2 A similar number of both white (57 percent) and black (60 percent) South Africans polled indicated that they likewise agreed that progress had been made towards reconciliation (ibid.).

Appendix: interviewees

Date	Name	Title/Organization	Location
11/02/2008	Sue Divin	CRO/Derry City Council	Derry, NI
12/02/2008	Stephen Ryan	Lecturer/University of Ulster	Derry, NI
13/02/2008	Paul Arthur	Professor/University of Ulster	Derry, NI
13/02/2008	Christine Bell	Director/Transitional Justice Institute	Derry, NI
14/02/2008	Paul O'Connor	Director/Pat Finucane Centre	Derry, NI
14/02/2008	Michael Doherty	Director/Peace and Reconciliation Group	Derry, NI
14/02/2008	Brandon Hamber	Director/INCORE	Derry, NI
23/03/2008	Gladys Ganiel	Lecturer/Irish School of Ecumenics	Belfast, NI
10/04/2008	Eamonn Deane	Director/Holywell Trust	Derry, NI
11/04/2008	Brian Dougherty	Director/St. Columb's Park House	Derry, NI
14/04/2008	Seamus Dunn	Professor Emer./University of Ulster	Coleraine, NI
14/04/2008	Ed Cairns	Professor/University of Ulster	Coleraine, NI
14/04/2008	Arthur Williamson	Professor/University of Ulster	Coleraine, NI
14/04/2008	Frances McLernon	Lecturer/University of Ulster	Coleraine, NI
14/04/2008	Anne Gallagher	Director/Seeds of Hope	Belfast, NI
14/04/2008	"Peter"	Former UDA Paramilitary/Sds. of Hope	Belfast, NI
14/04/2008	"Patrick"	Former PIRA Paramilitary/Sds. of Hope	Belfast, NI

14/04/2008	Matthew Cannon	Director/Irish Institute for Peace	Limerick, IE
15/04/2008	Orla Muldoon	Professor/University of Limerick	Limerick, IE
15/04/2008	Tom Lodge	Professor/University of Limerick	Limerick, IE
17/04/2008	David Stevens	Director/Corrymeela Community	Belfast, NI
17/04/2008	Bill Rolston	Professor/University of Ulster	Belfast, NI
17/04/2008	Kieran McEvoy	Professor/Queen's University Belfast	Belfast, NI
21/04/2008	Colin Knox	Professor/University of Ulster	Belfast, NI
21/04/2008	Caitlin Donnelly	Lecturer/Queen's University Belfast	Belfast, NI
21/04/2008	Kate Turner	Director/Healing Through Remembering	Belfast, NI
21/04/2008	Michael Wardlow	CEO/NICIE	Belfast, NI
21/04/2008	Ray Mullan	Director of Communications/CRC	Belfast, NI
21/04/2008	Mike Ritchie	Director/CAJ	Belfast, NI
22/04/2008	Jaqueline Irwin	CEO/CRC	Belfast, NI
22/04/2008	Patricia Lundy	Lecturer/University of Ulster	Belfast, NI
23/04/2008	Neil Jarman	Director/Institute for Conflict Research	Belfast, NI
24/04/2008	Louise McNeil	Researcher/GRU/Belfast City Council	Belfast, NI
24/04/2008	Colm Campbell	Director/Transitional Justice Institute	Belfast, NI
24/04/2008	Mary O'Rawe	Lecturer/Transitional Justice Institute	Belfast, NI
24/04/2008	Olive Hobson	Director/Quaker House Belfast	Belfast, NI
24/04/2008	Pete Shirlow	Lecturer/Queen's University Belfast	Belfast, NI
24/04/2008	Joanne Hughes	Professor/Queen's University Belfast	Belfast, NI
24/04/2008	Chris O'Halloran	Coordinator/Belfast Interface Project	Belfast, NI
25/04/2008	Ken Fraser	Head/Racial Equality Unit/OFMDFM	Belfast, NI

25/04/2008	Drew Haire	Director/Good Relns. Unit/OFMDFM	Belfast, NI
28/04/2008	Jennifer Todd	Professor/University College Dublin	Dublin, IE
29/04/2008	David Bloomfield	Director/Glencree Centre	Wicklow, IE
29/04/2008	Wilhelm Verwoerd	Researcher/Glencree Centre	Wicklow, IE
16/06/2008	Alex Boraine	Director/ICTJ (TRC Deputy Chair)	Cape Town, SA
16/06/2008	Hugo van der Merwe	Programme Manager/ CSVR	Cape Town, SA
17/06/2008	Amanda Gouws	Professor/Stellenbosch University	Stellenbosch, SA
17/06/2008	Pierre du Toit	Professor/Stellenbosch University	Stellenbosch, SA
18/06/2008	Fanie du Toit	Director/IJR	Cape Town, SA
18/06/2008	Natalie Jaynes	Project Leader/IJR	Cape Town, SA
22/06/2008	Shirley Gunn	Director/Human Rights Media Centre	Cape Town, SA
22/06/2008	Vincent Williams	Director/IDASA	Cape Town, SA
23/06/2008	Jan Hofmeyr	Head of Programme/IJR	Cape Town, SA
23/06/2008	Mary Burton	Former TRC Commissioner	Cape Town, SA
24/06/2008	Andre du Toit	Professor/University of Cape Town	Cape Town, SA
24/06/2008	Don Foster	Professor/University of Cape Town	Cape Town, SA
24/06/2008	Howard Varney	ICTJ (Head TRC Investigations Unit)	Cape Town, SA
24/06/2008	Nahla Valji	Project Manager/CSVR	Cape Town, SA
25/06/2008	Glenda Wildschut	Former TRC Commissioner	Cape Town, SA
25/06/2008	Kader Asmal	Former ANC Cabinet Minister	Cape Town, SA
25/06/2008	Marcella Naidoo	Director/Black Sash	Cape Town, SA
26/06/2008	Helen Scanlon	Director, Gender Justice Prog./ICTJ	Cape Town, SA

26/06/2008	S. Crawford-Brown	Head of Service Delivery/ TCSVT	Cape Town, SA
26/06/2008	Deon Snyman	CEO/Fndn. for Church-Led Restitution	Cape Town, SA
01/07/2008	Piers Pigou	Director/SAHA (TRC Invest. Unit)	Cape Town, SA
01/07/2008	Tlhoki Mofokeng	Director/Khulumani Support Group	Johannesburg, SA
02/07/2008	Garth Stevens	Professor/University of Witwatersrand	Johannesburg, SA
02/07/2008	Norman Duncan	Professor/University of Witwatersrand	Johannesburg, SA
03/07/2008	Deborah Posel	Director/WISER	Johannesburg, SA
04/07/2008	Oupa Makalemele	Researcher/CSVR	Johannesburg, SA
04/07/2008	Faizel Randerra	Former TRC Commissioner	Johannesburg, SA
06/07/2008	Piet Meiring	Former TRC Commissioner	Pretoria, SA
06/07/2008	Ivor Jenkins	Managing Director/ IDASA	Pretoria, SA
06/07/2008	Yasmin Sooka	Former TRC Commissioner	Pretoria, SA
06/07/2008	Hanif Vally	TRC Chief Legal Advisor	Pretoria, SA
07/07/2008	Tshepo Madlingza	Ntl. Advocacy Coordinator/Khulumani	Pretoria. SA
07/07/2008	Ivor Chipkin	Chief Research Specialist/ HSRC	Pretoria, SA
08/07/2008	Madeleine Fullard	TRC Senior National Researcher/NPA	Pretoria, SA
09/07/2008	Thapelo Mokushane	TRC Unit (Department of Justice)	Pretoria, SA
09/07/2008	Jacob Seekoe	Director/TRC Unit (DOJ)	Pretoria, SA
09/07/2008	Vivia Jacobs	TRC Unit (Department of Justice)	Pretoria, SA
10/07/2008	Michele Ruiters	Researcher/Inst. for Global Dialogue	Midrand, SA
10/07/2008	Emmanuel Kisiangani	Researcher/Inst. for Global Dialogue	Midrand, SA

Bibliography

Abdelal, R., McDermott, R., Herrera, Y.M. and Johnston, A.I. (2006) "Identity as a Variable," *Perspectives on Politics* 4, no. 4: 695–711.

Abbott, L., Dunn, S. and Morgan, V. (1998) *Integrated Education in Northern Ireland: An Analytical Review*, Coleraine: University of Ulster.

Abrahamsen, T. and van der Merwe, H. (2005) "Reconciliation through Amnesty? Amnesty Applicants' Views of the South African Truth and Reconciliation Commission," in *CSVR Research Reports*, Cape Town: CSVR.

Abu-Nimer, M. (ed.) (2001) *Reconciliation, Justice, and Coexistence: Theory and Practice*, New York: Lexington Books.

Abu-Nimer, M., Abdul, A.S. and Lakshitha, S.P. (2001) "The Long Road to Reconciliation," in M. Abu-Nimer (ed.) *Reconciliation, Justice, and Coexistence: Theory and Practice*, New York: Lexington Books.

Adam, H. and Moodley, K. (2005) *Seeking Mandela: Peacemaking between Israelis and Palestinians*, Philadelphia: Temple University Press.

Adler, E. and Barnett, M. (1998) "A Framework for the Study of Security Communities," in E. Adler and M. Barnett (eds) *Security Communities*, Cambridge: Cambridge University Press.

Aiken, N.T. (2008) "Post-Conflict Peacebuilding and the Politics of Identity: Insights for Restoration and Reconciliation in Transitional Justice," *Peace Research: The Canadian Journal of Peace and Conflict Studies* 40, no. 2: 9–38.

—— (2009) "The (Re)Construction of a Culture of Human Rights: Transitional Justice and Human Security," *Human Security Journal* 8: 10–18.

—— (2010) "Learning to Live Together: Transitional Justice and Intergroup Reconciliation in Northern Ireland," *The International Journal of Transitional Justice* 4, no. 2: 166–188.

—— (2012) "Putting the Past to Rest: The Bloody Sunday Inquiry and Intergroup Reconciliation in Northern Ireland," paper presented at the ISA Annual Convention, San Diego, CA, 2 April 2012.

Algappa, M. (1998) "Rethinking Security: A Critical Review and Appraisal of the Debate," in M. Algappa (ed.) *Asian Security Practice: Material and Ideational Influences*, Stanford: Stanford University Press.

Allport, G.W. (1954) *The Nature of Prejudice*, Cambridge, MA: Perseus.

Amnesty International. (2005) "The Finucane Case: Judiciary Must Not Take Part in Inquiry Sham." Online. 6 March 2005. Available at: http://www.amnesty.org/en/

library/asset/EUR45/014/2005/en/ca9a5de3-fa1e-11dd-999c-47605d4edc46/
eur450142005en.pdf (accessed 15 July 2012).

Amstutz, M.R. (2005) *The Healing of Nations: The Promise and Limits of Political Forgiveness*, Lanham: Rowman & Littlefield.

Anderson, B. (1997) *Imagined Communities*, New York: Verso.

Annan, K. (2004) *The Rule of Law and Transitional Justice in Conflict and Post-Conflict Societies: Report of the Secretary General (S/2004/616)*, New York: United Nations, 23 August 2004.

Arbour, L. (2007) "Economic and Social Justice for Societies in Transition," *N.Y.U. Journal of International Law and Politics* 40, no. 1: 1–27.

ARK. (2001) *Northern Ireland Life and Times Survey 2000*. Online. June 2001. Available at: http://www.ark.ac.uk/nilt/2000 (accessed 15 July 2012).

—— (2002) *Northern Ireland Life and Times Survey 2001*. Online. June 2002. Available at: http://www.ark.ac.uk/nilt/2001 (accessed 15 July 2012).

—— (2004) *Northern Ireland Life and Times Survey 2003*. Online. June 2004. Available at: http://www.ark.ac.uk/nilt/2003 (accessed 15 July 2012).

—— (2005) *Northern Ireland Life and Times Survey 2004*. Online. June 2005. Available at: http://www.ark.ac.uk/nilt/2004 (accessed 15 July 2012).

—— (2008) *Northern Ireland Life and Times Survey 2007*. Online. June 2008. Available at: http://www.ark.ac.uk/nilt/2007 (accessed 15 July 2012).

—— (2011) *Northern Ireland Life and Times Survey 2010*. Online. June 2011. Available at: http://www.ark.ac.uk/nilt/2010 (accessed 15 July 2012).

Arthur, P. (ed.) (2010) *Identities in Transition: Challenges for Transitional Justice in Divided Societies*, Cambridge: Cambridge University Press.

Ashmore, R.D., Jussim, L. and Widler, D. (eds) (2001) *Social Identity, Intergroup Conflict, and Conflict Reduction*, Oxford: Oxford University Press.

Auckerman, M.J. (2002) "Extraordinary Evil, Ordinary Crime: A Framework for Understanding Transitional Justice," *Harvard Human Rights Journal* 15: 40–97.

Azar, E. (1990) *The Management of Protracted Social Conflict: Theory and Cases*. Aldershot: Dartmouth.

Backer, D. (2003) "Civil Society and Transitional Justice: Possibilities, Patterns, and Prospects," *Journal of Human Rights* 2, no. 3: 297–313.

—— (2005) "Evaluating Transitional Justice in South Africa from a Victim's Perspective," *Journal of the International Institute* 12, no. 2: 1–3.

—— (2009) "Cross-National Comparative Analysis," in H. van der Merwe, V. Baxter and A.R. Chapman (eds) *Assessing the Impact of Transitional Justice: Challenges for Empirical Research*, Washington DC: United States Institute of Peace Press.

Baines, E.K. (2007) "The Haunting of Alice: Local Approaches to Justice and Reconciliation in Northern Uganda," *The International Journal of Transitional Justice* 1, no. 1: 91–114.

Ball, H. (1999) *Prosecuting War Crimes and Genocide: The Twentieth Century Experience*, Lawrence: University of Kansas Press.

Bar-Siman-Tov, Y. (2004) "Dialectics between Stable Peace and Reconciliation," in Y. Bar-Siman-Tov (ed.) *From Conflict Resolution to Reconciliation*, Oxford: Oxford University Press.

Bar-Tal, D. (2000) "From Intractable Conflict through Conflict Resolution to Reconciliation: Psychological Analysis," *Political Psychology* 21, no. 1: 351–365.

Bar-Tal, D. (2003) "Collective Memory of Physical Violence: Its Contribution to the Culture of Violence," in B. Einar, M. Boas and G. Saether (eds) *Ethnicity Kills? The Politics of War, Peace and Ethnicity in Subsaharan Africa*, New York: St. Martin's Press.

Bar-Tal, D. and Bennink, G.H. (2004) "The Nature of Reconciliation as an Outcome and as a Process," in Y. Bar-Siman-Tov (ed.) *From Conflict Resolution to Reconciliation*, Oxford: Oxford University Press.

Bayley, D.H. (2008) "Post-Conflict Police Reform: Is Northern Ireland a Model?" *Policing: A Journal of Policy and Practice* 2, no. 2: 233–240.

BBC News. (30 October 1998) "Mandela Addresses Truth Report Ceremony," *BBC News*. Online. Available at: http://news.bbc.co.uk/2/hi/special_report/1998/10/98/truth_and_reconciliation/204104.stm (accessed 15 July 2012).

—— (22 January 2007) "Reactions to Ombudsman's Report," *BBC News*. Online. Available at: http://news.bbc.co.uk/2/hi/uk_news/northern_ireland/6286657.stm (accessed 15 July 2012).

—— (23 August 2007) "Northern Ireland Division Costs £2.5bn a Year," *BBC News*. Online. Available at: http://news.bbc.co.uk/2/hi/uk_news/northern_ireland/6961077.stm (accessed 15 July 2012).

—— (25 February 2009) "Woodward Rules out Troubles Cash," *BBC News*. Online. Available at: http://news.bbc.co.uk/2/hi/uk_news/northern_ireland/7909625.stm (accessed 15 July 2012).

—— (15 June 2010a) "Bloody Sunday Report Published." *BBC News*. Online. Available at: http://www.bbc.co.uk/news/10322708 (accessed 15 July 2012).

—— (15 June 2010b) "Bloody Sunday: PM David Cameron's Full Statement," *BBC News*. Online. Available at: http://www.bbc.co.uk/news/10322295 (accessed 15 July 2012).

—— (15 March 2011) "Progressive Unionist Party Accuses HET of Arrests 'Bias,'" *BBC News*. Online. Available at: http://www.bbc.co.uk/news/uk-northern-ireland-12747620 (accessed 15 July 2012).

—— (22 June 2011) "Photographer Shot in Second Night of Belfast Rioting," *BBC News*. Online. Available at: http://www.bbc.co.uk/news/uk-northern-ireland-13869210 (accessed 15 July 2012).

—— (11 October 2011) "Pat Finucane's Family Anger after PM Rules Out Inquiry," *BBC News*. Online. Available at: http://www.bbc.co.uk/news/uk-northern-ireland-15262449 (accessed 15 July 2012).

—— (12 October 2011) "Owen Paterson says Pat Finucane Review will Uncover the Truth." *BBC News*. Online. Available at: http://www.bbc.co.uk/news/uk-northern-ireland-15276132 (accessed 15 July 2012).

—— (5 April 2012) "Work of Historical Enquiries Team to be Reviewed." *BBC News*. Online. Available at: http://www.bbc.co.uk/news/uk-northern-ireland-17619308 (accessed 15 July 2012).

—— (5 September 2012) "Missiles Thrown at Police During North Belfast Trouble," *BBC News*. Online. Available at: http://www.bbc.co.uk/news/uk-northern-ireland-19483426 (accessed 15 September 2012).

Bell, C. (2002) "Dealing with the Past in Northern Ireland," *Fordham International Law Journal* 26, no. 1: 1095–1147.

Benewick, R. (1974) "British Pressure Group Politics: The National Council for Civil Liberties," *Annals of the American Academy of Political and Social Science* 413, no. 1: 145–157.

Biggar, N. (ed.) (2001) *Burying the Past: Making Peace and Doing Justice after Civil Conflict*, Washington DC: Georgetown University Press.

Bloomfield, K. (1998) *We Will Remember Them: Report of the Northern Ireland Victims Commissioner*, Belfast: Northern Ireland Office, April 1998.

Blumer, H. (1969) *Symbolic Interactionism: Perspective and Method*, Englewood Cliffs: Prentice-Hall.

Boraine, A. (2000) "Truth and Reconciliation in South Africa: The Third Way," in R.I. Rotberg and D. Thompson (eds) *Truth v. Justice: The Morality of Truth Commissions*, Princeton: Princeton University Press.

Borer, T.A. (ed.) (2006) *Telling the Truths: Truth Telling and Peace Building in Post-Conflict Societies*, Notre Dame: University of Notre Dame Press.

Boulding, K. (1978) *Stable Peace*. Austin: University of Texas Press.

Boyd, D. and Doran, S. (2006) *The Viability of Prosecution Based on Historical Enquiry: Observations of Counsel on Potential Evidential Difficulties*, Belfast: Healing Through Remembering, October 2006.

Braham, E. (2007) "Uncovering the Truth: Examining Truth Commission Success and Impact," *International Studies Perspectives* 8, no. 1: 16–35.

Brass, P.R. (1994) *Ethnicity and Nationalism*. New Delhi: Sage Press.

Brewer, M.B. (2001) "Intergroup Identification and Intergroup Conflict: When Does Ingroup Love Become Outgroup Hate?" in R.D. Ashmore, L. Jussim and D. Wilder (eds) *Social Identity, Intergroup Conflict, and Conflict Reduction*, Oxford: Oxford University Press, 2001.

Brewer, M.B. and Campbell, D.T. (1976) *Ethnocentrism and Intergroup Attitudes*. New York: Sage Press.

Brewer, M.B. and Gaertner, S.L. (2001) "Toward Reduction of Prejudice: Intergroup Contact and Social Categorization," in R. Brown and S.L. Gaertner (eds) *Blackwell Handbook of Social Psychology: Intergroup Processes*, Oxford: Blackwell.

Bruland, P. and Horowitz, M. (2003) "Research Report in the Use of Identity in Comparative Politics," Cambridge: Harvard Identity Project.

Buckland, P. (1979) *The Factory of Grievances: Devolved Government in Northern Ireland, 1921–1939*, Dublin: Gill & Macmillan.

Buford, W. and van der Merwe, H. (2004) "Reparations in South Africa," *Cahiers d'Etudes Africaines* 44, no. 1: 263–322.

Burgess, P. (2006) 'A New Approach to Restorative Justice: East Timor's Community Reconciliation Process," in N. Roht-Arriaza and J. Mariezcurrena (eds) *Transitional Justice in the Twenty-First Century: Beyond Truth Versus Justice*, Cambridge: Cambridge University Press.

Burns, J.F. (2009) "Payment Plan for Northern Ireland Reconciliation Provokes Outrage," *New York Times*. 28 January 2009. Online. Available at: http://www.nytimes.com/2009/01/29/world/europe/29ireland.html?_r=2 (accessed 15 July 2012).

Byrne, S. (1995) "Conflict Regulation or Conflict Resolution: Third-Party Intervention in the Northern Ireland Conflict; Prospects for Peace," *Terrorism and Political Violence* 7, no. 2: 1–24.

Byrne, S. and Irvin, C. (2001) "Economic Aid and Policy Making: Building the Peace Dividend in Northern Ireland," *Policy & Politics* 29, no. 1: 413–429.

Cairns, E. and Darby, J. (1998) "The Conflict in Northern Ireland: Cause, Consequences, and Controls" *American Psychologist* 53, no. 7: 754–760.

Cairns, E. and Hewstone, M. (2002) "The Impact of Peacemaking in Northern Ireland on Intergroup Behaviour," in G. Salomon and B. Nevo (eds) *The Nature and Study of Peace Education*, Hillsdale: Erlbaum.

Cairns, E. and Roe, M.D. (2003) "Why Memories in Conflict?" in E. Cairns and M.D. Roe (eds) *The Role of Memory in Ethnic Conflict*, New York: Palgrave.

Campbell, C. and Ni-Aolain, F. (2002) "Local Meets Global: Transitional Justice in Northern Ireland," *Fordham International Law Journal* 26, no. 1: 871–892.

Campbell, D. (1998) *Writing Security: United States Foreign Policy and the Politics of Identity*. Minneapolis: University of Minnesota Press.

Cassel, D., Kemp, S., Pigou P. and Sawyer, S. (2006) *Report of the Indepdendent International Panel on Alleged Collusion in Sectarian Killings in Northern Ireland*. Notre Dame: Center for Civil and Human Rights, October 2006.

Centre for Conflict Resolution. (2012) *About CCR*. Online. Available at: http://www.ccr.org.za/index.php?option=com_content&view=article&id=49&Itemid=55 (accessed 15 July 2012).

Centre for the Study of Violence and Reconciliation. (2011) *Amnesty, Accountability and Ex-Combatant Reintegration*. Online. Available at: http://www.csvr.org.za/index.php?option=com_content&view=article&id=2375:amnesty-accountability-and-ex-combatant-reintegration&catid=143:transitional-justice-programme&Itemid=20 (accessed 15 July 2012).

Chapman, A.R. (2008) "Truth Recovery through the TRC's Institutional Hearing Process," in A.R. Chapman and H. van der Merwe (eds) *Truth and Reconciliation in South Africa: Did the TRC Deliver?*, Philadelphia: University of Pennsylvania Press.

——— (2009) "Approaches to Studying Reconciliation," in H. van der Merwe, V. Baxter and A.R. Chapman (eds) *Assessing the Impact of Transitional Justice: Challenges for Empirical Research*, Washington DC: United States Institute of Peace Press.

Chapman, A.R. and Ball, P. (2008) "Levels of Truth: Macro-Truth and the TRC," in A.R. Chapman and H. van der Merwe (eds) *Truth and Reconciliation in South Africa: Did the TRC Deliver?*, Philadelphia: University of Pennsylvania Press.

Chapman, A.R. and van der Merwe, H. (2008a) "Did the TRC Deliver?," in A.R. Chapman and H. van der Merwe (eds) *Truth and Reconciliation in South Africa: Did the TRC Deliver?*, Philadelphia: University of Pennsylvania Press.

——— (2008b) "Introduction: Assessing the South African Transitional Justice Model," in A.R. Chapman and H. van der Merwe (eds) *Truth and Reconciliation in South Africa: Did the TRC Deliver?*, Philadelphia: University of Pennsylvania Press.

——— (2008c) "Reflections on the South African Experience," in A.R. Chapman and H. van der Merwe (eds) *Truth and Reconciliation in South Africa: Did the TRC Deliver?*, Philadelphia: University of Pennsylvania Press.

Checkel, J.T. (2001) "Why Comply? Social Learning and European Identity Change," *International Organization* 55, no. 3: 553–588.

Chinapen, R. and Vernon, R. (2006) "Justice in Transition," *Canadian Journal of Political Science* 39, no. 1: 117–134.

Clark, P. (2008) "Hybridity, Holism and 'Traditional' Justice: The Case of the Gacaca Courts in Post- Genocide Rwanda," *George Washington International Law Review* 39: 765–837.

—— (2010) *The Gacaca Courts. Post-Genocide Justice and Reconciliation in Rwanda*, Oxford: Oxford University Press.

Clarke, L. (2011) "PUP Needs to Get a Sense of Proportion Over HET Arrests," *Belfast Telegraph*, Online. 18 March 2011. Available at: http://www.belfasttelegraph. co.uk/opinion/columnists/liam-clarke/pup-needs-to-get-a-sense-of-proportion-over-het-arrests-15116844.html (accessed 15 July 2012).

Clio Evaluation Consortium. (2002) *Evaluation of the Core Funding Program for Victims/Survivors' Groups*, Belfast: Clio, March 2002. Online. Available at: http://cain.ulst. ac.uk/issues/victims/docs/cec02.pdf (accessed 15 July 2012).

Cobb, S. (2003) "Fostering Coexistence in Identity-Based Conflicts: Towards a Narrative Approach," in A. Chayes and M. Minow (eds) *Imagine Coexistence: Restoring Humanity after Violent Ethnic Conflict*, San Francisco: Jossey-Bass.

Coleman, P.T. (2002) "Polarized Collective Identities: A Review and Synthesis of the Literature," New York: Columbia University.

Colletta, N.J. and Cullen, M.L. (2000) *Violent Conflict and The Transformation of Social Capital*, Washington DC: The World Bank.

Colvin, C.J. (2006) "Overview of the Reparations Program in South Africa," in P. de Greiff (ed.) *The Handbook of Reparations*, New York: Oxford University Press.

Community Relations Unit. (2005) *A Shared Future: Policy and Strategic Framework for Good Relations in Northern Ireland*. Belfast: OFMDFM, March 2005.

Conflict Archive on the Internet. (2012) *Malcolm Sutton: An Index of Deaths from the Conflict in Ireland*. Available at: http://cain.ulst.ac.uk/sutton/chron/index.html (accessed 15 July 2012).

Connor, W. (1994) *Ethnonationalism*, Princeton: Princeton University Press.

Consultative Group on the Past Northern Ireland. (2008) "Full Text of Speech Given By Lord Robin Eames and Denis Bradley At The Innovation Centre, Titanic Quarter Belfast," CGPNI. Online. 29 May 2008. Available at: http://www. patfinucanecentre.org/truth/eames.pdf (accessed 15 July 2012).

—— (2009) *Report of the Consultative Group on the Past*, Belfast: CGPNI, January 2009. Online. Available at: http://www.irishtimes.com/focus/2009/troubles/index.pdf (accessed 15 July 2012).

Coogan, T.P. (1995) *The Troubles: Ireland's Ordeal 1966–1996 and the Search for Peace*. London: Hutchinson.

Corrigan, A. (1969) *Eyewitness in Northern Ireland*, Belfast: Voice of Ulster.

Cory, P. (2003) *Cory Collusion Inquiry Report*, Dublin: Department for Justice, Equality, and Law Reform, December 2003.

Crawford-Pinnerup, A. (2000) "An Assessment of the Impact of Urgent Interim Reparations," in H. van der Merwe and T. Mofokeng (eds) *From Rhetoric to Responsibility: Making Reparations to the Survivors of Past Political Violence in South Africa*, Johannesburg: CSVR.

Cronin, B. (1999) *Community Under Anarchy*, New York: Columbia University Press.

Cronin, S. (1980) *Irish Nationalism: A History of Its Roots and Ideology*, Dublin: Academy Press.

Darby, J. (1976) *Conflict in Northern Ireland: The Development of a Polarized Community*, Dublin: Macmillan.

—— (1995) "Conflict in Northern Ireland: A Background Essay," in S. Dunn (ed.) *Facets of the Conflict in Northern Ireland*, Basingstoke: Macmillan.

Darby, J., Murray, D., Batts, D., Dunn, S., Farren. S. and Harris, J. (1977) *Education and Community in Northern Ireland: Schools Apart?*, Coleraine: University of Ulster.

Des Forges, A. and Longman, T. (2004) "Legal Responses to Genocide in Rwanda," in E.Stover and H.M. Weinstein (eds), *My Neighbor, My Enemy: Justice and Community in the Aftermath of Mass Atrocity*, Cambridge: Cambridge University Press.

DeBrito, A.B., Gonzalez-Enriquez, C. and Aguilar, P. (eds) (2001) *The Politics of Memory: Transitional Justice in Democratizing Societies*, Oxford: Oxford University Press.

DeGreiff, P. (ed.) (2006) *The Handbook of Reparations*, Oxford: Oxford University Press.

DeLaet, D.L. (2006) "Gender Justice: A Gendered Assessment of Truth-Telling Mechanisms," in T.A. Borer (ed.) *Telling the Truths: Truth Telling and Peace Building in Post-Conflict Societies*, Notre Dame: University of Notre Dame Press.

Deloitte. (2001) *Evaluation of Services to Victims and Survivors of the Troubles: Summary Report*, Belfast: Deloitte & Touche, October 2001. Online. Available at: http://cain.ulst.ac.uk/issues/victims/docs/deloittetouche01.pdf (accessed 15 July 2012).

Devine, P., Kelly G. and Robinson, G. (2011) "An Age of Change? Community Relations in Northern Ireland," *ARK Research Update* 72: 1–4.

Devine-Wright, P. (2003) "A Theoretical Overview of Memory and Conflict," in E. Cairns and M.D. Roe (eds), *The Role of Memory in Ethnic Conflict*, New York: Palgrave.

Dickinson, L.A. (2003) "The Promise of Hybrid Courts," *The American Journal of International Law* 97, no. 2: 295–310.

Dion, D. (1998) "Evidence and Inference in the Comparative Case Study," *Comparative Politics* 30, no. 2: 127–145.

Dolan, A. (2006). "Killing and Bloody Sunday, November 1920," *The Historical Journal* 49, no. 1: 789–810.

Donnelly, J. (2003) *Universal Human Rights in Theory and Practice*, Ithaca: Cornell University Press.

Drumbl, M.A. (2005) "Collective Violence and Individual Punishment: The Criminality of Mass Atrocity," *Northwestern University Law Review* 99, no. 2.

—— (2007) *Atrocity, Punishment, and International Law*, Cambridge: Cambridge University Press.

du Bois-Pedain, A. (2007) *Transitional Amnesty in South Africa*, Cambridge: Cambridge University Press.

Duckitt, J. and Mphuthing, T. (1998) "Political Power and Race Relations in South Africa: African Attitudes before and after the Transition," *Political Psychology* 19, no. 4: 809–832.

Dugard, J. (1978) *Human Rights and the South African Legal Order*, Princeton: Princeton University Press.

Durkheim, E. (1984) *The Division of Labour in Society*, New York: Free Press.

Durrheim, K. and Dixon, J. (2005) *Racial Encounter: The Social Psychology of Contact and Desegregation*, New York: Routledge.

Duster, T. (1971) "Conditions for Guilt-Free Massacre," in N. Sanford and C. Comstock (eds) *Sanctions for Evil*, San Francisco: Jossey-Bass.

Dyzenhaus, D. (1998) *Judging the Judges, Judging Ourselves: Truth, Reconciliation and the Apartheid Legal Order*, Oxford: Hart.

Eder, K., Gisen, B., Schmidtke, O. and Tambini, D. (2002) *Collective Identities in Action: A Scoiological Approach to Ethnicity*, Aldershot: Ashgate.

Elliott, S. and Flackes, W.D. (1989) *Northern Ireland: A Political Directory 1968–88*, Belfast: Blackstaff.

Ellis, D.G. (2006) *Transforming Conflict: Communication and Ethnopolitical Conflict*, New York: Rowman & Littlefield.

Ellis, S. (1998) "The Historical Significance of South Africa's Third Force," *Journal of South African Studies* 24, no. 2: 261–299.

Elshtain, J.B. (2001) "Politics and Forgiveness," in N. Biggar (ed.) *Burying the Past: Making Peace and Doing Justice after Civil Conflict*, Washington DC: Georgetown University Press.

Elster, J. (ed.) (2006) *Retribution and Reparation in the Transition to Democracy*, Cambridge: Cambridge University Press.

English, R. (2003) *Armed Struggle: A History of the IRA*, Oxford: Oxford University Press.

Equality Commission for Northern Ireland. (2008) *Monitoring Report No. 18: A Profile of the Northern Ireland Workforce 2007*, Belfast: Equality Commission for Northern Ireland.

Eriksen, T.H. (2001) "Ethnic Identity, National Identity, and Intergroup Conflict," in R.D. Ashmore, L. Jussim and D.Wilder (eds) *Social Identity, Intergroup Conflict, and Conflict Reduction*, Oxford: Oxford University Press.

Ernest, C. (2004) "A Quest for Truth and Justice: Reflections on the Amnesty Process of the Truth and Reconciliation Commission of South Africa," paper presented at the Conference "In Ten Years of Democracy in South Africa: Historical Achievement, Present State, Future Prospects," University of South Africa, Pretoria, 23–25 August 2004.

Evenson, E.M. (2004) "Truth and Justice in Sierra Leone: Coordination Between Commission and Court," *Columbia Law Review* 104: 730–768.

Exline, J.J., Worthington, E.L., Hill, P. and McCullough, M.E. (2003) "Forgiveness and Justice: A Research Agenda for Social and Personality Psychology," *Personality and Social Psychology Review* 7, no. 4: 337–348.

Fahey, T., Hayes, B.C. and Sinnott, R. (2006). *Conflict and Consensus: A Study of Values and Attitudes in the Republic of Ireland and Northern Ireland*, Boston: Brill.

Farquharson, K. and Marjoribanks, T. (2003) "Transforming the Springboks: Re-imagining the South African Nation through Sport," *Social Dynamics* 29, no. 1: 27–48.

Fay, M.T., Morrissey, M., Smyth, M. and Wong, T. (2001) *The Cost of the Troubles Study – Report on the Northern Ireland Survey: The Experience and Impact of the Troubles*, Derry: INCORE.

Fearon, J.D. and Laitin, D.D. (2000) "Violence and the Social Construction of Ethnic Identity," *International Organization* 54, no. 4: 845–877.

Fein, H. (1999) "Testing Theories Brutally: Armenia (1915), Bosnia (1992) and Rwanda (1994)," in L. Chorbajjan and G. Shirinian (eds) *Studies in Comparative Genocide*, New York: St. Martin's Press.

Finnemore, M. and Sikkink, K. (1998) "International Norm Dynamics and Politics Change," *International Organization* 52, no. 4: 887–917.

—— (2001) "Taking Stock: The Constructivist Research Program in International Relations and Comparative Politics," *Annual Review of Political Science* 4, no. 1: 391–416.

Fisher, R.J. (2001) "Social-Psychological Processes in Interactive Conflict Analysis and Reconciliation," in M. Abu-Nimer (ed.) *Reconciliation, Justice, and Coexistence: Theory and Practice*, New York: Lexington Books.

Fitzduff, M. (2002) *Beyond Violence: Conflict Resolution Process in Northern Ireland*, New York: United Nations University Press.

Fitzduff, M. and O'Hagan, L. (2009) "The Northern Ireland Troubles," Derry: INCORE.

Fletcher, L.E. and Weinstein, H.M. (2002). "Violence and Social Repair: Rethinking the Contributions of Justice to Reconciliation," *Human Rights Quarterly* 24: 572–639.

Foster, D. (2005) "Racial Relations and the Microecology of Contact," *South African Journal of Psychology* 35, no. 1: 494–504.

Foster, D. and Finchilescu, G. (1986) "Contact in a 'Non-Contact' Society: The Case of South Africa," in M. Hewstone and R. Brown (eds) *Contact and Conflict in Intergroup Encounters*, Oxford: Blackwell.

Frazer, H. and Fitzduff, M. (1994) *Improving Community Relations: A Paper Prepared for the Standing Advisory Commission on Human Rights*, Belfast: Community Relations Council.

Freeman, M. and Hayner, P. (2003) "Truth-Telling," in D. Bloomfield, T. Barnes, and L. Huyse (eds) *Reconciliation After Violent Conflict: A Handbook*, Stockholm: IDEA, 2003.

Gaertner, S.L. (1994) "The Contact Hypothesis: The Role of a Common Ingroup Identity on Reducing Intergroup Bias," *Small Group Research* 25, no. 2: 224–249.

Gaertner, S.L. and Dovidio, J.F. (2000). *Reducing Intergroup Bias: The Common Ingroup Identity Model*, Philadelphia: Psychology Press.

Gaertner, S.L., Rust, M.C., Dovidio, J.F., Bachman, B.A. and Anastasio, P.A. (1994) "The Contact Hypothesis: The Role of A Common Ingroup Identity on Reducing Intergroup Bias," *Small Groups Research* 25, no. 2: 224–249.

Gallagher, A.M. (1995) *Majority Minority Review – Education in a Divided Society: A Review of Research and Policy*, Coleraine: University of Ulster.

Gallagher, F. (1957) *The Indivisible Island: The Story of the Partition of Ireland*, London: Gollancz.

Galtung, J. (1969) "Violence, Peace, and Peace Research," *Journal of Peace Research* 6, no. 3: 167–191.

—— (1985) "Twenty-Five Years of Peace Research: Ten Challenges and Some Responses," *Journal of Peace Research* 22, no. 2: 141–158.

—— (2001) "After Violence, Reconstruction, Reconciliation, and Resolution: Coping with Visible and Invisible Effects of War and Violence," in M. Abu-Nimer (ed.) *Reconciliation, Justice, and Coexistence: Theory and Practice*, New York: Lexington Books.

George, A.L. and Bennett, A. (2004) *Case Studies and Theory Development in the Social Sciences*, Cambridge, MA: MIT Press.

Gibson, J.L. (2002) "Truth, Justice, and Reconciliation," *American Journal of Political Science* 46, no. 3: 540–556.

—— (2004) *Overcoming Apartheid*, New York: Russell Sage.

—— (2006a) "The Contributions of Truth to Reconciliation: Lessons from South Africa," *Journal of Conflict Resolution* 50, no. 1: 409–432.

—— (2006b) "Do Strong Group Identities Fuel Intolerance?: Evidence from the South African Case," *Political Psychology* 27, no. 5: 665–705.

Gibson, J.L. and Gouws, A. (1997) "Support for the Rule of Law in the Emerging South African Democracy," *International Social Science Journal* 15, no. 2: 172–191.

Gibson, J.L. and Macdonald, H. (2001) *Truth – Yes, Reconciliation – Maybe: South Africans Judge the Truth and Reconciliation Process*, Cape Town: Institute for Justice and Reconciliation, June 2001.

Goldie, R. and Ruddy, B. (2010) *Crossing the Line: Key Features of Effective Practice in the Development of Shared Space in Areas Close to an Interface*, Belfast: Belfast Interface Project.

Goldstone, R.J. (2004) "Justice and Reconciliation in Fragmented Societies," in A. Wimmer et al. (eds) *Facing Ethnic Conflicts: Toward a New Realism*, New York: Rowman & Littlefield.

Good Relations Unit. (2006) *Community Engagement, Good Relations and Good Practice: Guidelines on Good Practice to Community Engagement to Promote Good Relations in Northern Ireland*, Belfast: Belfast City Council, September 2006.

Government of Ireland. (1997) *Bloody Sunday and the Report of the Widgery Tribunal: The Irish Government's Assessment of the New Material Presented to the British Government in June 1997*, Dublin: Government of Ireland, June 1997.

Government of Northern Ireland. (1922) *Civil Authorities (Special Powers) Act (Northern Ireland) 1922*, Belfast: HMSO.

—— (1969a) *"The Cameron Report" – Disturbances in Northern Ireland: Report of the Commission Appointed by the Governor of Northern Ireland*, Belfast: NIO.

—— (1969b) *"The Hunt Report" – Report of the Advisory Committee on Police in Northern Ireland*, Belfast: NIO.

—— (1998) *"The Belfast Agreement" – The Agreement: Agreement Reached in the Multi-Party Negotiations*, Belfast: NIO.

—— (2000) *Review of the Criminal Justice System in Northern Ireland*, Belfast: NIO.

—— (2009) *Police (Northern Ireland) Act 2000: Review of Temporary Recruitment Provisions*, Belfast: NIO.

Government of South Africa. (1950) *Supression of Communism Act, No. 44 of 1950*, Pretoria: GSA, June 1950.

—— (1994) *Interim Constitution of the Republic of South Africa 1994*, Pretoria: GSA, April 1994.

—— (1995) *Promotion of National Unity and Reconciliation Act 1995*, Pretoria: GSA, July 1995.

—— (1996) *Constitution of the Republic of South Africa No. 108 1996*, Pretoria: GSA, December 1996.

Graybill, L.S. (2002) *Truth and Reconciliation in South Africa: Miracle or Model?*, London: Lynne Rienner.

Graybill, L.S. and Lanegran, K. (2004) "Truth, Justice, and Reconciliation in Africa: Issues and Cases," *African Studies Quarterly* 8, no. 1: 1–18.

Greenbaum, B. (2006) *External Assessment of Centre for the Study of Violence and Reconciliation (CSVR) Ex-Combatants Reintegration and Restorative Justice Project*, Johannesburg: CSVR, February 2006.

Gross-Stein, J. (2002) "Psychological Explanations of International Conflict," in W. Carlsaes, T. Risse and B.A. Simmons (eds) *The Handbook of International Relations*, Thousand Oaks: Sage.

Guembe, J.M. (2006) "Economic Reparations for Grave Human Rights Violations: The Argentinean Experience," in P. De Grieff (ed.) *The Handbook of Reparations*, Oxford: Oxford University Press.

Gutto, S. (2001) *Equality and Non-Discrimination in South Africa: The Political Economy of Law Making*, Cape Town: New Africa Books.

Hall, P.A. (2007) "Systematic Process Analysis: When and How to Use It," *European Political Science* 7, no. 1: 1–14.

Halpern, J. and Weinstein, H.M. (2004) "Rehumanizing the Other: Empathy and Reconciliation," *Human Rights Quarterly* 26, no. 1: 561–583.

Hamber, B. (1998) "The Past Imperfect: Exploring Northern Ireland, South Africa, and Guatemala," in B.Hamber (ed.) *Past Imperfect: Dealing with the Past in Northern Ireland and Societies in Transition*, Derry: INCORE, 1998.

—— (1999) "Have No Doubt It Is Fear in the Land: Continuing Cycles of Violence in South Africa," *South African Journal of Child and Adolescent Mental Health* 12, no. 1: 5–18.

—— (2001) "Does The Truth Heal? A Psychological Perspective on Political Strategies for Dealing with the Legacy of Political Violence," in N. Biggar (ed.) *Burying the Past: Making Peace and Doing Justice after Civil Conflict*, Washington DC: Georgetown University Press.

—— (2002) "'Ere their Story Die': Truth, Justice and Reconciliation in South Africa," *Race and Class* 44, no. 1: 61–79.

—— (2003) "Rights and Reasons: Challenges for Truth Recovery in South Africa and Northern Ireland," *Fordham International Law Journal* 26, no. 1: 1074–1094.

—— (2009) *Transforming Societies after Political Violence: Truth, Reconciliation, and Mental Health*, New York: Springer.

Hamber, B. and Kelly, G. (2005) *A Place for Reconciliation? Conflict and Locality in Northern Ireland*, Belfast: Democratic Dialogue.

Hamber, B., Magill, C. and Smith, A. (2009) *The Role of Education in Reconciliation: The Perspectives of Children and Young People in Bosnia and Herzegovina and Northern Ireland*, Belfast: University of Ulster.

Hamber, B., Nageng, D. and O'Malley, G. (2000) "Telling It Like It Is: Understanding the Truth and Reconciliation Commission from the Perspective of Survivors," *Psychology in Society* 26, no. 1: 18–42.

Hamber, B. and Wilson, R.A. (2003) "Symbolic Closure through Memory, Reparation and Revenge in Post-Conflict Societies," in E. Cairns and M.D. Roe (eds) *The Role of Memory in Ethnic Conflict*, New York: Palgrave.

Hamilton, A., Moore, L. and Trimble, T. (1995) *Policing a Divided Society: Issues and Perceptions in Northern Ireland*, Coleraine: University of Ulster.

Hansson, U. (2005) *Troubled Youth? Young People, Violence and Disorder in Northern Ireland*, Belfast: Institute for Conflict Research.

Hastings, A. (1997) *The Construction of Nationhood: Ethnicity, Religion, and Nationalism*, Cambridge: Cambridge University Press.

Hayes, B.C., McAllister, I. and Dowds, L. (2007) "Integrated Education, Intergroup Relations, and Political Identities in Northern Ireland," *Social Problems* 54, no. 4: 454–482.

Hayner, P. (1994) "Fifteen Truth Commissions – 1974 to 1994: A Comparative Study," *Human Rights Quarterly* 16, no. 4: 597–655.

—— (2000) "Same Species, Different Animal: How South Africa Compares to Truth Commissions Worldwide," in C. Villa-Vincencio and W.Verwoerd (eds) *Looking Back, Reaching Forward: Reflections on the Truth and Reconciliation Commission of South Africa*, Cape Town: University of Cape Town Press.

—— (2002) *Unspeakable Truths: Facing the Challenges of Truth Commissions*, London: Routledge.

Healing Through Remembering. (2002) *The Report of the Healing through Remembering Project*, Belfast: Healing Through Remembering, June 2002.

—— (2012) "A Day of Reflection." HTR. 21 June 2012. Online. Available at: http://www.dayofreflection.com/ (accessed 15 July 2012).

Hegarty, A. (2002) "The Government of Memory: Public Inquiries and the Limits of Justice in Northern Ireland," *Fordham International Law Journal* 26, no. 1: 1148–1192.

—— (2004) "Truth, Law, and Official Denial: The Case of Bloody Sunday," in W.A. Schabas and S. Darcy (eds) *Truth Commissions and Courts: The Tensions Between Criminal Justice and the Search for Truth*, Norwell: Kluwer.

Hermann, T. (2004) "Reconciliation: Reflections on the Theoretical and Practical Utility of the Term," in Y. Bar-Siman-Tov (ed.) *From Conflict Resolution to Reconciliation*, Oxford: Oxford University Press.

Hewstone, M. and Brown, R. (eds) (1986) *Contact and Conflict in Intergroup Encounters*, Oxford: Oxford University Press.

Hewstone, M., Cairns, E.,Voci, A., Paolini, S., McLernon, F., Crisp, R.J. and Niens, U. (2005) "Intergroup Contact in a Divided Sociey: Challenging Segregation in Northern Ireland," in D. Abrams, M.A. Hogg and J.M. Marques (eds) *The Social Psychology of Incusion and Exclusion*, Philadelphia: Psychology Press.

Hewstone, M. and Greenland, K. (2000) "Intergroup Conflict," *International Journal of Psychology* 35, no. 2: 136–144.

Hewstone, M., Hughes, J. and Cairns, E. (2008a) *Can Contact Promote Better Relations? Evidence from Mixed and Segregated Areas of Belfast*, Belfast: OFMDFM, June 2008.

Hewstone, M., Kenworthy, J.B., Cairns, E., Tausch, N., Hughes, J., Tam, T., Voci, A., Von Hecker, U. and Pinder, C. (2008b) "Stepping Stones to Reconciliation in Northern Ireland: Intergroup Contact, Forgiveness, and Trust," in A. Nadler, T.E. Malloy and J.D. Fisher (eds) *The Social Psychology of Intergroup Reconciliation*, Oxford: Oxford University Press.

Hillyard, P. (1983) "Law and Order," in J. Darby (ed.) *Northern Ireland: The Background to the Conflict*, Belfast: Appletree Press.

Hirshowitza, R. and Orkin, M. (1997) "Inequality in South Africa: Findings from the 1994 October Household Survey," *Social Indicators Research* 41, no. 1: 119–136.

Hobsbawm, E. and Ranger, T. (eds) (1991) *The Invention of Tradition*, Cambridge: Cambridge University Press.

Hofmeyr, J. (2007) *Report of the Seventh Round of the SA Reconciliation Barometer Survey*, Wynberg: Institute for Justice and Reconciliation, December 2007.

Hogg, M.A. and Abrams, D. (1998) *Social Identifications: A Social Psychology of Intergroup Relations and Group Processes*, New York: Routledge.

Holden, M. and McGrath, M. (1986) "Economic Outlook: Retrospect," *Indicator South Africa* 34, no. 1: 44.

Homer-Dixon, T. (1994) "Environmental Scarcities and Violent Conflict," *International Security* 19, no. 1: 76–116.

Homer-Dixon, T. (1999) *Environment, Scarcity, and Violence*, Princeton: Princeton University Press.

Honaker, J. (2005) "Unemployment and Violence in Northern Ireland: A Missing Data Model for Ecological Inference," paper presented at the Summer Meetings of the Society for Political Methodology, Tallahassee, Florida, July 2005.

Hoogeveen, J.G. and Ozler, B. (2005) "Not Separate, Not Equal: Poverty and Inequality in Post-Apartheid South Africa," in *William Davidson Institute Working Paper Series No. 739*, Ann Arbor: University of Michigan, January 2005.

Hopf, T. (1998) "The Promise of Constructivism in International Relations Theory," *International Security* 23, no. 1: 171–200.

Horowitz, D. (1975) "Ethnic Identity," in N. Glazer and D. Moynihan (eds) *Ethnicity: Theory and Experience*, Cambridge, MA: Harvard University Press.

—— (1994) "Democracy in Divided Societies," in L. Diamond and M. Plattner (eds) *Nationalism, Ethnic Conflict, and Democracy*, Baltimore: Johns Hopkins University Press.

—— (2000) *Ethnic Groups in Conflict*, Berkeley: University of California Press.

Horowitz, M. (2002) "Research Report on the Use of Identity Concepts in International Relations," Cambridge, MA: Harvard Identity Project, July 2002.

Hughes, J. and Carmichael, P. (1998) "Community Relations in Northern Ireland: Attitudes to Contact and Integration," in G. Robinson, D. Heenan, A.M. Gray and K. Thompson (eds) *Social Attitudes in Northern Ireland: The Seventh Report*, Aldershot: Ashgate.

Hughes, J. and Knox, C. (1997) "For Better or Worse? Community Relations Initiatives in Northern Ireland," *Peace & Change* 22, no. 3: 330–355.

Hughes, J., Donnelly, C., Robinson, G. and Dowds, L. (2003) "Community Relations in Northern Ireland: The Long View," Belfast: ARK, March 2003.

Hughes, J., Campbell, A., Hewstone, M. and Cairns, E. (2007) "Segregation in Northern Ireland: Implications for Community Relations Policy," *Policy Studies* 28, no. 1: 35–53.

Human Sciences Research Council. (1995) *Omnibus Survey: May 1995*. Pretoria: HSRC/Mark Data, May 1995.

—— (1998) *Survey: Perceptions*, Pretoria: HSRC/Mark Data, November 1998.

—— (2004) *Fact Sheet: Poverty in South Africa*, Pretoria: HSRC, July 2004.

Huyse, L. (2003) "Justice," in D. Bloomfield, T. Barnes, and L. Huyse (eds) *Reconciliation After Violent Conflict: A Handbook*, Stockholm: IDEA.

Huyse, L. and Salter, M. (eds) (2008) *Traditional Justice and Reconciliation after Violent Conflict: Learning from African Experiences*, Stockholm: IDEA International Press.

Ignatieff, M. (1998) *The Warrior's Honor: Ethnic War and the Modern Conscience*, New York: Henry Holt.

Imbleau, M. (2004) "Initial Truth Establishment by Transitional Bodies and the Fight against Denial," in W.A. Schabas and S. Darcy (eds) *Truth Commissions and Courts: The Tension between Criminal Justice and the Search for Truth*, Dordrecht: Kluwer.

Institute for Democracy in South Africa. (1994) *National Elections Survey: August 1994*, Cape Town: IDASA.

Institute for the Healing of Memories. (2011) *History*. Online. Available at: http://www.healing-memories.org/about/mission (accessed 15 July 2012).

Jarman, N. (2002) *Managing Disorder: Responding to Interface Violence in North Belfast*. Belfast: OFMDFM.

—— (2004) "From War to Peace? Changing Patterns of Violence in Northern Ireland: 1990–2003," *Terrorism and Political Violence* 16, no. 3: 420–438.

—— (2006) *Working at the Interface: Good Practice in Reducing Tension and Violence*, Belfast: Insitute for Conflict Research.

Jeong, H.W. (2005) *Peacebuilding in Post-Conflict Societies: Strategy and Process*, London: Lynne Rienner.

Jesse, N.G. and Williams, K.P. (2005) *Identity and Institutions: Conflict Reduction in Divided Societies*, New York: SUNY Press.

Johnstone, G. and Van Ness, D. (2007) "The Meaning of Restorative Justice," in G. Johnstone and D. Van-Ness (eds) *Handbook of Restorative Justice*, Portland: Willan.

Katzenstein, P. (ed.) (1996) *The Culture of National Security*, New York: Columbia University Press.

Kaufman, S. (1996) "Spiraling to Ethnic War," *International Security* 21, no. 2: 108–138.

—— (2001) *Modern Hatreds: The Symbolic Politics of Ethnic War*, New York: Cornell University Press.

—— (2006) "Escaping the Symbolic Politics Trap: Reconciliation Initiatives and Conflict Resolution in Ethnic Wars," *Journal of Peace Research* 43, no. 2: 201–218.

Keck, M. and Sikkink, K. (1998) *Activists Beyond Borders*, New York: Cornell University Press.

Kelman, H.C. (1973) "Violence without Moral Restraint: Reflections on the Dehumanization of Victims and Victimizers," *Journal of Social Issues* 29, no. 4: 25–61.

—— (1997) "Social-Psychological Dimensions of International Conflict," in I.W. Zartman and J.L. Rasmussen (eds) *Peacemaking in International Conflict: Methods and Techniques*, Washington DC: United States Institute of Peace Press.

—— (1999) "Transforming the Relationship between Former Enemies: A Social-Psychological Analysis," in R.L. Rothstein (ed.) *After the Peace: Resistance and Reconciliation*, Boulder: Lynne Rienner.

—— (2001) "The Role of National Identity in Conflict Resolution," in R.D. Ashmore, L. Jussim and D. Wilder (eds) *Social Identity, Intergroup Conflict, and Conflict Reduction*, Oxford: Oxford University Press.

—— (2004) "Reconciliation as Identity Change: A Social-Psychological Perspective," in Y. Bar-Siman-Tov (ed.) *From Conflict Resolution to Reconciliation*, Oxford: Oxford University Press.

—— (2008) "Reconciliation from a Social-Psychological Perspective," in A. Nadler, T.E. Malloy and J.D. Fisher (eds) *The Social Psychology of Intergroup Reconciliation*, Oxford: Oxford University Press.

Kenworthy, J.B., Turner, R.N., Hewstone, M. and Voci, A. (2005) "Intergroup Contact: When Does It Work and Why?" in J.F. Dovidio, P. Glick and L.A. Rudman (eds) *On The Nature of Prejudice: Fifty Years after Allport*, Oxford: Blackwell.

Kerr, R. and Mobekk, E. (2007) *Peace and Justice: Seeking Accountability after War*, Cambridge: Polity Press.

Kiss, E. (2000) "Moral Ambition within and Beyond Political Constraints: Reflections on Restorative Justice," in R.I. Rotberg and D. Thompson (eds) *Truth v. Justice: The Morality of Truth Commissions*, Princeton: Princeton University Press.

Klaaren, J. and Varney, H. (2003) "A Second Bite at the Amnesty Cherry? Constitutional and Policy Issues around Legislation for a Second Amnesty," in C. Villa-Vicencio and E. Doxtader (eds) *The Provocations of Amnesty: Memory, Justice, and Impunity*, Claremont: Africa World Press.

Knox, C. (1994) "Conflict Resolution at the Microlevel: Community Relations in Northern Ireland," *Journal of Conflict Resolution* 38, no. 4: 595–619.

Knox, C. and Hughes, J. (1996) "Crossing the Divide: Community Relations in Northern Ireland," *Journal of Peace Research* 33, no. 1: 83–98.

Knox, C. and Monaghan, R. (2002) *Informal Justice in Divided Societies: Northern Ireland and South Africa*, New York: Palgrave.

Knox, C. and Quirk, P. (2000) *Peacebuilding in Northern Ireland, Israel, and South Africa*, New York: St. Martin's Press.

Kriesberg, L. (1982) *Social Conflicts*, Englewood Cliffs: Prentice-Hall.

—— (1998) "Intractable Conflicts," in E. Weiner (ed.) *The Handbook of Interethnic Coexistence*, New York: Continuum.

—— (2001) "Changing Forms of Coexistence," in M. Abu-Nimer (ed.) *Reconciliation, Justice, and Coexistence: Theory and Practice*, New York: Lexington Books.

—— (2004) "Comparing Reconciliation Actions within and between Countries," in Y. Bar-Siman-Tov (ed.) *From Conflict Resolution to Reconciliation*, Oxford Oxford University Press.

—— (2005) "Identity Issues," in G. Burgess and H. Burgess (eds) *Beyond Intractability*, Boulder: University of Colorado Press.

Kritz, N. (ed.) (1995) *Transitional Justice: How Emerging Democracies Reckon with Former Regimes*, Washington DC: United States Institute of Peace Press.

Kruger, C. (2006) "Spiral of Growth: A Social Psychiatric Perspective on Conflict, Reconciliation, and Relationship Development," in N.N. Potter (ed.) *Trauma, Truth, and Reconciliation*, Oxford: Oxford University Press.

Lake, D.A. and Rothchild, D. (1996) "Containing Fear: The Origins and Management of Ethnic Conflict," *International Security* 21, no. 2: 41–75.

LaMarche, G. (2008) "Integrated Education: Essential to a Shared Future in Northern Ireland," *Atlantic Philanthropies*, Online. 17 April 2008. Available at: http://www. atlanticphilanthropies.org/currents/integrated-education-essential-shared-future-northern-ireland (accessed 15 July 2012).

Lambourne, W. (2009) "Transitional Justice and Peacebuilding after Mass Violence," *The International Journal of Transitional Justice* 31, no. 1: 28–48.

Lederach, J.P. (1997) *Building Peace: Sustainable Reconciliation in Divided Societies*, Washington DC: United States Institute of Peace Press.

—— (1998) "Beyond Violence: Building Sustainable Peace," in E. Weiner *The Handbook of Interethnic Coexistence*, New York: Continuum.

Leebaw, B.A. (2008) "The Irreconcilable Goals of Transitional Justice," *Human Rights Quarterly* 30, no. 1: 95–118.

Lefko-Everett, K., Lekalake, R., Penfold, E. and Rais, S. (2010) *2010 Reconciliation Barometer Survey Report*, Cape Town: Institute for Justice and Reconciliation.

Lefko-Everett, K., Nyoka, A. and Tiscornia, L. (2011) *SA Reconciliation Barometer Survey: 2011 Report*, Cape Town: Institute for Justice and Reconciliation.

Lerche, C. (2000) "Peace Building through Reconciliation," *Peace Studies* 5: 1–10.

Levine, V. (1997) "Conceptualizing 'Ethnicity' and 'Ethnic Conflict:' a Controversy Revisited," *Studies in Comparative Development* 32, no. 2: 45–75.

Lewin, K. (1948) *Resolving Social Conflcits*, New York: Harper and Row.

Linklater, A. (1998) *The Transformation of Political Community*, Columbia: University of South Carolina Press.

Llewellyn, J. (2006) "Restorative Justice in Transitions and Beyond: The Justice Potential of Truth Telling Mechanisms for Post-Accord Societies" in T.A. Borer (ed.) *Telling the Truths: Truth Telling and Peace Building in Post-Conflict Societies*, Notre Dame: University of Notre Dame Press.

—— (2007) "Truth Commissions and Restorative Justice," in G. Johnstone and D. Van Ness (eds) *Handbook of Restorative Justice*, Portland: Willan.

Llewellyn, J. and Howse, R. (1999) "Institutions for Restorative Justice: The South African Truth and Reconciliation Commission," *The University of Toronto Law Journal* 49, no. 3: 355–388.

Lombard, K. (2003) *Report of the First Round of the SA Reconciliation Barometer Survey*, Rondebosch: Institute for Justice and Reconciliation.

Long, W.J. and Brecke, P. (2003) *War and Reconciliation: Reason and Emotion in Conflict Resolution*, London: MIT Press.

Lundy, P. (2007) "Can the Past Be Policed? Lessons from the Historical Enquiries Team Northern Ireland," *Transitional Justice Institute Research Paper No. 09–06*, Jordanstown: Transitional Justice Institute, November 2007.

—— (2012) "Research Brief: Assessment of HET Review Processes and Procedures in Royal Military Police Investigation Cases," Institute for Research in Social Science: University of Ulster, April 2012. Online. Available at: http://eprints.ulster.ac.uk/21809/ (accessed 15 July 2012).

Lundy, P. and McGovern, M. (2001) "The Politics of Memory in Post-Conflict Northern Ireland," *Peace Review* 13, no. 1: 27–33.

—— (2005) *Community, Truth-Telling, and Conflict Resolution: Research Report Submitted to the Northern Ireland Community Relations Council*, Belfast: Community Relations Council, January 2005.

—— (2008) "Whose Justice? Rethinking Transitional Justice from the Bottom Up," *Journal of Law and Society* 35, no. 2: 265–292.

Lundy, P. and McGovern, M. (eds) (2002) *Ardoyne: The Untold Truth*, Belfast: Beyond the Pale.

Lynch, R. (2006) *The Northern IRA and the Early Years of Partition: 1920–1922*, Dublin: Irish Academic Press.

Macdonald, H. (2000) *2000 Pilot Reconciliation Survey*, Cape Town: Institute for Justice and Reconciliation, July 2000.

Mack, J.E. (1990) "The Psychodynamics of Victimization among National Groups in Conflict," in V.D. Volkan, J.V. Montville and J.A. Demetrios (eds) *The Psychodynamics of International Relationships*, Toronto: Lexington.

MacLean, R., Coyle, A. and Oliver, J. (2010) *The Billy Wright Inquiry – Report*, London: HMSO, September 2010.

Mallinder, L. (2007) "Can Amnesties and International Justice Be Reconciled?" *The International Journal of Transitional Justice* 1, no. 2: 208–230.

Mamdani, M. (2001) "A Diminished Truth," in W. James and L. van de Vijver (eds) *After the TRC: Reflections on Truth and Reconciliation in South Africa*, Athens: Ohio University Press.

Mani, R. (2001) "Rebuilding an Inclusive Political Community after War," *Security Dialogue* 36, no. 4: 511–526.

Mani, R. (2002) *Beyond Retribution: Seeking Justice in the Shadows of War*, Cambridge: Polity Press.

—— (2008) "Dilemmas of Expanding Transitional Justice, or Forging the Nexus between Transitional Justice and Development," *The International Journal of Transitional Justice* 2, no. 1: 253–265.

Maoz, I. (2004) "Social-Cognitive Mechanisms in Reconciliation," in Y. Bar-Siman-Tov (ed.) *From Conflict Resolution to Reconciliation*, Oxford: Oxford University Press.

Markel, D. (1999) "The Justice of Amnesty? Towards a Theory of Retributivism in Recovering States," *The University of Toronto Law Journal* 49, no. 3: 389–445.

McCauley, C. (2002) "Psychological Foundations," in C. Rittner, J.K. Roth and J.M. Smith (eds) *Will Genocide Ever End?*, St. Paul: Paragon House.

McEvoy, K. (1998) "Prisoners, The Agreement, and the Political Character of the Northern Ireland Conflict," *Fordham Law Review* 22, no. 4: 1539–1576.

—— (2006) *Making Peace with the Past: Options for Truth Recovery Regarding the Conflict in and About Northern Ireland*, Belfast: Healing Through Remembering, October 2006.

McEvoy, K. and Eriksson, A. (2006) "Restorative Justice in Transition: Ownership, Leadership and 'Bottom-up' Human Rights," in D. Sullivan and L. Tifft (eds) *A Handbook of Restorative Justice*, New York: Routledge.

McEvoy, K. and McGregor, L. (eds) (2008) *Transitional Justice from Below: Grassroots Activism and the Struggle for Change*, London: Hart.

McEvoy, K. and Mika, H. (2002) "Restorative Justice and the Critique of Informalism in Northern Ireland," *British Journal of Criminology* 42, no. 3: 534–562.

McEvoy, K. and Shirlow, P. (2008) *Beyond the Wire: Former Prisoners and Conflict Transformation in Northern Ireland*, Michigan: University of Michigan Press.

McEvoy-Levy, S. (2001) "Youth, Violence, and Conflict Transformation," *Peace Review* 13, no. 1: 89–96.

McGlynn, C., Niens, U., Cairns, E. and Hewstone, M. (2004) "Moving out of Conflict: The Contribution of Integrated Schools in Northern Ireland to Identity, Attitudes, Forgiveness, and Reconciliation," *Journal of Peace Education* 1, no. 2: 147–163.

McGrath, M. (1984) "Global Poverty in South Africa," *Social Dynamics* 10, no. 2: 38–44.

McKittrick, D. (2012) "Poison of Bloody Sunday Finally Seeps Away as Derry Moves On," *Belfast Telegraph*. Online. 30 January 2012. Available at: http://www. belfasttelegraph.co.uk/news/local-national/bloody-sunday/poison-of-bloody-sunday-finally-seeps-away-as-derry-moves-on-16110644.html (accessed 15 July 2012).

Mead, G.H. (1934) *Mind, Self, and Society*, Chicago: University of Chicago Press.

Mehl-Madrona, L. (2006) "Healing Relational Trauma through Relational Means: Aboriginal Approaches," in N.N. Potter (ed.) *Trauma, Truth, and Reconciliation*, Oxford: Oxford University Press.

Melaugh, M. (1992) "Housing," in P. Stringer and G. Robinson (eds) *Social Attitudes in Northern Ireland: The Second Report*, Belfast: Blackstaff.

—— (1995) "Majority–Minority Differentials: Unemployment, Housing, and Health," in S. Dunn (ed.) *Facets of the Conflict in Northern Ireland*, Basingstoke: Macmillan.

Mendez, J.E. (2006) "The Human Right to Truth: Lessons from Latin American Experiences with Truth Telling," in T.A. Borer (ed.) *Telling the Truths: Truth Telling and Peace Building in Post-Conflict Societies*, Notre Dame: University of Notre Dame.

Miall, H. (2004) "Transforming Ethnic Conflict: Theories and Practices," in A. Wimmer et al. (eds) *Ethnic Conflict and International Relations*, Aldershot: Dartmouth.

Miall, H., Ramsbotham, O. and Woodhouse, T. (2000) *Contemporary Conflict Resolution: The Prevention, Management and Transformation of Deadly Conflicts*, Cambridge: Polity Press.

Mika, H. (2006) *Community-Based Restorative Justice in Northern Ireland*, Belfast: Institute of Criminology and Criminal Justice, December 2006.

Miller, Z. (2008) "Effects of Invisibility: In Search of the 'Economic' in Transitional Justice," *International Journal of Transitional Justice* 2, no. 3: 266–291.

Millward Brown Ulster. (2008) *Public Opinion Survey Report: Integrated Education in Northern Ireland*, Belfast: Millward Brown Ulster.

Minow, M. (1998) *Between Vengeance and Forgiveness: Facing History after Genocide and Mass Violence*, Boston: Beacon Hill Press.

—— (2002) "Memory and Hate: Are There Lessons from around the World?" in M. Minow (ed.) *Breaking the Cycles of Hatred: Memory, Law, and Repair*, Princeton: Princeton University Press.

Monroe, K.R., Hankin, J. and Van Vechten, R.B. (2000) "The Psychological Foundation of Identity Politics," *Annual Review of Political Science* 3, no. 1: 419–447.

Montville, J.V. (1990) "The Pathology and Prevention of Genocide," in V.D. Volcan, J.V. Montville and D.A. Julius (eds) *The Psychodynamics of International Relationships*, Toronto: Lexington Books.

Morland, M., Strachan, V. and Burden, A. (2011) *The Rosemary Nelson Inquiry Report*, London: HMSO, May 2011.

Moses, R. (1990) "On Dehumanizing the Enemy," in V.D. Volcan, J. Montville and D.A. Julius (eds) *The Psychodynamics of International Relationships*, Toronto: Lexington Books.

Muldoon, O., McNamara, N., Devine, P. and Trew, K. (2008) "Beyond Gross Divisions: National and Religious Identity Combinations," *ARK Research Update* 58, no. 1: 1–4.

Mullan, D. (2007) *Eyewitness Bloody Sunday: The Truth*, Dublin: Merlin Publishing.

Murphy, C. and Adair, L. (2004) *A Place for Peace: Glencree Centre for Reconciliation 1974–2004*, Dublin: Liffey Press.

Murray, D. (1985) *Worlds Apart: Segregated Schools in Northern Ireland*, Belfast: Appletree.

Murtagh, B. (1994) *Ethnic Space and the Challenge to Land Use Planning: A Study of Belfast's Peace Lines*, Belfast: Centre for Policy Research, University of Ulster.

Muvingi, I. (2009) "Sitting on Powder Kegs: Socioeconomic Rights in Transitional Societies," *International Journal of Transitional Justice* 3, no. 2: 163–182.

Nadler, A. and Liviatan, I. (2006) "Intergroup Reconciliation: Effects of Adversary's Expressions of Empathy, Responsibility, and Recipient's Trust," *Personality and Social Psychology Bulletin* 32, no. 4: 459–470.

Nadler, A. and Shnabel, N. (2008) "Instrumental and Socioemotional Paths to Intergroup Reconciliation," in A. Nadler, T.E. Malloy and J.D. Fisher (eds) *The Social Psychology of Intergroup Reconciliation*, Oxford: Oxford University Press.

Nadler, A., Malloy, T.E. and Fisher, J.D. (2008) "Intergroup Reconciliation: Dimensions and Themes," in A. Nadler, T.E. Malloy and J.D. Fisher (eds) *The Social Psychology of Intergroup Reconciliation*, Oxford: Oxford University Press.

Newman, E. (2002) "Transitional Justice: The Impact of Transnational Norms and the U.N.," *International Peacekeeping* 9, no. 2: 31–50.

Ni Aolain, F. (2000) *The Politics of Force: Conflict Management and State Violence in Northern Ireland*, Belfast: Blackstaff.

Northern Ireland Council for Integrated Education. (n.d.) "About Us," NICIE. Online. Available at: http://www.nicie.org/aboutus/ (accessed 15 July 2012).

Niens, U., Cairns, E. and Hewstone, M. (2003) "Contact and Conflict in Northern Ireland," in O. Hargie and D. Dickson (eds) *Researching the Troubles: Social Science Perspectives on the Northern Ireland Conflict*, Edinburgh: Mainstream.

Niyodusenga, A. and Karakashian, S. (2008) *Program Evaluation of Healing of Memories Workshops*, Cape Town: Institute for Healing of Memories, March 2008.

Northern Ireland Affairs Committee. (2009) *The Report of the Consultative Group on the Past in Northern Ireland: Second Report of Session 2009–2010*, London: NIAC, December 2009.

Northern Ireland Memorial Fund. (2012) "A Little Bit About Us," Northern Ireland Memorial Fund. Online. Available at: http://www.nimemorialfund.co.uk/about.html (accessed 15 July 2012).

Northern Ireland Human Rights Commission. (2003) *Human Rights and Victims of Violence*. Belfast: NIHRC, June 2003. Online. Available at: http://cain.ulst.ac.uk/issues/victims/docs/nihrc03victims.pdf (accessed 15 July 2012).

Northern Ireland Statistics and Research Agency. (2005) *Northern Ireland Multiple Deprivation Measure 2005*, Belfast: HMSO, May 2005.

Northern Ireland Policing Board. (2012) *Public Perceptions of the Police, DPPs and the Northern Ireland Policing Board: January 2012 Omnibus Survey*, Belfast: NIPB, May 2012.

Northrup, T.A. (1989) "The Dynamic of Identity in Personal and Social Conflict," in L. Kriesberg, T.A. Northrup and S.J. Thorson (eds) *Intractable Conflicts and Their Transformation*, Syracuse: Syracuse University Press.

Oberschall, A. (2007) *Conflict and Peace Building in Divided Societies: Responses to Ethnic Violence*, New York: Routledge.

Oduro, F. (2007) *What Do We Understand by "Reconciliation?" Emerging Definitions of Reconciliation in the Context of Transitional Justice*, Ottawa: International Development Research Centre, March 2007.

Office of the First Minister and Deputy First Minister. (2008) "Significant Increase in Funding for Victims and Survivors," Belfast: OFMDFM. Online. 28 July 2008. Available at: http://www.northernireland.gov.uk/news-ofmdfm-220708-ofmdfm-significant-increase (accessed 15 July 2012).

—— (2009) *Strategy for Victims and Survivors*, Belfast: OFMDFM, November 2009.

—— (2011) *2010 Labour Force Survey Religion Report*, Belfast: OFMDFM, December 2011.

O'Leary, B. and McGarry, J. (1993). *The Politics of Antagonism: Understanding Northern Ireland*, London: Athlone Press.

O'Loan, N. (2007) *Investigative Report: Statement by the Police Ombudsman for Northern Ireland on Her Investigation into the Circumstances Surrounding the Death of Raymond*

McCord Junior and Related Matters, Belfast: Police Ombudsman for Northern Ireland.

Olson, W. (2004) "Triangulation in Social Research: Qualitative and Quantitative Methods Can Really Be Mixed," in M. Holborn (ed.) *Developments in Sociology*, Ormskirk: Causeway Press.

Orenlichter, D.F. (1991) "Settling Accounts: The Duty to Prosecute Human Rights Violations of a Prior Regime," *The Yale Law Journal* 100, no. 8: 2537–2615.

Orr, W. (2000) "Reparation Delayed Is Healing Retarded," in C. Villa-Vicencio and W. Verwoerd (ed.) *Looking Back Reaching Forward: Reflections on the Truth and Reconciliation Commission of South Africa*, Cape Town: University of Cape Town Press.

Osiel, M.J. (2000) "Why Prosecute? Critics of Punishment for Mass Atrocity," *Human Rights Quarterly* 22.1: 118–147.

Pat Finucane Centre. (1999) *Submission to the Independent Commision into Policing*, Belfast: PFC. Online. Available at: http://www.patfinucanecentre.org/policing/submiss1.html (accessed 15 July 2012).

—— (2005) "Press Release: Canadian Judge Peter Cory Slams Finucane Inquiry Legislation," Online. 15 March 2005. Available at: http://www.patfinucanecentre.org/cory/pr050315.html (accessed 15 July 2012).

Peskin, V. (2005) "Beyond Victor's Justice? The Challenge of Prosecuting the Winners at the International Criminal Tribunals for the Former Yugoslavia and Rwanda," *Journal of Human Rights* 4, no. 2: 213–231.

Petonito, G. (2000) "Racial Discourse and Enemy Construction," in P.G. Coy and L.M. Woehrle (eds) *Social Conflicts and Collective Identities*, Oxford: Rowman and Littlefield.

Pettigrew, T.F. (1998) "Intergroup Contact Theory," *Annual Review of Psychology* 49, no. 1: 65–85.

Phakathi, T.S. and van der Merwe, H. (2008) "The Impact of the TRC's Amnesty Process on Survivors of Human Rights Violations," in A.R. Chapman and H. van der Merwe (eds) *Truth and Reconciliation in South Africa: Did the TRC Deliver?*, Philadelphia: University of Pennsylvania Press.

Philpott, D. (ed.) (2006) *The Politics of Past Evil: Religion, Reconciliation, and the Dilemmas of Transitional Justice*, Notre Dame: University of Notre Dame Press.

Pierson, P. (2004) *Politics in Time*, Princeton: Princeton University Press.

Pigou, P. (2008) "Reaping What You Sow: Political Parties, the TRC, and the Quest for Truth and Reconciliation," in A.R. Chapman and H. van der Merwe (eds) *Truth and Reconciliation in South Africa: Did the TRC Deliver?*, Philadelphia: University of Pennsylvania Press.

Police Service of Northern Ireland. (2010) "Historical Inquiries Team: Introduction from the Chief Constable," Online. 8 November 2010. Available at: http://www.psni.police.uk/historical-enquiries-team/historical-enquiries-team (accessed 15 July 2012).

—— (2012a) *Freedom of Information Request F-2010–02443*. Online. 10 April 2012. Available at: http://www.psni.police.uk/cases_investigated_het.pdf (accessed 15 July 2012).

—— (2012b) "Workforce Composition Figures," Online. 4 July 2012. Available at: http://www.psni.police.uk/index/updates/updates_statistics/updates_workforce_composition_figures.htm (accessed 15 July 2012).

Putnam, R. (1993) *Making Democracy Work: Civic Traditions in Modern Italy*, Princeton: Princeton University Press.

—— (2000) *Bowling Alone: The Collapse and Revival of American Community*, New York: Simon and Schuster.

Quinn, J. (2007) "Social Reconstruction in Uganda: The Role of Informal Mechanisms in Transitional Justice," *Human Rights Review* 8, no. 4: 173–190.

—— (2010) *The Politics of Acknowledgement: Truth Commissions in Uganda and Haiti*, Vancouver: UBC Press.

Rabushka, A. and Shepsle, K. (1972) *Politics in Plural Societies: A Theory of Democratic Instability*, Columbus: Charles R. Merrill.

Ragin, C. (1987) *The Comparative Method*, Berkeley: University of California Press.

Ramirez-Barat, C. and van der Merwe, H. (2005) "Seeking Reconciliation and Reintegration: Assessment of a Pilot Restorative Justice Program," Cape Town: CSVR, February 2005.

Reiger, C. (2006) "Hybrid Attempts at Accountability for Serious Crimes in Timor Leste," in N. Roht-Arriaza and J. Mariezcurrena (eds) *Transitional Justice in the Twenty-First Century: Beyond Truth Versus Justice*, Cambridge: Cambridge University Press.

Reychler, L. and Paffenholz, T. (eds) (2001) *Peacebuilding: A Field Guide*, London: Lynne Rienner.

Rigby, A. (2001) *Justice and Reconciliation: After the Violence*, London: Lynne Rienner.

Risse-Kappen, T. (1996) "Collective Identity in a Democratic Community: The Case of Nato," in P. Katzenstein (ed.) *The Culture of National Security*, New York: Columbia University Press.

Roche, D. (2007) "Retribution and Restorative Justice," in G. Johnstone and D. Van Ness (eds) *Handbook of Restorative Justice*, Portland: Willan.

Roht-Arriaza, N. (2006) "The New Landscape of Transitional Justice," in N. Roht-Arriaza and J. Mariezcurrena (eds) *Transitional Justice in the Twenty-First Century: Beyond Truth Versus Justice*, Cambridge: Cambridge University Press.

Roht-Arriaza, N. and Mariezcurrena, J. (eds) (2006) *Transitional Justice in the Twenty-First Century: Beyond Truth Versus Justice*, Cambridge: Cambridge University Press.

Ronnquist, R. (1999) "Identity and Intra-State Ethnonational Mobilization," in H. Wiberg and C.P. Scherrer (eds) *Ethnicity and Intra-State Conflict: Types, Causes, and Peace Strategies*, Aldershot: Ashgate.

Ropers, N. (2004) "From Resolution to Transformation: Assessing the Role and Impact of Dialogue Projects," in A. Wimmer et al. (eds) *Facing Ethnic Conflicts: Toward a New Realism*, New York: Rowman & Littlefield.

Rosenblum, N.L. (2002) "Justice and the Experience of Injustice," in M. Minow (ed.) *Breaking the Cycles of Hatred: Memory, Law, and Repair*, Princeton: Princeton University Press.

Ross, M.H. (2004) "Ritual and the Politics of Reconciliation," in Y. Bar-Siman-Tov (ed.) *From Conflict Resolution to Reconciliation*, Oxford: Oxford University Press.

Rotberg, R.I., and Thompson, D. (eds) (2000) *Truth v. Justice: The Morality of Truth Commissions*, Princeton: Princeton University Press.

Rothman, J. (1997) *Resolving Identity-Based Conflict in Nations, Organizations, and Communities*, San Francisco: Jossey-Bass.

Rowthorn, B. and Wayne, N. (1988) *Northern Ireland: The Political Economy of Conflict*, London: Polity Press.

Ruane, J. and Todd, J. (1996) *The Dynamics of Conflict in Northern Ireland: Power, Conflict, and Emancipation*, Cambridge: Cambridge University Press.

Rubin, H. and Rubin, I. (1995) *Qualitative Interviewing: The Art of Hearing Data*, Thousand Oaks: Sage.

Rushton, B. (2006) "Truth and Reconciliation: The Experience of Truth Commissions," *Australian Journal of International Affairs* 60, no. 1: 125–141.

Ryan, S. (1995) *Ethnic Conflict and International Relations*, Aldershot: Dartmouth.

——— (2007) *The Transformation of Violent Intercommunal Conflict*, Aldershot: Ashgate.

Santa-Barbara, J. (2007) "Reconciliation," in C. Webel and J. Galtung (eds) *The Handbook of Peace and Conflict Studies*, New York: Routledge.

Sarat, A., Douglas, L. and Umphrey, M.M. (eds) (2005) *The Limits of Law*, Stanford: Stanford University Press.

Sarkin, J. (2001) "The Tension Between Justice and Reconciliation in Rwanda: Politics, Human Rights, Due Process and the Role of the Gacaca Courts in Dealing With The Genocide," *Journal of African Law* 45, no. 2: 143–172.

——— (2008) "An Evaluation of the South African Amnesty Process," in A.R. Chapman and H. van der Merwe (eds) *Truth and Reconciliation in South Africa: Did the TRC Deliver?*, Philadelphia: University of Pennsylvania Press.

Savage, M. (1987) "The Cost of Apartheid," *Third World Quarterly* 9, no. 2: 601–621.

Saville, M., Hoyt, W. and Toohey, J. (2010) *Report of the Bloody Sunday Inquiry*, London: HMSO.

Schabas, W.A. (2006) "The Sierra Leone Truth and Reconciliation Commission," in N. Roht-Arriaza and J. Mariezcurrena (eds) *Transitional Justice in the Twenty-First Century: Beyond Truth Versus Justice*, Cambridge: Cambridge University Press.

Schabas, W.A. and Darcy, S. (eds) (2004) *Truth Commissions and Courts: The Tension between Criminal Justice and the Search for Truth*, Dordrecht: Kluwer.

Schirch, L. (2001) "Ritual Reconciliation: Transforming Identity/Reframing Conflict," in M. Abu-Nimer (ed.) *Reconciliation, Justice, and Coexistence: Theory and Practice*, New York: Lexington Books.

Schlemmer, L. (1992) "Public Attitudes and South Africa's Future Democracy," *Information Update* 2, no. 4: 1–4.

Schubotz, D. and McCartan, C. (2008) "Cross-Community Schemes: Participation, Motivation, Mandate," *ARK Research Update* 55, no. 1: 1–4.

Schubotz, D. and Robinson, G. (2006) "Cross-Community Integration and Mixing: Does It Make a Difference?" *ARK Research Update* 43, no. 1: 1–4.

Schutt, R.K. (2009) *Investigating the Social World: The Processes and Practice of Research*, London: Sage Press.

Seekings, J. and Nattrass, N. (2004) "The Post-Apartheid Distributional Regime," in *Centre for Social Science Research Working Paper Series No. 76*, Centre for Social Science Research: University of Cape Town.

Sharpe, S. (2007) "The Idea of Reparation," in G. Johnstone and D. Van Ness (eds) *Handbook of Restorative Justice*, Portland: Willan.

Shirlow, P. (2001) "Fear and Ethnic Division," *Peace Review* 13, no. 1: 67–74.

Shirlow, P. and Murtagh, B. (2006) *Belfast: Segregation, Violence and the City*, London: Pluto Press.

Shriver, D. (2001) "Where and When in Political Life Is Justice Served by Forgiveness?," in N. Biggar (ed.) *Burying the Past: Making Peace and Doing Justice after Civil Conflict*, Washington DC: Georgetown University Press.

Sikkink, K. (2011) *The Justice Cascade*, New York: Norton.

Simkin, C. (1984) "What Has Been Happening to Income Distribution and Poverty in the Homelands?," *Development Southern Africa* 1, no. 2: 142–152.

Simpson, G. (1997) "Reconstruction and Reconciliation: Emerging from Transition," *Development in Practice* 7, no. 4: 475–478.

Smith, A. (1986) *The Ethnic Origins of Nations*, Oxford: Blackwell.

Smith, A. and Dunn, S. (1990) *Extending Inter-School Links: An Evaluation of Contact between Protestant and Catholic Pupils in Northern Ireland*, Coleraine: University of Ulster.

Smyth, J. (1997) "Dropping Slow: The Emergence of the Irish Peace Process," in A. O' Day (ed.) *Political Violence in Northern Ireland: Conflict and Conflict Resolution*, Westport: Praeger.

Snyder, J. and Vinjamuri, L. (2003) "Trials and Errors: Principle and Pragmatism in Strategies of International Justice," *International Security* 28, no. 3: 5–44.

Sonis, J. and van der Merwe, H. (2004) "Survivor Perspective in the South African TRC," in *CSVR Research Reports*, Johannesburg: Centre for the Study of Violence and Reconciliation.

South African Coalition for Transitional Justice. (2012) "Press Release: Zuma's Presidential Pardons Process Unconstitutional," Online. 6 June 2012. Available at: http://brandonhamber.blogspot.com/2012/06/zumas-presidential-pardons-process.html (accessed 15 July 2012).

Special EU Programs Body. (2006) *Peace III: Operational Programme*, Belfast, SEUPB.

Sriram, C.L. (2004) *Confronting Past Human Rights Violations: Justice vs. Peace in Times of Transition*, London: Frank Cass.

Stanley, E. (2002) "What Next? The Aftermath of Organized Truth Telling," *Race & Class* 44, no. 1: 1–15.

Staub, E. (1978) *Positive Social Behaviour and Morality: Social and Personal Influences*, New York: Academic Press.

—— (1989) *The Roots of Evil: The Origins of Genocide and Other Group Violence*, New York: Cambridge University Press.

—— (2000) "Genocide and Mass Killing: Origins, Prevention, Healing and Reconciliation," *Political Psychology* 21, no. 2: 367–382.

—— (2001) "Individual and Group Identities in Genocide and Mass Killing," in R.D. Ashmore, L. Jussim and D. Wilder (eds) *Social Identity, Intergroup Conflict, and Conflict Reduction*, Oxford: Oxford University Press.

—— (2006) "Reconciliation after Genocide, Mass Killing, or Intractable Conflict," *Political Psychology* 27, no. 6: 867–894.

Staub, E. and Bar-Tal, D. (2003) "Genocide, Mass Killing, and Intractable Conflict: Roots, Evolution, Prevention, and Reconciliation," in D.O. Sears, L. Huddy and R. Jervis (eds) *Oxford Handbook of Political Psychology*, Oxford: Oxford University Press.

Stephan, W.G. and Stephan, C.W. (2001) *Improving Intergroup Relations*, London: Sage.

Stevens, J. (2003) *Stevens Enquiry: Overview and Recommendations*, Belfast: Director of Public Prosecutions Northern Ireland, April 2003.

Stover, E. and Weinstein, H.M. (2004) "A Common Objective: A Universe of Alternatives," in H.M. Weinstein and E. Stover (eds) *My Neighbor, My Enemy: Justice and Community in the Aftermath of Mass Atrocity*, Cambridge: Cambridge University Press.

Sumner, W.G. (1906) *Folkways: A Study of the Sociological Importance of Usages, Mannsers, Customs, Mores, and Morals*, Boston: Ginn.

Sutton, M. (2010) *An Index of Deaths from the Conflict in Ireland*, Derry: CAIN.

Tajfel, H. (ed.) (1982) *Social Identity and Intergroup Relations*, Cambridge: Cambridge University Press.

Tajfel, H. and Turner, J. (1979) "An Integrative Theory of Intergroup Relations," in W. Austin and S. Worchel (eds) *The Social Psychology of Intergroup Relations*, Monterey: Brooks.

Tausch, N., Hewstone, M., Kenworthy, J., Cairns, E. and Christ, O. (2007) "Cross-Community Contact, Perceived Status Differences, and Intergroup Attitudes in Northern Ireland," *Political Psychology* 28, no. 1: 53–68.

Teitel, R.G. (2000) *Transitional Justice*, Oxford: Oxford University Press.

The Independent Commission on Policing for Northern Ireland. (1999) *"The Patten Report" – a New Beginning: Policing in Northern Ireland*, Belfast: HMSO, September 1999.

Thiessen, G. (2008) "Object of Trust and Hatred: Public Attitudes Towards the TRC," in A.R. Chapman and H. van der Merwe (eds) *Truth and Reconciliation in South Africa: Did the TRC Deliver?*, Philadelphia: University of Pennsylvania Press.

Treble, P. (2009) "IRA Killings Escalate as Recession Hits," *Macleans*. Online. 26 March 2009. Available at: http://www2.macleans.ca/2009/03/26/ira-killings-escalate-as-recession-hits (accessed 15 July 2012).

Treiman, D.J. (2005) "The Legacy of Apartheid: Racial Inequalities in the New South Africa," in *California Center for Population Research Working Paper Series*, Los Angeles: UCLA, October 2005.

Trew, K. (1986) "Catholic–Protestant Contact in Northern Ireland," in M. Hewstone and R. Brown (eds) *Contact and Conflict in Intergroup Encounters*, Oxford: Blackwell.

Truth and Reconciliation Commission. (1998) *Truth and Reconciliation Commission of South Africa Final Report*, Cape Town: Department of Justice, October 1998.

Tutu, D. (2000) *No Future without Forgiveness*, New York: Random House.

Valji, N. (2004) "Race and Reconciliation in a Post-TRC South Africa," paper presented at the "Ten Years of Democracy in South Africa Conference," Queen's University, Canada, May 2004.

Vandeginste, S. (2003) "Reparation," in D Bloomfield, T. Barnes, and L. Huyse (eds) *Reconciliation After Violent Conflict: A Handbook*, Stockholm: IDEA.

Van der Berg, S., Burger, R., Louw, M. and Yu, D. (2006) "Trends in Poverty and Inequality," in *Development Policy Research Institute Working Paper Series No. 104*, Development Policy Research Institute: Stellenbosch University, March 2006.

van der Merwe, H. (2001a) "National and Community Reconciliation: Competing Agendas in the South African Truth and Reconciliation Commission," in N. Biggar (ed.) *Burying the Past: Making Peace and Doing Justice after Civil Conflict*, Washington DC: Georgetown University Press.

van der Merwe, H. (2001b) "Reconciliation and Justice in South Africa: Lessons from the TRC's Community Interventions," in M. Abu-Nimer (ed.) *Reconciliation, Justice, and Coexistence: Theory and Practice*, New York: Lexington.

Van Ness, D. (2002) "The Shape of Things to Come: A Framework for Thinking About a Restorative Justice System," in E. Weltekamp and H.J. Kerner (eds) *Resorative Justice: Theoretical Foundations*, Portland: Willan.

Van Ness, D. and Strong, K.H. (1997) *Restoring Justice*, Cincinnati: Anderson Publishing.

van Zyl, P. (1999) "Dilemmas of Transitional Justice: The Case of South Africa's Truth and Reconciliation Commission," *Journal of International Affairs* 52, no. 2: 647–668.

Varney, H. and Gould, C. (2012) "Special Presidential Pardons Undermine Truth and Reconciliation in South Africa," Insitute for Security Studies. Online. 29 June 2012. Available at: http://www.iss.co.za/iss_today.php?ID=1509 (accessed 15 July 2012).

Väyrynen, T. (1999) "Socially Constructed Ethnic Identities: A Need for Identity Management?," in H. Wiberg and C.P. Scherrer (eds) *Ethnicity and Intra-State Conflict: Types, Causes, and Peace Strategies*, Aldershot: Ashgate.

Victims Unit. (2002) *Reshape, Rebuild, Achieve: Deriving Practical Help and Services to Victims of the Conflict in Northern Ireland*, Belfast: OFMDFM, April 2002.

Villa-Vicencio, C. (2000a) "Getting on with Life: A Move Towards Reconciliation," in C. Villa-Vicencio (ed.) *Looking Back, Reaching Forward: Reflections on the Truth and Reconciliation Commission of South Africa*, Cape Town: University of Cape Town Press.

—— (2000b) "Restorative Justice: Dealing with the Past Differently," in C. Villa-Vicencio and W. Verwoerd (eds) *Looking Back, Reaching Forward: Reflections on the Truth and Reconciliation Commission of South Africa*, Cape Town: University of Cape Town Press.

—— (2001) "Restorative Justice in Societal Context: The South African Truth and Reconciliation Commission," in N. Biggar (ed.) *Burying the Past: Making Peace and Doing Justice after Civil Conflict*, Washington DC: Georgetown University Press.

—— (2006) "The Politics of Reconciliation," in T.A. Borer (ed.) *Telling the Truths: Truth Telling and Peace Building in Post-Conflict Societies*, Notre Dame: University of Notre Dame Press.

Waddell, N. and Clark, P. (eds) (2008) *Courting Conflict? Justice, Peace and the ICC in Africa*, London: Royal African Society.

Walaza, N. (2000) "Insufficent Healing and Reparation," in C. Villa-Vicencio and W. Verwoerd (eds) *Looking Back, Reaching Forward: Reflections on the Truth and Reconciliation Commission of South Africa*, Cape Town: University of Cape Town Press.

Walker, K. (2004) "The History of South Africa: A Twice-Told Tale," *Carnegie Reporter* 2, no. 4: 2–13.

Weiner, E. (1998) "Coexistence Work: A New Profession," in E. Weiner (ed.) *The Handbook of Interethnic Coexistence*, New York: Continuum.

Weinstein, H.M. and Stover, E. (eds) (2004) *My Neighbor, My Enemy*, Cambridge: Cambridge University Press.

Wendt, A. (1992) "Anarchy Is What States Make of It," *International Organiation* 46, no. 2 (1992): 391–425.

—— (1994) "Collective Identity Formation and the International State," *The American Political Science Review* 88, no. 2: 384–396.

—— (2000) *Social Theory of International Politics*, Cambridge: Cambridge University Press.

—— (2003) "Why a World State Is Inevitable," *European Journal of International Relations* 9, no. 4: 491–542.

Whyte, J. (1983) "How Much Discrimination Was There under the Unionist Regime, 1921–1968," in T. Gallagher and J. O' Connell (eds) *Contemporary Irish Studies*, Manchester: Manchester University Press.

Wilmer, F. (2002) *The Social Construction of Man, the State, and War: Identity, Conflict, and Violence in the Former Yugoslavia*, New York: Routledge.

Zehr, H. (1990) *Changing Lenses: A New Focus for Crime and Justice*, Scottsdale: Herald Press.

—— (2002) "Journey to Belonging," in E. Weltekamp and H.J. Kerner (eds) *Restorative Justice: Theoretical Foundations*, Portland: Willan.

Index

Abrams, Dominic 14
accountability: and Belfast Agreement 112;
    lack of/Bloody Sunday Inquiry 123; norm
    of/international community 1; Northern
    Ireland/Troubles 62; of perpetrators 41,
    111; and reconciliation 212
acknowledgment: as form of justice 150,
    151; of victims and healing 115, 151; of
    victims/socioemotional learning 152
actors: international 49–50; societal 217–18
Adams, Gerry 57, 175, 218
Adler, Emmanuel 27, 37
All Children Together (ACT) 83
Allister, Jim 123–4
amnesty: changing perceptions of 205;
    conditional 70; hearings 94; and Interim
    Constitution 67; numbers taking part
    140, 149, 161n14; process 204, 209;
    process/resistance to 153; and prosecution
    155; and sacrifice of justice 150–1
Amnesty Committee (AC) 70, 93–4, 140,
    141, 180
Amnesty International 125
ANC (African National Congress party):
    administrations/structural reforms 187;
    civil disobedience resistance 64; human
    rights violations 141; lack of prosecutions
    of members 154; lack of prosecutions
    under 155; MK (Umkhonto we Sizwe)
    65, 141; and move to democracy 66; and
    Truth and Reconciliation Commission 71,
    208
Anglo-Irish Treaty 1921 55
apartheid 62–3; abuses under/secrecy and
    denial of 138; complicity of white South
    Africans 205, 207; as crime against
    humanity 140–1, 203, 204;
    dehumanizing effects of 90; era/

prosecutions of abuses 155; law 63,
    89–90; legacies of 188–90; petty/grand
    63, 177; racial identity under 12n4;
    structural elements of 143, 148, 183; as
    untenable 65; white views of 148, 181–3
Ardoyne Commemoration Project (ACP)
    133–4
Ardoyne: The Untold Truth 133
Arthur, Paul 175
Atlantic Philanthropies 119
atrocities, mass/and group membership 17
Attwood, Alex 127
Azanian People's Liberation Army (APLA)
    66

B-Specials 165, 166, 167
Backer, David 156
Ball, Patrick 142
Ballymurphy Massacre 131
Bantu Authorities Act 1951 64
Bantu Education Act 1953 63
Bantu education system 65, 177
Bantustans 64
Bar-Siman-Toy, Yaacov 20, 26
Bar-Tal, Daniel 21, 43, 46
Barnett, Michael 27, 37
Battle of the Bogside, The 56
Belfast 75, 80, 83, 165, 170, 176
Belfast Agreement (BFA) 59–60; and
    accountability 112; and continuing
    violence 77, 176; differing perceptions of
    61–2; and inequalities 169; needs of
    victims 114; and prisoner release 117; and
    reforms 169, 174; role of ex-paramilitaries
    118
Belfast Interface Project (BIP) 81, 175
beliefs, biased 44
Bell, Christine 87, 120

benign cycle of positive affect 14
Berkeley Human Rights Center 220
Biggar, Nigel 40–1
Bilko, Steve 65
Bill of Rights for Northern Ireland 169
Bill of Rights, South Africa 187
Black Consciousness Movement 65
Black Economic Empowerment Act (BEE) 188, 209
black liberation movement 91
Black Sash 189, 193
Blair, Tony 121
Bloody Sunday 57, 72n1, 121, 160n1
Bloody Sunday Campaign 121
Bloody Sunday Inquiry (BSI) 121–4
Bloomfield, Kenneth 113
Bloomfield Report 113–14, 116
Boraine, Alex 64, 69, 139
Borer, Tristan Anne 42, 43
Bosnia 220
Botha, P.W. 65, 71
Brecke, Peter 44
British Army: and Bloody Sunday 122; collusion with RUC 126; evidence tampering 127; see also British security forces; British soldiers
British Irish Rights Watch 128
British Northern Ireland Affairs Committee 137
British security forces: casualties 58; criminal responsibility of 130–1; killings by 55; and marquee murders 124, 125; role in Troubles 123, 198, 200; see also British Army; British state
British soldiers, preferential treatment of/giving evidence 130
British state: collusion in violence 112, 126, 198; collusion with paramilitaries 126; role in Troubles 112–13, 123, 125, 200; see also British Army; British security forces
Burton, Mary 100, 147, 183, 193
business community, and distributive reforms/South Africa 183–4
Buthelezi, Mangosuthu 65, 72

Cairns, Ed 173
Cameron Commission 163, 164, 166, 193n2–3
Cameron, David 122, 124, 125
Canadian International Development Research Centre 25

Cannon, Matthew 116, 119
Center for Conflict Resolution (CCR) 106
Center for the Study of Violence and Reconciliation (CSVR) 91, 94, 105–6, 110n18, 153, 186, 208
Chapman, Audrey 2, 66, 95, 97, 139, 142, 143, 148, 149, 151, 155, 177, 181, 184
Checkel, Jefferey 32
Chilean National Commission for Truth and Reconciliation 67
civil rights movements, Northern Ireland 56–7, 163, 164, 166, 201
civil society initiatives: Northern Ireland 79–82, 131–3; South Africa 105–8, 204
civil society sector: Northern Ireland 78; South Africa 108
civilian casualties, Northern Ireland 58, 72n2–4
Claudy Bombing 161n5
cognitive dissonance, and TRC 100
Cohesion, Sharing, and Integration 108n3
collective identification: and gross human rights violations 3; and Self/Other 20–1; and social learning 30n8; see also collective identity
collective identity 13, 14, 15, 19, 26; see also collective identification; group identity
collusion: British state/in violence 112, 126, 198; police/Loyalist paramilitaries 127, 167
Commission for Victims and Survivors (CSVNI) 114
Committee on the Administration of Justice (CAJ) 118, 128, 129
Common Ingroup Identity Model 30n7, 35
communal divisions, and conflict 77
communication: bridging 37; controlled 39; interracial/South Africa 90; and social learning process 27; social networks of 27; transformative 38; see also dialogue
Community Foundation for Northern Ireland (CFNI) 81, 114
community initiatives, local/Northern Ireland 131–5
community relations: community relations programs 84–5, 87; and equality/Northern Ireland 202; following BFA/Northern Ireland 176–7; government interventions/Northern Ireland 78–9; and integrated education/Northern Ireland 85–6; rebuilding/Northern Ireland 62, 74–5, 77–83, 84, 199

Community Relations Council (CRC) 80, 108n4, 114, 170
Community Relations Officers (CROs) 79
Community Relations Unit (CRU) 78–9, 108n1
Community Restorative Justice Ireland (CRJI) 119, 120
compensation: Northern Ireland 114, 137; South Africa 70–1, 151, 152, 179, 181, 184; for victims of violence 47–8
conflict, and communal divisions 77
Conflict Archive on the Internet (CAIN) 113
conflict transformation literature 19, 27, 32
conflict transformation scholarship 3
Constitution, South Africa 66, 67, 68, 187
constructivist scholars, and role of institutions/structures 27, 28
constructivist theory 32
Consultative Group on the Past (CGPNI) 197, 200
contact hypothesis 4, 34–7, 74
contact, interracial/South Africa 89–90, 92, 93–6
contact work, short term 87
controlled communication 39
Cory, Peter 124
Cox, David 128
Crawford-Brown, Sarah 90, 151
Crawford-Pinnerup, Anna 186
crimes against humanity 1
criminal justice system: Northern Ireland 169; Western 220
cross-community contact 84
Cultural Heritage 82
culture of human rights, and culture of violence 21
culture of silence 134
culture of violence: and culture of human rights 21; South Africa 156, 209

Darby, John 165, 173
Day of Private Reflection 132–3
Day of Reflection and Reconciliation 136
DCCRP (District Councils Community Relations Programme) 79
De Klerk, F.W. 65, 71–2
De Kock, Eugene 161n9
Deane, Eamonn 199–200
decentralized transitional justice, Northern Ireland 8, 60–2
deeply divided societies, and politics of identity 13–17

dehumanization, of the Other 16
Deloitte 115
democracy: Northern Ireland 167; South Africa 66, 67
Democratic Unionist Party (DUP) 57, 60, 128, 174–5, 196
Department of Education for Northern Ireland 82
deprivation, Northern Ireland 170, 175, 176; see also inequalities
Derry 56, 75, 80, 87, 108n5, 124, 165, 166, 170, 199
Development and Reconciliation Fund 181–2
devolved governance, Northern Ireland 61
dialogue: creating space for 98; CSVR 110n18; groups 38; intercommunal 88; processes/recent enemies 39; processes/storytelling 88, 105; and reconciliation 92; reflexive 38; societal 39, 96–105, 204; strategies/divided societies 39; transformative 37–40, 74; and Truth and Reconciliation Commission 96–108; workshops 106, 107; see also communication
dignity, and victims' healing processes 42
Direct Rule, Northern Ireland 57
discrimination: Northern Ireland 55–6, 60, 163–4, 165, 167; racial/South Africa 63
distributive equality, Northern Ireland 173–4
distributive interventions, outside TRC process 187–93
distributive learning 5, 33, 45–8; Northern Ireland 162, 163–77, 198; South Africa 162, 205, 207; and structural/material reforms 216; and Truth and Reconciliation Commission 177–83
distributive reforms 47; Northern Ireland 166–70
divided societies, social learning/reconciliation in 209–12
Divin, Sue 87–8
divisions, structural/material 22
Dixon, John 104
Doherty, Michael 87, 88, 89
domination, Northern Ireland 55–6
Drumbl, Mark 2, 17
Du Toit, Fanie 100, 141, 143, 190, 191
Duduza 150
Durrheim, Kevin 104

Eames, Robin 137
economic development, as lever for change
    176–7
economic prosperity, and interracial contact
    190–1
economic redistribution, and reconciliation
    179
economic wealth, inequalities in 45–6
Eder, Klaus 15
education: Bantu education system 65, 177;
    black South Africans 63, 188; integrated/
    Northern Ireland 83, 85–6, 108n7,
    109n8; mixed/South Africa 191;
    segregated/Northern Ireland 76, 82; and
    transitional justice institutions 39
Education for Mutual Understanding 82
education initiatives, Northern Ireland 82–3
Education Reform (Northern Ireland) Order
    1989 82
egoism of victimization 44; and moderating
    truth 45
elections, South Africa 66; see also voting
    rights
electoral bias, Northern Ireland 164–5,
    193n2
electoral system, reform/Northern Ireland
    167, 169
elites: black South Africans 209; role of
    conducive 49–50, 217
Ellis, Donald 38
employment: discrimination in/Northern
    Ireland 163–4; inequalities/South Africa
    178–9; reforms/Northern Ireland 168,
    171, 172
Employment Act 1989 168
Employment Equity Act 188
engagement, and Truth and Reconciliation
    Commission 100–1
entrepreneurs, role of conducive 49–50, 217
equality: and collective identification 22; of
    material/social resources 33; and
    reconciliation 202; reforms/Northern
    Ireland 62, 171–2, 173, 196; of status/
    reconciliation 36, 37; white South
    Africans reaction to 209; see also
    inequalities
Equality Commission 169
Equality Unit 169
equity, and justice 170
Ervine, Brian 130
ethnocentrism, universal 14
ethnonational identities, and violence 16

ethnonational violence, and group/collective
    identity 3
European Union, Programme for Peace and
    Reconciliation (PEACE) 81, 115
evaluation, victims' initiatives/Northern
    Ireland 115
evidence: destruction of by NP government
    143; preferential treatment of British
    soldiers 130; tampering RUC/British
    Army 127
Ex-Combatants Programme 80
Ex-Combatants Reintegration and
    Restorative Justice Project 105–6

Fair Employment Agency (FEA) 168
Fair Employment and Treatment Order
    1998 169
Fair Employment Commission (FEC) 168
Families Acting for Innocent Relatives
    (FAIR) 115
Finucane, Pat 124, 125, 126
Fitzduff, Mari 76, 167, 171
Foster, Don 104–5
Fullard, Madeleine 98, 144, 179, 182, 187
funding: prisoner reintegration 117–18;
    victims initiatives/Northern Ireland 115;
    see also resources

Gaertner, Samuel 35
Galtung, Johan 46
Gender and Sexual Orientation Unit 169
gerrymandering, Northern Ireland 164, 165,
    167
Gibson, James 91, 100, 101, 145, 146, 148,
    150, 151, 157, 181, 184
Gibson, William 90
Glencree Centre for Peace and Reconciliation
    (Glencree) 80–1, 88, 201
Glover Report 73n5
Good Friday Agreement 1998 see Belfast
    Agreement (BFA)
Gould, Chandre 158
Gouws, Amanda 153, 181, 189
government: British/Ireland 57; Northern
    Ireland 55–6, 60; see also British state;
    Government of Northern Ireland (GNI);
    South African state
government interventions, community
    relations/Northern Ireland 78–9
Government of Northern Ireland (GNI) 56,
    78, 82, 115, 117, 131, 163; reforms
    167–8

grand apartheid 63, 177
Greater Shankill Alternatives 119
Group Areas Acts 63–4, 177
group identity, new perceptions of/Northern
    Ireland 197; *see also* collective identity
group membership, and atrocities/human
    rights violations 17
Growth, Employment, and Redistribution
    (GEAR) initiative 188

Hall, Peter 6
Hamber, Brandon 48, 109n12, 116, 147
Hamill inquiry 125
Hamill, Robert 124
Hani, Chris 66
Hayner, Priscilla 141
healing: and acknowledgement of victims
    115, 151; and distributive reforms 48;
    intercommunal 131; personal 94; and
    reparations/South Africa 184
Healing Through Remembering (HTR)
    129, 131–3, 197
Hegarty, Angela 121, 125
Hermann, Tamar 38
Hewstone et al. 85
Hewstone, Miles 77, 196
Historical Enquiries Team (HET) 128–31,
    161n6
history: coming to terms with/Northern
    Ireland 210; confronting 44;
    disagreements over interpretation 200;
    Northern Ireland/Troubles 163–6; official
    record of past violence 45, 71, 111, 112,
    204; and Truth and Reconciliation
    Commission 139, 140, 210
Hofmeyr, Jan 191
Hogg, Michael 14
Holywell Trust 199
Home for All Campaign Initiative 181
Homelands system, black 64
housing allocation: discrimination in/
    Northern Ireland 163–4, 166; reforms/
    Northern Ireland 172
housing, South Africa 178
Hughes et al. 174
Hughes, Joanne 198–9, 200
human rights: culture of 21; universal 1
human rights-based approach, transitional
    justice 212
Human Rights Commission 169
human rights violations: and collective
    identity 3; and criminal trials 220–1; and

dividing Self from Other 18; and group
    membership 17; South Africa/addressing
    72; and Truth and Reconciliation
    Commission 93, 139
Human Rights Violations Committee
    (HRVC) 69, 70–1, 93, 140, 141–2, 147,
    180
humanizing, and Truth and Reconciliation
    Commission 98
Hunt Committee 167

identification: collective and the truth 43;
    common 22
identity: collective identity 3, 13, 14, 15,
    19, 26; conflicts 16, 17; as construction
    15, 18; and gross human rights violations
    3; group/Northern Ireland 84, 197;
    groups 14; and intergroup reconciliation
    207; national/Northern Ireland 61;
    politics of 4, 13–17, 26, 210; racial under
    apartheid 7, 12n4; and reconciliation 3,
    210, 211; South African national 101;
    and transitional justice 207, 211;
    widening 20
identity negotiation, and intergroup
    dialogue 37
Immorality Act 1950 63
Independent Commission on Policing for
    Northern Ireland (ICPNI) 169
Independent Consultative Group on the Past
    (CGPNI) 136–8
indigenous approaches, justice 215
inequalities: arrest and conviction rates
    Northern Ireland 130; in dealing with
    past/Northern Ireland 123; distributive/
    Northern Ireland 201; Northern Ireland
    56, 62, 163, 168–70, 198, 202; and
    reconciliation 22, 37, 45–8, 170–1; and
    social learning process 192–3; South
    Africa 177–80, 185, 188–9, 194n11,
    205, 209; structural 46–8, 62; *see also*
    equality
ingroup/outgroup 14
injustice: and instrumental learning 52n1;
    and lack of prosecutions/South Africa 155;
    official recognition of 152; and pardon
    process/South Africa 159; and reparations/
    South Africa 153, 207; and return to
    violence 41; and social learning process
    156
Inkatha Freedom Party (IFP) 65, 66, 72, 96,
    141, 142, 154

INLA (Irish National Liberation Army) 124, 125
Inquiries Act 2005 124, 125
Institute for Democracy in South Africa (IDASA) 92, 206
Institute for Global Development 104, 192
Institute for Healing of Memories (IHOM) 105, 106, 208
Institute for Justice and Reconciliation (IJR) 92, 102, 190
institutional design, and justice/ reconciliation 25–6, 52
Institutional Hearings 140, 183
institutional responses, transitional justice 23
institutions: shared societal and social learning 26–8; state/abuses of apartheid 148
instrumental learning 4, 32–3, 34–40; and injustice 52n1; Northern Ireland 74, 75–89, 199; South Africa 75, 89–108, 204, 208; and Truth and Reconciliation Commission 92–3; and victimization/ injustice 52n1
instrumental reconciliation 32
intergroup violence 17
interaction: interracial/South Africa 91–2; and social learning process 27
Interactive Conflict Resolution strategies 38
intercommunal dialogue 88
intergroup conflicts, and collective identity 19
intergroup dialogue: and identity negotiation 37; and social learning 38
intergroup hostility 14
intergroup reconciliation 19–22, 34, 162; Northern Ireland 62, 173, 195, 199; and social psychology 32; South Africa 195
intergroup relations: Northern Ireland 62, 196–7; South Africa 203
intergroup violence 16, 17
Interim Constitution, South Africa see Constitution
interim reparations grant (IRG) 186
Intermediary Funding Bodies (IFBs) 81, 114, 115, 117
International Center for Transitional Justice (ICTJ) 64, 67
International Conflict Research Institute (INCORE) 113, 116
International Criminal Court 1

International Criminal Tribunal of Yugoslavia (ICTY) 53n3
International Criminal Tribunals 1
International Fund for Ireland 81
internment, Northern Ireland 57, 165
interracial contact: and economic prosperity 190–1; South Africa 89–90, 93–6
interracial interaction, South Africa 91, 103
interracial relations, South Africa 206
Investigation Unit, HRVC 71, 140, 142–3
IRA (Irish Republican Army) 55, 57; see also PIRA (Provisional Irish Republican Army); Real IRA (RIRA)
Irish Free State 55
Irish Peace Institute 116, 119
Irish War of Independence 55

Jaynes, Natalie 102
Jeong, Ho-Won 49
judicial purview, limiting of/Northern Ireland 124
Junction, The 108n5
just war, struggle against apartheid as 146
justice: and addressing past violence 40; and amnesties/South Africa 150; and Bloody Sunday 122–3; calls for/Northern Ireland 112; and dignity/moral worth of victims 42; and equity 170; indigenous approaches 215; initiatives/Northern Ireland 121; international/and reconciliation 212; lack of/Northern Ireland 129; philosophy of 42; and reparations 150, 185; restorative/ retributive 213; and social learning 40–2, 214–15; and socioemotional learning 5, 111; and Truth and Reconciliation Commission 149–60
justice mechanisms: and institutional design 25–6; and large-scale violence 2; and peace/post-conflict societies 2
justness, of political violence/South Africa 66–7

Katorus 150
Kelman, Herbert 19, 44
Khulumani Support Group 99, 152, 155, 159, 179, 186, 189
killings: and collusion RUC/UDA 126; by Inkatha Freedom Party 141; revenge/ Northern Ireland 58; see also murders; violence

Kingsmill Massacre 161n5
Kiss, Elizabeth 139

Lagan College 83
Land Acts 177
Lapsley, Michael 105
law(s): disregard for rule of/South Africa
    156, 157, 209; South Africa 63–5, 68–9,
    89–90, 177
learning, strategic learning 20; see also social
    learning
Lederach, John Paul 21
Legacy Commission 136
legislative power, Northern Ireland 164
legitimacy, of peace-building/Northern
    Ireland 118
liberation movements, and HRVC 142
LIVE Programme 80
living conditions, South Africa 178
Llewellyn, Jennifer 93
Lodge, Tom 152
Londonderry see Derry
Long War, Northern Ireland 58
Long, William 44
Loyalist Volunteer Force (LVF) 124
Loyalists: arrest/conviction rates of 130;
    collusion with British state 112; Northern
    Ireland 58
Lundy, Patricia 130, 133, 134, 135

Macdonald, Helen 150, 151, 157, 181, 184,
    206
Mack, John 44
Madikizela-Mandela, Winnie 71
Making Peace With the Past: Options for Truth
    Recovery Regarding the Conflict in and about
    Northern Ireland 132
Mandela, Nelson 65, 66, 68, 69, 71, 73n8,
    187, 203, 218
Mandela, Winnie see Madikizela-Mandela,
    Winnie
Mani, Rama 219
marquee murders, security force collusion
    124, 125
marriages, mixed/Northern Ireland 76
material inequalities, Northern Ireland 62
Mbeki, Thabo 107, 157, 159, 186, 188, 218
McArt, Pat 124
McCord, Raymond Jr. 126–7
McEvoy, Kevin 118, 119, 120
McEvoy, Kieran 129
McGovern, Mark 133, 134, 135

McGuinness, Martin 60
media coverage, Truth and Reconciliation
    Commission 101–2, 109n15, 143
media, under apartheid 65, 139
Mehl-Madrona, Lewis 38
Meiring, Piet 187
Millward Brown Ulster 86
Minimal Group Paradigm 29n1
Minow, Martha 41
Mitchell, Brian 95–6
MK (Umkhonto we Sizwe) 65, 141
moderating truth, and egoism of
    victimization 45
Mofokeng, Tlhoki 99, 152, 155, 156, 159,
    179, 189
moral community, extension of boundaries
    of 21
moral growth 38
moral order: development of equitable 21;
    disruption of 16; shared 22
moral responsibility, and peace process/
    Northern Ireland 62
morality, reversal of 35
Muldoon et al. 84
Mullan, Ray 76, 170
murders, RUC/UDR involvement in 126,
    127; see also killings; violence
myths, reevaluation of national 44

Nadler, Arie 32, 33, 52n1, 135
Naidoo, Marcella 189, 193
National Party (NP): abuses by/lack of
    justice 138; and Amnesty Committee
    process 142; and apartheid 62, 65, 66;
    destruction of evidence 143; lack of
    prosecutions of members 154; and Truth
    and Reconciliation Commission 71, 142
National Prosecuting Authority (NPA) 155,
    157–8, 159
National Unity and Reconciliation Act 180
nationalism, South African 101
nationalist, term 11n3
nationalists: and Bloomfield Report 116;
    Northern Ireland/BFA 61; Northern
    Ireland/victimization 60; views of
    violence 112
Nelson Inquiry 125
Nelson, Rosemary 124, 125
networks: peace-building partnership 80;
    of trust/communication 27
Northern Ireland: creation of 55; post-
    conflict experience 60; Troubles 7, 54–62

Northern Ireland Alternatives (NIA) 119, 120
Northern Ireland Assembly 114, 169, 175
Northern Ireland Association for the Care and Resettlement of Offenders (NIACRO) 117, 119
Northern Ireland Civil Rights Association (NIACRA) 56
Northern Ireland Commissioner for Administration 168
Northern Ireland Council for Integrated Education (NICIE) 83, 198
Northern Ireland Executive 115
Northern Ireland Government 60; see also Government of Northern Ireland (GNI)
Northern Ireland Housing Executive (NIHE) 166, 172
Northern Ireland Life and Times (NILT) survey 75–6, 85, 109n10, 116, 172, 173–4, 197
Northern Ireland Memorial Fund (NIMF) 114
Northern Ireland Office (NIO) 60, 78, 114
Northern Ireland Policing Board (NIPB) 173
Northrup, Terrell 20

Office of the First Minister and Deputy First Minister (OFMDFM) 79, 108n3, 114, 131, 169
Office of the Police Ombudsman for Northern Ireland (OPONI) 126, 128
O'Halloran, Chris 175
O'Leary, B. & McGarry, J. 60–2
O'Loan Enquiry 127
O'Loan, Nuala 126
Omagh 73n6
Operation Ballast 130
Operation Demetrius 131
oppression, structural/South Africa 180
Orange Order 56, 165
Orr, Wendy 187
Other: dehumanization of 16; humanizing of 88; learning about 37; and prejudice 15; rehumanization of 21, 34–5, 39, 91; and Self 14, 16, 17, 18, 20, 21, 26

Paisley, Ian 60, 218
Pan African Congress (PAC) 65, 66
paramilitaries, ex/and peace-building 118
paramilitary organizations: and deprivation 176; Northern Ireland 57, 58

pardon process, South Africa 158–9, 160
partitioning, of Ireland 55
Pass Laws 65, 177
Pat Finucane Centre (PFC) 128
Paterson, Owen 126
Patten Commission/Report 169–70, 172
peace: groups South Africa 108n2; and justice 40; negative 7, 22, 49, 50; Northern Ireland 196; positive 22; and public truth-telling 44; sustainable 18, 25, 30n8, 50–1; see also peace process
Peace and Reconciliation Group (PRG) 87
peace-building, and ex-combatants 118–19
peace-building partnership networks 80
peace process: Northern Ireland 59, 61–2, 73n6, 77, 168, 201; South Africa 67
peace-systems, and war-systems 21
peace walls 75
perpetrators of crimes: accountability of 41, 111; lack of prosecutions/South Africa 149–50, 154–5, 159, 205, 206, 209; reconciliation with victims 96; and Truth and Reconciliation Commission 153
petty apartheid 63, 177
Phakathi, T.S. 96, 150, 153
philosophy of justice 42
Pienaar, Francois 73n8
Pigou, Piers 190
PIRA (Provisional Irish Republican Army) 57, 58
Plantation of Ulster, The 55
polarization, intercommunity/Northern Ireland 175–6
police: Northern Ireland 127, 165, 166, 167–8, 169–70, 172–3, 194n6; violations by South African 145, 148; see also Police Service of Northern Ireland (PSNI)
Police Act 1970 167
Police Authority for Northern Ireland 167
police enquiries, Northern Ireland 126–8
Police (Northern Ireland) Acts 126, 170
Police Ombudsman 170
Police Service of Northern Ireland (PSNI) 119, 120, 170, 172; see also police
Policing Board 170
Policy Appraisal and Fair Treatment (PAFT) 168
Political Dialogue Workshops 80
political reforms, South Africa 187
political representation, Northern Ireland 169
political system, South Africa 177

politicians, and pardon process/South Africa 158
politics, of identity 4, 13–17, 26, 210
Posel, Deborah 90, 156–7
positive intergroup contact 34–7
post-conflict experience, Northern Ireland 60
post-conflict societies, politics of identity 4
poverty, South Africa 66, 178, 188–9, 19; *see also* inequalities
power: legislative/executive in Northern Ireland 164; socioeconomic/sociopolitical 46
power-sharing government, Northern Ireland 60, 61
prejudice, and the Other 15
President's Fund 185
prisoner release/reintegration, Northern Ireland 117–20
problem-solving workshops 38
process-tracing 6–7, 8
Programme for Peace and Reconciliation (PEACE) 81, 115
Progressive Unionist Party (PUP) 130
Prohibition of Mixed Marriages Act 1949 63
Promotion of National Unity and Reconciliation Act 1995 68–9, 149
prosecutions: lack of/South Africa 149–50, 154–5, 157, 159, 205, 206, 209; resulting from inquiries/Northern Ireland 125, 127, 129
Protestant Loyalists 57
Protestant Orange Order 56, 165
Protestant unionists 55
psychological divisions, Northern Ireland 77
psychosocial processes, of social learning 28–9, 32
public enquiries, Northern Ireland 120–6
public hearing process, South Africa 97–8, 99, 100, 102, 145, 204
public institutions, and intergroup communication 39

Queen's University Belfast 84, 116, 118, 129, 133, 198

racial categories, South Africa 63
racial discrimination, South Africa 62–3
racial divisions, South Africa 103, 104, 206
Racial Equality Unit 169
racial identity, under apartheid 12n4

racial stereotypes 90, 99, 178, 203
racism: institutionalized/South Africa 66, 177; interlocking/South Africa 90; reverse racism 182
Rainbow Nation 69, 101, 209
Real IRA (RIRA) 73n6
reconciliation 18–23; and accountability 212; community based 78; and confronting history 44; conversation of 107; and conversational/dialogical space 38; and criminal trials 220; and dialogue 92; and distributive reforms 48; divided societies 209–12; and economic redistribution 179; and identity 3, 210, 211; and inequalities 22, 37, 45–8, 170–1; and institutional design 25–6, 52; intergroup 19–22, 32, 34, 162; intergroup/Northern Ireland 62, 173, 195, 199; intergroup/South Africa 195; interpersonal/South Africa 68; interracial/South Africa 91, 96, 98, 101–2; key learning mechanisms of 34; lack of funding/South Africa 107; and lack of prosecutions/South Africa 157; and lack of socioeconomic change 188–9; Northern Ireland 196–202; and politics of identity 210; as a process 29, 52n1; and reflexive dialogue 38; and reparations/South Africa 184; role of ex-combatants 118, 119; and social psychology 32; societal 7–8; socioemotional/instrumental 32; South Africa 202–9; and Special Pardons/South Africa 159; and structural divisions/South Africa 179; top-down and bottom up/Northern Ireland 78; and transitional justice 3, 4, 25, 28, 210, 211–12, 213; in transitional societies 2; and truth 42–5, 135; and Truth and Reconciliation Commission 100, 146, 147, 203–9
Reconciliation Forum 136
reconciliation processes, perpetrators/victims 94–5
Reconstruction and Development Programme (RDP) 187–8
redistribution, societal/South Africa 181, 182, 183, 207, 209; *see also* inequalities
reflexive dialogue, and reconciliation 38
reforms: distributive/restitutive 47, 48; and social learning 216; structural/South Africa 187
Register of Reconciliation 140
rehumanization, South Africa 92

Relatives for Justice (RFJ) 115, 116, 131
remembrance, Northern Ireland 131
reparations: and healing/South Africa 184; and justice 185; and Truth and Reconciliation Commission 184–7
Reparations and Rehabilitation Committee (RRC) 70, 150, 152, 180, 185
reparations programs 47, 48; Urgent Interim Reparations (UIR) program 185–6
reparations scheme: Northern Ireland 137; South Africa 150, 152, 153, 205, 207; view of white South Africans 194n9
Report on the Consultative Group on the Past 136
repression: apartheid era 91; compensation for 47–8
Republican paramilitary groups 57, 58
Republicans 55; views of violence 112
research: design/methodology 6–11; future avenues 217–21
Research Department, HRVC 71, 140
Reservation of Separate Amenities Act 1953 63
resettlement, forced/South Africa 64
Reshape, Rebuild, Achieve 114, 131
resources, duplication of/Northern Ireland 174, 198–9; *see also* funding
responsibility, for past violence/Northern Ireland 135, 197
restitutive reforms 47; views of white South Africans 181
restorative approaches, transitional justice 24
restorative justice 213; South Africa 215; and Truth and Reconciliation Commission 68, 112
restorative justice initiatives, and ex-combatants 119–20
retributive approaches, transitional justice 23–4
retributive justice 149, 213, 218, 219–20
reunification, Ireland 61
revictimization 187
Review of the Criminal Justice System in Northern Ireland, The 169
Ritchie, Mike 118, 129
Robinson, Peter 137, 175
Roman Catholic Irish nationalists 54–5
Ropers, Norbert 39
Rothman, Jay 38
Royal Ulster Constabulary (RUC): and civil rights riots 56; collusion with British

Army 126; collusion with Loyalist paramilitaries 126, 127, 167; demilitarization of 167; discrimination by 194n7; discrimination in structure of 165; evidence tampering 127; and Nelson murder 125
Ruane, Joseph 46, 163
Ruiters, Michele 104, 192
Rushton, Beth 40
Rwanda 220

St. Andrews Agreement 2006 60
St. James Massacre 66
sectarian violence, Northern Ireland 176
segregated neighborhoods, interface zones 75
segregation: Northern Ireland 56, 75, 76–7, 82, 196; and onset of violence 16; self/informal 104; South Africa 90, 190, 208
Self, and Other 14, 16, 17, 18, 20, 21, 26
Separate Representation Acts 177
Shared Future, A 79, 82, 85, 108n3
Sharpeville Massacre 65
Shirlow, Pete 77, 116, 118
Shnabel, Nurit 32, 52n1, 135
shoot-to-kill policy 167
single-identity work 89, 115, 133, 134
Sinn Féin (SF) 57, 60, 118, 174
Snyman, Deon 90–1
social capital: bridging 29n4; and communal identity conflicts 16
social construction, and identity groups 15
Social Democratic and Labour Party (SDLP) 57, 127, 175
social identity, defined 14; *see also* collective identity
Social Identity Theory (SIT) 13–15, 52–3n2
social learning: and cessation of violence 26; and collective identification 30n8; divided societies 209–12; and illegitimacy of violence 21; and intergroup dialogue 38; and intergroup inequality 47; and justice 42, 214–15; key mechanisms of 50; and lack of socioeconomic change 188–9; as long-term process 216–17; and material inequality 192–3; Northern Ireland 196–202; permissive conditions for 48–50; processes of 4–5, 32, 212, 214; psychosocial processes of 28–9, 32; and reconciliation 19; and retributive justice 219–20; and sense of injustice 156; and shared societal institutions 26–8; South

Africa 202–9; successful 19–22; and transitional justice 3–5, 31–4, 50–2, 211, 213–14, *see also* chapter 3; and truth telling 44, 45

social persuasion, and Truth and Reconciliation Commission 100

social psychology: Contact Hypothesis 34; and intergroup reconciliation 32

social relationships, South Africa 102–3

social segregation 75

social status, inequalities in 45–6

socialization, and transitional justice institutions 39

societal dialogue 39, 204

socioeconomic discrimination, Northern Ireland 56

socioeconomic power, inequalities in 46

socioemotional learning 5, 32–3, 40–5, 212; barriers to 136; and Bloody Sunday Inquiry 124; and instrumental learning 52n1; and justice 111; Northern Ireland 135–8, 197; South Africa 111–12, 204; and Truth and Reconciliation Commission 144–9, 151–60; white South Africans 146

socioemotional reconciliation 32

sociopolitical power, inequalities in 46

Sooka, Yasmin 180

South African Coalition for Transitional Justice (SACTJ) 158–9

South African Communist Party (SACP) 65, 66

South African Defence Force, and Amnesty Committee process 142

South African Foundation for Human Rights 63

South African government, destruction of evidence 143; *see also* South African security forces; South African state

South African History Archive (SAHA) 190

South African Human Science Research Council (HSRC) 206

South African Institute for Security Studies 158

South African military, lack of involvement in TRC 142

South African Reconciliation Barometer (SARB) study 92, 102, 159, 190–1, 203

South African security forces: lack of involvement in TRC 142; and pardon process 158; violations by 145, 148

South African state: collusion with IFP 141;

human rights violations 141, 148; *see also* South African government; South African security forces

Soweto 65

space, conversational/dialogical 38, 98, 106, 134

spaces, for interaction/South Africa 91–2

Special Pardons, South Africa 158–9

Special Powers Act 1922 165–6

Special Theme hearings 140

spoilers, domestic 50

Spratt, Jim 128

Springboks 73n8

Stanley, Elizabeth 48

state, discrimination by/Northern Ireland 163

state institutions, and abuses of apartheid 148

Staub, Ervin 21, 39, 46

stereotypes: racial 90, 99; reducing/Northern Ireland 197

Stevens Enquiry 126, 127

Stevens, Garth 91, 188, 192

Stevens, John 126

storytelling 88, 105, 109n12, 134

strategic learning 20

structural inequalities 46–8, 62

structural violence 46

Suppression of Communism Act 1950 64–5

symbolic identifiers 76

Symbolic Interactionism School (SIS) 35, 52–3n2

taboo subjects 134

Targeting Social Need (TSN) 168

Tausch, Nicole 47

tax, wealth tax/South Africa 183

Teitel, Ruti 28

telling, informal system of/Northern Ireland 76

territorial demarcation, Northern Ireland 75

theoretically-oriented systematic process analysis 6

thick social/psychological changes, and peace 18

thin/negative coexistence 18

Todd, Jennifer 46, 163, 171

township settlements 66

Traditional Unionist Voice Party 123

transformative communication 38

transformative dialogue 37–40, 74

transitional justice 1, 23–6; based on

process 214; best practices 212–17; broad/narrow 30n9; goals of 25; human rights-based approach 212; and identity 207, 211; institutions 24, 28, 36, 39, 45, 48; interpretations of 33; literature 2, 25; Northern Ireland 111, 195–6, 215; and reconciliation 3, 4, 25, 28, 210, 211–12, 213; and social learning 3–5, 31–4, 50–2, 211, 213–14, *see also* chapter 3; South Africa 196, 215; strategies 24; and Truth and Reconciliation Commission 150
transitional justice initiatives, actors roles in 50
Transitional Justice Institute 87, 120
transitional justice institutions 24, 28, 36, 39, 45, 48
transitional justice program, decentralized/ Northern Ireland 8
transitional justice strategies 2; dialogue processes promoted by 39; and distributive learning 162; and inequalities 47; Northern Ireland 7, 54–62, 197; permissive conditions for 48–50; South Africa 6, 54–62, 62–72
transitional processes, and societal reconciliation 2
transitional societies, reconciliation in 2
Trauma Centre for Survivors of Violence and Torture 151
trials, v. truth 23
Tribunals of Inquiry (Evidence) Act 1921 121
Troubles, Northern Ireland 7, 54–62
trust: and contact 35, 191; mutual 20, 22; social networks of 27
Trust Feed Massacre 95–6
truth: calls for/Northern Ireland 112, 113; establishing 111; initiatives/ Northern Ireland 121, 131–3; micro/macro level 141–2, 143, 161n7; process of gathering 45, 129; and reconciliation 42–5, 135; and shared narrative 40; and socioemotional learning 5; and Truth and Reconciliation Commission 140–9, 153–4, 210; v. trials 23
Truth and Reconciliation Commission (TRC) 7, 67–72; distributive interventions within 183–7; and distributive learning 177–83; encounter/ dialogue in 105–8; and encounter/ interracial contact 93–6; final report 143–4, 161n10, 177, 179–80, 184, 186;

and history 139, 140, 210; Institutional Hearings 140, 183; and instrumental learning 92–3; Investigation Unit 142–3; and justice 149–60; mandate of 138, 143, 194n8, 205; and Mbeki administration 218; perceptions of white South Africans 206; as perpetrator-centered 153; public hearing process 97–8, 99, 100, 102, 145, 204; recommendations of 184; and reconciliation 100, 146, 147, 203–9; reparations through the 184–7; and restorative justice 68, 112; and societal dialogue 96–105; socioemotional learning from 144–9, 151–60; and truth 140–9, 153–4, 210; undermining of 215–16
truth commissions 45, 138
truth recovery processes 43, 132–3, 134
truth recovery/truth-telling frameworks 23
Truth Seeking Program for the ICTJ 67
truth-telling processes, and reconciliation 44, 45
truths, competing 134–5
Tutu, Desmond 68, 69, 101, 203, 218

ubuntu 68
Ulster Defence Regiment (UDR) 167
Ulster Unionist Party (UUP) 57, 175
Ulster Volunteer Force (UVF) 57, 127, 130
unemployment: Northern Ireland 164, 168, 170, 171–2; South Africa 178, 188
unionist, term 11n3
unionists, Northern Ireland/BFA 61
United Nations 1
universal ethnocentrism 14
University of Cape Town 90, 104, 106
University of Limerick 84, 116
University of Stellenbosch 153, 181
University of Ulster 84, 116, 120, 130, 175
University of Witwatersrand 90, 91, 188, 192
upward mobility, black South Africans 191
Urgent Interim Reparations (UIR) program 185–6

Valji, Nahli 153, 159, 190, 191
Vally, Hanif 63
van der Merwe, Hugo 66, 91, 95, 96, 97, 139, 143, 148, 149, 150, 151, 153–4, 155, 177, 181, 184
van der Merwe, Johann 158
Varney, Howard 67, 99, 142, 147, 154, 155, 158

Väyrynen, Tarja 18
Verwoerd, Wilhelm 88, 147, 201
Victim-Offender Mediation pilot project
    106
victim services, Northern Ireland 115
victim status, white South Africans 182
victim support/acknowledgement, Northern
    Ireland 113–17
Victim Survivors Core Funding Scheme 114
victimhood: double 135; polarization/
    Northern Ireland 116
victimization: ego of 44; and instrumental
    learning 52n1; Northern Ireland 60,
    135–6; perceptions of/white South
    Africans 209; revictimization 187; sense
    of/Unionists 198
Victims and Survivors Forum 114–15
Victims and Survivors Service 115
Victims' Commission 113
Victims' Liaison Unit (VLU) 114
Victims' Minister 114
victims of violence: acknowledgment of 111,
    150, 151; and Belfast Agreement 114;
    and healing 115; hierarchy of/Northern
    Ireland 116, 133–4, 137; Northern
    Ireland 160n1; reconciliation with
    perpetrators 96
Victims Survivors Development Scheme 114
Victims' Unit 114, 131
Villa-Vicencio, Charles 98, 147
violence: antagonistic perceptions of/
    Northern Ireland 116; apartheid era
    12n4, 66, 91; breaking cycle of 50;
    communality of 2; continuing in
    Northern Ireland 176, 196, 199, 202;
    crime/South Africa 91; culture of/South
    Africa 156, 209; dissident/Northern

Ireland 196; dynamics of 16; and
    ethnonational identities 16; and group/
    collective identity 3; and inequalities/
    Northern Ireland 170; intergroup 16, 17;
    interracial 66; intracommunity/South
    Africa 65; large-scale 2; mass 18;
    Northern Ireland 58–9, 60, 62;
    paramilitary punishment 119–20;
    protracted intergroup 16–17;
    responsibility for/Northern Ireland 112,
    113; sectarian/Ireland 55, 58, 77, 176;
    and segregation 16; and social learning
    21, 26; South Africa 203, 209; structural
    46, 209
Vlok, Adriaan 158, 161n9
voting rights, South Africa 64, 177

War of Independence, Irish 55
war-systems, and peace-systems 21
Wardlow, Michael 83, 198
WAVE Trauma Centre 115
We Will Remember Them 113
Wendt, Alexander 35
Weston Park talks 124
Whyte, John 164
Widgery Inquiry 121, 123
Wildschut, Glenda 92, 107
Williams, Vincent 92, 100, 103, 106–7
Wilson, Richard 48, 147
Wits Institute for Social and Economic
    Research (WISER) 90, 156
Woodward, Shaun 137
Wright, Billy 124, 125
Wright Inquiry 125

Zehr, Howard 42
Zuma, Jacob 158, 159

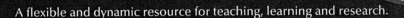

CPSIA information can be obtained
at www.ICGtesting.com
Printed in the USA
FFOW01n1603200915
.17039FF